ORGANIZED FOR PROHIBITION

☆ ORGANIZED ☆
FOR
PROHIBITION

A NEW HISTORY
OF THE
ANTI-SALOON LEAGUE

☆☆ K. AUSTIN KERR ☆☆

YALE UNIVERSITY PRESS
NEW HAVEN AND LONDON

Published with assistance from the Louis Stern
Memorial Fund.

Designed by Sally Harris
and set in Baskerville type by The Saybrook Press, Inc.
Printed in the United States of America by
BookCrafters, Inc., Chelsea, Michigan.
Library of Congress Cataloging in Publication Data
Kerr, K. Austin.
Organized for prohibition.
Bibliography: p.
Includes index.
1. Anti-saloon League of America—History.
2. Prohibition—United States—History. I. Title.
HV5287.A64K47 1985   363.4'1'06073   85–3131
ISBN 0–300–03293–5 (alk. paper)

The paper in this book meets the guidelines for
permanence and durability of the Committee on
Production Guidelines for Book Longevity
of the Council on Library Resources

10 9 8 7 6 5 4 3 2 1

To John C. Burnham,
scholar, colleague, friend,
and to my son, Jonathan,
who missed my last book

CONTENTS

ILLUSTRATIONS

The illustrations are published by courtesy of the Board of Trustees of the Westerville (Ohio) Public Library, the Ohio Historical Society, and the Ohio Council on Alcohol Problems.

following page 114

PREFACE

I decided to write this book in 1974 when the Ohio Historical Society acquired the remaining records of the Anti-Saloon League from its Westerville, Ohio, headquarters. When I sampled those materials and saw their huge volume and nature, I realized that the manuscripts, magazines, and books constituted a major archival source that no other scholar had been able to explore previously. Not only did these materials seem to reveal fundamentally new information about the modern prohibition movement, but they showed that prohibition was a movement that reached deep into the heart of American society over a period of half a century. As I worked further, my conviction of the archive's importance grew and matured. Now that it is catalogued, processed, and microfilmed, other scholars will, I am sure, gain fresh insights into the American past as I have.*

Both the Anti-Saloon League and the political campaigns it mobilized so successfully in the Progressive era have long interested historians and scholars in other disciplines. Usually the attraction is one of fascination with how evangelical zeal led to political excesses, stories of rum running, agents emptying bottles of illicit hooch into sewers, flappers listening to jazz in speakeasies, and preachers moralizing about the improvement of society through righteous, abstemious behavior. A large literature in this vein fills library shelves and sporadically appears in textbooks.

But about the same time the records of the Anti-Saloon League

---

*The film project included materials in the Michigan Historical Collections and the records of the Woman's Christian Temperance Union. The WCTU materials had, for the most part, been closed to scholars. Persons interested in using them should consult *Guide to the Microfilm Edition of Temperance and Prohibition Papers,* ed. Randall C. Jimerson, Francis X. Blouin, and Charles A. Isetts (Ann Arbor, 1977).

became available in a public repository, historians were reinterpreting the story of prohibition, portraying it as a response in the mainstream of American reform to real social problems of alcohol use. The outstanding volume in this new tradition is the brilliant essay by Norman Clark, *Deliver Us From Evil: An Interpretation of American Prohibition* (New York, 1976), which appeared in time to guide my own research. Thanks to the work of Clark and other scholars, we now understand that the desire for prohibition conformed to a broader vision within the evangelical Protestant churches for enlarging the power of government to strike at social conditions that inhibited human freedom and denied men and women their potential. Prohibition was part of the social gospel. It was one quest for a social system wherein private behaviors conformed to the social good. And most reformers agreed that the good society, the public interest, required the legal extinction of the venal industries that plied citizens with intoxicating drink.

This book accepts, indeed, confirms the reinterpretation of prohibition. I, too, look at the liquor business and its opposition. I have not sought to break new ground in our understanding of the ideology of the dry movement, already thoroughly and well explored by other scholars who used the plethora of printed sources that the movement generated. Instead, I have focused on the inner workings of the Anti-Saloon League, the nuts and bolts of how it appeared, developed, succeeded, and failed, doing so in the context of the activities of the industries it opposed.

To my surprise, there was yet more to be discovered. Over a period of years, carefully researched, informative monographs about the prohibition movement in particular states were published, but, I found, students of the national movement had omitted a systematic exploration of the manuscript materials already available. Citations to the papers of such key figures as Woodrow Wilson, E. Y. Webb, and Andrew Volstead simply have not appeared in books about the national politics of prohibition after 1912. This book, therefore, tells the story of the Anti-Saloon League not just from the league records acquired by the Ohio Historical Society in 1974 but from the records of other important actors as well. My story is new, in part, because it is the first full history of the national politics of the Anti-Saloon League and prohibition.

There was a special motivation in my quest for the history of the league. Although I personally am unattracted by its ultimate goal, the league is interesting not only for the values that it expressed, but also because it was a pioneering political organization. The men who organized and led the Anti-Saloon League had learned, somehow, both a nonpartisan political strategy and techniques for mobilizing the large numbers of Americans who wanted prohibition for a successful, long-term campaign. Observers had recognized for a long time that the league represented something special in American political history, that it had developed as a single issue, nonpartisan pressure group not quite like its predecessors or contemporary counterparts. The league mobilized a mass constituency for uncompromising action on an emotional issue that the existing party system could not accommodate. I wanted to write the history of this development in the framework of the recent understanding of the significance of prohibitionist ideology and in the context of the scholarly awareness of the importance of private associations in modern American life.

Whatever merits this book may have, thus, rest in part on the new materials I have examined. They also come from the help that friends and colleagues have provided. The staff of the Ohio Historical Society went out of their way to provide help. Mary S. Higley and Laurel G. Bowen, who prepared the microfilm edition, deserve special thanks for a job well done. The board of trustees of the Ohio State University generously granted a year's professional leave. Dean Jules R. LaPidus of the graduate school and Diether H. Haenicke of the college of humanities provided essential research funds. Lewis L. Gould and Norman Clark added important suggestions as well as words of encouragement. Jack S. Blocker, Jr., offered able criticisms of an earlier version of chapter 2. My wife, Rita, and my children, Julie, Katie, and Jonathan, deserve credit for immeasurable patience.

Finally, throughout the preparation of this book my friend Professor John C. Burnham always provided sage advice, although we ultimately have differing judgments concerning drinking in general and prohibition in particular. The errors of fact and interpretation are my own; to him should go most of the credit for whatever insights I have conveyed. He has shown, over the years, what the word *colleague* should mean and I cannot adequately express my appreciation.

ABBREVIATIONS FOR MANUSCRIPT SOURCES

AIP   American Issue Publishing Company series, Temperance and Prohibition Papers, Ohio Historical Society microfilm

AJV   Andrew J. Volstead papers, Minnesota Historical Society

ASLA   Anti-Saloon League of America series, Temperance and Prohibition Papers, Ohio Historical Society microfilm

ASLAN   Anti-Saloon League of America series, Samuel E. Nicholson subseries, Temperance and Prohibition Papers, Ohio Historical Society microfilm

BH   Benjamin Harrison papers, Library of Congress microfilm

CD   Charles Dick papers, Ohio Historical Society

DCASL   District of Columbia Anti-Saloon League series, Temperance and Prohibition Papers, Ohio Historical Society microfilm

DR   Daniel C. Roper papers, Duke University

ECe   Ernest Cherrington series, Executive Committee file, Temperance and Prohibition Papers, Ohio Historical Society. I examined the Cherrington papers in their original.

ECg   Ernest Cherrington series, General Office file, Temperance and Prohibition Papers

ECp   Ernest Cherrington series, personal file, Temperance and Prohibition Papers.

ED   Edwin Dinwiddie papers, Library of Congress

EYW   E. Y. Webb papers, Southern Historical Collections, University of North Carolina

FSM	Francis Scott McBride series, Temperance and Prohibition Papers, Ohio Historical Society microfilm
GKN	George K. Nash papers, Ohio Historical Society
HC	Heriot Clarkson papers, Southern Historical Collections, University of North Carolina
HCK	Henry Churchill King papers, Oberlin College Archives
HH	Howard Russell series, Temperance and Prohibition Papers. I examined the Russell papers in their original.
HU	Harriet Upton papers, Western Reserve Historical Society
IPA	Intercollegiate Prohibition Association series, Temperance and Prohibition Papers. I examined the IPA papers in their original.
IRS	Records of the Internal Revenue Service, Record Group 58, U.S. National Archives
IWM	I. W. Metcalf papers, Oberlin College Archives
JB	James Beaver papers, Pennsylvania Historical Collections, Pennsylvania State University
JBr	Johnson Brigham papers, Division of Historical Museum and Archives, Iowa State Historical Department
JC	James Cannon papers, Duke University
JDR	John D. Rockefeller, Sr., papers, Rockefeller Archive Center
JM	James Monroe papers, Oberlin College Archives
JRG	James R. Garfield papers, Library of Congress
KN	Knute Nelson papers, Minnesota Historical Society
MH	Myron Herrick papers, Ohio Historical Society
MWWCTU	Minutes of the Wilkinsburg, Pa., WCTU, Archives of Industrial Society, University of Pittsburgh
NF	Newton H. Fairbanks papers, Ohio Historical Society
OASL	Ohio Anti-Saloon League series, Temperance and Prohibition Papers, Ohio Historical Society microfilm
OGC	O. G. Christgau papers, Minnesota Historical Society
PP	Prohibition Party series, Temperance and Prohibition Papers, Ohio Historical Society microfilm
PPMR	Private papers of the Messrs. Rockefeller, Rockefeller Center, New York
STF	Scientific Temperance Federation series, Temperance and Prohibition Papers, Ohio Historical Society microfilm

USFA   Records of the U.S. Food Administration, Record
            Group 4, U.S. National Archives
WA   William H. Anderson papers, University of Chicago
WCTU   Woman's Christian Temperance Union series, Tem-
            perance and Prohibition papers, Ohio Historical
            Society microfilm
WDF   William D. Foulke papers, Library of Congress
WGH   Warren G. Harding papers, Ohio Historical Society
            microfilm
WM   William Mitchell papers, Minnesota Historical Society
WW   Woodrow Wilson papers, case file 144, Library of
            Congress microfilm

INTRODUCTION

On December 22, 1914, Richmond P. Hobson, a decorated veteran of the Spanish-American War and a lame-duck representative from Alabama, rose on the floor of the House of Representatives in Washington, D.C., to try to persuade his colleagues to submit to the states an amendment to the United States Constitution that would prohibit the manufacture and sale of alcoholic beverages. To plead their case Hobson and his supporters marshaled a variety of arguments about the evils of alcoholic beverages and presented a petition bearing six million names and stretching for 150 feet across the visitors' gallery and hanging to the House floor at both ends. At the end of the day, when the roll was called, a majority supported the resolution, but it failed for lack of the necessary two-thirds margin. Nevertheless the campaign for national prohibition, announced the preceding year at the twentieth-anniversary convention of the Anti-Saloon League, had begun in earnest.

Hobson and his fellow prohibitionists were pursuing arguments that the American prohibition movement had expressed for decades. Similar resolutions had been introduced, unsuccessfully, in the Congress from the 1870s. All sought to improve society and the lives of individual Americans by eliminating their legal right to manufacture and sell alcoholic beverages. "We do not try to force old drinkers to stop drinking . . . ," Hobson explained. "What is the object of this resolution? It is to destroy the agency that debauches the youth of the land and thereby perpetuates its hold upon the Nation." It was "the liquor trust," he explained, that managed "a systematic, organized debauching of our youth through tens of thousands of agencies throughout the land." The agencies were, of course, the saloons. Here was the evil: a business system with millions of dollars of capital at its disposal that worked to ensnare Americans in a lifetime habit of drinking the poison, alcohol. "Men here may try to

1

escape the simplicity of the problem," said Hobson. "They can not." Alcohol is a harmful substance, he continued, and even its temperate use produces "harm to society." The solution was clear. Enact constitutional prohibition, and "the liquor trust of necessity would disintegrate. The youth would grow up sober."[1]

Hobson presented succinctly prohibitionist arguments and rhetoric, a culmination of agitation, debate, legislation, and inquiry that had proceeded since the 1850s. Within four years of the congressional presentation of that 1914 Christmas season, the prohibition movement that Hobson represented achieved national political power. That political power was the result of skillful and innovative organization by the Anti-Saloon League of America, the main subject of this book. By the twentieth century, American prohibitionists were convinced that the only effective method of dealing with the evils of beverage alcohol was through the eradication of the business system that foisted drink upon the American people. It was "the liquor traffic" at which the Eighteenth Amendment to the Constitution struck, not drink per se, nor the individual who rushed a growler of beer to his workplace or relaxed in the evening with a glass of wine—or even bourbon.[2]

The Americans who worked for national prohibition chose to emphasize this strategy through the selection of the name of their most powerful organization. It was the Anti-Saloon League, not the Anti-Liquor or Anti-Beer League. Of course the ultimate goal was the reform of society and hence of the individual, but the only practical means toward that goal seemed to be the destruction of the

1. *Congressional Record*, December 22, 1914, pp. 602–08. Excerpts from Hobson's and other's speeches in the debate are reprinted in my *The Politics of Moral Behavior: Prohibition and Drug Abuse* (Reading, Mass., 1973), pp. 95–116. For an account of the debate, see David F. Musto, *The American Disease, Origins of Narcotic Control* (New Haven, 1973), pp. 65–68. That same December Congress passed the Harrison Act, which outlawed the use of narcotics. There were significant differences between the two measures. Regarding narcotics, Musto explains, the issue was "*how* to control, not (as in the case of liquor) whether to control." Hobson, however, closely associated alcohol and narcotics, and in the 1920s led an antinarcotic organization.

2. There are popular misconceptions that prohibition somehow attempted to forbid drinking. The distinction between these misconceptions and the actual case is important for a clear understanding of how the dry forces fit in with the general reform spirit of their time. Furthermore, my study profited from John C. Burnham's seminal essay, "New Perspectives on the Prohibition 'Experiment' of the 1920s," *Journal of Social History* 2 (Fall 1968): 51–68, which shows, among other matters, how earlier historical conceptions of prohibition as an "experiment" rather than as a reform had led to misleading interpretations of the subject.

industries that supplied drink. The officers and supporters of the Anti-Saloon League made no secret of the fact that they were opposed to the consumption of alcoholic beverages, but they consistently emphasized that the means toward their objective of uplifting the individual was the legal destruction of the systems of manufacturing and distributing dangerous beverages.

In the reform movement that culminated after 1913 in the campaign for a national prohibition amendment, the leaders pursued a twofold strategy. They used, as have subsequent historians, the words *temperance* and *prohibition* to describe that strategy. Temperance reformers exhorted the individual to abstain from drink by trying to persuade him of its harmful effects. Temperance reformers sought to convince their fellow citizens that the sober, abstemious life was far healthier, happier, and more socially beneficial than an existence that included the imbibing of alcohol. Temperance as such was a reform movement that antedated efforts for prohibition, and it continued while the campaign to outlaw the saloon proceeded. By the early twentieth century the activities of temperance reformers included the generation and propagation of scientific information regarding the dangers of alcoholic beverage consumption to the individual and to society. The Anti-Saloon League was tied to this temperance movement ideologically, financially, and through overlapping leadership.

But the league's main purpose was to pursue the second part of the strategy, prohibition. This aspect was overtly political. Prohibitionists struggled for over half a century to use political institutions to destroy the liquor traffic, and this book is a study of their political action. It will begin with an explanation of what the dry forces believed the liquor traffic was and of what historical inquiry reveals it to have been. As we shall see, there was a difference between the belief and the actuality, and an understanding of that difference will allow an explanation of the eventual political victory of the prohibition movement.

It was in its standing as a political organization that scholars first recognized the significance of the Anti-Saloon League. During the 1920s, when the public perceived the league to be at the zenith of power, political scientist Peter Odegard observed that, as a pressure group, it had uncovered a new meaning for the phrase "the people shall rule." When only the two major parties exist they are not always adequate democratic instruments, he remarked, because they "invariably include adherents whose wills are hopelessly at variance upon all but a few questions." The league had shown a new way for "minor associations" to organize and achieve their objectives. Odegard thus saw the league as a pioneering pressure group, one that was important for comprehending the emerging American system of political expression.[3]

This approach to understanding the Anti-Saloon League was new when Odegard completed his classic *Pressure Politics* in 1928. Much, however, escaped that creative political scientist. He had but a limited historical perspective, and of course he did not have access to the private papers of the league's leaders. This book will try to broaden and deepen our knowledge and show that the league was even more important than Odegard realized. The league was not only a pioneering pressure group, but it was born and won its victories at a time when America was experiencing what historians now realize was an "organizational revolution" of major dimensions. The league, in fact, was part of that revolution. The history of the league not only confirms that change but extends our understanding of it. It is in this context that we must understand the league.[4]

The organizational impulses in American life grew rapidly in the late nineteenth century and in the Progressive era of the early twentieth century. Most impressive both to contemporaries and to later scholars was the appearance of "big business" firms that developed new managerial techniques and bureaucratic hierarchies to combine and control the modern flow technologies of production with the acquisition of raw materials and the distribution of finished products to an expanding network of urban markets. During the 1880s this "managerial revolution" enabled important manufacturing achievements that impressed not only the world of business at large but also observers from other walks of life. When reformers came together in the 1890s to form the Anti-Saloon League, they consciously thought of emulating the achievements of the new business organizations in their own field of interest, prohibition.[5]

---

3. *Pressure Politics: The Story of the Anti-Saloon League* (New York, 1928), p. vii.

4. The term "organizational revolution" was probably first coined by Kenneth Boulding. See his *The Organizational Revolution: A Study in the Ethics of Economic Organization* (New York, 1953). The first historian who tried to explain its significance for the Progressive era was Samuel P. Hays. See his *Response to Industrialism, 1885– 1914* (Chicago, 1957), especially the chapter titled "Organize or Perish."

5. The now classic study of the rise of big business is Alfred D. Chandler, Jr., *The Visible Hand: The Managerial Revolution in American Business* (Cambridge, Mass., 1977). The developments he analyzed are used for understanding the emergence of the Anti-Saloon League in my essay "Organizing for Reform: The Anti-Saloon League and Innovation in Politics," *American Quarterly* 32 (Spring 1980): 37–53.

The managerial revolution that transformed the internal structures of the firms that increasingly dominated important sectors of
the American economy was thus not the only dimension of the
organizational revolution. The number of private associations of all
kinds began to explode in the 1890s. Private associations, of course,
had existed from the founding of the American nation. It was the
number of associations and the widening scope of activities that
those numbers implied that were dramatically on the rise. So too was
the specialization of these groups. In the world of business, not only
did general associations, such as chambers of commerce, multiply
rapidly in this period, but so too did the various trade associations
intended to serve particular industries or particular groups of firms
within industries. In politics, specialized groups formed to transform the governmental structures of particular cities, to work for
the election of reform slates of candidates, and to lobby for particular legislation. In social reform matters, the Progressive era witnessed the appearance of associations composed usually of members
of the emerging scientific, educational, and administrative elites,
who worked for specific changes in institutions that provided education, for instance, or public health services. The settlement houses
of the time gave those more specialized social reform efforts a
geographical focus in the teeming urban-industrial centers and,
through personal contact with some of the nation's worst social
sores, provided a personal impetus for many of the reformers.[6]

The Anti-Saloon League fit within this context of expanding and
specializing associational activity. The league focused the reform
movement for which Hobson spoke on particular political goals,
arranged in stages: local option legislation to ban the saloon from
particular districts, state prohibition laws, and, after 1913, an amend-

6. The expansion of the number of private associations has no general scholarly
history, but specialists in a number of fields have observed the growth. The importance of this literature for interpreting American history is explained by Louis
Galambos, "The Emerging Organizational Synthesis of Modern American History,"
Business History Review 44 (Autumn 1970): 279–90, and "Technology, Political
Economy, and Professionalization: Central Themes of the Organizational Synthesis,"
ibid. 57 (Winter 1983): 471–93. The literature of political science on the subject is
large and important, for the growth of associational activity prompted the development of pluralist theory. Grant McConnell, *Private Power and American Democracy*
(New York, 1966), is an important critique of the growth of private associations,
although it focuses mainly on economic groups. For a brilliant analysis of how the
growth of associational activity has reshaped the structure of the American polity, see
Theodore M. Lowi, *The End of Liberalism: The Second Republic of the United States* (New
York, 1979).

ment to the federal Constitution to outlaw the manufacture, distribution, and sale of alcoholic beverages. The prohibition movement arose in the 1850s, the league not until the 1890s. In the intervening four decades dry reformers had worked, for the most part, either through general associations or local, ad hoc groups. The Prohibition party that formed at the end of the 1860s sought to win its goal by operating as an open, democratic organization offering candidates committed to prohibition and, usually, taking stands on other issues. The Woman's Christian Temperance Union (WCTU), started in 1874, worked for a broad range of reform goals, not the least of which was prohibition. The Anti-Saloon League was different, and it was that difference that attracted the attention of Odegard and other observers. The league specialized by focusing continuing attention on a single issue, prohibition, and by refusing direct involvement with other issues. Like its predecessor dry organizations, the league tried to mobilize millions of supporters across the nation and to win new recruits for the cause; but unlike them, the league consistently refused to distract attention, and potentially to lose supporters, by straying from its single purpose.[7]

The league, as we shall discover, differed from its predecessor prohibition organizations in another important respect: the way it was managed. Social theorists in the early twentieth century began to notice what Robert Michels called the "iron law of oligarchy," the tendency of the leaders of private associations to exert control regardless of whatever formal trappings of democracy their constitutions might contain.[8] The Anti-Saloon League suffered the same affliction, except that in its case control by the leaders was implanted from the start. The formal definitions of constituency control of the organization's direction came later, and they had no significant impact on the exercise of power within the league. Started as a conscious effort to pattern a reform organization on the successful business firms that had undergone the managerial revolution, the Anti-Saloon League always remained a single-issue institution controlled and operated by a leadership cadre who mobilized a mass

7. I have profited greatly from Jack S. Blocker, Jr., *Retreat from Reform: The Prohibition Movement in the United States, 1890–1913* (Westport, Conn., 1976), although my perspective is different from his. Blocker argues that the Prohibition party represented a middle-class reform effort concerned with the well-being of all social classes, whereas the Anti-Saloon League was more narrow-minded, representing a middle-class retreat from fundamental social changes.

8. For a discussion of Michels's insights for the American setting, see McConnell, *Private Power and American Democracy*, especially chapter 5, "Private Government."

constituency that donated funds and supplied votes on election day. The emulation of business techniques meant that the men and women who formed and ran the league were attempting to devise a modern bureaucracy, complete with separate departments managed by professional experts who coordinated their activities through a central office.

If the Anti-Saloon League was a distinct part of the organizational revolution that swept through American society during its lifetime, it was also part of the broad reform phenomenon that historians call progressivism. Progressivism appeared during the time of the organizational revolution and in part reflected the various goals of the disparate associations that were forming in American society. The many facets of progressivism—it had economic and political aspects as well as social, intellectual, and cultural—have led to much dispute among its interpreters. To understand the league, however, we need not stray too far in the historians' thickets. Because the political power of the Anti-Saloon League was reaching its peak at the same time that progressivism was flowering, and because many of the same people were involved both as "progressives" and as prohibitionists, it is easy to associate the two.[9]

The ideology of the prohibition movement—the thoughts that Hobson and his colleagues were voicing—was closely integrated with the main strands of reform expressions during the first two decades of the twentieth century. One of those threads was the appearance of new systems of government—business relations. At first glance, the prohibition amendment and the growth of governmental agencies to control business may seem far apart in spirit as well as purpose. This book will show that the politics of the league conformed closely to the general tendency of the time of increasing expectations of government intervention in the economy.

Government regulation of business and the genesis of new agencies such as the independent regulatory commissions had two main political sources. Historians have long recognized the complaints of the owners of small firms and of commercial farmers about what seemed the inordinate power of the large corporations that had emerged from the managerial revolution and the machinations of financiers like J. P. Morgan. Their complaints created political support in Congress and state legislatures for new laws asserting the dominance of "the public interest" over special interests. The other

9. The key work associating prohibition and progressivism is James H. Timberlake, *Prohibition and the Progressive Movement, 1900–1920* (Cambridge, Mass., 1963).

source of government regulation, understood only more recently, came from the business executives who were responsible for large organizations capitalized with huge sums and who thus desired more stable and predictable social environments. When the corporate leaders thought they could achieve their goals through private associations, they erected them, but they did not hesitate otherwise to seek the assistance of the government.[10] The distillers and brewers sometimes responded to the dry forces by seeking protective regulation.

Hobson's complaints about the liquor trust provide a clue that the prohibition movement was part of this more general phenomenon of Americans turning to politics to control aspects of business behavior. The prohibition movement thus was part of progressivism insofar as it was part of the more general growth of the politics of government–business relations. Except, in this case, the reformers were not small businessmen or farmers fulminating about the powerful and hurtful intrusions of corporate giants into the traditional market economy. Instead, the reformers were church men and women who believed that an evil concentration of power had arisen in the form of the liquor trust, power that they could break only with a constitutional declaration of the illegality of the business systems that organized the manufacture and distribution of alcoholic beverages. The public interest, in their view, required no less than the destruction of the brewing and distilling industries.

If the Anti-Saloon League and its supporters were engaged in an exercise in government-business relations, the drys were acting in a spirit that was cultural, not economic. It was this cultural spirit that perhaps distinguished progressivism. There was an idealism, evangelism, and moralism that welled up in American life in the decade preceding the nation's entry into the First World War which the league helped promote and which it voiced. Evangelism, moralism, and idealism had long been present in American culture, but in this progressive phase Americans expressed those emotions and thoughts optimistically and with an insistence that they could define the public weal. Reformers from many walks of life and from different parts of the nation came somehow to the belief that they could successfully apply the principles of Christian brotherhood to reshape America for the better. Reform and a concern for the public

---

10. The literature of government-business relations is too large to cite briefly. For a survey of recent scholarship, see Thomas K. McCraw, "Regulation in America: A Review Article," *Business History Review* 49 (Summer 1975): 159–83.

interest as defined by Christian tenets enjoyed widespread social support. These progressive reformers came to express the possibilities of "character and service" in changing the ways individuals related to society: to "live and help live." This was a hope that Americans believed they could accomplish in various ways, from invigorating a peace movement to founding the Boy Scouts and the Campfire Girls.[11] Americans stated their optimism through voluntary associations of many kinds, not the least of which was the Anti-Saloon League. The league came, in the years surrounding Hobson's proposal to the House of Representatives, to enjoy nationwide political support and to command very large budgets from the contributions of hundreds of thousands, if not millions, of church people. In those years the league wanted to reach out to enlist the support of organized labor as well as the nation's businessmen. Some dry leaders wanted to work sympathetically with the teeming immigrant populations of the cities to persuade those peoples, in their native languages, if not to support prohibition laws, then at least to understand their purpose.

The cultural confidence and optimism expressed by the progressive reformers who were most directly concerned with improving society, as opposed to engaging in traditional partisanship or bargaining for economic advantages, came to a crashing halt shortly after the First World War. The Anti-Saloon League suffered as a result. League leaders had expected to continue commanding a well-funded, broadly supported movement that, among other matters, would extend American prohibition doctrine to other nations while continuing to educate and uplift American's own wet populations. Other leaders expected to wield power in American politics and to maintain vigilance against a resurgence of the liquor traffic. None of these goals, as events turned out, was supportable. By 1920 the league leaders had to scale down their budgets dras-

11. The essay by John C. Burnham in John D. Buenker, John C. Burnham, and Robert M. Crunden, *Progressivism* (Cambridge, Mass., 1977), pp. 3–29, is especially incisive. Burnham explains that progressivism was a coalescence that came together around 1907 and can best be understood as a cultural phenomenon, not as a set of political events. He addresses the especially sticky problem of how progressivism came to encompass older reform movements, including prohibition, and the voluntary tradition; progressivism was an outburst of a widespread ethos of optimism about improving the public good. "Insistence of the public weal," he explains, "was what made progressivism so distinctive." See also, Ferenc M. Szaz, "The Stress on 'Character and Service' in Progressive America," *Mid-America* 63 (October 1981): 145–56.

tically, and by 1930 league officials were failing to replace an aging leadership with a younger generation.

The 1920s proved a curious decade for the Anti-Saloon League, in part because the depth of optimism that had buoyed progressivism was gone and in part because the league was itself ill-structured to cope with the new situation it faced. The league was a successful organization when it worked to achieve prohibition. It effectively rallied voters to support its single cause. But the league's structure was less well suited for an educational campaign to uplift Americans and maintain or enlarge its base of support. The struggle to achieve passage of the Eighteenth Amendment, as this book reveals, was not as prolonged as dry leaders had anticipated. They thought that an extended period of education and proselytizing was required, and they began working to marshall the resources for the required missionary work.

But the league never had to complete that task, as events turned out, in order to win its political victory, and so when the progressive confidence died in the 1920s, the league had few resources, organizational or financial, with which to try to revive it. After the dry forces struck what they thought was a deadly and permanent blow to the liquor traffic, they were able to maintain a facade of enormous and virtuous political power. It was that facade that Odegard observed. But underneath the facade the inner league structure was crumbling away. Meanwhile, also fading from predominance in American civilization was the broad cultural progressivism upon which the league had capitalized.

The varying responses of prohibition leaders to this situation of the 1920s revealed that the league had mobilized a coalition that agreed on the enactment of the Eighteenth Amendment but did not agree upon a proper church strategy within a legally dry America. The Anti-Saloon League, it turns out, split into two factions after 1920. One, led by Wayne Wheeler, captured most of the public's attention. He wanted the league to control appointments to law enforcement agencies. He wanted to obtain ever stricter enforcement statutes. The other faction, led by Ernest Cherrington, was less visible to the general public. Cherrington wanted to leave law enforcement to the government, conducted by a professional civil service encouraged by the league. The Anti-Saloon League, in the meantime, should effectively reconstitute itself as a grand *temperance* organization, using its skills and resources to conduct educational campaigns and keep the progressive spirit of uplift and the public weal kindled. This basic dispute over strategy dominated the story of the Anti-Saloon League after 1920. One result of the dispute was to abet the disintegration of the dry coalition.

The disintegration of the dry coalition was not apparent until after the stock market crash of 1929. Facing the candidacy of the dry Democrat, Al Smith, the league had helped elect Herbert Hoover in 1928. The Hoover landslide seemed to provide, for a very brief period, a revival of the old confidence that government could help reshape a progressive society. Following the elections the dry margins in Congress were at their highest point in the decade. The Hoover administration was willing to lead the reorganization of the prohibition enforcement agencies and to ask Congress for financial support for an educational campaign on behalf of law observance. But suddenly after 1929 the political winds shifted. Hoover and the Republicans were blamed for the collapse of the American economy. When the Democrats swept into office after 1930 the dry legislative support evaporated, public support for prohibition seemed to be dying, and the repeal movement raged through most of the nation like a prairie fire. The Anti-Saloon League leaders observed these changes helplessly, for their organization was a faded shadow of its former self little more than a decade earlier.

No one could have foreseen these changing circumstances while Hobson preached to the House of Representatives that December day in 1914. When he voiced complaints about the liquor trust, his words were not an aberration; the sentiment he expressed did not stand apart from a wider set of public concerns. Moreover, the propaganda of the dry forces regarding the liquor traffic persuaded millions of Americans because it contained elements of observable truth. In particular, by 1914 the point of retail sale of most beer and whiskey, the saloon, was in many places under the control of brewing firms that were themselves often big businesses. Where it was not outlawed or regulated, the saloon was a ubiquitous institution, a highly visible part of the alcoholic beverage industries. Complaining drys commonly observed saloons that were tied to gambling and prostitution activities and saloon keepers who bought police protection, helped finance city political bosses, and otherwise corrupted local government and society. To understand these elements—and therefore to understand the rise of the Anti-Saloon League—we must first turn to the history of the brewing and distilling industries and examine their exercise of power in American society and politics.

1

THE BUSINESS
OF DRINK

The prohibition movement of the late nineteenth and early twentieth centuries was convinced that it was fighting the liquor trust. That much is clear from the rhetoric spoken by Representative Hobson in 1914 and from the countless pages of broadsides, leaflets, posters, and articles the reformers produced over the decades. At one level the notion of the liquor trust was a simple rhetorical device for focusing the attention of reform sentiment. As a rhetorical device, the notion was something of a myth for, as we shall see, there was no single business institution that organized the manufacture, distribution, and sale of alcoholic beverages. But at another level, the notion of the liquor trust addressed reality, for there was a business system penetrating city neighborhoods and rural areas alike for the marketing of beer and spirits. It was that business system that prohibitionists sought to destroy, and in order to understand their actions, and the long struggle that the reformers faced, we must first explore the evolution of the distilling, brewing, and saloon industries. Understanding the outline of the history of those businesses will allow us to separate myth from reality in the prohibition crusade and especially to comprehend the reasons behind the reformers' convictions that to deal effectively with the social problems of alcohol use the nation must engage in a new venture in government-business relations. Furthermore, the rivalries within the business of drink will help account for the rapid success of the Anti-Saloon League after 1913.

The distilling of spirits and the brewing of beer were enterprises nearly as old as the first European settlements in North America. Each industry evolved independently, and by the post-Civil War decades each experienced fundamentally different patterns of organization and marketing. Peculiar taxation policies, technological developments, and marketing opportunities changed both industries after the Civil War. The preference of drinkers was shifting

12

from spirits to beer in the new industrial age. The history of the brewing industry produced the ubiquitous saloon, whose presence fired the emotions of reformers, persuaded them of the reality of a liquor trust, and gave them cause, in 1893, to name their new political organization the Anti-Saloon League.

Exposing the Liquor Traffic

Long before the Anti-Saloon League was organized or became a powerful political force, dry reformers were convinced that the permanent improvement of American society required the extinction of the liquor traffic. Their logic was simple. The social good required abstention. Yet America permitted businessmen to seek profit from the manufacture and sale of alcoholic beverages. The profit motive of the liquor traffic produced a condition in which it was in the interests of distillers and brewers to encourage Americans to drink—more Americans to drink, and to drink more alcohol. Politicians, in the reformers' view, all too often participated if for no other reason than to enjoy tax revenues from whiskey, beer, and saloons. The combination of the profit motive and the pecuniary interests of the government, from the local to the federal levels, produced an undesirable social and governmental system. The way to break this system, to change it for the better, was to declare illegal the manufacture and sale of alcoholic beverages and thereby substantially reduce, if not remove, the impetus of businessmen constantly seeking to enlarge their markets. Once the business of drink was illegal, as Hobson so emotionally explained, the enticement of Americans to a life of drink would recede, and the nation would become sober.[1]

The first step in the crusade for a sober nation seemed to be to expose the liquor traffic. Once the traffic's practices were brought to light, the reformers were convinced, an indignant public would insist on prohibition. The saloons, and the attendant abuses, were apparent to all citizens who cared to observe them. But apart from the point of retail sale, "the liquor trust" or "the liquor traffic" was a

---

1. Here and elsewhere my study relies on the able work of other scholars who have explained the ideology of the dry crusade. An excellent, brief overview is the paper commissioned by the National Research Council, Paul Aaron and David Musto, "Temperance and Prohibition in America: A Historical Overview," in *Alcohol and Public Policy: Beyond the Shadow of Prohibition*, ed. Mark H. Moore and Dean R. Gerstein (Washington, 1981), pp. 127–81.

more hidden affair. From the 1870s through the 1890s prohibition organizations called for full public disclosure of the liquor traffic. The drys were confident that if Congress empowered a national commission to collect statistical data, hear expert testimony, and subpoena the records of firms and trade associations, it would report evidence persuasive of the evils of beverage alcohol and of the business system that supplied it. On seven occasions in the late nineteenth century the U.S. Senate passed resolutions to establish such a Commission of Inquiry into the Liquor Traffic, but in no case did the House of Representatives ever vote upon them. Congress did, however, authorize the U.S. commissioner of labor, Carroll D. Wright, to investigate and issue a report, *Economic Aspects of the Liquor Problem*, in 1898.[2]

Wright confined his investigation to the production, consumption, distribution, and taxation of alcoholic beverages. He deliberately refrained from exploring the social and moral consequences of the liquor traffic. He gathered statistical data from the census and from the commissioner of internal revenue, selected districts intended to represent the nation as a whole for a more exhaustive survey, and sent questionnaires to 30,000 employers regarding their attitudes toward drink and the workplace. In the report, which mostly comprised statistical tables and explanations of the means used to derive them, Wright drew few conclusions. He seemed most interested in the 7,025 responses from employers, not in describing the liquor traffic as prohibitionists construed it. What Wright found "most interesting" were data unsympathetic to prohibitionist arguments: the employers who stated that prohibition legislation only increased the thirst among laborers for alcoholic beverages.[3]

The scope of this federal investigation of the liquor traffic was certainly unsatisfactory from the viewpoint of the prohibition movement. The report said little about the human effects of the liquor traffic and nothing about the political activities of its business firms or of their efforts to enlarge and control the markets for alcoholic beverages. But Wright's data did describe important trends in the industries. In the production of both beer and liquor between 1880 and 1890 there was a concentration of firms, an expansion of capital investment, and a significant increase in the value of products.

2. "Alcoholic Liquor Traffic Commission," *House Report* 1789, 54th Cong., 1st sess., 1896; *Twelfth Annual Report of the Commissioner of Labor, 1897, Economic Aspects of the Liquor Problem* (Washington, 1898).

3. *Economic Aspects*, p. 80.

Between 1880 and 1890 the number of breweries declined from
2,191 to 1,248 and distilleries from 844 to 440. But the capitalization
of those industries increased, for breweries from $91.2 million to
$232.5 million and for distilleries from $24.2 to $31 million. In a
time of general monetary deflation the value of the products of
breweries increased from $101 to $182.7 million and of distilleries
from $41.1 to $104.2 million.[4] Here was evidence that prohibitionists could interpret as a confirmation that the alcoholic beverage
industries were tending to place larger sums of money in the hands
of fewer firms. There was, thus, in the late nineteenth century a
trend toward the production of a larger volume of alcoholic beverages, by fewer firms, using large and growing capital investments.

The problem with such a conclusion, however—and it was not one
that Wright's report drew—was that it overlooked two important
facts. When adjusted for the growth in the population and expressed in per capita terms, the consumption of distilled spirits was
noticeably decreasing and the imbibing of beer dramatically rising.
Wright reported Treasury Department figures showing that between 1840 and 1896 the per capita consumption of "proof gallons"
of distilled spirits had declined from 2.52 to 1.00, while that of malt
liquors had risen from 1.36 to 15.16 gallons.[5] One could conclude—
again, Wright did not do so—that American society had become
much more temperate in its use of alcoholic beverages. Second, as
the consumption data hinted, there was intense competition for
markets within the drink business with the brewers increasingly
capturing the preferences of consumers.

Richmond P. Hobson and other prohibition advocates chose to
overlook this information, if they were aware of it, in their accusa-
tions about a liquor trust and in their complaints about the saloon.
The histories of the distilling and brewing industries in the United
States that led to the abuses of the saloon system help explain how
such an oversight was possible. Those same histories will also explain
how the liquor trust was overrated as a political force. The whiskey
and beer industries were, in fact, so much in competition with one
another that, until they faced extinction by Hobson and the Anti-
Saloon League's campaign for a federal constitutional amendment,
they were unable to agree on a common political organization and
strategy for their survival.

4. Ibid., pp. 19–21.
5. Ibid., p. 35.

Drink, Business, and Social Customs in a Traditional Society

The growth of large corporations for the manufacture and distribution of alcoholic beverages was a relatively recent phenomenon that paralleled similar developments in other business fields after 1880. In the beverage industries, as in many other manufacturing enterprises, growth occurred with changing consumer preferences and waves of migration to American cities. The liquor traffic evolved from a long sequence of changes in the American economy. When the United States was born, Americans commonly drank rum and cider. In the colonial years rum was both an important product in the export market and an item of barter in a cash-poor society. But with the changes in political policy and ideology that occurred with the American Revolution, American drinkers began to shift from rum to whiskey. This was especially true with the opening of the trans-Appalachian frontier at the turn of the nineteenth century.[6]

When farmers first grew grain west of the Appalachian mountains, they discovered that they could not market that grain conveniently and profitably. For a farmer in Kentucky or Ohio in the early nineteenth century there were two potential markets for grain, New Orleans or the eastern seaboard. The cost of transporting grain overland to seaports was prohibitive, and the river journey to New Orleans was a long one with an uncertain price at its terminal. But grain could be easily converted to whiskey and then shipped economically to market, where it was more likely to receive a profitable price. The prospects of profit attracted investments in thousands of small distilleries in the new West after 1800. Soon whiskey was in plentiful supply, and it replaced rum as an item of barter in the cash-poor economy.

At the same time that the supply of whiskey was expanding, Americans began consuming it in larger quantities. By 1825 the annual per capita consumption of whiskey in the United States was not quite five gallons. Americans were also drinking large quantities of cider, along with smaller amounts of beer and wine, so that the annual per capita consumption of absolute alcohol by adult Americans stood at about seven gallons. (By comparison, the figure in 1975

6. W. J. Rorabaugh, *The Alcoholic Republic: An American Tradition* (New York, 1979), pp. 53–108, explains early American drinking customs and their industries. The data below on consumption are drawn from this study and from Norman Clark, *Deliver Us from Evil: An Interpretation of American Prohibition* (New York, 1976), pp. 19–20.

was 2.7 gallons.) This was a high rate of consumption, and travelers and commentators consistently reported seeing widespread drunkenness. Drunkenness, historians have concluded, was a result of both a plentiful supply of beverage alcohol and of underlying tensions in a society experiencing rapid growth and change. The temperance movement of the early nineteenth century was a response to this situation. Its spokesmen exhorted Americans to drink less or not at all, and Americans who pledged to abstain formed fraternal societies for mutual support and for propagating the temperance message.

At about the time of the emergence of the American temperance movement, the economic conditions that had fostered the widespread production of whiskey were changing. The opening of canal systems in the 1820s and 1830s allowed farmers profitable opportunities to export grain to East Coast markets. Whiskey production began to concentrate in large distilleries in Cincinnati, Pittsburgh, and southeastern Pennsylvania, locations where transportation costs for shipping grain to market remained relatively high. By 1845 the annual adult per capita consumption of whiskey was down to about 2.1 gallons, of absolute alcohol to 1.8 gallons.

Distilled spirits, or whiskey, were not the only alcoholic beverages that Americans consumed in this period, although in alcoholic content they were by far the most significant. Farmers turned plentiful apple crops into cider. There were small vineyards that produced wine, and local breweries operated in the cities. In 1845 the American annual per capita consumption of beer was about 1.4 gallons. This beer, however, differed from the later product. It was brewed in vats with a top-floating yeast of English origin. It stored poorly and was costly to ship, so the site of production was almost always in the larger cities near the retail outlets. At the time of the Civil War the preferred alcoholic beverage of Americans was still whiskey.

The Evolution of the Whiskey Business in Urban Industrial Society

Americans bought two types of whiskey in the decades before prohibition. There were firms in Kentucky and Pennsylvania, making bourbon and rye whiskey, respectively, that distilled grain mash, aged it in wooden casks for a period of years, and sold it under brand labels. This so-called straight whiskey was not, however, the common product. Americans drank mostly rectified whiskey in their saloons, a product made by a two-stage process. First, a distiller produced alcohol from grain—what we would call grain neutral spirits—and then sold the alcohol either for industrial or beverage purposes. For drinking, the rectifier diluted the alcohol with water and flavored it in one of several ways: with aged whiskey or even fruit juices, or, for gin, with the oil of juniper berries. He sold his products to wholesale firms that in turn distributed them to retail outlets.[7]

This industry was deeply affected by federal tax policy. During the Civil War the government turned to spirits as a source of tax revenue. Before the war, a 100 proof gallon of spirits sold in New York for 24 cents, on the average. Then the government began to tax alcohol, increasing the rate to $2 per gallon by January 1, 1865. But the government did not levy those taxes retroactively on spirits already manufactured and held in storage. The manufacturing of spirits required relatively small investments of capital, so speculators entered the business, setting up new distilleries and holding the alcohol in storage in anticipation of a higher future tax levy. In 1865 it cost about 25 cents to manufacture a gallon of 100 proof spirits. The cost of "new" spirits thus was $2.25 per gallon, and it was possible to sell "old" spirits well below that figure and still turn a handsome profit. So the tax policy had two harmful effects on the industry. The policy created incentives that led to a considerable overexpansion of productive capacity relative to market demand, and it raised the price of alcohol to levels that prohibited its economical use for fuel, or in varnishes, perfumes, and the like. The ease of entry, the expansion of productive capacity, and the destruction of part of the market for industrial alcohol meant that at the end of the nineteenth century distilling firms suffered from internecine competition.[8]

The center of the distilling industry after the Civil War was Peoria, Illinois. Distillers there were favored with nearby supplies of grain and coal, ample water, and good rail connections. Peoria was close to the Chicago livestock market, important for the firms that fed their cooked grain mash to cattle. Peoria-based firms led the industry in a strategy of controlling productive capacity and thereby prices and profits. The forms of the strategy followed a classic pattern in American business history. In the early 1880s the distilling firms formed the Western Exporters' Association, a pool intended to

7. *Preliminary Report on Trusts and Industrial Combinations, United States Industrrial Commission* (Washington, 1900), vol. 1, pp. 75–76.

8. Ibid., p. 81; Jeremiah W. Jenks, "The Development of the Whiskey Trust," *Political Science Quarterly* 4 (June 1889): 296–300.

include between seventy and eighty members. That pool failed when Cincinnati- and New York−based firms refused to enter and subsequently undercut prices. In 1887 the Distillers' and Cattle Feeders' Trust was formed; by 1889 eighty-six firms had placed control of their stock in the hands of the trustees. Fearing the intervention of the courts, the trust was incorporated in Illinois in 1890. Nevertheless, in 1894 the Illinois Supreme Court ruled that the Distillers' and Cattle Feeders' Company was in fact a combination in restraint of trade and ordered it dissolved.[9]

What ensued was a labyrinth of receiverships, corporate organization and reorganization. In 1895 the American Spirits Manufacturing Company took over the plants of the old Distillers' and Cattle Feeders' Company and then, in 1896, formed a subsidiary, the Spirits Distributing Company, to control the rectifying bussiness. A rival firm, the Standard Distilling and Distributing company, formed in New York in 1898. It had a marketing organization as well as distilling and rectifying facilities. By 1899 American Spirits controlled about 55 percent of the nation's spirits production, Standard about 35 percent. The Kentucky Distillers and Warehouse Company formed that year to control the production of about 90 percent of the manufacture of straight bourbon. In 1899 these four firms were brought together under a holding company, the Distilling Company of America; it was reorganized in 1902 as the Distillers Securities Corporation.[10]

This corporate maneuvering was a manifestation of a fundamental shift in business strategy. The goal of the Distillers' and Cattle Feeders' Company, and of the pools that had preceded it, was to control the volume of production. The Distillers' Company had resorted to a rebate scheme in the 1890s in an effort to enforce its power. Wholesale dealers who purchased a prescribed gallonage from the trust received a rebate. The intention of this plan was to prevent potential competitors from having the opportunity to market spirits. But when the Distillers' Company had to use its funds to buy out competitors rather than pay the wholesalers, it issued them mortgage bonds. The wholesalers, who never liked the rebate

9. Earnest E. East, "The Distillers' and Cattle Feeders' Trust, 1887−1895," *Journal of the Illinois State Historical Society* 45 (Summer 1952): 101−23; *Preliminary Report on Trusts and Industrial Combinations*, vol. 1, pp. 76−78; *Bonfort's Wine and Spirits Circular*, Feb. 10, 1886, p. 172, and June 25, 1886, p. 87.

10. *Preliminary Report on Trusts and Industrial Combinations*, vol. 1, p. 76; Alfred D. Chandler, Jr., "The Beginnings of 'Big Business' in American Industry," *Business History Review* 33 (Spring 1959): 1−31.

scheme in the first place, foreclosed on the bonds and forced the manufacturing firm into receivership at about the same time the Illinois court ruled that it was an illegal combination in the restraint of trade.[11] These conditions led to the development of an entirely different corporate strategy by the successor firms, one that was similar to the forms of business organization developed in other industries that processed agricultural goods for human consumption: vertical integration.

The strategy of vertical integration that the Distillers Securities Corporation pursued in the early twentieth century did not seek the complete control of the distillation of spirits. Instead, the reorganized firm sought to lower the costs of production and to secure its own markets through the ownership of selected wholesale firms and the brand name identification of its products with consumers. The firm's size allowed it to offer wholesalers a full line of various spiritous liquors while it lowered management and distribution costs. This strategy of vertical integration combined with the size of the firm meant that it was able to maintain a position as the price leader in the industry. The efficiency and size of Distillers Securities effectively brought order out of the chaos of the Gilded Age industry.[12]

The strategy of vertical integration did not insure whiskey's hold on the growing urban markets, however. The Distillers Securities Corporation proved to be a profitable enterprise. It paid dividends quarterly until 1913 and thereafter substantially reduced its bonded indebtedness. The company reported a surplus on hand of almost $8,500,000 in 1916. But in spite of the financial health of the firm and its industry, whiskey was losing ground to a competing beverage, beer. The vertical integration of the industry did not extend to retail sales in saloons. They were increasingly coming under the control of the brewing companies, and sales of spiritous liquors in saloons declined relative to beer.

The Rise of the American Brewing Industry

In spite of the importance of the American distilling industry, it was the brewing industry that fueled the modern prohibition move-

---

11. *Preliminary Report of Trusts and Industrial Combinations*, vol. 1, pp. 83–84.
12. Ibid., pp. 178, 241, 814–19, 834–45; Jeremiah W. Jenks and Walter E. Clark, *The Trust Problem*, 4th ed. (New York, 1919), pp. 141–49; Chandler, *The Visible Hand*, p. 328.

ment. The simple fact of the matter was that as the modern prohibition movement was gaining strength, the preference of American drinkers was shifting from spirits to beer. The average per capita consumption of distilled spirits declined after 1865, when it stood at 2.1 gallons. In 1915 Americans consumed, on the average, 1.2 gallons of spirits. During the same half-century, beer sales rose dramatically, from 3.5 gallons per capita in 1865 to 20.2 gallons in 1915. The largest increase in beer consumption occurred between 1880 and 1885, from 6.9 gallons to 11.4 gallons per capita.[13] This expansion of the brewing industry meant that the annual adult consumption of absolute alcohol was increasing, even as Americans drank less whiskey. In 1880 adult Americans drank about six-tenths of a gallon of absolute alcohol in beer. By 1915 that consumption had quadrupled. This dramatic rise in beer consumption meant that we must explore the history of the brewing industry in order to understand how American reformers responded.

The brewing of beer in North America was nearly as old as European settlement, but the modern industry did not emerge until the period between 1840 and 1880. Before 1840 brewing was a local industry using English techniques that produced a beverage we would now call ale or porter. The modern industry emerged after 1840, when brewers introduced German yeast cultures that resulted in a light beer that they could store (lager). Lager beer appealed to American tastes, and by 1867 there were about 3,700 separate brewing firms manufacturing and marketing beer in every state and territory in the nation. These were still mostly small operations supplying local markets. Beer was too bulky a product to ship long distances economically, and in the age before pasteurization and mechanical refrigeration even lager beer did not keep easily.[14]

The industry underwent rapid change after the Civil War. A number of important scientific and technological breakthroughs allowed expansion to occur, and the growth of cities and the completion of the railroad network opened new marketing opportunities. The discoveries of Pasteur led to a greater understanding of the brewing process and offered brewers the opportunity to market a less perishable product. Lager beer required fermentation at cool temperatures, and the introduction of mechanical refrigeration de-

13. Jenks and Clark, *The Trust Problem*, pp. 141–49; Rorabaugh, *The Alcoholic Republic*, p. 207.

14. Stanley Baron, *Brewed in America: A History of Beer and Ale in the United States* (Boston, 1962), pp. 173–83.

vices in the 1880s relieved brewers of dependence on the capricious natural ice industry. With mechanical refrigeration brewers could more closely control the temperatures required for fermentation, and they could also supply ice for cooling freight cars and distribution centers. By the 1890s brewers had developed labor saving devices, refrigeration facilities, and scientific knowledge to allow the economical production in large volumes of a uniform product that satisfied popular tastes.[15]

By the latter part of the nineteenth century, thus, important conditions for change in the brewing industry were appearing. Not only were the technologies of brewing and distributing beer advancing, but market conditions provided important new opportunities. Between 1873 and 1893 the potential market for beer increased dramatically as the population concentrated in towns and cities larger than 8,000 persons doubled. Enterprising brewers, led by Pabst, Schlitz, and Blatz in Milwaukee, Anheuser-Busch and Lemp in St. Louis, and Moerlein in Cincinnati, took advantage of these conditions and reinvested their profits to compete for sales on a national basis. Dozens of other firms sought to expand their operations regionally. So a modern business structure emerged in the brewing industry to satisfy the firms' marketing strategies. It was part of the management revolution generally experienced by transportation and manufacturing firms at the time. The larger breweries adapted advanced technological and scientific knowledge to the manufacturing of beer and developed integrated marketing structures in order to sell it in larger volumes. The vertical integration of brewing firms included purchasing agents, production departments, transportation facilities, and networks of distribution centers in their marketing regions. By the 1880s breweries were also seeking control of retail outlets, and by the twentieth century they became heavily involved in the actual ownership of saloons.[16]

The evolving business strategy and structure of the brewing industry did not lessen competition at the retail level. If anything, competition increased. Before the adoption of modern production

15. Ibid., pp. 228–46; Thomas C. Cochran, *The Pabst Brewing Company: The History of an American Business* (New York, 1948), pp. 102–28.

16. Cochran, *The Pabst Brewing Company*, pp. 70–78; Chandler, *The Visible Hand*, pp. 301–02; Ronald J. Plavchan, *A History of Anheuser-Busch, 1852–1933* (New York, 1976), pp. 66–98; Perry Duis, "The Saloon and the Public City: Chicago and Boston, 1880–1920," (Ph.D. diss., University of Chicago, 1975), pp. 391–421. Duis has subsequently revised and shortened his work as *The Saloon: Public Drinking in Chicago and Boston, 1880–1920* (Urbana, Ill., 1983).

and distribution technologies, small local firms had largely satisfied local markets, but with the more advanced techniques—supplemented by the late 1890s with successful procedures for bottling
beer—in any given city competition increased when the so-called
shipping breweries entered the field. The Chicago market provides
a good example, for the city's growth made it important to the
brewing industry. By the 1870s the Milwaukee and St. Louis firms
were competing there among themselves and also with local breweries. The result was a price war that drove margins to unprofitable
levels.

The response of the brewers in the Chicago market was to seek
ways of stabilizing their markets and restoring their profits. They
ended the price war in 1881 with an agreement to fix the minimum
price of beer at $8 a barrel and to refrain from giving away signs,
free advertising, and other favors to saloon keepers. This agreement
lasted for a few years, but by the mid-eighties the Chicago market
was again chaotic. The problems from the brewers' viewpoint lay in
the system of independent saloons that allowed the retailers to
bargain with suppliers for lower prices. The vertical integration of
the brewing industry had not yet reached the retail level. When the
saloons operated as independent businesses they were visited by
salesmen from competing firms who tried to place their products in
them. Trying a new brand of whiskey was no problem for the saloon
keeper, for a case, or even a barrel, of spirits would store easily. Beer
was another matter. It came in barrels holding from 31 to 55 gallons
apiece that required an expensive tapping apparatus. Most saloons
had sufficient capital for only two barrels at one time, one in use, the
other in storage. So the saloon was limited effectively to only one
brand of beer, and salesmen from the breweries offered a variety of
inducements, ranging from secret rebates to gifts of signs and other
paraphernalia, for the saloon to sell their brand. By the mid-eighties
in Chicago the price of beer had slipped from the profitable $8
figure to an unprofitable $4 per barrel.[17]

The brewers' response was to extend their strategy of vertical
integration to the saloon. Brewers began to finance saloon keepers

17. Duis, "The Saloon and the Public City." The same pattern occurred at the same
time in Cincinnati. William L. Downard, *The Cincinnati Brewing Industry: A Social and
Economic History* (Athens, Ohio, 1973), pp. 48–49, 89–92. In Michigan overpro-
duction and competition led to unsuccessful attempts to control production and then
to the tied-house system. Larry Engelmann, "O Whiskey! The History of Prohibition
in Michigan" (Ph.D. diss., University of Michigan, 1971), pp. 84–89.

in exchange for agreements to handle the firm's product exclusively. In this "tied house" system, as it was called, the brewing firm held the mortgages on the saloons. By 1898 in Chicago the breweries were making large outright investments in real estate in order to place their product in desirable locations, such as major intersections. This further integration of the industry ended the competitive relationships between saloon keepers and brewers, but not, of course, among the integrated firms themselves. The desire to secure and expand market shares continued among the brewers, and the institution of the saloon, now well financed, proliferated.[18]

So the saloon by the late nineteenth century had become a ubiquitous institution thanks to the competition within the brewing industry. When, in the face of heavy criticism from the prohibition movement, the industry began to consider a strategy of cleaning up its operations after 1900, its goal in important urban markets was to limit the ratio of saloons to one per 500 population. This enormous growth in the number of saloons in areas where the government did not control their number meant that saloon keeping was, at best, a marginal business in most cases because the market was saturated. At the retail level there was little if any profit to be made in beer sales. This situation tempted saloon keepers to encourage customers to drink more at an earlier age, to violate government regulations of their hours, and to engage in sidelines such as prostitution and gambling. To maintain such operations saloon keepers often had to bribe police officials and offer their money and services to urban political machines.[19] The proliferation of these abuses supplied the prohibition movement with its most telling arguments, and thus with the name, Anti-Saloon League, for the organization that became so powerful after 1893.

"The Liquor Trust" as Myth and Reality

Spokesmen for the Anti-Saloon League were well aware that their own rhetoric about "the liquor trust" was more an exercise in myth-making than a description of reality. That is, there was no centralized liquor business force. The league's newspaper, the *American Issue*, began carrying accounts of rivalry and internal disputes among wet organizations as early as 1900. According to these reports, only

18. Duis, "The Saloon and the Public City," pp. 391–421.
19. Ibid.; Engelmann, "O Whiskey!," pp. 128–29; *Brewers' Journal* 33 (Nov. 1, 1908): 13.

when the league began to achieve legislative victories were wet leaders moved to call for unity among all branches of the trade for their mutual self-defense. "Those who read liquor journals with any degree of comprehensiveness," the editor told his readers in 1902, "know that between the brewers and distillers . . . there is a perpetual feud." The purpose of these early accounts in the history of the league was to assure dry supporters that they had little to fear from the liquor traffic—"those who know it best fear it least." Much later, in 1917 when the league was at the peak of its power, James Cannon, in charge of lobbying before Congress, noted that the brewers and distillers remained deeply suspicious of one another in spite of their large investments in a common, defensive political movement.[20]

It was more than useful, however, for the dry reformers to perpetuate the myth of the liquor trust. Because of the large presence of saloons, the complaints about the trust contained sufficient elements of truth, and jibed closely with personal observations, to serve as a powerful weapon of political propaganda. *Trust* in the popular lexicon was the same as *big business*, and the brewing and distilling industries were dominated by wealthy, vertically integrated firms whose arms extended to the neighborhoods and villages of the nation. But "the liquor trust" did not fit more precise definitions of either monopoly or oligopoly, nor did it exist in any permanent political organization.

The political operations of the brewers and distillers, moreover, fueled the Anti-Saloon League's rhetoric. These political activities were one essential ingredient that allowed the myth of the liquor trust to flourish. The brewers and distillers formed political organizations to fight prohibition campaigns, often cooperating to wage specific battles in particular local and state jurisdictions. In those instances their politics seemed to confirm the claim about the liquor trust. But because of the market rivalry between spirits and beer, at the national level the brewers and distillers failed to agree on a consistent political strategy and, consequently, no long-running national political organization united the two industries.

It was common for businessmen to try to influence public policy through the system of political parties that governed the United States in the period. The brewers and spirits men were no exception. They donated campaign funds, served occasionally in party and public offices, and expected the party caucuses in Congress and in

20. Virginius Dabney, *Dry Messiah: The Life of Bishop Cannon* (New York, 1949), p. 127; *American Issue* 8 (Sept. 1900): 11, and January 24, 1902, p. 6.

the legislatures in turn to restrain hostile legislation. Prohibition reformers were unable to break the industries' power in the two-party system during the nineteenth century and sought to circumvent the system by organizing their own third party, and, in the 1880s, by arranging referendum campaigns for the state constitutional amendments. The fight against the referendum required more visible associational activity on the part of the brewers and distillers. They developed techniques of reaching individual voters directly with arguments in refutation of prohibition and of mobilizing those voters on election day. Those techniques lapsed after the wave of prohibition agitation receded at the end of the decade, but what did persist, on the other side, was the conviction of many reformers that they were fighting a well-organized conspiracy.

The public political operations of the industries in the 1880s were a product also of associational impulses common to American business. These impulses came first from the brewers, and their trade association developed the furthest, but the impulses were present among the distillers, wholesalers, and retailers as well. By the end of the century there were national associations of brewers, distillers, and wholesale and retail liquor dealers as well as state and local branches and groups. One function of these associations was resistance to the prohibition movement. On the national level, however, there was no systematic cooperation among them in that regard, and leaders of the groups seldom had even informal contacts with one another.

On the state and local level this organizational diversity was apparent, although cooperative political action among the branches of the trade was much more common. In Ohio, for instance, there were three wet trade associations after 1893: the Ohio Brewers' Association, the Ohio Wine and Spirit Association, and the Ohio State Liquor League, the latter representing the retailers. These groups employed small staffs and appointed committees to guard against unfavorable legislation. They raised funds for donations to party treasuries and jointly mobilized sympathetic voters. In Oregon in 1906 the brewers and wholesalers united to enlist the aid of the retailers in turning out voters opposed to both prohibition and woman suffrage. It is no wonder that prohibitionists spoke of the liquor trust. In their immediate experience in those and other states it was no myth at critical times. But they were seeing local responses to concrete and immediate threats to the trade. At the national level, by contrast, rivalry between the spirits and brewing trades prevented common action, much less argreement on a common strategy of mutual protection.[21]

The United States Brewers' Association (USBA) was the first and most highly developed trade association concerned with a defense against the prohibitionists. Formed in 1862 to fight a federal tax imposed on the industry, the USBA soon grew to include all of the larger brewing firms, and as the industry expanded its markets, it became a significant example of the trade association movement generally. The USBA promoted the general interests of brewing by widening the acceptance of beer in the marketplace, helping its members learn about new techniques of production, fostering ample supplies of raw materials, and securing favorable tariff legislation. What set the USBA apart from other trade associations was that it served an industry constantly threatened with extinction through political action. The association began to voice antagonism toward prohibition legislation in 1866, and it continually professed that beer, with concentrations of alcohol far lower than that of liquor, was truly a "temperance beverage," a "liquid bread."[22]

As an organization, however, the USBA did not reflect the managerial revolution that its large members were experiencing. To attract small firms to its fold, the large breweries allowed each member to have an equal vote, while dues were assessed according to a member's volume of production. The association operated through a system of annual conventions, a board of trustees that governed its affairs, and committees appointed for specialized tasks. By the 1880s it maintained a small headquarters in New York City, where it employed a secretary, a literary manager, and a clerical staff. An attorney represented its interests in Washington, D.C. The USBA was in many ways an informal and loosely structured organization whose components overlapped in their functions and interests. The vigilance committee corresponded with members and collated information about the activities of the prohibition movement, while the

---

21. Brewers' and Wholesale Liquor Dealers' Association to Sir, May 21, 1906, HU; *Dayton Daily Journal*, Mar. 31, 1893; *Columbus Evening Dispatch*, Feb. 7, 1894; *Anti-Saloon* 1 (Nov. 1893): 4.

22. Brewers' Industrial Exhibition, *Essays on the Malt Liquor Question* (New York, 1876), p. 15; Nuala M. Drescher, "The Opposition to Prohibition, 1900–1919" (Ph.D. diss., University of Delaware, 1964), pp. 97–98. The notion of beer as "liquid bread" was probably more than advertising hyperbole, rooted as it was in the brewers' German cultural background. In Germany today, brewers still tout their product as liquid bread.

committee on hostile legislation reviewed applications from local firms for financial assistance to fight dry campaigns. The publication committee took charge of generating and distributing the industry's propaganda. The organization committee sought new members and encouraged the formation of state and local brewers' groups. The overlapping responsibilities did not concern the members. Because the persons involved worked closely together, President Hermann B. Scharmann assured the 1884 convention that there was "complete harmony of action." Aside from hiring Gallus Thomann in 1883 to take charge of the literary effort, the association made no effort to employ a staff to develop specialized knowledge regarding prohibition campaigns or to pay full-time attention to them. Instead, the brewers relied on ad hoc expenditures of funds and on their personal attention whenever they felt the need to react to a prohibition initiative.[23]

The reason the brewers did not transfer the managerial revolution from their firms to their trade association no doubt stemmed from the success of the industry and the USBA. The last three decades of the nineteenth century witnessed the steady expansion of beer production and marketing in the United States. The prohibition movement, the regulation of saloons, and licensing measures seemed to have little impact on the industry overall. The wave of prohibition campaigns in the 1880s was of course a matter of concern, so much so that in 1887 the USBA doubled its dues assessments in order to provide political funds. But that wave of prohibition agitation waned, and dry sentiment seemed not to extend to cities, which provided almost the entire market for beer. The brewers took comfort in the notion that the public would eventually realize that beer was a desirable temperance beverage compared with whiskey. "Manly and decided" action seemed, by the 1890s, to have beaten back the prohibitionists. The publication committee reported to the USBA convention in 1895 that prohibition strength had proven "ephemeral." The brewers had exposed the fallacious dry arguments, and the market for beer was flourishing. Promotion of a laissez-faire environment remained their policy.[24]

The brewers wanted the law of supply and demand to regulate the market because they were convinced that, in the absence of govern-

23. USBA, *Proceedings of the 23rd Convention* (New York, 1883), pp. 12–13, 18–19, and *Proceedings of the 24th Convention* (New York, 1884), p. 17.

24. USBA, *Proceedings*, 1883, p. 13; *Proceedings of the 27th Convention* (New York, 1887), p. 80; *Brewers' Journal* 19 (July 1, 1895): 384–85.

mental regulation, beer would replace whiskey. America would then become a temperate society. As one brewer remarked to a colleague, "All people hate drunkards and whiskey makes them. Men drinking beer exclusively may become 'funny' but never drunk." This anti-prohibition argument was inseparable from the industry's marketing strategy. Both made the brewers highly suspicious of the distilling interests.

Brewers expressed suspicion that distillers were in league with the prohibitionists. They were aware that beer was a bulky product that required an elaborate and technologically sophisticated marketing system for sales at any distance from the site of production. Small packages of liquor, on the other hand, could be shipped easily to individuals even though they resided in dry areas, as years of local legislation had demonstrated. The brewers therefore accused the spirits interests of aiding the prohibition movement in order to damage the brewing industry.[25] These attitudes, and the marketplace rivalries that bred them, effectively prevented meaningful cooperation between the distillers and the brewers in national affairs.

The leaders of the distilling industry, on the other hand, sought a political partnership with the brewers for a vigorous campaign to fend off prohibition. The problem was that their strategy was the opposite of the brewers'. The spirits men and the independent retailers wanted government regulation as a protective measure. Their pitch was for state and city "model license laws" that would regulate the operations of saloons and limit their numbers. Revenue from license fees would insure the support of government officials and help win the sympathy of other taxpayers. Restrictions on the saloon would prevent the abuses that gave the most fanatical prohibitionists arguments for persuading their more moderate neighbors.

The desire for regulation and for taking the offensive against dry agitators led to the first national organization of the distilling industry in 1886. *Bonfort's Wine and Spirit Circular* served the industry, and when the prohibition wave of the 1880s was cresting, one of the

25. Drescher, "Opposition to Prohibition," pp. 97–98; B. Adoue to Otto Wahrmund, Jan. 28, 1902, in *The Brewers and Texas Politics* (San Antonio, 1916), p. 1138. In 1883 the vigilance committee told the USBA that prohibitory laws were "really aimed at skillfully fermented drinks" because they did not prevent customers from purchasing liquors. *Proceedings*, 1883, p. 19. In 1899 the trustees baldly stated that "wherever the brewing industry is to be injured by any law whatever there you will find actively at work the distiller by the side of the Prohibitionist." *Brewers' Journal* 23 (July 1, 1899): 408–09.

staff writers, J. T. Pratt of Louisville, began calling for the formation of a national association to unite distillers, brewers, and dealers in a common resistance. Successful local partnerships had turned back prohibition referendum campaigns and had influenced legislators to deny dry petitions, but there was no national movement either to answer charges regarding the evils of drink and the saloon or to share political resources. In 1886 the *Circular* published several letters asserting the need for a national organization of all the businessmen concerned to raise thousands, if not millions, of dollars for public education and for the teaching of successful political techniques. One writer argued that "a strong, active organization, backed by money and inspired by brains, could well ignore small politicians and laugh at Prohibition fanatics." Another man warned that without such an association, the industries should expect a national prohibition statute.[26]

The National Protective Association formed at a meeting called by Pratt in Chicago that October of 1886. The meeting failed to unite the spirits and brewing industries in a common defense. The four hundred delegates who attended, mostly dealers, asserted that they favored temperance and law observance, not prohibition; that theirs was a respectable business. The delegates endorsed a system of licensing saloons to restrict their number and prevent the abuses that arose from competition, and they promised to refrain from engaging in political activity that was extraneous to the fight against the drys. The convention elected W. J. Lemp, a prominent St. Louis brewer and a trustee of the USBA, vice-president of the association, and invited the brewing industry to join forces with it. But the strategy of promoting model license laws was contrary to the laissez-faire views of most brewers, and Lemp was unable to persuade the USBA.[27]

Even without the assistance of the brewers, the National Protective Association was still able to mount a noticeable effort. It raised funds from dealers and distillers to purchase advertisements in local newspapers during referendum campaigns, hire lecturers and publish literature to counter dry publicity, and make certain that saloon keepers and their customers knew which political candidates op-

26. *Bonfort's Wine and Spirits Circular*, May 15, 1871, p. 1; April 25, 1886, pp. 288–89; May 10, 1886, pp. 8–9; June 10, 1886, p. 65; July 10, 1886, p. 107; August 25, 1886, pp. 192–93.

27. Ibid., Oct. 25, 1886, p. 293; *Chicago Tribune*, Oct. 17, 19, 20, 1886.

posed prohibition. But when the prohibition movement waned in the 1890s, the organization lapsed.

State and local associations remained, however, and in their permanence lay the truth of the prohibitionists' claims about a liquor trust. For example, the Liquor Dealers' and Manufacturers' State Protective Association of Illinois was organized according to senatorial districts and dedicated "to use every effort to defeat oppressive legislation and to maintain and support the cause of personal liberty." The Illinois group provided legal and financial support for any member who faced prosecution under the state's dram shop statute. In partisan politics the association, like state and local liquor groups elsewhere, was neutral, always prepared to help its friends with cash and votes.[28]

During the 1890s two more national groups formed. They represented the third element, the dealers. In 1893 the National Retail Liquor Dealers' Association (NRLDA) organized to protect the interests of independent businessmen. The NRLDA, later called the National Liquor League, worked for the enforcement of licensing laws against illegitimate competitors and, or course, worked against prohibitory legal restrictions. In 1896 the National Wholesale Liquor Dealers' Association (NWLDA) organized to serve distillers, wholesalers, and wineries. Price cutting that threatened the value of inventories prompted the formation of the wholesalers' association. The group initially directed its attention to securing favorable federal tax and tariff legislation. By 1902, only 302 firms had joined, a small fraction of the 4,000 wholesale dealers in business across the country.[29]

The Political Failure of the Business of Drink

Key parts of the context in which the modern prohibition movement developed thus were competitive rivalries among the industries supplying alcoholic beverages and within the brewing industry itself. The spirits industry recognized that the proliferation of saloons fed the fires of dry rhetoric, but the whiskey men were unable to

28. John E. George, "The Saloon Question in Chicago," American Economic Association, *Economic Studies* 2 (1882): 106–08; James R. Turner, "The American Prohibition Movement, 1865–1897" (Ph.D. diss., University of Wisconsin, 1972), p. 361.

29. *The South-West*, Feb. 3, 1893, pp. 2–3; *Bonfort's Wine and Spirits Circular*, Aug. 10, 1896, pp. 220–21; Oct. 25, 1896, p. 378; June 25, 1902, pp. 161–67; *New York Times*, June 10, 1904.

secure the cooperation of the brewers in obtaining either the laws or the corporate policies needed to remedy the condition. They desired a partnership to control the retailing of alcoholic beverages but were unable to secure it until 1913, when Congress passed the Webb-Kenyon bill that forbad the interstate shipment of alcoholic beverages to dry areas. This action shocked the brewers and prompted them to accept the liquor dealers' appeals for a united front. But before 1913 there simply was no liquor trust of national dimensions. There were, however, sufficient examples of associational and cooperative activities at the city and state level to feed dry perceptions of a well-heeled, determined, and when occasion demanded, united enemy.

The failure of the brewers to accept the appeals for national unity was a result of their observation of the beer market. In spite of the storm of protest that the Anti-Saloon League was mobilizing, before 1913 beer sales steadily improved. The dry sentiment appeared to be overwhelmingly rural when the votes in local option contests and state referendums were tallied. The brewers realized that the market for beer was almost entirely urban and that the proportion of Americans living in cities was growing steadily. As new waves of European immigrants swelled tenement districts, the market for beer enlarged. The brewing industry, in short, was experiencing unprecedented good health. "Legislation of an unfavorable character has been undertaken by the legislatures of many states," USBA President John Gardiner told the convention in 1907, "and notwithstanding the sales of beer have increased wonderfully." Maybe an explanation of the paradox would surface, "but, meanwhile we are justified in concluding the correctness of our old contention that beer will always be kept off the list of proscribed articles of diet."[30]

The setting in which the Anti-Saloon League rose had still another important aspect that fit in with the confidence that Gardiner expressed. In spite of the managerial skills of individual brewers, the structure of their trade association was grossly inadequate for responding adequately to the prohibition movement. Until 1908, when the USBA formed an organization bureau staffed by full-time persons, it failed to mobilize fully even the resources of the brewing industry. The committee system reflected the absence of central direction. In 1903, for instance, the trustees reported that the industry was surrounded by enemies "thoroughly organized and splendidly equipped for aggressive warfare;" it was "imperative" that the

---

30. USBA, *Proceedings of the 47th Convention* (New York, 1907), p. 13.

industry perfect its organization. At the same convention, on the other hand, the vigilance committee noted the "manifest decline of prohibition." The next year the publication committee asserted that the effect of prohibition literature "appears to be in inverse proportion to its growth." For evidence the committee cited the growth of beer sales. Nor was the USBA in a position to take charge and coordinate the activities of state and local brewers' organizations. In 1899, when the association was mounting an effort to have a burdensome war tax repealed, it rejected proposals for a hierarchy within the industry capable of exercising authority in the political struggle.[31]

In contrast to the USBA, the NWLDA moved much more quickly to mobilize its resources. "It is apparent," its executive committee reported in 1902, "that a wave of prohibition sentiment is again beginning to sweep the land . . . . Prompt action is imperative." The association formed a protective bureau, chose Cyrus C. Turner, who had served the old National Protective Association, as its general manager, and embarked on a campaign to solicit memberships, raise funds, and warn the public about the dry fanaticism. The alarm brought in new members; by 1904 the association included 590 firms from 100 cities.[32]

The protective bureau went to work quickly to develop a long-range strategy of presenting the industry's side of the prohibition issue. Critical of earlier "spasmodic" efforts that had "squandered" money, its executive committee believed the work was "permanent." Turner focused on propaganda and a positive approach short of initiating political campaigns. Industry leaders recognized that there were abuses in the saloon system that required remedies if they were to eliminate the appeal of the Anti-Saloon League. The trade association asked wholesalers, in effect, to boycott saloons that affronted standards of decency, and it revived the idea of promoting a model license law among state legislatures that would stop the proliferation of saloons and lessen the competitive pressures that were the source of lawbreaking at the retail level. In so doing they were ahead of the brewers in recognizing the strength of the Anti-Saloon League and the kind of industry-wide efforts required to check it.[33]

31. *Brewers' Journal* 23 (July 1, 1899): 414; USBA, *Proceedings of the 43rd Convention* (New York, 1903), pp. 19–21, 71; *Proceedings of the 44th Convention* (New York, 1904), p. 79.

32. *Bonfort's Wine and Spirits Circular*, April 25, 1902, p. 566.

33. National Wholesale Liquor Dealers Association of America, *One Year's Work* (n.p., 1902); *Bonfort's Wine and Spirits Circular*, June 10, 1903, p. 111.

The protective bureau, however, encountered serious problems. Although the Distillers Securities Corporation provided all of its administrative expenses, including Turner's salary, the bureau's funds were too limited, and its organization inadequate, to promote political efforts of its own. In local option campaigns, the bureau mailed literature directly to individual voters, but without a field organization of its own, it had to rely on the sales representatives of wholesalers to inform it of local political conditions around the nation. The problem with the procedure was that the wholesale firms did not always know in advance of local elections. Even when the association was well informed, its resources were inadequate. In its first year the bureau spent only $14,000, nearly two-thirds of that sum in Texas alone.[34] The bureau's budget limited its contributions to advice and literature for wet candidates and campaigns.

So the drink business was hardly the all-powerful, well-heeled trust whose tentacles reached out to envelop the nation in the conspiratorial ways depicted by the Anti-Saloon League. Liquor interests were often effective in specific local campaigns, as the drys witnessed. But in general the drink business comprised several industries engaged in bitter competitive rivalries. As the losers in the competitive warfare, the whiskey men were prescient in their understanding of the Anti-Saloon League, but they were also unable to generate the money needed to counteract its thousands of zealous followers. The brewers, engaged in a far more financially healthy enterprise, were simply unable to face the realities of dry political power. When they eventually did so, in 1908, the Anti-Saloon League was well established. The drink business, far from being a liquor trust, was simply a set of industries and a collection of entrepreneurs who were able to do little more than react to the initiatives of their foes.

The prohibitionists had not always been so well unified or aggressive as they were in 1908 and 1913, either. The history of the prohibition movement and its organizations stretched back for the better part of a century. That history also involved disunity, rivalries that included the questions of whether or not to engage in political action at all, of whether to develop a partisan or nonpartisan political strategy, and of how to mobilize supporters. The Anti-Saloon League that held the drink business in its grip during World War I was a product of those rivalries.

---

34. *Bonfort's Wine and Spirits Circular*, June 10, 1904, pp. 114–15; *One Year's Work*.

2

PARTISANSHIP AND PROHIBITION IN THE GILDED AGE

The birth of the Anti-Saloon League in 1893 occurred after more than forty years of agitation for dry laws. By 1850 Americans had substantially reduced their consumption of alcohol. Temperance agitation undoubtedly helped cause this reduction. But although the United States was a far more sober nation at midcentury than it had been earlier, reformers nevertheless found liquor a deplorable social evil and advocated further action, namely, prohibition. Thinking in much the same terms as Hobson two generations later, they embarked on a wave of agitation for state laws making the manufacture and sale of alcoholic beverages illegal. Maine passed the first prohibition law in 1850, and in the ensuing decade twelve other states enacted "Maine laws." This was the first of three waves of prohibition agitation. The Maine laws, for the most part, were repealed during the Civil War. The second wave came in the 1880s, when reformers used the provisions in state constitutions allowing voters directly, through referendums, to enact amendments. The third wave, led by the Anti-Saloon League, would come in the Progressive era of the early twentieth century.

To understand the strategy and structure of the Anti-Saloon League, we must explore the earlier experiences of prohibition reformers, especially the wave of agitation in the 1880s, for it was from the failure of this movement that the league directly emerged. In the latter part of the nineteenth century two main organizations promoted prohibition. The first was the Prohibition party, founded in 1869 to seek a new coalition of reform-minded voters to change the face of American politics. The second was the WCTU, formed in 1874 to embody unenfranchised women and to provide a channel for political action to persuade the men who monopolized political power that women's concerns, especially prohibition, deserved attention.

Each of these organizations played an important role in the emergence of the Anti-Saloon League. In one sense, their importance was negative, for both failed to win widespread victories in the 1880s, and their failure created a political vacuum that eventually the league filled. In a more positive sense, both the Prohibition party and the WCTU were significant because they represented strategies and structures characteristic of the terms in which nineteenth-century reformers thought about politics. In structural matters, leaders of both organizations thought of democracy as a participatory process through which members of reform organizations directly shaped their affairs. In contrast, the founders of the Anti-Saloon League, having seen the political failures of predecessor organizations, would build a new kind of organization controlled from the top down by leaders who sought the support of followers but not control by followers. The twentieth-century structure of the Anti-Saloon League would look very different from the nineteenth-century structures of other prohibition organizations.

That structure would differ, moreover, because the strategy of the league differed from the approaches of the earlier drys. Nineteenth-century reformers thought of political action as an affair of political parties presenting platforms for change to voters. Politics in their language meant party politics in ours. The Anti-Saloon League founders, on the other hand, would struggle to implant an idea of politics taking place independently of the nomination of candidates and the writing of platforms that comprised the agenda of a political party. This strategy of the league grew out of a controversy within the WCTU. In the 1880s the WCTU set the stage upon which leaders struggled to distinguish partisan and nonpartisan politics, a controversy that culminated in the 1880s when the WCTU affiliated with the Prohibition party. That action aroused the ire of Republican drys and divided the WCTU, and from the turmoil of that division would eventually arise a new clarification of partisan and nonpartisan politics and the strategy of the Anti-Saloon League.

Prohibition, Antislavery, and Political Strategy

The underlying sentiment of the prohibition movement throughout each phase of its long history was essentially religious. By the middle of the nineteenth century the evangelical churches rooted in the British reformation had developed a theology that called for an extension of government power to make society moral, to create

God's Kingdom on Earth. Acting on the belief that the individual should be free to worship his or her Creator, evangelicals sought to destroy institutions that fettered that freedom and seemed to prevent conversion to the faith. Politically they advocated governments that would regulate human affairs and remove the barriers, the work of the devil, that enslaved humans. Laws should be wide-ranging and powerful, these reformers believed; for instance, laws should insure that Sunday was a day set aside for the pious. The power of legislation, so the belief continued, could break the chains of demon rum, the distilleries, breweries, and saloons who profited from enshackling men in a dissolute life of drink. According to the uplift spokespersons, most important was that government should break the power of the southern slavocracy and set all Americans free.[1]

The fight to abolish slavery posed an awful dilemma for some evangelical reformers, however, and it was from that dilemma that the partisan prohibition strategy evolved. The combination of abolition and prohibition was incompatible with the realities of American electoral politics. The antislavery movement, and the new Republican party that expressed the antislavery ambition politically, needed to attract the broadest possible support. To do so the leaders had to play down prohibition. In particular, the Republicans hoped to attract German-American voters who opposed slavery but who were not necessarily attracted to the prohibition banner. In New York in 1856, for instance, Republican leaders told John Marsh, president of the American Temperance Union, that "temperance, for humanity's sake, must yield." Marsh reported that "thousands of men, we were told, there were in the State, who would vote for an anti-slavery Governor, who would not vote for prohibition."[2] The Republican strategy of concentrating on a few issues meant that Americans like John Marsh were forced to rank their opposition to slavery higher than their opposition to the liquor traffic.

The result of the choice was important in the history of prohibition. The dry organizations of the 1850s withered, and eight of the thirteen states that had enacted Maine laws repealed the statutes by the early 1860s. The sapping of the prohibition movement by the

1. For a discussion of the relationship of prohibition to antebellum reform, see Clark, *Deliver Us from Evil*, pp. 45–50. For a recent, thoughtful analysis of the antebellum temperance movement, see Ian R. Tyrrell, *Sobering Up: From Temperance to Prohibition to Antebellum America, 1800–1860* (Westport, Conn., 1979).

2. *Temperance Recollections* (New York, 1866), pp. 266–67.

antislavery cause meant that the dry reform, at the end of the Civil War, was at a nadir.[3]

If the choice of priorities led to the decline in prohibition laws, the success of the Republican strategy was nevertheless impressive to dry reformers. The Republican victories seemed to point the way for effecting change in the American political system; they seemed to provide a victorious reform strategy and show that goals could be achieved through a party dedicated to them. For a generation the success of the Republicans, which had followed extended agitation and education regarding the evils of slavery, shaped the thinking of prohibition advocates. The temperance movement had spoken against the abuse of alcoholic bevarages for decades. Should not that education continue, while a new movement formed to strike the liquor traffic directly?

The rise of an issue-oriented party, moreover, fit in with Americans' faith in and practice of democratic values. Not only did a party in its platforms and candidates ideally present the voters with clear positions on issues, but once in office it was the mechanism for forwarding legislative programs as well. The party itself, at least in theory, was a democratic entity. It rested upon the activities of thousands of supporters, dispersed over vast regions, caucusing in their local townships and wards to choose delegates to the conventions that wrote platforms and nominated candidates.

But when the prohibitionists sought to move their cause to the top of the evangelical political agenda, they encountered serious problems. The Republican party did not disappear with the victory over slavery. It continued to seek and receive the support of Americans who wanted a positive government program of economic development as well as laws to enhance the moral order of society. After 1865 Republican leaders faced the reality that theirs was still a minority party (there was no national majority party before the voter realignments of the 1890s). Republican success still depended on retaining the support of voters arrayed on both sides of the highly emotional prohibition issue.[4] Moreover, many dry voters retained a

---

3. Ernest H. Cherrington, *The Evolution of Prohibition in the United States of America* (Westerville, Ohio, 1920), pp. 235–45; D. Leigh Colvin, *Prohibition in the United States: A History of the Prohibition Party and of the Prohibition Movement* (New York, 1926), pp. 31–43.

4. Morton Keller, *Affairs of State: Public Life in Late Nineteenth Century America* (Cambridge, Mass., 1977), pp. 238–69. Before the voter realignment occurred, a liquor dealers' paper in Cincinnati observed that a usual dry bill was introduced in the Ohio legislature, but the Republican leaders would not allow the measure to surface,

devotion to the Republican party. They spoke of the need for a period of public education, followed at some future time by pressures within the party to have it declare for prohibition, or for having voters decide the issue directly. Another, smaller group of drys, however, asserted that with the achievement of abolition the Republican party had outlived its usefulness and should be replaced by a new organization that would focus on prohibition. Their actions provoked a furious discussion over practical methods for achieving the prohibition reform.

This debate over strategy raged within the dry camp throughout the Gilded Age. Indeed its echoes were still heard after enactment of the Eighteenth Amendment in 1920. The debate first flared with the formation of the Prohibition party in 1869. It continued after the woman's crusade of 1873–74 resulted in the organization of the WCTU. Then, while the WCTU campaigned for state referendums, in 1884 the Prohibition party successfully wounded the Republicans. On the surface the Gilded Age appeared to be a time of stagnation for the prohibition movement, with dry laws repealed except in rural and remote areas of the countryside. But in spite of the defeats, or perhaps because of them, prohibitionists were clarifying the political methods that victory required. Eventually out of this contention and body of experience the Anti-Saloon League emerged.

The National Temperance Society

In the years following the Civil War, hundreds of local temperance groups appeared, but there were three organizations that transcended local communities to provide national forums. Of the three, the Prohibition party and the WCTU were politically most important, but the oldest, the National Temperance Society, had roots in the antebellum movement. The society, whose main function was to produce an enormous amount of educational literature, revealed that many drys were unconvinced of the efficacy of political action.

The Sons of Temperance, the Independent Order of Good Templars, and the American Temperance Union all survived the war and gave birth to the new society. The first two were fraternal organizations that provided members with continuing support for having

---

for they "cannot afford to alienate the large German and other liberal elements in the big cities." In the editor's view, everyone except "temperance cranks" wanted to keep the saloon out of politics. *The South-West*, Jan. 20, 1893, p. 2.

taken an abstinence pledge. The Templars, the largest group, not only included women, but also worked for passage of prohibition laws. The American Temperance Union had prospered for fifteen years before the war, sponsoring temperance congresses and providing, through the pages of its *Journal*, for the discussion of temperance and related social and political strategies. But by 1865 the union was all but dead.[5]

The union was revived in 1865 as the National Temperance Society and Publication House at a National Temperance Congress. When 378 delegates from the Good Templars, the Sons of Temperance, and concerned churches gathered in Saratoga Springs, the upstate New York site of earlier national conventions, dissension appeared. In part, the delegates argued about the proper relationship between temperance organizations and the churches. But most of all, they disputed just what course of action they should take to achieve a more temperate nation, whether or not to rely on simple persuasion or to seek prohibition statutes and, if so, whether or not to work within the established political parties.[6]

The new society, incorporated in 1866, avoided these controversies by dedicating itself to educational work. Its first president was William E. Dodge, a Republican congressman and merchant capitalist, who called for "one grand, earnest, continuous onset against the combined powers of rum and darkness." He meant education. When Dodge called a temperance convention in 1868, he warned the delegates that, although political action might be feasible in rural areas, it was not in cities like New York, where large numbers of foreign-born voters not only sought free license for the sale of intoxicants, but "demand[ed] that the Lord's Day shall be desecrated" as well. When state prohibition campaigns began in earnest in the 1880s, the society supplied literature and speakers but not political leadership. Theodore S. Cuyler, the prominent Brooklyn Presbyterian pastor who served as the society's third president from 1885 to 1893, believed that money spent on "abortive" political efforts was wasted. Temperance organizations should, he said, concentrate their

5. *Standard Encyclopedia of the Alcohol Problem*, 6 vols. (Westerville, Ohio, 1925–30), 1:59–60; 3:1332–36; 6:2474–75; Turner, "American Prohibition Movement," pp. 7–8, 22, 203.

6. *Proceedings of the Fifth National Temperance Convention* (New York, 1865), pp. 54–59, 90; John J. Rumbarger, "The Social Origins and Functions of the Political Temperance Movement in the Reconstruction of American Society, 1825–1927" (Ph.D. diss., University of Pennsylvania, 1968), pp. 56–58; Turner, "American Prohibition Movement," pp. 8–16.

resources "to make converts to temperance [and] save our tempted youth." The society remained steadfast in the evangelical Christian tradition that tried to convert people one by one, not by groups.[7]

Even the educational strategy was a struggle for the society, for it did not obtain a sound financial footing until 1880. At first it existed largely on the beneficence of President Dodge. Finally in 1880 he raised $60,000 from the likes of Cornelius Vanderbilt, J. P. Morgan, and John D. Rockefeller, who began an annual donation of $1,000. With this support, the society published two monthly magazines, the *National Temperance Advocate* and *Youth's Temperance Banner*. With hundreds of writers supplying material, the society printed millions of copies of books and pamphlets. Literature went to thousands of churches and Sunday schools, usually free of charge. The society staged conventions and sponsored exhibitions at fairs, distributing literature to all who would accept it.[8]

The Prohibition Party

Although the educational focus of the National Temperance Society reflected disagreement among dry Americans as to the propriety of political action, some of its leaders helped organize the Prohibition party in order to present the issue clearly and directly to voters. When the society sponsored the National Temperance Convention in 1868, the delegates vigorously debated political matters. This time a majority agreed on the need for obtaining prohibition legislation. J. N. Stearns, editor of the *National Temperance Advocate*, heralded the resolution as the dawn of a "new era" for the temperance cause.[9] But there was no agreement among the society's officers on the important questions of political technique, and so political leadership came, after 1869, from the Prohibition party and, after 1874, from the WCTU.

At the time of the 1868 convention, a number of leaders were already convinced of the need to organize a new political party, and in 1869 they launched the Prohibition party. John Russell, a Method-

---

7. *Proceedings of the Sixth National Temperance Convention* (New York, 1868), pp. 20–28, 107–09; Cuyler to John D. Rockefeller, Sr., Feb. 2, 1886, JDR; Turner, "American Prohibition Movement," p. 20.

8. Turner, "American Prohibition Movement," pp. 203–04; Cuyler to Rockefeller, Feb. 2, 1886, Jan. 5 and 21, 1893; J. N. Stearns to Rockefeller, Jan. 3, 1894, JDR; *Sixteenth Annual Report of the National Temperance Society and Publication House* (New York, 1881), pp. 14–15.

9. Turner, "American Prohibition Movement," pp. 24–26.

ist clergyman and leader of the Good Templars in Michigan, was the principal spokesman.[10] Russell and his colleagues expressed faith that the new party would supplant the Republican party as the agent of the positive liberal state. They were convinced that an "oligarchy" of the liquor traffic controlled Democratic and Republican affairs alike. The Prohibition party would educate voters in revulsion against the saloon power and provide them with a practical political alternative. The saloon domination of the major parties left but two choices for temperance men: "either antagonize this force inside of the present parties, or out of them." The Maine law movement had failed, in Russell's view, because the contest between wets and drys in the existing parties was unequal. The liquor traffic could not possibly control the Prohibition party, which would gather men now scattered in the established parties where "minor political questions" distracted their attention. Not influenced by the curses of the saloon power, the third party would "tend to retrieve the lost honor of political life, and bring a better class of men before the people for their suffrages." Its caucuses would not meet in the "lowest grog-shops of the town or city;" the better class of citizens, not having to breathe there "the very fumes of hell," would be free to participate in political life. Their dry platforms would force discussion of the drink problem in the secular press and thereby increase sentiment favorable to prohibition.[11] Such was the view and hope of the new party leaders.

In organizing the Prohibition party, Russell and his colleagues revealed not just how the principal reform experience of their generation influenced their thinking, but they also showed a faith in democracy that was broadly shared by Americans in the Gilded Age. According to this faith, political parties were the instruments through which democratic man organized to express his views, the organizations where like-minded voters gathered to insure that their preferred candidates and policies were visible choices for the electorate. Party platforms thus were serious expressions of intent, commitments to social values.

The structure of the Prohibition party reflected this democratic view. It was a loose, informal organization that allowed broad, popular participation in its affairs. The national committee could include

10. Ibid., pp. 22–29; Colvin, *Prohibition in the United States*, p. 645; *Standard Encyclopedia of the Alcohol Problem*, 5:2217.

11. William Goodell to John Russell, May 2, 1876, unmarked clipping, Prohibition Leaflet file, Oberlin College Library; Russell, "A Plea for a National Temperance Party," *Proceedings of the Sixth National Temperance Convention*, pp. 117–19.

two representatives from each state and territory, chosen at conventions. On the local level any citizen, male or female, who supported temperance and agreed with the partisan strategy could participate in the nomination of candidates, the writing of platforms, and the selection of delegates to conventions in congressional districts and states. At conventions, credentials committees prevented disruption from Republican dissidents, but sometimes even they were allowed to join in the discussions of temperance matters, though not in the conduct of party business.[12]

The spontaneity of citizen participation upon which the party relied did not, of course, insure its rapid growth or financial well-being. The founders expected prohibition and other reform issues, at least in northern states, to foster a rapid voter realignment, with the party growing accordingly. But such did not occur, or even threaten to occur, before 1884. Despite the intent to concentrate on one issue, the party's platforms advocated a wide range of social and political reforms, including, somewhat equivocally, woman suffrage. In 1872 the party offered James Black as a presidential candidate in six states, where he received about six thousand votes. In 1876 the party gained ten thousand votes in eighteen states, but did no better in 1880 with the venerable Neil Dow, symbol of the old Maine law movement, as its presidential candidate. Meanwhile, the financially strapped party employed men to organize local meetings and obtain their salary from the collection basket.[13]

The party remained a rather small part of the prohibition movement throughout its life, and it certainly was insignificant in national politics until 1884. For that presidential campaign it chose a new national chairman to replace Russell and decided to concentrate on New York State. This new focus involved a subtle shift away from the earlier thoughts of the party founders. In the 1870s the party had been concerned with education, from which it hoped a voter realignment would emerge. Now, in 1884, the party leaders were bent on the disruption of the established partisan balance in American politics, consciously trying to damage and eventually destroy the Republican party, from the ruins of which the Prohibitionists hoped

12. J. W. Haggard, *History of the Prohibition Party* (Bloomington, Ill., 1888), pp. 10–11, 37; *National Prohibition Reform Party, Its Candidates, Platform, Address* (Detroit, 1876), p. 23; *Prohibition County Convention* (broadside; New Paris, Ohio, 1879), Ohio Historical Society.

13. *Delaware Signal Extra*, n.d., Ohio Historical Society; "Minutes of the State Central Committee of Michigan, Feb. 28, 1872, PP, reel 2; Blocker, *Retreat from Reform*, pp. 45, 105; Turner, "American Prohibition Movement," p. 30.

to emerge victorious. The new approach seemed, in 1884, to affect the outcome of the national election. That appearance, in turn, made the third party, for a time, a significant political institution within the prohibition movement, one whose strategy was discomforting to loyal, dry Republicans and whose existence threatened the older party.[14] The threat, which in the end proved illusory, provoked heated controversy over political methods. Before 1884, when temperance advocates debated whether or not to engage in political action, they usually meant, not attempting to influence the views of individual legislators or of engaging in referendum campaigns, but supporting the Prohibition party. After 1884, temperance Republicans began to think about a politics that separated party loyalty and prohibition activity. That consideration centered in the most important Gilded Age dry organization, the WCTU.

The Woman's Christian Temperance Union

The "woman's crusade" burst forth late in 1873 and lasted for about six months. The crusade involved at least 50,000 women, mostly in the East and Middle West, who visited saloons and prayed for drinkers to take abstinence pledges, saloon keepers to close their doors permanently, and local politicians to enforce restrictive ordinances and revoke saloon licenses. In the short run, at least, the actions were successful; hundreds of saloons closed their doors, at least temporarily, and tens of thousands of Americans took the pledge. Almost a year after the crusade began, the WCTU was organized at a meeting in Cleveland, Ohio, to embody permanently the ideals of the crusade and sustain temperance agitation.[15]

The birth of the WCTU signaled an important step in reform organization, and from its activities emerged the consideration of a new nonpartisan prohibition strategy eventually embodied by the Anti-Saloon League. In the 1870s and 1880s the WCTU channeled prohibition zeal, effectively organizing thousands of women and disturbing state politics in the North. As the WCTU evolved, it blended nineteenth-century democratic processes with some of the characteristics of modern bureaucracy that were emerging else-

---

14. *Standard Encyclopedia of the Alcohol Problem*, 5:2217–20.

15. Ruth Bordin, "A Baptism of Power and Liberty: The Women's Crusade of 1873–1874," *Ohio History* 87 (Autumn 1978): 393–404; Jed Dannenbaum, *Drink and Disorder: Temperance Reform in Cincinnati from the Washingtonian Revival to the WCTU* (Urbana, Ill., 1984), pp. 212–33.

where in American society. Yet the WCTU, as we shall see, did not develop as an organization capable of conducting fully coordinated activities on a continuing basis. Although the WCTU rested on a voluntary democratic base, by the mid-eighties a charismatic president, Frances Willard, determined its overall strategy, much to the dismay of other vigorous leaders. As a women's organization, moreover, prohibition was not the only reform on the WCTU's agenda.

The founders designed a democratic, federal organization to provide opportunities for women to engage in temperance agitation independently of any male concerns or control. Not a tightly knit structure, the WCTU recommended a model constitution for parallel groups in states that, in turn, rested on commitments of women in local communities. A woman joined by signing an abstinence pledge and paying annual dues of fifty cents; men could affiliate ex officio by taking the pledge and paying higher dues. The union was to function democratically, with conventions of women electing officers each year and choosing delegates to represent them in higher bodies. In the national union, power resided in an executive committee that included the officers; the president of each state union served on the committee as a vice-president of the national body. Initially a series of committees appointed by the president carried on the national work, corresponding with their counterparts in the states, which in turn communicated with the local members.[16]

The three women who figured most prominently in the WCTU during the nineteenth century were Annie Wittenmyer, Frances Willard, and Judith Ellen Foster. Of the three, in 1874 Wittenmyer was the eldest and best known. She was an independently wealthy widow. During the Civil War, Wittenmyer had assumed responsibility in the sanitary movement, a precursor of the American Red Cross. As a state sanitary agent in Iowa she fought attempts to merge her women's service with the male dominated U.S. Sanitary Commission. After the war, Wittenmyer moved to Philadelphia, where she continued to exemplify her belief that women enjoyed divinely derived abilities for social service. She helped found the Ladies' and Pastors' Christian Union in 1868, an organization that provided women with opportunities to serve the needy. Wittenmyer published her own magazine, the *Christian Woman*, and lectured widely on behalf of the idea of women's service to society. In 1874 she was a

16. Norton Mezvinsky, "The White-Ribbon Reform, 1874–1920" (Ph.D. diss., University of Wisconsin, 1959), pp. 48–60; *Standard Encyclopedia of the Alcohol Problem*, 6:2891, 2902–05.

leader of the crusade in Philadelphia. When the founders of the
WCTU chose Wittenmyer as its first president, she told them that
women enjoyed greater moral strength than men. In temperance
work, she said, men had a tendency to quit the battle, but women
persisted. "She believed that women could do anything on which
they set their hearts," the minutes noted, and that the crusade had
shown "they can face the cannon and the mob."[17]

Wittenmyer served as a president until 1879, when the WCTU
chose Frances Willard, a prominent educator, advocate of women's
rights, and temperance worker. Born in 1839, Willard had matured
feeling resentful of the inability of women to participate fully in
public life. Although she had only about four years of formal education, she became a teacher and, in 1871, president of the Evanston
College for Ladies, a new Methodist school affiliated with Northwestern University. She resigned that position at the end of the
1873–74 academic year because of disagreements with Northwestern's president. The crusade, and the resulting WCTU organization, provided Willard with an outlet for her considerable talents.
When the crusaders of Chicago formed their local organization they
asked Willard to lead it. When Illinois crusaders met that autumn to
form a state group, Willard became its secretary. After 1874, her
position as corresponding secretary of the national union, in charge
of organizational work, put her in contact with other state and local
leaders so that she soon became a well-known figure within the
entire organization.

As a national leader, Willard argued that the WCTU should
concern itself with a broad range of reforms, especially woman
suffrage. Annie Wittenmyer disagreed. Although Wittenmyer did
not dispute the principle of woman suffrage, she believed that the
union should concentrate its efforts on temperance matters. When
she tried to discourage Willard from diverting her attention from
that course, Willard, in 1877, resigned her national office and began
to oppose Wittenmyer's reelection as president. Willard was able to
express her views in the pages of *Our Union*, the WCTU paper, and
in 1879 the national convention chose her as its new president.
Willard held the office until her death in 1898.[18]

17. *Minutes of the First Annual Meeting of the National Woman's Christian Temperance
Union*, 1874, p. 17. Regretably these *Minutes* do not directly quote Wittenmyer. See
also Mezvinsky, "White-Ribbon Reform," pp. 61–62, and Frank L. Byrne, "Annie
Wittenmyer," in *Notable American Women*, 3 vols., ed. Edwin T. James (Cambridge,
Mass., 1971), 3:636–38.

18. Mary Earhart Dillon, "Frances Willard," in *Notable American Women*, 3:613–19;
Mary Earhart, *Frances Willard: From Prayers to Politics* (Chicago, 1944), p. 110; Mezvinsky, "White-Ribbon Reform," pp. 62–65.

As president of the WCTU, Frances Willard commanded tremendous faith from her followers. Remarkably popular as a public speaker, she had a charisma that endeared her to audiences and moved them to support her causes. Although Willard believed in a wide range of reforms to alleviate the harsh life that so many workers and city dwellers suffered, she never deviated from her devotion to the eradication of the liquor traffic. To her, the liquor traffic was like the Chicago fire, which she had witnessed, in its capacity to destroy homes. In seeking liquor's abolition and in arguing the right of suffrage for women, Willard claimed she was seeking protection for the American home.[19]

J. Ellen Foster was one of the persons attracted to Frances Willard. "I loved her with a chivalrous devotion not common among women," Foster wrote in 1889. "My admiration was absolute and unquestioning." Foster began temperance work at about the same time as Willard but believed her to be the more skilled leader; Willard, after all, had experience as an educator while Foster was rearing children. So, with the woman's crusade, "I gave to Miss Willard the ardor of a personal devotion, which drew to itself the religious fervor of that Holy War. Her words were to me, almost as sacred as the spirit of the movement itself."[20]

However devoted she may have been to Frances Willard, however, Ellen Foster even before the 1874 crusade was hardly a typical nineteenth-century American woman. Born in 1840, this devout daughter of a Wesleyan Methodist minister attended public schools in Boston and, as a teenager, spent a year at a seminary. She married at nineteen, bore her first two of four children, and then divorced. By now living in Chicago, she met her future husband, E. C. Foster, while doing Sunday school work in the slums. After their marriage, the Fosters moved to Clinton, Iowa, he to practice law, she to bear two more children and read law in her husband's office. The Iowa bar admitted her in 1872. Clinton was a wide open river town, and Mrs. Foster became a crusader in 1874. Gaining a local reputation as a superb public speaker, she went to Cleveland to help found the WCTU. There this Iowa attorney took charge of drafting the union's constitution.[21]

Foster was thus closely involved with the formation of the WCTU.

19. *Minutes of the Fourth Annual Meeting of the National Woman's Christian Temperance Union*, 1877, p. 138.

20. Judith Ellen Foster, *The Truth in the Case, Concerning Partisanship and Non-Partisanship in the W.C.T.U.* (Clinton, Iowa, 1889), p. 150.

21. Frank L. Byrne, "Judith Ellen Foster," in *Notable American Women*, 1:651–52; David C. Mott, "Judith Ellen Foster," *Annals of Iowa* 19 (July 1933): 126–38.

Believing with Willard that the pursuit of a broad, "do everything" policy would enhance the growth of the movement, Foster supported the president in her efforts to broaden the union's appeal to women on a wide range of social reforms. Further, each state should have the freedom to plan and execute its own work according to local conditions. Willard claimed that Wittenmyer had failed to insure the collection of dues assessments by national headquarters. In Willard's view, a sound financial basis, as well as the wresting of the presidency from Wittenmyer to insure the "do everything" strategy, would allow the national union to promote the formation of local unions, especially in the largely unorganized South and West, and thereby build the movement into a powerful women's agency for social change.[22]

The new WCTU president first turned her attention to reorganization and expansion. Willard appointed Foster head of a special "Committee on Plan of Work" and instructed it with a "schedule" of the various functions she envisioned, divided into seven categories: "Educational," "Evangelistic," "Social," "Legal," "Extending our Organization," "Preventive," and a general rubric, "Instigated and Inspired by Our Unions." Foster's committee recommended the formation of departments to replace the existing corresponding committees. Each department would have a single National Superintendent. When the convention in 1880 approved the reorganization, Willard expressed her desire to provide small salaries to some leaders so that they might devote their full attention to their particular interests. Willard believed that having more paid workers—whom she termed *our protestant nuns*"—was desirable. "This is the age of experts and specialists," she told the 1880 convention. "We must find out what each woman who makes this cause her life-work can do best, and then set her at that and see that she is taken care of." Although she refused a personal salary, Willard wanted each state union and the larger locals to establish headquarters and pay a secretary to run them. To accomplish this feat, the national WCTU raised its dues assessment from five to ten cents per member in 1886. The organization had already, in 1881, decided to apportion delegates to its conventions according to the number of dues-paying members. Under this scheme, by 1920 at least forty-one WCTU leaders had received salaries.[23]

22. Earhart, *Willard*, p. 151; Willard, *Glimpses of Fifty Years* (Chicago, 1889), p. 369.

23. *Minutes of the Seventh Annual Meeting of the Woman's National Christian Temperance Union*, 1880, pp. 146–47. By 1890 there were thirty-nine departments, which Willard classified into categories of labor, temperance, and woman. Earhart, *Willard*,

The new structure was a shift away from a completely volunteer, spontaneous organization toward a bureaucratic one. Yet under Willard the WCTU failed to become fully bureaucratic by a number of tests. The organization had no hierarchical staff structure and no lateral lines of coordination among the departments, even though their activities overlapped. The WCTU lacked clear definitions of the superintendents' functions. The only coordination was through the annual meetings of the large executive committee. Some departments were issue-oriented, while others were concerned with general operations. Thus there was a department for "Influencing the Press" and one for "Temperance Legislation," but there was no formal mechanism for the person devoting her time to press relations to coordinate her activities with those of the superintendent trying to persuade legislatures to enact a desired law. "Temperance Legislation" meant obtaining particular statutes to restrict or forbid the drink business, but one of the principal legislative activities of the WCTU fell under a separate department, "Scientific Instruction." Mary Hunt headed this effort from 1880 to 1906, working in state capitols for legislation requiring "scientific" instruction in the public schools regarding the evils of alcohol.

Within this situation, job descriptions were often imprecise. Willard tried to rectify this fault in 1881. She reported her satisfaction with the superintendent system to the convention. "But there is room," Willard indicated, "for much clearer definitions of their duties." By this comment she meant, however, not a clarification of the organizational chart but instructions regarding particular duties. Willard thought, for instance, that the women concerned with scientific temperance education should regard visits to all national and state teachers' conventions as an obligation to their office.[24]

The organization that Willard and Foster devised, moreover,

---

p. 184; Mezvinsky, "White-Ribbon Reform," pp. 73–74; *Minutes of the National Woman's Christian Temperance Union*, 1879, p. 67, and 1880, pp. 18–21, and 1881, p. cxii. Willard looked forward to a time when women would view WCTU work as a vocation comparable to teaching. There might be unmarried women available who no longer needed to be called spinsters because they could do much more than spin. Or such women might come from the ranks of those with grown children who had left home.

24. *Minutes of the Seventh Annual Meeting of the Woman's National Christian Temperance Union*, 1880, pp. 104–05; *Minutes of the Eighth Annual Meeting of the W.N.C.T.U.*, 1881, p. lxiv. By 1889 the superintendents were meeting separately just before the national convention to share their methods. *Chicago Inter-Ocean*, undated clipping, Foster file, Schlesinger Library for the History of Women, Radcliffe College.

lacked the essential attribute of a bureaucracy: an assurance of continuity apart from the lives and careers of its occupants. The continuity of the WCTU's operations, thus, was assured only by the reappointment of a particular individual such as Mary Hunt. Nor was there any means of assuring that the national plan of work, adopted annually at the convention, was actually carried on by the state and local unions save through the urgings of the national officers. There was no mechanism for disciplining superintendents, with local and state unions and individuals free to focus their attention as their fervor of the moment indicated. Instead of a disciplined, coordinated, and bureaucratic organization, Willard saw the entire structure as desirably democratic and spontaneous. Local unions sent delegates to state conventions, which in turn elected representatives to the national meeting, where policy was set and officers chosen. "The convention," in her words, "is the only source of power."[25]

Willard vigorously promoted the organization. When she took office in 1879, the WCTU had 26,843 members in 1,118 locals in 24 states and territories. Willard paid women to travel among local communities to recruit new members. Willard herself embarked on extended tours of the South and the West in the 1880s, and she sent Foster on at least one such tour in 1883. By that year there were 73,176 members of 2,580 local unions in 42 states and territories, and the growth continued into the 1920s. At the same time, WCTU activities expanded, ranging from the maintenance of "friendly inns" in city slum districts to the promotion of social purity. But what probably accounted for the largest share of growth in the early 1880s was political activity. State referendum campaigns gave thousands of women a concrete reason to join.[26]

The Continuing Crusade of the 1880s

The 1880s proved crucial for the prohibition movement. The decade began with dry Americans confident that they could achieve their goals through the popular referendum. It ended with bitter, acrimonious dispute over political strategy. The emotions that

25. *Minutes of the Eleventh Annual Meeting of the National Woman's Christian Temperance Union*, 1884, p. 53. After 1889 the superintendents were elected at the convention, but only upon the nomination of the executive committee. *Minutes of the Fifteenth Annual Meeting of the N.W.C.T.U.*, 1888, n.p.

26. Mezvinsky, "White-Ribbon Reform," p. 68; Cherrington, *Evolution of Prohibition*, pp. 176–84.

welled up split the WCTU, disturbed national partisan politics, and eventually led to a clarification of what nonpartisan politics entailed. Only then, in the 1890s, could the Anti-Saloon League's nonpartisan strategy emerge, a reflection of the experiences of the preceding decade.

State prohibition referendum campaigns began in 1880 because dry leaders believed that sixty years of agitation sufficed to produce favorable majorities. The referendum had the added appeal of skirting the tangle of party caucuses. "The whole country," Ellen Foster concluded from a state-by-state survey in 1880, is "slowly but surely waking up to the iniquity of the liquor traffic, and the duty of the State to put it away." The constitutional referendum seemed the way to accomplish the feat. As the editors of the *National Temperance Advocate* pointed out, the liquor industry used its superior financial resources to corrupt the legislative process. But a popular vote reduced that advantage because the saloon men "cannot so easily control and debauch the whole body of voters." The way seemed open to a durable solution to the evils of the liquor traffic.[27]

Events in Kansas sparked the decade's amendment campaigns, and the zeal of the WCTU fueled them. In 1876 a Kansas state senator, John St. John, publicly refused the Republican gubernatorial nomination on the grounds that party leaders had asked him to compromise his views on prohibition. When he threatened to run on the Prohibition party ticket, the Republicans in 1878 nominated him with a platform plank that promised to submit an amendment to the voters. St. John's election and the subsequent approval of the Kansas amendment in 1880 led the WCTU, under Foster's leadership as national superintendent for legislation, to embark on amendment campaigns elsewhere. Let a prohibition law not be a party "but a people's measure," Foster wrote. Women could maintain this apolitical posture because, "as active workers . . . having no political existence, [they] must neutralize very much what otherwise might be tinged." The WCTU typically called a convention of a particular state's prohibitionists to plan the campaign. The union provided speakers for rallies and church meetings, circulated petitions asking for submission of an amendment, and, in the campaign, canvassed individual voters. On election day, as church bells tolled, women

27. S. D. Hastings, "A Constitutional Amendment," *National Temperance Advocate* 13 (Oct. 1878): 148–49; 16 (Dec. 1881): 200; *Minutes of the Woman's National Christian Temperance Union*, 1880, p. 75; Turner, "American Prohibition Movement," pp. 237–42.

gathered at polling places prayerfully to encourage their supporters.[28]

The results were mixed and, on the whole, disappointing. In Ellen
Foster's home state of Iowa, the WCTU and its allies had what
seemed a resounding success. After Foster proposed an amendment
campaign in 1878, the drys secured the support of the Republican
party. In 1882 the voters approved an amendment, but in 1883 the
state supreme court disallowed it on a technicality. Only then did the
Republican-dominated legislature enact a prohibition law. The
Democrats remained wet, and the state's parties were clearly polarized. In 1889 the Democrats elected their first governor since 1852,
and the Republicans, seeking to broaden their appeal to the voters,
began to soften their position, so that, in effect, after 1894 Iowa
licensed saloons and allowed local option. But until 1889, thanks to
the WCTU, Iowa was a dry bastion.[29]

The prohibitionists were less successful in most other states. In
Ohio matters were confused by the constitution of 1851 that forbad
the licensing of liquor sales. The state supreme court varied its
interpretation of that stricture, however, according to which group,
wet or dry, controlled its majority. The effect of the clause was
that saloons flourished without the restraints that licensing could
have imposed. In 1883, pressured by the WCTU, the Republican-
dominated legislature supplied a clear choice to voters: a ballot
proposal to allow the licensing of saloons, and a second amendment
for outright prohibition. The outcome of the election, after the
WCTU set the state "ablaze with truth," showed a plurality of votes
for the second amendment but not the required majority of the total
vote cast in the general election.[30]

In Pennsylvania the prohibitionists' campaign lasted the entire
decade and ended in failure. In 1880 the state WCTU formed a
constitutional amendment committee headed by Wittenmyer. With

28. Judith Ellen Foster, *Constitutional Amendment Manual* (New York, 1882), pp.
53–66; Clark, *Deliver Us from Evil*, pp. 73–74.
29. Mott, "Judith Ellen Foster," pp. 126–38; Ballard C. Campbell, "Did Democracy Work? Prohibition in Late Nineteenth Century Iowa: A Test Case," *Journal of
Interdisciplinary History* 8 (Summer 1977): 87–116.
30. Francis M. Whitaker, "A History of the Ohio Woman's Christian Temperance
Union, 1874–1920" (Ph.D. diss., Ohio State University, 1970), pp. 275–76; Samuel
Unger, "A History of the National Woman's Christian Temperance Union" (Ph.D.
diss., Ohio State University, 1933), pp. 57–58.

the cooperation of a male group, by 1883 she had flooded the legislature with 400,000 petitions for a referendum. But only after 1885, when they threatened to throw their support to the third party, did the drys obtain support from the Republican boss, Matthew Quay. The WCTU helped elect a dry Republican governor, James Beaver, who took office in 1887. Wittenmyer told Beaver that she did not expect him, or the Democrats for that matter, "to champion Prohibition. All we ask is . . . respect [for] the demands of the people for the exercise of their undoubted rights." The constitution required successive sessions of the legislature to approve submission of an amendment, so the actual vote came in 1889. The Prohibition party tried to take control of the campaign, and the bitter division within the temperance ranks contributed to an overwhelming defeat at the polls.[31]

In spite of the best efforts of the WCTU, then, there were few successes. At the end of the decade only Iowa, the Dakotas, Vermont, New Hampshire, and Maine were dry states, although others had passed local option statutes. What the state amendment campaigns did provide was much political emotion. By 1890 American prohibition reformers were bitterly divided on a basic political strategy. The rancor increased thanks to the rise of the Prohibition party and the danger that it seemed to pose to the Republican party. In Kansas, Iowa, and Pennsylvania, amendments had appeared on the ballot only after their supporters had threatened to bolt the Republican ticket. For Republican leaders, the problem of maintaining a coalition that included both wets and drys remained. The partisan balances of the Gilded Age were generally close, so when drys threatened to cast votes for the third party, they threatened defeat for Republican candidates. The referendum had offered a way for the politicians to declare that prohibition was no longer a "political" issue, but one for the people directly to decide.

But for the leaders of the Prohibition party that declaration, and the reliance on the referendum, was unacceptable. They asserted that prohibition, and especially its enforcement, required party action. The new strategy of 1884 allowed the party to claim the

31. Earl C. Kaylor, "The Prohibition Movement in Pennsylvania, 1865–1920" (Ph.D. diss., Pennsylvania State University, 1963), pp. 253–79; Annie Wittenmyer to James Beaver, Dec. 1, 1886, JB.

balance of power, and countless observers agreed with its analysis.[32] Reaction within both the Republican party and the temperance movement was swift. For instance, Pennsylvania Republican leaders allowed the prohibition referendum to proceed in order to defuse the partisan nature of the issue. Nor did most Republican drys suddenly desert their party. Instead, they angrily assailed the partisan strategy while defending the nonpartisan, referendum approach to reform.

Frances Willard and the Politics of the 1880s

The WCTU and Frances Willard were in the thick of these events. Willard believed that a partisan strategy was not simply the best vehicle for achieving prohibition, but a desirable means of promoting other social reforms as well. She began to maneuver to ally the WCTU with the Prohibition party. In this quest Willard was both patient and hardworking.

Willard broached the subject at the union's national convention in 1881. She explained to the delegates that she had always been "a Staunch Republican," but now changed her views for two reasons. One basis of her earlier commitment was a fear that the South might reopen the issues of the Civil War. But her travels convinced her otherwise, that it was possible for North and South truly to reunite. But neither the Republican nor the Democratic party, each vested with the emotions of the rebellion, could do the task, she said; a new party was necessary. Second, echoing the arguments of the Prohibition party founders, she noted that the liquor evil was the great question of the day, and yet neither of the established parties dealt with it adequately because they had both wets and drys among their supporters. It was time, Willard concluded, for the Republican party to die; it had accomplished its goals. "Parties are the moulds into which God pours the principles that are to bless humanity," she told the convention. "But when these have crystallized into the law and life of a people God breaks the mould for which he has no further

32. That the Prohibition party claim regarding New York in the presidential election of 1884 was a false one is irrelevant here. The GOP was in a period of long-term decline in its appeal to voters in presidential elections, and Republican leaders viewed further defections to the Prohibition party with some alarm. For a modern analysis of the results of 1884, see Lee Benson, "Research Problem in American Political Historiography," in *Common Frontiers of the Social Sciences*, ed. Mirra Komarovsky (Glencoe, Ill., 1957), pp. 113–83. Blaine lost New York by a tiny 1,140 vote margin, and with it the nation. St. John had 25,000 votes in the state.

use." That fracture had occurred for the Republicans. They had fought and won free territory, preservation of the Union, and the abolition of slavery, she continued. The party had gone as far as it could with "negro enfranchisement" and civil rights legislation; further attainment of those goals would have to await "education."

Willard went on to review her activities on behalf of third-party politics. Inspired by the Illinois union, she had formed a Home Protection party to offer candidates who were committed to prohibition, civil service reform, compulsory education, and antimonopoly and anti-Mormon legislation. She expected it to combine with the Prohibition party to form one grand Prohibition Home Protection party. But she cautioned her followers that the newly invigorated party should "hold [itself] in abeyance in states where a prohibition amendment was pending." On the woman suffrage issue the party should allow each state to decide its own position, because so many southern drys were steadfast in their opposition. Finally, Willard did not ask for the union's endorsement, for she recognized "the fact that we are a non-partisan society, working through moral suasion." But Willard welcomed the expressions of sympathy already received from state conventions.[33]

In 1882 and 1883 Willard moved closer to achieving her dream of fusion with the third party. In 1882 The Home Protection and Prohibition parties merged. In that autumn's WCTU convention, aware that most of the women were unprepared to make an explicit party endorsement, she asked Foster and the Iowa union, so prominently identified with the referendum strategy, to present a vaguely worded resolution of sympathy toward any party that supported prohibition. Then in 1883 the union went further toward an alliance. Prior to the WCTU convention, Willard told the readers of the *Union Signal* (the new title of the union's paper) that she was a third-party person; but as for the Iowa Republican party that had supported a prohibition law, "Let us stand by them." Moreover, if she resided in a state where the Democrats advocated prohibition, she would follow its banner. When she discussed politics in her annual presidential address at the convention, Willard remarked that the important referendum campaigns "must be done *through non-partisan methods*." But once enacted, dry laws required the Prohi-

33. *Minutes of the Eighth Annual Meeting of the Woman's National Christian Temperance Union*, 1881, pp. lxxv–lxxxv. Willard was not always wholeheartedly dedicated to reforms. She voiced commitment to woman suffrage, for instance, but did not consistently support it in her behavior.

bition party in office to insure adequate enforcement, and the WCTU members were its "natural allies." Still, Willard recommended that the national union "*applaud the loyalty of any party to Prohibition.*" When it came time to introduce a resolution on the matter, she again asked Foster to do so. Willard cleverly worded the statement so that it could either be interpreted as a reaffirmation of the nonpartisan character of the WCTU or used to support the Prohibition party. After the convention, in an unsigned commentary, the *Union Signal* assured its readers that the nonpartisan interpretation was probably correct. The editor characterized "the expression" as "very cautious." The resolution "may mean the prohibition party or it may refer to either of the two great political organizations of the country, as the situation in different localities shall indicate."[34]

But Willard also had the 1883 convention open the route to an exclusive alignment with the national Prohibition party. The convention authorized her to visit the party conventions to seek adoption of a platform plank favoring submission of a prohibition amendment to the U.S. Constitution. Willard did so, after arranging for the Prohibition party convention to occur after those of the two major parties. When she presented her plank to the Republican platform committee, it chose to adopt a vague statement intended to please both wets and drys. After this failure, Willard said she "had no heart" to ask the Democratic or Greenback parties to adopt her proposal, although the latter did declare for prohibition.[35]

In the campaign of 1884 Willard acted as if there were a formal alliance between the Prohibition party and the WCTU. It was no secret that she would seek a formal WCTU endorsement of the party. She scheduled the national convention for October, before the elections, rather than for the usual November date. In August, when a reader of the *Union Signal* inquired as to the meaning of the 1883 resolution, Willard explained that neither the Democrats nor the Republicans had "done anything for Prohibition *nationally.*" She

34. The resolution read, "We will lend our influence to that party, by whatever name called, which shall furnish the best embodiment of prohibition principles, and will most surely protect our homes." *Minutes of the National Woman's Temperance Union*, 1883, p. 31. Also see p. 49. *Union Signal*, Nov. 8, 1883, p. 1; *Twelfth Annual Meeting of the Iowa WCTU*, 1885, pp. 1–2; Turner, "American Prohibition Movement," pp. 275–81.

35. Gail Hamilson, "Prohibition in Politics," *North American Review* 140 (March 1885): 509–20; *New York Times*, Jan. 7, 1884.

concluded that "the National WCTU will lend its influence to the Prohibition party." At the end of the month, in an "Address to the National Officers" printed in the paper, Willard told her followers how to help: by becoming informed, circulating the *Union Signal* (now editorially supporting St. John) among friends, reading local papers and writing to correct their errors, and helping party rallies and campaign staffs. "No individual member," Willard assured the readers, "—local, auxiliary, or state union—is in any way bound to receive what we have said in the way of sisterly counsel." But Willard believed that she was reflecting majority sentiment in the national union.[36]

Willard's perception of her support was accurate. Foster, Wittenmyer, and Hunt opposed the endorsement but were unable to gather much support. Foster wrote to Hunt, pleading with her to explain to the members that the endorsement would impair lobbying efforts among legislators. "I do feel so lonely," Foster said. "I wish somebody of 'our set' would come to the rescue." Wittenmyer tried arguing that a national prohibition campaign was premature. In her view, votes for St. John were in effect votes for Cleveland, "and . . . the Prohibition party is in fact, if not in plan, Democratic." But she did not have a large following within the national union. When Foster, who did, publicly complained of Willard's actions, she was called a "client" of the Republicans.[37]

At the October convention debate on the matter was vigorous. In support of her resolution to have the national WCTU "lend its influence" to the Prohibition party, Willard repeated the now familiar arguments for a partisan strategy. Foster led the opposition. Foster's chief complaint was that the alliance would tend to weaken the independence of women—so hard-won through the WCTU—because it bound their organization to the actions of the party. Women, she believed, should follow the banner of prohibition, not politicians; to do otherwise changed the feminist character of their organization. The endorsement, moreover, would hurt the conduct of other lines of women's work. "This resolution," Mary Hunt said in support of Foster's position, "if passed, will make my work more difficult." Willard tried to soothe her opponents by assuring that the action meant only that the national union would help the national

---

36. *Union Signal*, Aug. 21, 1884, p. 4, and Aug. 28, 1884, p. 9.
37. Foster to Hunt, Sept. 14, 1884, STF, reel 2; Wittenmyer to Joseph Weeks, Oct. 2, 1884, in *The Press*, WCTU, reel 34; *Union Signal*, Sept. 25, 1884, p. 4.

party. Individual members remained free to "go their own way."[38]

Willard won her way by a vote of 195 to 48. The convention sanctioned her earlier partisan activities. It refused to accept a resolution offered by the Iowa delegation that explicitly would free national officers to follow their individual consciences and that would allow state unions to veto any local operation of the national party endorsement. Willard expected criticism to recede after the election, but it did not. Foster felt forced to resign as national superintendent for legislation. She advocated her views, beginning in 1885, as president of the Iowa union, a position that automatically made her a vice-president of the national union.[39]

The Campaign of 1884 and the Strategy of the Prohibition Movement

The Prohibition party campaign of 1884 and the WCTU endorsement shocked the dry movement. The events of that year prompted a hailstorm of criticism from abused Republicans that the partisan strategy was impractical. Critics attacked the third party; some leaders searched for alternative organizations. The most prominent Methodist spokesman for prohibition worked with Ellen Foster and her husband, E. C. Foster, to try to form a new nonpartisan prohibition organization, while other Republicans organized a pressure group within their own party in an effort to evoke a forthright prohibition plank in its 1888 platform. Neither effort was successful. Meanwhile, Frances Willard was steadily working to solidify her alliance with the Prohibition party.

The Republican complaints about the partisan prohibition strategy repeated familiar arguments but with a new sense of urgency after 1884. The vision of building the Prohibition party into a national coalition of reformers was illusory and impractical, in this view. Even within the third party, consensus on issues other than prohibition was unlikely, critics observed. To be successful, in the words of one Methodist editorial, the party "must ignore all other public interests, except its own specialty—which the great body of citizens will not do, and ought not." Even if a broad agreement was reached on other principles, it would simply take too much time and

38. *Minutes of the National Woman's Christian Temperance Union*, 1884, pp. 66–69; *Union Signal*, Oct. 30, 1884, pp. 21–22; Mezvinsky, "White-Ribbon Reform," p. 122.

39. Mezvinsky, "White-Ribbon Reform," pp. 125–26; Earhart, *Willard*, pp. 214–18; *Twelfth Annual Meeting of the Iowa WCTU*, 1885, p. 2; Foster, *Truth in the Case*, p. 58.

cost too much money to win elections. Meanwhile, not only would important temperance work, especially education, suffer, but the short-run outcome would be the election of wet Democrats like Grover Cleveland. Senator Henry Blair of New Hampshire, the best-known congressional advocate of prohibition, warned that the partisan strategy threatened his own reelection chances. Ellen Foster noted that congressmen who favored a federal inquiry into the liquor traffic, a goal of virtually every temperance organization, saw their seats endangered.[40]

The sense of urgency was expressed not just in rhetoric but also in organizational activity. Shortly after the defeat of the Republican James Blaine in the presidential election of 1884, Daniel Dorchester, a Massachusetts pastor who headed the Methodists' committee on temperance and prohibition, announced the formation of the National League for the Suppression of the Liquor Traffic. He sought to unite drys who opposed "political or sectarian alignments" in favor of educational work. Dorchester did not explain how his new group would differ from the National Temperance Society, but in the late winter its political purpose was clarified. John D. Rockefeller began to make small monthly donations that paid E. C. Foster, Ellen Foster's husband, to serve the new league as a full-time executive. The league began to issue pamphlets, a key one of which Ellen Foster wrote, touting the nonpartisan route to political change. "Give me *bread, documents* and *stamps*," Mr. Foster wrote to Rockefeller that March, "and I will agree to create a non-partisan epidemic." He wanted to build a network of local affiliates enlisting nonpartisan temperance workers who would support the structure with their dues.[41]

The league, all of whose officers were Republicans, appeared to Prohibition party leaders to be nothing more than a front designed to keep Republican voters in line. Although the *Union Signal*, while noting the "partisanship of nonpartisanship" welcomed the league as a coworker in the battle for dry laws, privately Frances Willard called it "that curious League;" its purpose was to keep "temperance Republicans from going into the Prohibition party." That summer

40. "The Prohibition Movement," *Methodist Review* 67 (March 1885): 277–80; Foster, *Partisanship and Non-Partisanship* (Boston, 1885).

41. Daniel Dorchester, *Non-Partisanship in Temperance Effort* (Boston, 1885); *New York Times*, Jan. 5, 1885; E. C. Foster to John D. Rockefeller, March 5 and July 2, 1885, JDR; Lora B. Pine, "The Attitude of the Methodist Episcopal Church Toward Temperance and Prohibition," (M.A. thesis, University of Pittsburgh, 1931), p. 59.

she publicly called it "a special contribution box for 'wealthy Republicans.' "[42]

By the end of the year the national league was dead, a victim of inadequate financing and ill-formed ideas about organizing supporters on the local level. Aside from distributing a large volume of literature, it had accomplished little. In the meantime a group of temperance Republicans was taking another route. Rather than breaking away from the nineteenth-century political theory of the party as the appropriate instrument for change, they hoped to build an Anti-Saloon Republican League to press for a prohibition platform. Led by Albert Griffin of Kansas, who called the first meeting late in 1885, the group proposed to combine those Republicans who merely wanted to restrict the functioning of the saloon with those who advocated outright prohibition of the liquor traffic. That union, whose aim was to put an end to the ideological bickering that had so divided temperance forces over the years, seemed most sensible to Griffin, who asserted that it was time to work together to achieve the most widely accepted goals.[43]

Griffin and his followers had a rather grand organization in mind. They believed that the party machinery was generally controlled by the liquor interests, even though they were but a tiny minority in each state, because the saloon men were united while the temperance forces were divided. Thus the new league was to provide "a permanent, watchful and aggressive organization." Its leaders hoped to recruit sympathizers in each of the nation's precincts. The network of local and state leagues would secure the assistance of Republican newspapers and help other temperance organizations with information and lecturers, while endorsing appropriate slates of candidates. This would be done in an unselfish manner, in what Griffin thought was the great tradition of the Republican party. "It is the early triumph of a great reform," he wrote, with a barb thrown at the third party, "not the transient instrument of that reform, that is chiefly sought."[44]

42. *Union Signal*, Jan. 15, 1885, p. 1; Sept. 3, 1885, p. 8; Sept. 10, 1885, p. 1; Willard to her mother, May 8, 1885; Willard to editor of *Golden Censor* (Rockford, Ill.), July 29, 1885, WCTU, reel 34. Joseph Weeks served both the national Republican party and the league as treasurer. His wife was active in the Pennsylvania WTCU.

43. *The Nation*, Sept. 23, 1886, p. 244; Albert Griffin, *Anti-Saloon Republicanism, An Address Delivered in Cortland, N.Y., Dec. 1, 1886*, Oberlin College Library.

44. *Address of the National Committee of Anti-Saloon Republicans*; *General Plan of Work*; both in Oberlin College Library; E. W. Metcalf to I. W. Metcalf, Nov. 16, 1886, IWM.

Griffin's league attracted attention from the Republican press, but it never approached the grand design of its founder. On the eve of the Republican convention in 1888, the league's meeting in New York was "a partial disaster," with less than one-third of the expected delegates attending; and the most prominent figures were not among those who did come. Ellen Foster was a featured speaker, and both she and Griffin presented their views to the Republican platform committee the next month and expressed pleasure with the outcome. But the party refused to finance the league, and by the next year it had disappeared, with Griffin personally bankrupted for his efforts.[45]

Ellen Foster led the WCTU opposition to Willard until the end of 1889. The Iowa union, when it elected Foster president in 1885, recorded its "unfailing loyalty to the National Woman's Christian Temperance Union in all its established departments of work" and, by a three-to-one margin, declared that it would remain nonpartisan and active in political work. To prepare for a debate in the national convention in Philadelphia that autumn, Foster collected information on the successful use of the nonpartisan strategy in securing scientific temperance education laws and received personal financial assistance from her good friend John D. Rockefeller. Although she saw "no visible sign of any change in policy on the part of Miss Willard," she told him, "I have faith that somehow God will help us." Foster and Willard met privately in an unsuccessful attempt to resolve their differences. The 1885 convention delegates again endorsed the Prohibition party, by a margin wider than the previous year. When Foster concluded the two-hour debate, she heard hisses of disapproval from some delegates, whom Willard, in the chair, quickly gaveled to silence. Foster privately referred to the convention as "the Philadelphia persecution."[46]

Foster did not give up the fight. Secure in the support of a majority of the Iowa members and encouraged by leaders in at least five other states, she tried again in 1886 to have the national union reverse its position. "I shall make my stand and rally what few women there will dare to follow," she wrote Rockefeller. "The best

45. Both Theodore Roosevelt and John D. Rockefeller were members of the league. Griffin to Rockefeller, Aug. 1, 1887; May 10 and June 13, 1888; Jan. 23, 1889; Oct. 10, 1890, JDR; *New York Times*, May 1, 2, and 4, 1888.

46. *A Statement by the WCTU of Cleveland, July 20, 1885*; Foster to Mary Hunt, undated, 1885, and Dec. 8, 1885, STF, reel 2; *National WCTU Bulletin*, undated, Willard scrapbook, WCTU, reel 34; E. C. Foster to Rockefeller, Oct. 18 and Nov. 10, 1885, JDR. *Twelfth Annual Meeting of the Iowa WCTU*, 1885, pp. xxii–xxv.

women, those who think as we do will not be there. They do not like
contention and will stay at home. I shall do what I can to stem the
tide." At the convention, Foster's protest was referred to the executive committee, and she was refused permission to read it to the
delegates. The convention adopted a new rule that in the future any
questions regarding "our attitude toward political parties" had to be
voted upon without discussion; its author simply said she was weary
of the arguments. The following year Foster's only avenue was
offering an amendment to the constitution that would have declared
the national union nonpartisan and nonsectarian. The convention
turned it down.[47]

The bitterest fight occurred at the convention in New York in
1888. Prior to the assembly, writers in the *Union Signal* attacked
Foster personally, stating that she had "ceased to be in spirit if not in
name a Christian Temperance Union woman." An indignant and
sorrowful Foster repudiated "the libel." "I am pained at the lowered
moral tone, and the mental obliquity which permits it." She was sad
that the *Signal* attack denied "the oft-repeated claim that woman's
presence would purify politics." When Foster asked the national
executive committee to censure the editor responsible, not only did
it refuse, but it applauded her work. Foster was no more successful
on the convention floor. The delegates did repeal their ban on
discussion of party affiliations, but that action did not help Foster.
Willard postponed the debate until the last evening "in order that
the real work of the Convention should not be interfered with," in
one of her follower's words. Only a small minority of delegates
supported Foster. The Illinois delegation even offered a resolution
that would have forbidden any member of the WCTU from speaking on any public platform against the party endorsement. But that
was too extreme a measure even for Frances Willard to accept, and
the convention defeated it.[48]

The final break came at the national convention of 1889. It surprised no one. Before the convention, Frances Willard told a reporter that she did not expect the minority to make another attempt
to amend the constitution. To do so required a year's notice; that

47. Foster to Rockefeller, Sept. 26, 1886, JDR; Mezvinsky, "White-Ribbon Reform," pp. 126–28.
48. Willard, *Glimpses of Fifty Years*, pp. 456–60; *Union Signal*, July 12, 1888,
pp. 4–5, and Nov. 8, 1888, p. 9; *New York Tribune*, Oct. 19 and 21, 1888; *New York
Times*, Oct. 21 and 24, 1888; *Minutes of the National Woman's Christian Temperance Union*,
1888, p. 41; Earhart, *Willard*, pp. 222–23.

notice was given but "by some mistake it did not go in the record." Willard denied that this was a deliberate failure: "It was simply one of those mistakes which will sometimes occur." She expected Foster's small following to withdraw from the convention, although she would not try to force such an action. Foster and her supporters were watching to see if there was any chance that the national union might retract its partisan strategy. If not, they were prepared to form a separate organization. When Foster finally led the Iowa delegation from the convention floor, Frances Willard, according to one observer, "rose to her feet, and swaying back and forth in her excitement, cried out in an exultant voice, 'This is not unexpected although we regret it,' showing in voice and manner only gladness." Then followed "a perfect pandemonium, . . . hisses, laughter, cheers." "It *had to be*," Foster wrote to Rockefeller. She and her supporters no longer wished to expend their strength in the battle over strategy, preferring instead to return to temperance work.[49]

Frances Willard's final victory in the six-year struggle over the political strategy of the WCTU was costly. Her opponents claimed that the endorsement of the Prohibition party caused thousands of women to abstain from joining, faithful workers to withdraw, churches to refuse their rooms for meetings, ministers to decline to read notices to their congregations, and donors to withhold funds lest they go to the party. To such charges Willard retorted that the WCTU had never been stronger. But whatever the endorsement may or may not have cost the union in support, Willard's actions on its behalf diminished her esteem among the great majority of prohibition supporters who did not choose to affiliate with the third party. In its internal affairs the union ceased to be fully democratic as the president maneuvered. As Mary Aldrich, an Iowa leader, put it, Willard's behavior "would be condemned as demagogic in politicians." Overlooking the substance of the complaint, Willard noted in answer that the delegate majorities favoring the endorsement were ever increasing. She was unwilling to allow fair procedures to stand in the way of her convictions.[50]

49. Foster to Rockefeller, Nov. 26, 1889, JDR; *Oberlin Weekly News*, Dec. 12, 1889; *The Non-Partisan Journal* 2 (Nov. 1889): 1; James Clement Ambrose, "Women of Reform," *The Independent*, Nov. 21, 1889, p. 14; *Chicago Inter-Ocean*, undated clipping, Foster file, Schlesinger Library.

50. Foster, *Truth in the Case*, pp. 24–25, 91; Ellen M. Watson to James A. Beaver, Nov. 12, 1886, JB; Mattie F. Weeks to Mary Hunt, Oct. 14, 1889, STF, reel 3. Willard liked to claim that the large delegate majorities that favored her views were a product

Willard sought a wide range of reforms, with herself and the WCTU leading the way. She saw Ellen Foster only as a loyal Republican, part of a Republican effort to undercut the new party of reform. The rewards for the Fosters were public acclaim and federal patronage. Willard rejected the argument that parties must strike compromises. Her definition of a party was simple: "A party means a part of the voting population that think one way." No complex affair that had to accommodate competing ideologies, "it implies another part who unite because they think a different way."

No matter how fervently she wanted to help the third party, however, Willard insisted that the WCTU was really nonpartisan. Women could not be otherwise until they had the vote. "But nonpartisan," she informed the convention in 1889, " . . . does not imply you cannot speak your good word, and show what side you are on." While in its "organic law" the WCTU was nonpartisan, the will of the majority, determined democratically, was rightfully sympathetic with a particular party. For her that meant "As women we can pray, plead, and work for the party that pledges itself to the protection of our homes." All the endorsement of the Prohibition party meant was that the WCTU was renewing "the methods of the crusade, no longer making the saloon but the *individual voter* our objective point.[51]

Willard's dreams and the Prohibition party soon encountered disappointment, however. The party had little impact on the national election of 1888. Willard wanted it to cooperate with other reformers seeking broad changes in American society, but by 1892 the People's party had become the vanguard of broad reform. By 1896 the Prohibition party itself was deeply divided between those who, like Willard, wanted to have a "broad gauge" platform addressing many social and economic injustices and those who thought it should limit itself to the "narrow gauge" of a single issue, prohibi-

---

of democratic decisions made at local, county, and state meetings. The Wilkinsburg, Pa., union, however, anticipating the decision soon to be reached at the state convention, found that its members could not agree on the wisdom of the party endorsement. So they decided that their delegate would have to decide for herself, and then, so as to save expenses, chose as their delegate a member who would be in the convention city on personal business. MWWCTU, Oct. 1, 1889.

51. Willard, "The Progress of the Prohibition party," *Union Signal*, Nov. 21, 1889, p. 11, Jan. 30, 1890, p. 5. Willard's words obscured the reality that, after the endorsement, the WCTU organizers she employed tried to help the Prohibition party, that programs the union recommended were intended to help the party, and that the *Union Signal* was, in effect, a party sheet.

tion. The latter group controlled party affairs in the 1890s. In the midst of these developments, Willard counseled patience. "Four years count for but little in the long life of a great movement for humanity," she wrote in 1890. "It is darkest just before the day." Finally, in 1896 she admitted to a reporter, "I do not think [the party] will ever come to power, but I am with it heart and soul."[52]

The disillusionment with a partisan reform strategy that even Frances Willard expressed by the middle of the 1890s did not mean that the entire prohibition movement judged that the reform was hopeless. Willard's drive for WCTU endorsement of the third party had provoked counterarguments, especially those by Ellen Foster, that clarified a distinction between loyalty to a party and commitment to a political cause regardless of party platforms. It was this clarification, and the resulting formation of a Nonpartisan WCTU, that paved the way for the birth of the Anti-Saloon League.

52. Willard, "The Progress of the Prohibition Party," *Our Day* 5 (March 1890): 185–94; G. T. B. Davis, "An Interview with Frances E. Willard," *Our Day* 16 (May 1896): 264; Blocker, *Retreat from Reform*, pp. 69–77.

3

THE BIRTH OF THE
ANTI-SALOON LEAGUE

The vacuum in the prohibition movement caused by organizational disunity and dissent over appropriate political techniques was the condition that the founders of the new Anti-Saloon League sought to end. Their goal was to provide both a clear political strategy and a new kind of political organization that could build and command the prohibition movement effectively. Two themes, thus, stand out in the birthing process. The first was the void caused largely by the actions of the Prohibition party and Frances Willard in the 1880s. One result of the turmoil was the emergence of Ellen Foster as a forceful spokesperson for an effective nonpartisan strategy, what became, in effect, the program of the new Anti-Saloon League. The other theme, which also appeared in the 1880s, was the rise of "big business" in manufacturing industries. These two themes, apparently so distant from one another in every aspect except the timing of their appearance, provide the keys for understanding the Anti-Saloon League.[1]

The significance of Ellen Foster's opposition to Willard was twofold. First, Foster's battle within the WCTU, and her loyalty to the Republican party and support from its patrons, caused her to speak

1. An earlier version of this chapter appeared as my "Organizing for Reform." For the ensuing account, I am indebted to Odegard, *Pressure Politics*, esp. pp. 1–10, and Blocker, *Retreat from Reform*, esp. pp. 154–75. My own work, however, differs substantially. Odegard's focus was upon the league as a structure, and he did not provide a narrative about its birth or explain the historical setting. Blocker, on the other hand, while a work of history, takes the Prohibition party far more seriously than I do. As Blocker's title indicates, his main interest lies in explaining how and why the league arose as a "retreat" from a middle-class concern with fundamental social change, which he believes the Prohibition party represented. I am interested, in contrast, more with the league itself, as an expression of mainstream tendencies in American life.

widely about distinguishing party loyalty from the particular issue of prohibition. Second, her actions resulted in 1889 in the formation of a dissident Nonpartisan WCTU that soon gave important succor to the new Anti-Saloon League.

The founder of the league was Howard Russell (no relation to the father of the Prohibition party). Russell and his supporters, who included leaders of the Nonpartisan WCTU, adopted Foster's point of view as their basic program. But Russell did much more than simply form a male counterpart to that woman's organization. He consciously set out to emulate the bureaucratic characteristics of the new, modern business firms in order to build a political organization that officially disregarded all but prohibition issues so as to unite the largest possible following to sustain pressure to outlaw the liquor traffic.

Ellen Foster and the Nonpartisan WCTU

Ellen Foster's thoughts about political strategy evolved as a response to Frances Willard's partisan actions. The success of the Iowa WCTU in gaining a state prohibition law through the action of the state's Republican party combined with Willard's alliance with the Prohibition party to lead Foster to her own independent consideration of political strategy. Foster had begun her career as a reformer who unquestioningly accepted the received wisdom that change was achieved through party action. As she told the WCTU convention in 1881, prohibition could "only be permanently secured through the agency of *a political party making this its central idea.*" Foster's thoughts changed only when, in 1884, she realized that Willard was leading the WCTU to affiliation with the Prohibition party, an affiliation that did not square with the successful achievement of prohibition in Iowa.[2]

After 1884 Foster felt compelled to defend the Republican record on prohibition and to define the proper relationship between the WCTU, or any other reform organization, and a political party. As for the Republican record on prohibition, Foster revealed only confidence. "The Republican party boldly challenges inspection," she told a meeting in Connecticut in 1888. The Republicans were dominant in every state that had a prohibition law. Other measures restricting liquor sales were either "secured by Republican votes or

---

2. *Minutes of the National Woman's Christian Temperance Union,* 1881, p. xviii.

defeated by Democratic vetoes." Nevertheless Foster was dissatisfied with the Republican record.[3]

Foster realized that successful political parties reflected the complexities of society, so that on emotional issues the party might not agree with zealous reformers. Her conclusion was that the public had to lead the party, not, as the Prohibition party leaders supposed, the party educate the people. Most important, reformers might have to abandon, at least temporarily, their party allegiance. By 1886 she was telling audiences that "when it comes to the temperance question, I am ready to see any party go down, if prohibition will result." But the appearance of Prohibition party candidates only served to elect wet Democrats. "I would be glad to assist in the defeat of a liquor Republican at any time anywhere," she told a follower in Connecticut, "*if in so doing his place should be filled by a temperance man of any other party.*" But she also urged Republican leaders not to subject temperance advocates to such a powerful cross-pressure. "From my standpoint of non-partisan temperance work," she wrote to James Beaver, the successful dry Pennsylvania Republican gubernatorial candidate in 1886, "I cannot trust the principle of prohibition to the sole advocacy of any political party . . . but from the standpoint of a Republican, I do desire the party to take that stand—I do not see how it can do more—I believe it cannot safely do less."[4]

The zealousness of some Prohibition party ideologues rankled Foster. Unlike them, she accepted halfway measures. License laws, for instance, however noxious, at least admitted the principle of government power. Local option laws merited the support of temperance workers if they were the only ones politically feasible. She had no patience with zealots who claimed that such halfway measures were a "covenant with the devil," writing in amazement to Rockefeller in 1889 that some Prohibition party leaders declared themselves against local option because a majority vote could not decide the will of God. She wondered if these "good people . . . will next dispute the foundation principle of popular government, and go back to the *divine right of Kings!!!*"[5]

In promoting their cause, drys, Foster believed, should carefully

3. Foster, "The Republican Party and Temperance," *The Independent*, Sept. 13, 1888, p. 7.

4. *Twelfth Annual Report of the Cleveland WCTU*, 1886, p. 13; Foster to James Beaver, Sept. 7, 1886, JB; Foster to Mrs. Whitmore, Sept. 11, 1886, published in *Putnam (Conn.) Patriot*, Sept. 17, 1886, reprinted in *Truth in the Case*; Foster to Harrison, July 19, 1888, BH.

5. Foster to Harrison, July 19, 1888, BH. Foster to Rockefeller, Feb. 20, 1889, JDR.

distinguish between ends and means and between their own organizations and political parties. Prohibition laws were a means toward the goal of achieving individual abstinence. Winning laws, thus, was no substitute for the "education of individuals as to personal duty." That, to her, was the problem with the Prohibition party; it was not an abstinence society but an organization that had substituted the means for the end. Such was the core of her objection to the affiliation of the WCTU with the party. The WCTU sought to persuade Americans to lead abstemious lives, and the women worked for prohibition laws as only one means among many for that persuasion. The Prohibition party operated on a different principle, in her view. It asked not for the people to pledge to lead drink-free lives but instead for them to vote for candidates dedicated to eradicating the drink traffic through expansion of police powers.[6]

When the WCTU endorsed the Prohibition party, it confused those ends and means. Foster thought the confusion understandable. It rested with women's disenfranchisement and lack of political experience. "They see . . . the Prohibition Party . . . men sincerely sympathize with the sorrow of the women and offer to champion their cause," she wrote privately to Republican presidential candidate Benjamin Harrison in 1888. "They say, 'We will fight your battles and avenge you of your adversaries.' It is not strange that women answer 'We accept your help and will lend our influence to your party;' it is not strange that women who have no knowledge of political methods and the possibilities of party action should make an unwise choice of agencies." The way out of the problem seemed clear to Foster. Women should have suffrage, but pending enfranchisement they should develop their political skills and knowledge. Separate organizations, one for party affiliation and one for nonpartisan prohibition work, would facilitate their political abilities. As individuals, temperance women should follow their partisan preferences, but, unlike Frances Willard, they should not try to merge their temperance organization with a political party. As prohibition workers, they should seek to persuade voters to elect committed candidates of whatever party. As persons with partisan loyalties, they should work through a separate organization to influence party policy.[7]

6. Foster, "The Woman's Christian Temperance Union in Politics," *The Independent*, Nov. 1, 1888, pp. 1–2.

7. Ibid.; Foster to Harrison, July 19, 1888, BH. She expressed these thoughts briefly in "The Iowa Memorial" to the national WCTU convention of 1888. *Union Signal*, Nov. 8, 1888, p. 9.

Ellen Foster followed her own prescription in her subsequent career. In 1888 she formed the Woman's Republican Association of the United States and served as its president until her death in 1910. The group was inspired by the Woman's Liberty Association, which Foster observed while vacationing in England in 1887. Just as the latter aided Gladstone on the Irish home rule issue, so Republican women's clubs could help educate women wage earners and homemakers as to the wisdom of the party's tariff policy. Thinking in broad terms about women's participation in political affairs, Foster believed not only in the ability of a women's organization to help the party but also in the desirability of women preparing themselves for the "happy day" when they received the right to vote. By becoming involved in politics, she told the Congress of Women at the World's Columbian Exposition in 1893, women could learn not just about the symptoms of social problems but about their causes as well. As head of the Woman's Republican Association, Foster lived according to her own rhetoric, accepting federal appointments to investigate conditions of women and child workers and the treatment of the female inmates of federal prisons.[8]

Foster persuaded only a small minority of WCTU delegates, but her supporters included several important leaders. The group that followed her out of the convention in 1889 went on to found the Nonpartisan WCTU to compete with the original union. The rival union embodied Foster's ideas, and although she did not assume an active role in it, as will become clear, it provided links between Foster's ideas and the program of the Anti-Saloon League.

While Foster for years chose to fight Willard from within the WCTU, other dissidents had already bolted the organization. The most significant rupture occurred in Ohio. There the president of the state union, Ellen J. Phinney of Cleveland, was appalled by the endorsement in 1884 of the St. John campaign. Phinney observed that the resolution prevented the union from influencing politicians in the established parties. So she exercised her control of the executive committee to disassociate the Ohio union from the national party endorsement. This action provoked a bitter fight for control of the Ohio presidency between Phinney and Mary Woodbridge, a

8. Byrne, "Judith Ellen Foster"; Foster, "Women in Politics," in *The Congress of Women*, ed. Mary Kavanaugh Oldham Eagle (Chicago, 1893), pp. 668–69; *Official Proceedings of the Tenth Republican National Convention*, 1892, pp. 114–15; Foster to Harrison, July 19, 1888, BH; *Chicago Inter-Ocean*, Sept. 29, 1888. Willard's biographer interpreted Foster's activity as stemming solely from a Republican effort "to woo the Union through Mrs. Foster." Earhart, *Willard*, p. 222.

member of the Prohibition party national committee and a past president of the Ohio union. Woodbridge and the party flooded the state with literature and, with the help of Willard at the state convention in 1885, won the office. Phinney and the Cleveland union, who believed they were the "legitimate child of the crusade," broke with the WCTU and organized a network of nonpartisan affiliates across the state. By 1886 the Nonpartisan Ohio WCTU had thirty chapters and about one thousand members; Woodbridge's group retained about six thousand members. Phinney asserted that the controversy not only hurt fund raising but caused women to refuse to join either union because the dispute, as opposed to prohibition work, seemed so all-consuming.[9]

The nonpartisan Ohio union hosted Foster's supporters who left the national WCTU convention in 1889. They met with Phinney, raised $500 for expenses, and planned an organizing convention for late January 1890 in Cleveland, symbolically in the same church that was the birthplace of the WCTU in 1874. Phinney found that "the interest is quite widespread." She thought the "outlook [was] at least hopeful," as women in Ohio, Pennsylvania, Iowa, Minnesota, and Maine expressed their interest in the new organization. "The country approves our course," Foster wrote to Rockefeller; "women everywhere are ready to respond . . . . I am not in any sense discouraged, but I feel very solemn in view of the great issues which will soon be determined by the course which our woman's temperance work now takes."[10]

The organizers of the new Nonpartisan WCTU sought to provide an alternative, not to damage the WCTU. "We do not wish to break down the old organization," Phinney told Rockefeller, "—we aim to gather in those who have dropped out of the work, and with them thousands who have not enlisted because of the partisan methods of work." Her strategy, as opposed to Willard's "do everything" policy,

9. *Union Signal*, July 12, 1883, p. 11; "The Ohio WCTU," *The Living Issue*, Willard scrapbook, WCTU, reel 34; Whitaker, "A History of the Ohio WCTU," pp. 295–97; Phinney to Rockefeller, Nov. 4, 1884; Anna Prather to Rockefeller, Nov. 21, 1884, and Jan. 17, 1885; Phinney to Rockefeller, May 20, 1885; June 8, 1885; Sept. 20, 1888; Nov. 26, 1888; *A Statement by the Woman's Christian Temperance Union of Cleveland, Ohio, July 20, 1885*, JDR; *New York Times*, Dec. 29, 1884; *Twelfth Annual Report of the WCTU of Cleveland*, 1886, pp. 11–12; *Sixteenth Annual Report of the WCTU of Cleveland*, 1889–90, p. 43.

10. Foster to Rockefeller, Nov. 26, 1889; Phinney to Rockefeller, Dec. 14, 1889, JDR; *First National Meeting of the Non-Partisan National Woman's Christian Temperance Union, Held at Cleveland, Ohio, January 22–23–24, 1890*, p. 38. Oberlin College Library.

was to focus attention more sharply on prohibition in order to avoid limiting appeal among dry advocates. The new group's purpose was to put "non-partisan temperance sentiment . . . in harness" and to make it "an available force."[11]

The Nonpartisan WCTU had a difficult time establishing itself. The attendance at the organizational meeting in Cleveland was disappointing. Only about forty delegates came from out of state. Foster declined the nomination as president, stating that she was tired of controversy and wanted to work as an individual on temperance matters. Privately, she expressed a desire to earn money on the lecture circuit and "open a bank account." Phinney was the group's first president, serving for five years.[12]

Reaction to the new organization from Frances Willard was swift. Although the dissenters were "Our Friends, the Seceders," according to the *Union Signal* editorial that followed the Cleveland meeting, the established union sought to place the burden of organization on them. The seceders were nothing more than "a movement in the interests of the dominant party of the hour, and are really partisans of the most decided character." The WCTU recommended that each local union immediately incorporate itself, if it had not already done so, so that "no property held in its name may be alienated by seceders." Although leaders of the established parties, out of fear of the new political movement, "will do their utmost to induce our members to go out," they must do the organizing; we are organized already." Willard instructed local unions to go about their business as usual, electing new officers as necessary.[13]

11. *First National Meeting of the NPWCTU*, pp. 34–35; *Cleveland Plain Dealer*, Jan. 24, 1890; *Worker's Manual for the Non-Partisan Woman's Christian Temperance Union* (Cleveland, 1893), p. 3, and Phinney to Rockefeller, Dec. 14, 1889, JDR; Phinney, "Call for a National Non-Partisan Convention at Cleveland," *Oberlin Weekly News*, Dec. 26, 1889; *News and Herald*, Jan. 23, 1890, Willard Scrapbook, WCTU, reel 35.

12. *Cleveland Plain Dealer*, Jan. 24, 1890; *First National Meeting of the NPWCTU, 1890*, pp. 29–30; Foster to Johnson Brigham, Sept. 18, 1891, JBr; Foster to Rockefeller, Dec. 16, 1889, JDR; *Minutes of the Twenty-Second Annual Meeting of the Non-Partisan Temperance Women of Ohio. The Tenth Annual Meeting of the Non-Partisan Woman's Christian Temperance Union, Cleveland, Oct. 16, 17, 18, 1895*, p. 45; Cherrington, *Evolution of Prohibition*, p. 174; *Standard Encyclopedia of the Alcohol Problem*, 5:1894.

13. *Union Signal*, Jan. 30, 1890, p. 8; "An Address from the National WCTU," Willard Scrapbook, WCTU, reel 32; *New York Times*, Jan. 28, 1890; MWWCTU, Jan. 7, 1890. Phinney wrote to Rockefeller that "we are getting quite accustomed to such pet names as 'frauds,' 'hypocrites,' 'deceivers,' 'Republicans,' which to them means 'enemies of all righteousness.' " June 24, 1890, JDR.

Although Frances Willard for the most part prevented the rival union from acquiring WCTU resources, she could not quiet the ideas it embodied. The nonpartisan union came to provide essential help in establishing the new Anti-Saloon League. Most important of all its help, Ellen Foster and the nonpartisan union provided the grand strategy for the birth of the modern prohibition movement. Russell and the Anti-Saloon League embodied that strategy in an innovative structure. The Nonpartisan WCTU helped the new league in very practical ways. Local nonpartisan unions eventually supplied small sums of cash to the league's founders and helped league officials contact potential supporters and patrons. Phinney counseled Howard Russell when he first sought to organize the Ohio league, and she arranged a meeting between Russell and John D. Rockefeller, whose wife belonged to the nonpartisan Cleveland union, when Russell was desperately short of funds. Annie Wittenmyer helped also. She served as the nonpartisan national president from 1896 to 1898 while also a trustee of the American Anti-Saloon League.

Dimmed Hopes, New Searches

The dispute between Willard and Foster and the formation of the nonpartisan union were but two symptoms, albeit highly visible ones, of what had happened to the prohibition movement by 1890. The bright prospects following the Kansas victory in 1880 had dimmed by the time of the WCTU split in 1889. With little to show for a decade of agitation and expenditure, church leaders, aside from the minority who supported the Prohibition party and Frances Willard, were arguing among themselves about how best to proceed, or even whether to proceed at all. There were developments between 1889 and 1893 that in retrospect indicate that a consensus was emerging that eventually benefited the Anti-Saloon League.

But in the short run the temperance movement was in chaos. Some churchmen still insisted that their task was to persuade

---

The controversy among the women finally ended at the beginning of the twentieth century. Frances Willard died in 1898, and her successors were not so closely committed to the Prohibition party. The Republican party, thanks to the depression of the 1890s and the debacle of the Bryan candidacies, had clearly emerged as the majority coalition in the nation, and the third party, itself deeply divided, showed no signs of becoming a viable vehicle for assuming power. In 1901 the national WCTU convention rejected party endorsement, and soon thereafter the Nonpartisan WCTU merged with the larger organization.

individuals—so-called gospel temperance—and refrain from political action. Others approved of "high license" laws severely restricting the numbers and the operations of saloons, while still others passionately decried such statutes as implicit government sanctions of the liquor traffic, all the more dangerous because they raised revenue through licensing fees and gave wet advocates another argument for opposing prohibitory laws. Looking back on the period as an Anti-Saloon League leader and historian, Ernest Cherrington observed that some temperance groups "to all appearances, possessed a hatred of other similar organizations stronger by far than their hatred of saloons." Throughout the period, some zealous leaders of the Prohibition party, certain that theirs was the only appropriate course, attempted to destroy any rival organization. But the decline of their own organization left a vacuum of leadership for the dry cause.[14]

The bitterness and the vacuum prompted the organization of several national forums intended to illuminate common ground within the movement. In New York, seven men called a National Temperance Congress in 1890. Pleased with the attendance, one observer described the discussion as filled with "excitement . . . life . . . vigorous and sometimes violent assertion . . . [and] protest." The results in 1890 were meager, but similar meetings by 1893 had produced agreement that "the saloons be made an objective point of attack on the part of all opponents of the drink traffic, whatever their differences of opinion as to other particulars." Even this understanding took years to emerge, and it excluded the means for attacking the saloon. No consensus was reached about whether restrictive license laws or local option campaigns was the most effective weapon. Aware that his own Prohibition party had instigated so much rancor among drys, late in 1890 I. K. Funk, a prominent editor and publisher, began "A Symposium—On What Line May All Enemies of the Saloon Unitedly Do Battle?" in the *Homiletic Review*, to search for common ground. But Funk held no hope for finding agreement on methods. The next year Edward Everett Hale responded to Funk's invitation to participate in the symposium by noting, "I was tempted to say . . . that everybody knew well enough what the ground is on which the enemies of the saloon may unite, but that everybody knew also that they would not unite on any ground."[15]

14. Cherrington, *History of the Anti-Saloon League* (Westerville, Ohio, 1913), p. 8.

15. Charles F. Deems, "The First National Temperance Congress," *Homiletic Review* 21 (Jan. 1891): 30–40. The congress of 1890 was not intended to pass resolu-

Leaders in the Methodist church especially were concerned about the divisions in the temperance movement. In 1892 the General Conference of the Methodist Church (North) adopted a statement for its *Book of Discipline* that urged Methodists to vote "to promote the rescue of the country from the guilt and dishonor which have been brought upon it by the criminal complicity with the liquor traffic." It suggested that "Christian men" should refuse to support political parties that failed to stand forthrightly against the saloon.[16] Although Methodists could read the statement as a plea for the Prohibition party, the action of the general conference was toward nonpartisan activity. The church had established specialized "boards" as separate legal corporations for particular tasks. The conference created a committee on temperance and prohibition in 1892, which in 1904 became a board. A. J. Kynett, a prominent Philadelphia clergyman and Methodist editor, headed the temperance committee.[17]

Kynett eventually led his church to support the Anti-Saloon League, and the road he took illustrates how circumstances came to favor the league. At the end of the 1880s he was active in the Pennsylvania amendment campaign, heading an ad hoc Union Prohibitory League. The campaign instructed Kynett in the power of the saloon interests and the weakness of the scattered temperance forces. He concluded that the nation needed a permanent nonpartisan organization that would unite church members across party and denominational lines. Kynett formed the Interdenominational Christian Temperance Alliance, which local Methodist conferences began to endorse; by 1893 it was forming in four states. The Ohio alliance merged with the Ohio Anti-Saloon League in the autumn of 1893.[18]

---

tions lest such actions divide temperance forces further. See James C. Fernald's "Preface" to *Proceedings of the National Temperance Congress, 1890* (New York, 1891). See also *Homiletic Review* 20 (Dec. 1890): 509–13, and 22 (Sept. 1891): 213–15.

16. Quoted in *Minutes of the 55th Annual Session of the North Ohio Conference of the Methodist Episcopal Church, 1894.*

17. Nolan B. Harman, "Structural and Administrative Changes," in *The History of American Methodism*, 3 vols., ed. Emory S. Bucke (New York and Nashville, 1964), 1: 3–4; Frederick A. Norwood, *The Story of American Methodism* (New York and Nashville, 1974), p. 349.

18. A. J. Kynett, "Christian Temperance Leagues and Alliances," in *Temperance in All Nations*, 2 vols., ed. J. N. Stearns (New York, 1893), 1: 328–30; Cherrington, *History of the Anti-Saloon League*, pp. 20–21; *National Temperance Advocate* 28 (May 1893): 77, and 28 (Oct. 1893): 164; *Official Minutes of the Central Ohio Conference of the Methodist Episcopal Church 1892*, p. 85.

The Methodists were not alone in thinking about the need for a new temperance organization. The Ohio alliance was headed by a Presbyterian pastor, and it included representatives from fourteen denominations. In 1892 a Congregational minister in Massachusetts, James Brand, headed a group that used the term *antisaloon* in its name. In the District of Columbia, church members were mobilizing to achieve the closer regulation of the saloon in their city. In 1895 the Presbyterians' Permanent Committee on Temperance, which heretofore had engaged only in small-scale educational activities, noted the growth of the Ohio Anti-Saloon League and began corresponding with bodies in other denominations regarding ways "to make temperance work more effective." This correspondence was part of the impetus behind the formation of the American Anti-Saloon League in December 1895.[19]

Howard Russell and the Founding of the Anti-Saloon League

None of these persons or organizations, however, proposed an innovative organization. Kynett was interested in uniting the temperance forces, not in providing bureaucratic control over the prohibition movement. Active as a minister in the 1850s and 1860s, he used rhetoric arising from his memories of the Civil War to persuade people to join the interdenominational alliance. He suggested that the northern experience with mobilization was a model for temperance work, but his thinking was bureaucratic only in the sense that he recognized the need to divide responsibilities among individuals in a military fashion.[20] Kynett's plans did not include notions of a bureaucracy providing a continuing effort apart from the lives and action of the individuals in it or, most important, providing full-time people to develop the expertise for handling problems through a departmentalized system of authority that passed from the top of a hierarchy downward. But it was just these contributions that set the Anti-Saloon League apart from preceding organizations, and they came from a Congregational minister, Howard Russell.

Russell was baptized to prohibition work in the thicket of Ohio politics, and he was encouraged to make the Anti-Saloon League his

19. *Fourteenth Annual Report of the General Assembly's Permanent Committee on Temperance, 1895*, pp. 1-2, 20; *The Permanent Committee on Temperance of the General Assembly of the Presbyterian Church in the U.S.A.; 15th Annual Report, 1896*, pp. 3–5.

20. "The Church Militant Against the Saloon," *National Temperance Advocate* 28 (Oct. 1893): 164; *Christianity in Earnest* 7 (Mar.–Apr. 1895): 65.

life's ministry by professors, students, and friends of Oberlin College. Russell had entered the ministry as a second career. He was a Corning, Iowa, attorney and Republican politician who experienced a religious conversion in 1883 and attended the theological seminary at Oberlin College from 1884 to 1888.[21] As an Oberlin student he was very much involved in the temperance cause, observing its internal disputes firsthand and participating in them with some dismay. As a seminarian he argued that a separate Prohibition party was a hopeless vehicle for achieving reform and held firm to his commitment to the Republican party. The Prohibitionist voters in the North, he noted, tended to advocate civil rights for the freedmen in the South; yet prohibitionist sentiment was growing most rapidly among white southerners. Prohibitionists North and South could never unite in a single political party that would inevitably have to address policy concerns other than temperance. Given that reality, he concluded that nonpartisan organization was the only one that seemed appropriate.[22]

Russell personally carried out successful nonpartisan temperance work during his senior year, and he began to develop a vision of a new way of conducting prohibition agitation. A group of prominent Oberlin temperance advocates formed the Ohio Local Option League, an ad hoc group to press for passage of a township local option bill by the 1888 Ohio General Assembly. They employed Russell as state canvasser. After the legislature enacted the desired township law, Russell promoted the idea of making the league a permanent organization.

His thoughts were not yet sharply focused on details, except for rhetoric that was conventional among Republicans who wanted to thwart the growth of the Prohibition party. In a public meeting in Oberlin in March, and in his written report to his followers, Russell ascribed the victory to the "*all*-partisan approach," an "organized effort to stimulate the public judgment in both Republican and Democratic counties." Temperance people, he warned, should take a leaf from the operations of the liquor and brewing interests, who "do not form a party" but instead exercised their influence over existing political organizations and their members. But his ideas were tending in the direction of applying the full-time efforts of an

21. Biographical sketches of Russell appear in Louis A. Banks, *The Lincoln Legion* (New York, 1903), pp. 173–92, and Harry M. Chalfant, *These Agitators and Their Ideas* (Nashville, 1931), pp. 156–61.
22. College vs. Seminary," May 22, 1885, HH.

expert to temperance agitation on an ongoing basis. The way for temperance advocates to accomplish their goal, he said, was to create a statewide network of local agitators knowledgeable in both local affairs and temperance politics, tied together with a semimonthly newspaper, and led by a full-time, salaried organizer. "An active man should be kept in the field canvassing for members and subscribers." By collecting annual dues of one dollar, this organizer could enroll 50,000 members for an Ohio Anti-Liquor League, funding his salary and the publication of the paper and insuring that each township had one local resident responsible for agitation and the gathering of information. Russell optimistically predicted that such a group could close 90 percent of the state's saloons within three years and then mount sufficient pressure to secure statewide prohibition.[23] Thus by 1888 Russell realized the importance of having a full-time staff, but otherwise his thoughts about organization did not carry beyond those of some previous groups, such as the WCTU.

Russell did not remain on the scene to follow through with the realization of his ideas. Upon graduating that spring, he began his ministerial career in an urban mission in Kansas City, Missouri, rising quickly to become head of the Armour Mission in the stockyard district of Chicago. Although Russell left Ohio to assume his ministry, a new group did begin to form in his absence. An Oberlin student, John R. Commons, who later became a prominent reformer and labor relations scholar, and his mother, Mrs. C. W. Commons, began a semimonthly paper, *The Temperance Herald*, backed by well-known professors and local merchants. It was here that the first ideas of bringing a business system to temperance work appeared. A "temperance trust," the Commonses argued, was necessary to counteract the superior business organization of the distillers and brewers. "We suggest a trust that will completely boycott the whole business. There are more temperance men than drinking men in this country . . . . Total abstinence and prohibition [should be] the requisition of membership" in the "temperance trust," which would work for prohibition laws in every state, the District of Columbia, and the federal territories. "Such a course is only the application of sound methods in regard to other business matters." Feeling that temperance organization should not await the moment

23. Russell, "To the Temperance Workers of Ohio," *The Temperance Herald* (Oberlin), Aug. 15, 1888; Russell to Monroe, Feb. 3 and Mar. 1, 1888, JM; *Elyria Chronicle-Telegram*, May 25, 1920.

of battle in a legislature, the Commonses and their supporters began an Anti-Liquor League in Lorain County, Ohio, and urged adoption of its constitution elsewhere. The Commonses' organization followed the suggestions Russell had made in 1888 after the campaign for the township option bill. When members paid dues they brought a "share in this stock company. The more shareholders the more interested parties."[24]

This early impulse toward bringing business organization to the temperance movement, however, never went further than this general rhetoric. In Russell's absence no full-time organizer was hired, and the constitution the Commonses published as the model for a new antiliquor organization failed to spell out any details of a system for mobilizing people or to include any plan for adapting the departmentalized hierarchy of a modern business firm to temperance work. After six months of publication, *The Temperance Herald* failed, John R. Commons left Oberlin for graduate school, and the Anti-Liquor League faded into oblivion. Its only legacy was the general notion that somehow new business methods might be used in prohibition agitation.

Russell did not leave temperance work altogether while serving in the urban missions, and his experiences in Kansas City and Chicago eventually reinforced his commitment to the cause so that he was willing, at considerable personal sacrifice, to embark on a full-time temperance ministry. In the stockyard districts he witnessed how abuse of alcoholic beverages could destroy otherwise productive lives, and his direct encounter there with cultural traditions foreign to an American evangelical Protestant appalled him. In the summer of 1890 he took a leave from his church to try to implement his ideas by organizing the Missouri Anti-Liquor League. Still, his organizational thoughts did not go beyond hiring a full-time staff member, and when he failed to secure a person he considered suitable, the Missouri group withered. By the spring of 1893, after considerable soul-searching and the decision of the Armour family to convert the mission into the Armour Institute of Technology, Russell decided to devote his full attention to temperance work.[25]

24. *The Temperance Herald*, Sept. 15, Oct. 15, 1888; Jan. 15, Apr. 1, and May 1, 1889; John R. Commons, *Myself* (Madison, 1963), p. 21.

25. Russell to Lillian Russell, Aug. 1, 1890; "First Trial Trip—Missouri Anti-Liquor League," Russell's autobiographical writings; "A Suggested Form for a Constitution, Aug. 12, 1890," HH; *Armour Mission Visitor* 5 (Feb. 1891): 2; "Pastor's Pencilings," ibid. 5 (May 1891): 2.

In May he returned to Oberlin, where he obtained support for a summer's fund-raising and organizing effort in northern Ohio. In early September, the Ohio Anti-Saloon League formed at a meeting in Oberlin, and Russell was employed as state superintendent. The new group was to be nonpartisan, willing to work with any government official or candidate for office if only he would support dry legislation and its enforcement. The league solicited support from all churches. As the name indicated, the saloon—with all the evils associated with it in the eyes of temperance advocates—was to be the object of attack, and further local option legislation was to be the immediate means of the saloon's destruction. The league hoped to focus on the saloon and avoid the divisiveness of other issues that were virtually destroying the Prohibition party.[26]

A Business Model

In forming the new league Russell clearly saw it as the kind of temperance trust that the Commonses had advocated. The league would guide temperance activities while asking older groups to develop ties with it and accept its leadership. "As corporations, trusts and combinations have succeeded by a union of forces in the commercial world," Russell recalled two years later, "so, it was urged, the powers of righteousness should be mobilized and federated for greater moral victories." But his thoughts went beyond simply bringing union to a nonpartisan strategy of achieving prohibition. Although there is no available evidence to show that he directly and consciously studied the structure of the modern, departmentalized business firm at Armour or elsewhere, by 1893 Russell had developed a plan for adapting that structure in the development of the

26. Records of the Oberlin Temperance Alliance, vol. 2, p. 21, Oberlin College Archives; G. W. Shurtleff to E. W. Metcalf, May 31, 1893, and June 8, 1893, IWM; Banks, *Lincoln Legion*, pp. 208–11; "The Founding of the Anti-Saloon League Movement," typescript, HH; *Provisional Constituion of the Anti-Saloon League of Ohio* (n.p., 1893). Later the executive committee was renamed the board of trustees. Joseph R. Gusfield, *Symbolic Crusade: Status Politics and the American Temperance Movement* (Urbana, 1963), p. 99, discusses the birth of the Anti-Saloon League as a shift away from a reform tradition espoused by the WCTU that sought to assimilate minority groups into evangelical Protestant traditions. The league, in his view, was evidence of a shift toward coercive reform, of rural Americans seeking to impose their values on urban Americans. The evidence I have seen, however, suggests that the choice of a name, Anti-Saloon League, resulted from a desire to suppress a business system in order to make possible the progress of evangelical Protestant values.

Anti-Saloon League. He divided the principal functions of the league into specialized departments: agitation, legislation, law enforcement, and finance. The agitation department was to prepare propaganda and educational materials and to arrange for an annual "Anti-Saloon Sunday" in a community's cooperating churches, with a league employee supplying the pulpit. The legislative department was to write desirable bills, keep watch over enemy political activities, and lobby in the statehouse. The law enforcement department was to provide expert assistance to regularly elected public officials in cases involving liquor regulations. The finance department had the important but, in the midst of a depression, unsuccessful task of raising the necessary funds. Russell even envisioned eventually forming paramilitary "boys' brigades" as a fifth department to perpetuate temperance sentiment among future generations. He wanted to divide the state into ten geographical districts, each with a full-time district superintendent and a supporting staff replicating the larger departments. Supervising and coordinating all operations, including publication of a monthly newspaper, was the state superintendent, with offices in the capital.[27]

From its inception the Anti-Saloon League was to be like a modern business firm, bureaucratic and not democratic. At the top was a self-perpetuating executive committee of ten members carefully selected by Russell, who made certain that all political parties and supporting churches were represented. Members of the committee elected officers, hired the state superintendent, and formed committees to assist the league's departments. Beginning in 1894 the league held annual meetings that thousands of supporters attended, but like the stockholders' meetings of the typical modern corporation, they were carefully staged events for exhortation and education, not for involving large numbers of people in reaching decisions vital to the organization.[28]

Nor was the league envisioned as a democratic organization at the local level. Russell was careful to point out that the governing boards of the local leagues should be selected, not elected. His method of organizing was to travel to a community, arrange to meet sympathetic pastors and lay leaders, and choose a steering committee. Such

27. Russell, "A State Anti-Saloon Syndicate," *The Congregationalist*, Oct. 17, 1895, pp. 557–58; *Anti-Saloon* 1 (Nov. 1893): 2.

28. *Provisional Constitution*; "Second Annual Report of the State Superintendent for the Year Ending June 30th, 1895," pp. 7–8, OASL; Russell, "Plan for Effective State Organization," *Christianity in Earnest*, 9 (July–Aug. 1897): 154–55.

selection insured that various temperance organizations, political parties, and denominations were represented, and that party prohibitionists hostile to the new rival organization could not destroy it from within. The role of the local members, therefore, was not to participate in shaping the league's direction but to contribute funds, listen to speakers, volunteer in distributing literature, canvass voters, and serve at the polls on election day.[29] Thus the league was within the voluntary tradition of the American Protestant churches in the sense that it was self-supporting, but as an organization it differed radically from those churches (including the Congregational, of which Russell was a minister) where lay members exercised control over leadership and policies.

Organizing the Anti-Saloon League

However attractive Russell's ideas about the new organization might have appeared in his rhetoric, he still faced the very practical problem of transmitting them to the state's evangelical Christians. He spent the remainder of 1893 setting up the new organization and publicizing it and attracted attention in 1894 by engaging in a specific legislative controversy.

Russell's goal in 1893 was to establish a state headquarters in Columbus and two district offices in nothern Ohio, where the highest concentration of sympathizers resided. Using the funds pledged to him at the Oberlin meeting, he rented a small office in Columbus, hired a headquarters clerk, and had 5,000 copies of the constitution prepared for distribution. In November, the first issue of *Anti-Saloon*, an eight-page monthly tabloid, appeared. The paper provided the league with a regular means of communicating its leaders' views and warning drys about their wet opposition. The first issue began with an optimistic note, Russell (presumably) arguing that the public was unorganized, despairing of the liquor problem, and anxious for the new "strength and hope of the Anti-Saloon League . . . its unity, permanency and aggressiveness."[30] The state executive committee announced that it had devised a systematic plan for helping local leagues organize.

---

29. "The Methods of a Live Local League," 1895 typescript, HH; Cherrington, *History of the Anti-Saloon League*, p. 45; *Anti-Saloon* 1 (Nov. 1893): 3.

30. *Anti-Saloon* 1 (Nov. 1893): 1–2; "Report of the State Superintendent to the State Executive Committee for the Year Ending June 30th, 1894," OASL; Russell's 1942 recollections, miscellaneous writing, HH.

By the end of the year Russell had organized about one hundred local leagues and had hired two district superintendents, based in Akron and Toledo. "It was difficult to get a foot-hold anywhere at first," he reported. "Anti-Saloon people everywhere were disheartened by the failures of the past." It took eighteen weeks of work in eight northwestern counties to obtain sufficient pledges to hire a district superintendent; the same task took three weeks in northeastern Ohio. Often Russell encountered hostility from Prohibition party activists. On one such occasion, he told his wife, "I think some of them are even more intensely partisan than their . . . neighbors in the Republican and Democratic parties." Prohibition party critics argued that all nominees, regardless of their position on the saloon, deserved the support of their party members; all dry voters therefore belonged in the Prohibition party, not in the league. Echoing the WCTU debate, the league's claim to nonpartisanship, the Prohibition party partisans said, meant that it was simply synonymous with "Republican." The organizers "should seek to build up" the party. Otherwise, according to the editor of the party's *New Era*, the league was simply a device "to put salve on the sore conscience of voters by making them believe that they are really doing something." This dissent depressed Russell, who thought of the league as a unifying agency.[31]

More inimical to the continued growth of the new nonpartisan organization were deteriorating economic conditions, which made it difficult to raise money. Without knowing it in advance, Russell was starting his venture at the very time the nation was beginning the worst economic depression yet experienced. Because purse strings were slow to open, by December Russell had to reduce his expenditures. For the next five years his plans remained larger than the league bank account's capacity to pay for them.

One way to gain attention, it occurred to the league's leaders, was to provoke a battle in the Ohio legislature, even if there was little hope for a dry victory. But Russell and his advisors expected that the attempt would foster the spread of local organizations and encourage financial support. E. W. Metcalf, a wealthy Elyria benefactor, took charge of the legislative operations. He drafted a bill modeled on laws in ten states that provided for automatic local option elections in each of Ohio's voting precincts every two years. Metcalf and Russell approached Joseph T. Haskell of Wellington, a member of

31. *New Era*, quoted in *The [Oberlin] Citizen*, Sept. 23, Nov. 4, 1893; "Mr. Russell's Endeavor," undated clipping, IWM; Russell to Lillian Russell, Dec. 7, 1893, HH.

the House Temperance Committee, to sponsor the legislation. Haskell resisted, arguing that other Republicans would resent the raising of the emotionally divisive issue. But then influential league friends "persuaded" him.[32]

Having obtained a sponsor, the league prepared for the campaign. It printed 50,000 copies of the Haskell bill, expanded circulation of the *Anti-Saloon* to 20,000 copies, and added to the staff of state headquarters. Although he was unsure of being able to pay the salary, Russell hired E. C. Dinwiddie, grand counselor of the Grand Lodge of Ohio of the Independent Order of Good Templars and former secretary of the Ohio Prohibition party, for four months to help in league organizational work. The headquarters staff prepared flyers explaining the bill and asked 3,500 pastors around the state to set aside an Anti-Saloon Sunday in their churches during March to rally the faithful. If passed, they explained, the bill would protect temperance people in cities from immigrant majorities by allowing local option in wards. The league wanted to force the bill out of committee and, in a roll call vote, determine who were its friends and enemies. The drys planned to gather tens of thousands of signatures on petitions, inform committee members that the league was raising a $40,000 fund for political activites in the forthcoming biennium, and promise the support of temperance voters for whoever voted positively in the roll call. To those who objected that the issue would cost the Republican party support, the league rejoined that the issue would cost the Republican party support, the league rejoined that the temperance vote was much stronger than the liquor vote—that no party which catered to the liquor vote could in the long run succeed.[33]

The bill, of course, failed of passage. But the league did have it reported from committees and voted upon in the House. Russell and his followers had aroused temperance voters around the state, and they looked forward to turning ad hoc organizations into permanent local leagues. Russell used the defeat to argue for further organizing efforts. We failed, he told the state executive committee, because of "the superior organization of the Liquor League. When the Anti-Saloon League has a permanent and aggressive organization in each county in the state, we shall be able to secure the passage

---

32. *Anti-Saloon* 1 (April 1894): 6; E. W. Metcalf, "The Haskell Bill," OASL; "The Haskell Bill Skirmish," autobiographical miscellaneous writings, HH.

33. Russell's 1942 recollections, miscellaneous writings; Dinwiddie to Russell, Jan. 2, 1894, HH; *Anti-Saloon* 1 (March 1894): 3, 6; "Report of the State Superintendent, 1894," OASL.

of radical bills, and enforce them after they are enacted."[34] To the league's followers, he wrote, the shrewdness of the liquor dealers showed the way. "They do not get excited. They do not rush off and organize new political parties. They put their efforts in the direction of the *individual politician*, and through their organization they exhibit their power to reward or punish." When the league was as well organized and as widespread as its opposition, it would prevail.[35]

Russell's task was to fulfill his expectation that the legislative battle would advance the league as an organization. He needed to obtain the active support of church and Prohibition party officials, secure a firmer financial base, and maintain enthusiasm among temperance voters. He spent much of his time visiting churches to convince them to maintain a local league and to pledge financial support. He was especially successful in his relationships with leaders of the Methodist Episcopal church. He recruited a Columbus minister, Purley A. Baker, to serve as first district superintendent in Cleveland, and he hired a young Methodist layman, Oberlin graduate Wayne B. Wheeler, to work as "an agitator and organizer." In 1894 the Methodist Central Ohio Conference endorsed the league as a "well founded monument." The state's presiding elders sent a letter explaining the league to each local pastor, asking him to read it to the congregation and seek support. Russell also obtained encouragement from state leaders of the Methodists' Epworth League and from the interdenominational United Society of Christian Endeavor, both of which were prominent and large Christian youth organizations.

These connections eased the fears of some Prohibition party leaders that the league was out to destroy the party. In 1894 Russell contracted with John G. Woolley, the party's most popular speaker, for engagements in the state. In time for the state election in 1895, J. W. Bashford, president of Ohio Wesleyan University and a party leader, wrote a form letter urging followers to vote for the regular Prohibition ticket except in legislative races where, regardless of partisan affiliations, candidates favoring the Haskell bill deserved their votes. These were encouraging signs to the league's staff, although friction with some Prohibition party activists remained chronic.[36]

34. "Report of the Superintendent, 1894," OASL; Russell to Committee Against the Saloon in Ohio, IWM.

35. *Anti-Saloon* 1 (May 1894): 3.

36. *Minutes of the Central Ohio Conference of the Methodist Episcopal Church, 1894*, pp. 457–58; "Second Annual Report of the State Superintendent for the Year Ending June 30th, 1895," OASL; Bashford form letter, Oct. 30, 1895, HH; Russell to E. W. Metcalf, May 9, 1894, IWM; *Anti-Saloon* 2 (June 1895): 5, and 2 (July–August 1895): 1.

These efforts meant that in its second year of existence, the league could boast of four hundred local affiliates in almost every county of the state, including strong local organizations in every major city except Cincinnati. Russell believed that the league's momentum was sufficient to move into Cincinnati, the bastion of Ohio's wet sentiment, in 1895 or 1896.[37]

The problems with the pledge system stemmed largely from the depression, but they were a result of another factor as well. Russell and the league organizers spoke constantly of the need for a long-running battle against the saloon. But antisaloon volunteers were not necessarily prone to such thinking, their waves of enthusiasm being easily diverted to other concerns. The league, like any voluntary organization, including the churches, always faced the possibility of evaporating donations as the popular mood shifted. The leaders recognized this condition when they emphasized "agitation" in the league program. The leaders knew, as well, that the league needed tangible victories in order to maintain public support.

Agitation work thus consumed much of the officers' time, energy, and talent. Their agitation effort included attempts to reach the uninitiated, but attention mostly went to constant exhortations to the dry faithful to maintain their pledged donations. League officials routinely visited local pulpits. The league also staged large public events. Late in 1894 the league held an Anti-Saloon Congress in Columbus, even though the event strapped its treasury. Setting a pattern for the future, the delegates did not determine basic policies. Rather, the congress was an event staged to attract public attention and exhort the faithful. During the three-day meeting, supporters listened to speeches and sang hymns. The league printed the speeches in a souvenir booklet for general distribution. The league also began an "anti-saloon contest," selling a book of readings to local leagues and church groups. They in turn were to charge admission for public recitations and award a medal, supplied from Columbus, to winning speakers.[38]

If staging events seemed important to keeping the faith of dry supporters, political victories were more so. The problem was that the league was still too weak and too poor to hope to influence political decisions on a statewide basis. So it chose to concentrate on

37. "Second Annual Report of the State Superintendent, 1895," OASL; Russell to Lillian Russell, Aug. 3 and Sept. 8, 1895; E. W. Metcalf to Russell, Aug. 20, 1894, HH.

38. *Anti-Saloon Contest Selections*, OASL; *A Souvenir Selection of the Anti-Saloon Addresses Delivered at the Annual Congress of the Ohio Anti-Saloon League at Columbus, December 11–13, 1894*; Russell to E. W. Metcalf, Feb. 4, 1895, IWM.

insuring that those who had voted for the Haskell bill were returned at the polls. The league also engineered the defeat of state senator John Locke, a Republican from Madison County who had fought the league. In the spring of 1895, Russell, Dinwiddie, and Wheeler worked quietly to pack the nominating conventions in Locke's district with their followers. In May they caught Locke by surprise, and the Republicans had a dry nominee for the autumn election.[39] The league's victory was not only tangible but spectacular and proved useful in exhorting its supporters and warning its legislative opponents.

Russell was quick to boast of this victory and to claim that in its first two years the league's agitation in communities had led to the closing of four hundred saloons. His skill in public relations and speaking, as well as the material results, attracted attention from outside the state. In 1894 and 1895 Russell was receiving requests for information, and several groups, including the National Temperance Society, were considering holding national conventions to found a new political movement. A. J. Kynett wrote to the District of Columbia Anti-Saloon League, a volunteer organization dedicated to working for the passage of legislation harmful to liquor dealers in the capital, asking it to sponsor a national meeting.[40]

The call of the resulting convention stressed the need for unity among the nation's prohibition reformers. "Heretofore we have agreed . . . in resolutions rather than in resolute action," the organizers observed; meanwhile, "the united enemy" has gained greater power. The goal was to start an organization for the suppression of the saloon through local, state, and national legislation, strictly enforced. Anyone who agreed was admitted as a delegate. Among those who came were Phinney, Foster, and Wittenmyer, the latter two women serving on the committee that drafted the constitution for the new American Anti-Saloon League. The National Temperance Society sent four representatives who assured the conference of the society's "readiness" to help "in any proper movement" so long as it did not usurp the society. When they perceived the new league as subordinating other groups, they reported their dissatisfaction. And in fact it came to pass that with the rise of the

39. *Anti-Saloon* 2 (Feb. 1895): 2; "Second Annual Report of the State Superintendent, 1895," OASL; "A New Kind of Politics," Russell's autobiographical writings, HH.

40. Banks, *Lincoln Legion*, pp. 211–27; James L. Ewin, *Birth of the Anti-Saloon League* (Washington, 1913), p. 12; Minutes, Board of Managers, National Temperance Society, May 14, 1895, Presbyterian Historical Society.

Anti-Saloon League, the National Temperance Society ceased to perform a leading part in the prohibition movement. The convention appointed an executive committee that included Wittenmyer and employed Russell as national superintendent. Hiram Price, an elderly, distinguished temperance warrior from Iowa, long an advocate of a nonpartisan approach, was the first president. Delegates pledged $1,000 in support, and Russell was to be paid $10 per day while doing national work. There was call for it. Even during the convention, drys in fifteen states were asking for assistance in organizing new nonpartisan groups for political action.[41]

The goal of the new American Anti-Saloon League was to organize and coordinate prohibition work across the nation, employing the strategy outlined by Ellen Foster and embodied in the Ohio league. No one present at the founding convention doubted that the struggle would be long and hard; and all agreed to the eventual goal of a national prohibition amendment. In the meantime, Russell and his supporters must work to build an organization resting on the widest possible agreement, eschewing other controversial, divisive issues. Victories could first be won in the communities with local option legislation, and as dry territory spread across the nation, the drys could work for further state and federal restrictions on the liquor traffic. Success would breed success, as Americans saw the social and human benefits of local dry laws and decided to support the larger campaigns.[42]

Much work remained for the new league, that much was clear. The Ohio league was still struggling to collect funds and survive, much less to support organizing activities elsewhere. Just as the National Temperance Society had refused to cooperate in the founding of the new league, so too would other, older dry organizations, especially elements of the Prohibition party, continue to

41. Minutes, Board of Managers, National Temperance Society, Oct. 10 & Dec. 12, 1895, & Jan. 16, 1896; *Proceedings, National Anti-Saloon Convention, 1895*, pp. iii–30; *Proceedings, National Anti-Saloon Convention, 1896*, pp. 29–30; Russell to E. W. Metcalf, July 2, 1896, IWM.

42. Odegard, *Pressure Politics*, pp. 1–35, clearly outlined the league's political strategy. Blocker, *Retreat from Reform*, pp. 162–66, describes the "balance of power" aspect of the strategy, where, in legislative elections, the league's well-organized dry supporters, although a minority, would control the outcome of liquor issues. Blocker ably summarizes the league as embodying "The Policies of Opportunism." Norman H. Clark, *The Dry Years: Prohibition and Social Change in Washington* (Seattle, 1965), pp. 72–81, explains how "local option" was initially the dry goal with the widest popular appeal.

attack Russell's group. Cooperation from the WCTU was uncertain at best so long as Frances Willard was in charge. At the end of 1895, thus, the vision of the Anti-Saloon League as a national power commanding and enlarging the numbers of the nation's dry voters still remained to be focused in its practical details.

Much work remained, also, that was unclear. The idea of a temperance trust was still a vision, the organizational details of which— matters of structure, administrative discipline, leadership succession, funding, and constituency influence—had yet to be considered in a practical, working manner. Overlooked in the hope of the moment, moreover, were fundamental issues of organizational goals. Those organizational goals were clear so long as the nation remained wet, although of course disputes over immediate tactics would arise in particular campaigns. Eventually, however, the Anti-Saloon League, to be successful, would have to decide fundamental questions of strategy for church reformers in a dry nation. Meanwhile, the leaders faced an uncertain future trying to turn their dream of political power into reality.

4

ESTABLISHING A MODEL LEAGUE: OHIO, 1895–1908

The founders of the new Anti-Saloon League faced a host of problems and dilemmas in adapting business methods to their reform program. The goal was clear enough: to do all that was feasible to achieve prohibition and to foster popular support for temperance so as to expand the horizons of what was legislatively possible. The league existed to unify temperance supporters, provide them with a businesslike method of operation, and engineer disciplined political action under able leaders. But these were only general ideals, and to achieve them in practice was no easy matter. There was no model to follow, no comparable reform organization. The selection of leaders, the raising of funds, the persuasion of individuals to the nonpartisan strategy, the acceptance of the league by churches, and the dissemination of the league organization around the nation were all matters that required clarification. They had to be worked out, moreover, in a particular context: the league was appealing to a mass following and encouraging voluntary action, and its methods and form of organization therefore had to achieve and maintain credibility. By solving these problems the league attained its key place in the evolution of American public politics.

The Ohio league was the mother organization that spawned the national movement, and it is events in Ohio that provide understanding of the emergence of basic practices that shaped the modern prohibition movement. The Ohio Anti-Saloon League, like the state in which it operated, was not a microcosm of the nation. But the Ohio league provided the organizational model that the American Anti-Saloon League advocated in other states. Moreover, the Ohio league provided key leaders to the national prohibition movement, served as the home base for its officers, and generated a large volume of propaganda materials that organizations in other states used. It was in Ohio, finally, with only a few significant exceptions, that national leaders received their baptism of fire and faced and resolved the practical problems of building an organization.

Ohio Society and Politics

The temperance issue had raged in Ohio for generations prior to the appearance of the Anti-Saloon League. Dry sentiment was deeply imbedded in the religious persuasion of many Ohioans, whose ancestry and religious tradition stretched back through New England to the dissenting churches of Great Britain. These Protestants evangelized their commitment to a life of abstinence and promoted the notion that God's kingdom could be brought closer to reality on earth through prohibition legislation. It was these peoples, residing for the most part in the northern counties around Cleveland known as the Western Reserve, and their churches that provided the social base for prohibition agitation.[1]

But these evangelical Protestants were a minority of the state's citizens and voters. Ohio had been settled by migrants from Virginia, and as the transportation and industrial revolutions of the nineteenth century reshaped the state's economy, persons unpersuaded by evangelical Protestant doctrines came to live there. Cincinnati, the rural areas, and some smaller cities like the capital, Columbus, had large populations of German and Irish ancestry whose liturgical customs included the use of wine in the religious service itself. As coal mines and factories grew in the late nineteenth century, the state began to build atop its agricultural base an economy of heavy industry. Cleveland in particular and to a lesser extent smaller cities in the northern part of the state were attracting southern and eastern European immigrants for whom abstention, and therefore prohibition, were simply alien.

The liquor laws of Ohio and the political parties reflected the emotional depths of these divergent views. When leaders had written a new constitution for the state in 1851, they tried to satisfy both wets and drys by including a provision outlawing the licensing of saloons while allowing the taxation of the liquor traffic. The WCTU,

---

1. Two scholars especially have pointed out the significance of ethnocultural tensions for understanding midwestern and Ohio politics in this period. See Richard Jensen, *The Winning of the Midwest: Social and Political Conflict, 1888–96* (Chicago, 1971); and Paul J. Kleppner, *The Cross of Culture: A Social Analysis of Midwestern Politics, 1850–1900* (New York, 1970), and *The Third Electoral System, 1853–1892, Parties, Voters, and Political Cultures* (Chapel Hill, 1979).

as we have seen, led a referendum campaign in 1883 that persuaded a plurality of voters but not the necessary majority. The only consolation that drys enjoyed by 1893 was the township local option bill for which Howard Russell successfully lobbied in 1888, a law that allowed city councils to declare their towns legally dry, and a high tax on saloons, $350 per year (the Dow Law, passed in 1886). Because of the tax, and the possibility that a court might someday interpret the constitution of 1851 as forbidding the liquor trade, the brewing, distilling, and saloon interests liked the legal situation only a little better than did the drys.[2]

The emotions on the question of prohibition, the conflict between the religious and cultural groups, ran so deep that they constantly threatened to upset the fortunes of the major political parties. In national politics Ohio was closely contested in the Gilded Age, and both the Democratic and Republican parties contained within their coalitions blocs of voters who were deeply committed to the wet or dry causes. It is entirely understandable, then, why party leaders had a vested interest in keeping the prohibition issues at bay. This was especially noticeable among Republican leaders. The party had roots in the Western Reserve that stretched far back to its antislavery origins. But the Republicans also commanded support among some more recent immigrants to the state, and they were consciously trying to attract voters who found prohibition, to say the least, unpalatable. Winning Ohio was important to the Republicans, who, among partisans, had a persuasive argument against dry appeals: prohibition laws must be turned back for the good of the party, of its control of the state, and ultimately of the nation.[3]

The intensity of major party rivalry and the national implications of the outcome made the Anti-Saloon League's task all the more difficult. The goal of the league was in one sense to undercut the Republican leaders' influence among individual legislators in Columbus. In the larger sense, of course, its goal was to convince voters that prohibition legislation was important enough to break party ties and support only those candidates, no matter of what party, whose views were acceptable to the league. The league thus faced a circular strategy: to persuade supporters that through

2. *Standard Encyclopedia of the Alcohol Problem*, 5:2042−55.
3. League lobbyists believed that Republican politicians and newspapers tried to suppress temperance legislation in order to protect the larger interests of their party. *American Issue* (June 1900): 8.

proper organization and nonpartisan action they could collectively
enjoy power sufficient to elect majorities of dry legislators, and to
persuade legislators that if they failed to do the league's bidding they
would feel the wrath of the state's "church vote." A great deal of
what the league had to do in its early years was to teach both voters
and politicians just what nonpartisan political action meant in practice, as occurred in the case of Senator Locke. The process was
circular in part because once the league was able to change votes in
the legislature it could use that fact to foster support from the
citizenry, but the league had to foster that support and organize it in
order to change votes. It was this achievement, the cutting into the
circle, for which the departmentalized structure of the new organization was intended.

Building an Organization

Russell and the other league founders envisioned much more than a
state headquarters structured on the departmentalized business
model and run by a professional, full-time salaried staff. They saw
the state organization as the apex of a hierarchy that stretched down
to the local church congregations. There were the armies of citizens
to be disciplined to spread the gospel of temperance among the
uninitiated, to vote for dry candidates, to encourage local authorities
to enforce the law, and to contribute the funds needed to keep the
organization alive. The role of local followers in shaping the policies
of the organization, however, remained unclear. The direction that
the league took from its earliest days in Ohio was toward control
from the top, managerial direction by the professional, salaried
superintendents running the various departments of league work,
down to and including the county level.

   In 1896 Russell published model constitutions for church, local,
and county leagues that revealed the kind of hierarchy he sought.
He suggested that each sympathetic church congregation should
have a league. Individuals, members of the congregation, or simply
local residents, could become members by signing an antisaloon
pledge and by making personal abstinence vows and a promise "to
induce others to abstain" and to work to abolish both saloons and the
manufacture and sale of alcoholic beverages. The church league
would have officers and an executive committee that included the
pastor, Sunday school superintendent, and "president of the Young
people's society." The executive committee would appoint members

to local committees that replicated the departments of the state organization.[4]

The next levels in the hierarchy were the local and county Anti-Saloon Leagues. Like the church league, a local league was open to any individual who signed an appropriate antisaloon pledge, to all of the members of the church leagues in the town, and to the members of other temperance societies. The local league would be run by an executive council to which each church league appointed its pastor and two other members, and each temperance society three members. For the county league, the executive body would include the presidents of all of the local leagues, and it would employ a superintendent whose principal task would be organizing and nurturing local and church leagues to insure that there was some organized body of drys devoted to the nonpartisan method in every voting precinct in the county.[5]

Russell never clarified just what balance, if any, should exist in league governance between the local members and the state trustees and salaried officials. The model constitutions he published in 1896 were unclear as to whether or not those persons who enrolled would have any say whatever in who their officers were, how funds might be collected or spent, what law enforcement activities might be practiced, or what political candidates promoted or opposed. Perhaps his silence on the matter was necessary, for Russell was, after all, appealing to denominations with differing traditions of hierarchical versus local control. In any event, he wanted to insure that local pastors and lay leaders were an integral part of the league at the local level.[6]

Russell worked out the details of the hierarchical structure, such as they were, from his organizing experience. Organizing the league at the local level was, in the first years at least, his main task. In performing that task, Russell followed a consistent pattern. He arranged with a local pastor or with a town's ministerial association to visit and explain the new organization and what it hoped to accomplish. Wherever he was welcomed Russell appeared before the congregations of local churches. His appeal was on a practical, local level. When Russell preached at a Sunday service, the preceding evening he visited local saloons to observe violations of regulations and to count the number of young men who were customers.

4. *Proceedings of the National Anti-Saloon Convention, 1896*, pp. 80–82.
5. Ibid.
6. "The Methods of Work of a Live Local League," 1895 typescript, HH.

On Sunday he dramatically revealed his finding as a way of graphically portraying the need for additional legislation and better local law enforcement. Before Russell left the area, he appointed pastors and lay persons as an executive body to start the organization.[7] By 1898 his successor, Purley A. Baker, reported that leagues were established in every county and in most municipalities in Ohio. Seven district headquarters operated in the regions of the state.[8]

The purpose of this hierarchy, of course, was to extend the departments of league work to the local level. Local leagues engineered local option referendums in the townships and supported the candidacies of dry councilmen. Local leagues encouraged officials to enforce liquor laws by employing private detectives to gather evidence of violations and hiring attorneys to assist in prosecutions. The state headquarters provided references to detective agencies and offered the help of its legal staff, time permitting, so long as the expenses were paid.

Thus the league men counseled a course of immediate, pragmatic progress. Reduce the number of saloons, curtail the hours of those that remained, and cut down thereby the temptations that led Americans to drink. "Do not strive after the impossible," local followers were admonished from state headquarters in 1900. "Study local conditions and reach after the attainable." These methods, leaders boasted, were effectively reducing the number of saloons and increasing the business costs of those that remained. The league, they said, was not interested in the martyrdom of lost battles. The league chose to fight where it had a chance of victory; otherwise it refused to waste resources.[9]

Agitation was a more important area of work for the league, in the eyes of the state officers, than achieving local legislation or even law enforcement. Changing the laws of the state, after all, seemed more significant than banning saloons in townships where marketing realities made them insignificant in any case. "The truth is," Russell told a reporter in 1894, "a strong public sentiment against the drink habit

7. Ibid.; *Anti-Saloon* 1 (Jan. 1894): 6; *A Mirror Held Up to Dayton* (1895 circular), IWM, reported that in one hour on one Saturday evening 397 young men, presumed minors, were observed entering local saloons.

8. Baker to John D. Rockefeller, Sr., January 14, 1898, PPMR.

9. *American Issue* 8 (Jan. 1900): 8; (Sept. 1900): 7; (Oct. 1900): 5; W. F. Whitlock and Purley Baker to board of trustees, Nov. 16, 1898, IWM. Baker wrote that in its first year the Ohio league stopped the growth of saloons; that in its second and third years it eliminated 400 and 1,000 saloons respectively. Purley A. Baker, "The Anti-Saloon Movement," *Christianity in Earnest* 9 (Nov.–Dec. 1896): 235.

and traffic is the main thing. Without public demand no law can be passed, and it is worthless when it is passed." Field work, as league staff members called it, was a high priority. In addition to monthly temperance meetings, the state headquarters wanted each town and each church at least annually to have an Anti-Saloon Sunday, with a league official addressing parishioners directly from the pulpit. Furthermore, league men traveled around the state speaking at rallies, projecting slides of saloon conditions to audiences wherever they could find them, and contrasting those conditions with the opulence of life in the homes of brewers.[10]

The state league supported agitation with a huge volume of pamphlets, broadsides, stereopticon slides, and a newspaper. The Ohio league changed its paper's name in 1896 to *The American Issue*, partly to attract subscribers in other states and bring in advertising revenue. The Rev. J. C. Jackson became its full-time editor, and in 1900 *The American Issue* began to publish weekly editions.[11] Jackson consistently preached the wise practicality of the league's politics, and he reprinted items from wet organs to convince readers of the need for persistence against a rapacious foe.

But the most important work of the local leagues, inevitably, was to raise money to support statewide and national activities. The league followed a policy of combining a few large donations with numerous small pledges throughout its history, although dependence on wealthy patrons was greatest in the early years. The financial difficulties brought on by the depression in the 1890s almost killed the Ohio Anti-Saloon League; it survived only because Russell convinced wealthy patrons to help. Most notable was the relationship Russell established with the state's wealthiest prohibitionist, John D. Rockefeller, in the autumn of 1894, a relationship that lasted on a financial level into the 1920s and on a personal level until the oil magnate's death. Rockefeller agreed to donate $2,000 toward the league's second year of operations.[12]

10. *Columbus Dispatch*, June 7, 1894, and Jan. 13, 1898; "The Methods and Work of a Live Local League" and "Anti-Saloon Contest Selections," OASL; *American Issue*, Nov. 23, 1900, p. 1; "Instructions to Our Superintendents," n.d., ED.

11. *Anti-Saloon* 1 (Nov. 1893): 2; Russell to Board of Trustees, March 16, 1896, and Headquarters Committee to Board of Trustees, March 16, 1896, IWM.

12. Ohio Anti-Saloon League, "Statement and Appeal of Finance Committee, Oct. 25, 1894," IWM; Russell to John D. Rockefeller, Sr., Sept. 17, 1894; Entry for Sept. 20, 1894, Pledge Books; J. G. W. Cowles to Rockefeller, Sept. 12, 1894; Rockefeller to Mary E. Ingersoll, Sept. 14, 1894. Ellen J. Phinney wrote that the league "is unifying the temperance forces beyond my most sanguine expectations." Phinney to Rockefeller, Sept. 14, 1894, JDR.

The depression and the consequent inability of Russell to raise small pledges, however, almost killed the organization. For this reason Russell's plan of operation was simply grander than the means at his disposal. He found that expenses were especially heavy during election campaigns and legislative sessions, which required borrowing funds from banks, from wealthy patrons, and, in the form of unpaid salaries, from league officers. Russell extended his personal credit to the limit. But even though the league was deeply in debt by early 1895, the trustees planned a budget of $40,000 for the third year, hoping to raise that sum by appointing a full-time fund raiser and by hiring college students for summer work, their pay to be half of what they collected. The result was that by 1896 the league was even more deeply in debt, its staff unpaid for months and living under the threat of imminent personal bankruptcy. Russell was forced to leave the state for speaking engagements, payment for which he could use to keep the league going.[13]

Finally, in 1897, with the Ohio league almost $8,000 in debt, the trustees investigated and determined that the problems lay not with mismanagement but with the "hard times." They eliminated the debt with special donations and by convincing employees to forego the salary owed them. Once this crisis passed, the Ohio league began a different policy, what Wayne Wheeler termed, "cut your feed." Each staff officer was required to raise sufficient funds to cover his own salary. The economies engendered by the new policy on salaries, together with the continuing income from donors like Rockefeller and the return of national prosperity in 1898, enabled the Ohio league to become financially healthy. Rockefeller promised to give 10 percent of whatever pledges the league received, but by 1904 he decided to set a ceiling of $5,000 because the league income exceeded $50,000 annually. By 1916 the Ohio league and affiliated organizations were able to raise and spend $500,000 for the state-wide referendum on prohibition.[14]

13. Report by Russell, 1896, ASLA; Russell to League Employees, July 21, 1896; R. R. Bane to E. W. Metcalf, Nov. 27, 1896; Russell to Metcalf, Feb. 4, 1895, and Dec. 3, 1896, IWM; "Ohio League Day at Lakeside," *Christianity in Earnest* 7 (Sept.–Oct. 1895): 187.

14. *The "Hard Times" Defeat of the League, Oct. 9, 1897* (Columbus, 1897); *Arise and Sing!* (Columbus, 1897); Wheeler to E. W. Metcalf, Sept. 9, 1898, IWM; John D. Rockefeller, Jr., to Russell, Jan. 24, 1901; Starr J. Murphy to John D. Rockefeller, Jr., Feb. 4, 1904, PPMR. Odegard showed that thousands of small donations provided the bulk of the league's funds during the years of its greatest power. *Pressure Politics*, pp. 188–98.

Political Methods

In spite of financial hardship in the 1890s, the league pressed ahead with political work. It was easy enough for Russell to see that striving for advanced temperance legislation would give concrete reasons for supporters to form local leagues and donate money. But it was one thing to agitate on the saloon problems in an abstract way, quite another to agitate in the concrete terms of gaining political strength to reduce the number of such problems through legislation. The Anti-Saloon League was innovative as a political organization, providing a system of rallying temperance voters behind the single issue, cutting through the tradition of party as the agency of political action in a democratic society.

The political methods of the modern prohibition work were first developed and applied in Ohio. Russell was obliged repeatedly to speak about the new league as an "all-partisan" or "omni-partisan" organization, embodying the only possible approach to dry victory. He admonished audiences that the inevitable defeats they would suffer should produce not despair but a redoubling of efforts. "In God's name and with His help," Russell assured the Christian Endeavor Society in 1896, "we will enter upon a permanent good citizenship campaign which shall mean the . . . victorious domination of Christian conscience, whose right it is to rule, in the politics of America." But he knew that much more than inspirational rhetoric was needed. The league should work for the selection of satisfactory candidates in each major party. Party caucuses and conventions, especially at the local level, were the occasions when the important decisions were made, Russell asserted; legislatures only put on "finishing touches." The drys had to choose their candidates, for legislative races as well as party posts, well in advance of party meetings. Place temperance supporters on party committees, he advised, "securing victories wherever we can."[15] Then, by election day, the

15. "Christian Politics and the Saloon," speech of July 9, 1896, HH. Russell's instructions to staff members organizing church and local leagues were to select officers carefully "from different parties" and, when choosing a local advisory board, to make certain it was "non-partisan." When he employed college students for a summer's organizing and fund-raising campaign in 1896, he gave explicit directions: "On general principles, it is wise to make no demonstration of your own party connection, and of course party discussion must be tabooed by our field workers." They might personally support any party they chose, he told them, "but our League cannot be made the vehicle for an exposition of political views. Our mission is to educate the people, irrespective of party or creed, for aggressive hostility against the saloon." "Official Instructions to Summer Organizers," 1896 typescript, ED.

league should have canvassed the state's voters and mobilized its supporters.

Essential to this scheme was the constant trumpeting of the success of league methods. The agitation department combined rhetoric about the evils of the saloon with claims of the keenness of league politics. It used every resource it could command, including images of saloons and surrounding poverty conditions surreptitiously photographed, to arouse Ohioans to the prohibition cause. The league always emphasized the need for political action under its leadership. It consistently buttressed its case with references to the power gained by wet organizations through nonpartisan practices. The league reprinted items found in the publications of the liquor and brewing industries, arranged to show that the wets thought the league and its methods were the gravest danger they faced. One reprinted headline from the August 20, 1896, issue of *Wine and Spirit News*, the paper of the state's retailers, read, "The Anti-Saloonists will Capture the Church and the Church will Capture the State; Then God have Mercy on the Balance of Mankind if They are Allowed to Live at All."[16]

Ohio Antisaloon Politics, 1896−1908

All the organizing and fund-raising work, of course, was to win political victories. After the Haskell Bill fight in 1894, the Ohio league pressed prohibition issues in each session of the legislature. The league first sought state laws requiring regular local option elections in wards and townships and then moved to achieve county option referendums. The objective was to increase the areas of the state that outlawed the liquor traffic, all the time adding to the league's power so that eventually it could win a statewide dry law.

After the success in unseating the wet Senator Locke, Russell proceeded to have a local option bill introduced in the 1896 session by Representative William S. Harris. A major battle loomed. There were rumors that the brewers had raised $500,000 and the saloon keepers $200,000 to use in petitioning and bribing legislators.

16. See Russell, *Memoranda of Some of the Political Victories of the Ohio Anti-Saloon League* (n.p., 1899), ED; Russell, "The Brewer's Christmas (1896)," in autobiographical writings, HH. Some of these photographs are in the Western Reserve Historical Society. While he was stationed in Cleveland, Purley Baker arranged for a photographer to record the Christmas celebration of the Leisy family, owners of brewery, to visit saloons under the guise of selling the images to customers, and recording surrounding slum conditions. The contrasting images were arranged into a slide program and shown to audiences around the state.

Nevertheless, Russell was confident of passage in the House of Representatives. The chairman and six of the seven members of the House Temperance Committee were committed to the Harris bill, and at one point Russell claimed that sixty-two members, five more than the fifty-seven votes required, supported it also. But in the end he and the league were bitterly disappointed. The leaders of the Republican majority wanted the bill to fail. A detective hired by the league arranged to overhear private conversations among leaders of the Republican legislative caucus. Senator Joseph B. Foraker, through his private secretary, Charles Kurtz, instructed the chairman of the Temperance committee, "That bill must not be allowed to pass." The committee reported the measure without a recommendation, and, on the day of debate, despite a deluge of telegrams and petitions and last-minute appeals from Russell and Dinwiddie in the lobbies, the Harris bill received only fifty favorable votes. The legislature later tried to pacify the drys by raising the annual tax on saloons from $350 to $500.[17]

The experience was instructive. In 1888 Russell had expressed his belief that a few short years of the right kind of temperance agitation would produce statewide local option legislation, and he apparently thought that victory might come in 1896 after only three years of agitation and politicking. But now Russell began advising that the destruction of the liquor traffic would be a long-term effort indeed, one that might well last several generations. When the league staff assembled for a midsummer conference, Russell told the trustees that the obstacles to prohibition in Ohio and similar states were enormous. Rural states, he said, can "win and hold state prohibition, and that without a permanent and expensive organization." But Ohio would be different. Here there were great cities where the liquor traffic was "thriving," and where "disreputable and immoral men like George Cox [the Republican boss of Cincinnati] dictate the politics and politicians must obey or step out." There were $20 million invested in breweries in Ohio; only New York, Pennsylvania, and Wisconsin had more brewers than Ohio. There was one saloon operating for every two hundred residents in Ohio; only New York and Illinois had more retail dealers. "These facts show the task we

17. *Proceedings, National Anti-Saloon Convention, 1896*, p. 13; "Greetings of the Ohio Anti-Saloon League," *Christianity in Earnest* 7 (Sept.–Oct. 1895): 186; R. R. Bane form letter, Dec. 26, 1895, ED; Russell and Dinwiddie to legislators, Jan. 28, 1896; Russell to E. W. Metcalf, Jan. 17, 18, and 28, 1896, IWM; Dayton *Daily Journal, Cleveland Plain Dealer, Cincinnati Enquirer*, Cincinnati *Commercial Gazette*, all Feb. 6, 1896; Russell, "Scouts on Watch (1896)," typescript, HH; *American Issue* 9 (June 1900): 7.

have before us," he concluded. "It is well to look the facts in the face and not expect too much at once." Further efforts at organizing dry citizens were required, and the drys should expect to fight for at least a generation.[18]

Subsequent political events seemed to confirm Russell's observations. The legislature that would select a U.S. senator was elected in 1897, and party leaders pleaded that the contest was more important than moral reform. In the 1898 General Assembly, which elected Mark Hanna senator, the league was helpless to prevent the choice of an unfriendly Speaker of the House and Temperance Committee. No local option bill came up for a vote. But these machinations only rekindled the determination of league officers, now in charge of a financially solvent organization, to persist. Dinwiddie, who had returned to Ohio from his new post as Pennsylvania state superintendent to help in the legislative effort, recommended more long-range fund raising and political planning for a "determined and heroic effort." That advice soon paid off.[19]

Important breakthroughs occurred in 1899 when the league conducted its first statewide campaign to defeat an obnoxious wet. By now the league had the names of 100,000 temperance voters classified, and it mailed messages directly to individuals informing them of the situation in their local districts. By the close of the campaign the league had one hundred men working in the field and had mailed 115,000 letters and 300,000 sample ballots around the state, in addition to a huge volume of literature. Legislators with whom the league was unfriendly were working overtime to gain support. In contests where wet Republicans were running, Democratic leaders invited the league to name a satisfactory opponent. In districts where the drys could not reasonably expect to nominate a friendly Republican they offered no opposition inside the party to wet candidates, planning instead to put up a dry Democrat so as to catch the saloon interests off guard.[20]

In 1899 this machinery influenced the race for lieutenant gover-

18. Untitled Russell Speech to Ohio Board of Trustees, July 31, 1896, ASLA.
19. Baker to John D. Rockefeller, Sr., Jan. 14, 1898, PPMR; *Rise, Progress, and Purpose of the Ohio Anti-Saloon League* (Columbus, 1897), p. 5; Dinwiddie to E. W. Metcalf, Sept. 8, 1898, IWM. Baker was preparing league followers in November for the following spring's party conventions. See Baker form letter, Nov. 20, 1900, ED.
20. Baker to E. W. Metcalf, Dec. 1, 1898, and May 10, 1899, IWM; 1899 Ohio Campaign Clippings, JRG; Russell, *Memorandum of Some of the Political Victories of the Ohio Anti-Saloon League*. Russell prepared this pamphlet to explain to prohibitionists elsewhere what proper organization was able to produce.

nor. The Republican party challenged the league when it nominated John A. Caldwell, former mayor of Cincinnati and an attorney for the Ohio Brewers' Association. His Democratic opponent, A. W. Patrick, according to Russell, was "a man of excellent character and sterling integrity." In a Republican year, Caldwell, who in the end was elected, saw his margin fall 34,000 votes short of Governor-elect George K. Nash, in spite of a well-financed effort by the brewers to enlarge his margin. The Anti-Saloon League claimed the episode as a victory, for, as the press of the state noted, it had clearly become a force to be reckoned with in Ohio politics.[21]

But the power that the league had generated was still insufficient to win in the General Assembly. The problem was the leadership of the Ohio Republican party, especially the faction led by Hanna, who saw party majorities as dependent on a coalition with the Cox "machine" in Cincinnati. In the interests of party harmony, and the high stakes of carrying the state for McKinley, Roosevelt, and the U.S. Senate, the party leaders prevented local option legislation from passing. It took three more battles, in 1900, 1902, and 1904, and intervention into the gubernatorial race of 1905, which ended Republican domination of the state's politics, for the league to obtain a law that allowed city voters to banish saloons.

When the General Assembly convened in 1900, league leaders thought that they had enough votes to begin closing saloons in Ohio's towns and cities. Representative Thomas H. Clark, a friendly Columbus attorney, introduced a bill requiring municipalities and wards within cities to hold local option elections, upon petition of one-fourth of the voters. The bill carried the House on February 7 by a comfortable margin of fifty-nine to forty votes. Then the serious fight began in the Senate. Again Baker and Wheeler thought they had sufficient support to win, if for no other reason than enough Democrats might support the measure in hopes of using it as a campaign issue against the Cox Republican organization in Cincinnati. But they had not counted on the machinations of Republican leaders. Although they had a pledge from Governor Nash to refrain from taking sides on the issue, the drys discovered that the Republican leaders were persuaded that passage of local option legislation might lead to Democratic victories in the state, as presumably had happened in the 1880s. The brewing and liquor interests, who had contributed heavily to campaign funds, called in their

21. Russell, *Memorandum*; Baker form letters, Oct. 25, 1899, and Nov. 2, 1899; Jos. A. Miller, form letter, Oct. 31, 1899, IWM.

debts. Lt. Governor Caldwell, Carl Hoster, a member of the governor's staff and president of the Ohio Brewers' Association, and Tim McDonough, head of the State Liquor League, conferred and began lining up votes. They used every device available, including promises of patronage plums and possibly bribery, to persuade Republican senators that the bill's passage would surely cost the party its Cincinnati majorities, while they discounted the league's ability to lead dry voters away from prominent party candidates like McKinley. When the roll was called in the Senate, the league discovered that three members reneged on their promises of support, and the Clark bill went down by a margin of one vote. The immediate postmortems were bitter. Clark personally blamed the loss on "ward politicians and local heelers"; Baker and Wheeler on the governor. "This is a declaration of so-called party leaders," they told the press, "that the saloons of Ohio are more important than the 250,000 church voters."[22]

These events convinced the league officers that it was necessary to redouble their campaign to demonstrate to dry voters the necessity of operating outside of the party framework if they were ever to achieve "advanced" temperance legislation in Ohio. "The Anti-Saloon League," an *American Issue* editorial stated that spring, "has to meet and overcome the political bosses, acting in concert with the combined liquor influences of the State, before the people can have a chance to express their will regarding the saloon at the polls." Hanna and Foraker had an "infernal compact" with the state's "saloonists" that must be exposed. "Unless we succeed in smashing party bossism," Baker wrote, "we might as well be Russian serfs." "The Anti-Saloon League is not going to fight the Republican party as a party," the editors said. "But for the effect on the party of uncovering all the facts it will not hold itself responsible."[23]

The league's campaign against "party bossism" did ultimately lead to the defeat of Myron T. Herrick for governor in 1905, an event that attracted national attention and firmly implanted the realiza-

22. Baker to John D. Rockefeller, Dec. 28, 1899, PPMR; *Minutes of the Twenty-Sixth Annual Meeting of the Non-Partisan Temperance Women of Ohio* (n.p., 1899), p. 57; L. B. Cherrington to Nash, Feb. 10, 1900, GKN; Cincinnati *Commercial Tribune*, Feb. 8, 11, and March 15, 1900; Columbus *Press Post*, Feb. 9, March 14 and 15, 1900; *American Issue* 8 (May 1900): 6; Randolph C. Downes, *The Rise of Warren Gamaliel Harding* (Columbus, 1970), p. 118. Four years later a brewer remarked that $47,000 had been spent to defeat the bill. *American Issue*, Feb. 12, 1904, p. 8.

23. *American Issue* 9 (April 1900): 6–7, 10.

tion of league power. The campaign began in the summer of 1900 when Baker picked a fight with senators Hanna and Foraker, most successfully with the latter. The league prepared a circular for general distribution that reviewed all of the events leading up to the defeat of the Clark bill and forwarded copies to both men with a cover letter asking for their comments prior to publication. The circular asserted that Hanna had directly told legislators to kill municipal local option lest the issues damage McKinley's reelection chances. During the Lincoln Day banquet in Cincinnati Foraker had conveyed the same message, that the bill must be defeated "in the interest of the party." In response Hanna denied having ever "used President McKinley's name in giving a reason why I thought it would be well that the temperance question rest where it was." Nor had he reached his position in exchange for campaign funds. "I do not think the methods of your circular are calculated to help your cause," was his terse advise to Baker.

Foraker, however, rose to the bait. "I have always been of the opinion that in large cities local option by wards would not materially promote good morals, but only Democratic victories," he told the Ohio superintendent. Then Foraker went on with a lengthy attack on Baker and his methods, flatly denying assertions in the league's circular. The problem was that Baker was prepared to support those assertions. All told, there were four exchanges of letters between the two men, all of which the *American Issue* happily published. It reprinted an 1899 interview in which ex-Governor Foster stated that the party had chosen Foraker as a standard bearer in the 1880s because he had no record on temperance and the credentials to straddle the issue. Now the league had flushed Foraker into an open admission of placing his party concerns above the saloon problem.[24]

This tactical success seemed to do little good for the league in the short run. George Cox resigned his seat on the Republican National Committee, apparently trying to mollify dry Republicans. The league insisted that it would take no part in the presidential race because it had "no direct bearing" on the local option issue. In the elections of 1901, the Republican party retained control of the General Assembly, and in 1902 returned Foraker to the U.S. Senate. That same legislature enacted the first important temperance measure in the ten-year history of the league, albeit in a substantially

24. *American Issue* 9 (June 1900): 1–15. The league encountered trouble mailing this *Issue* on the grounds that it was not complying with postal regulations. *American Issue* 9 (July 1900): 5.

watered down form. The Beal bill, as it was called, after a series of compromises in both houses, required a local option election in a municipality after 40 percent of its voters so petitioned. The law did not apply to wards or other districts within the cities. Both wets and drys claimed this law as a victory, the wets because its practical effect would be to eliminate saloons only in small towns, the drys because for the first time it gave temperance people a weapon for direct popular action against saloons in those towns. Theretofore only city councils could banish saloons, and in seeking such actions the league had faced the same partisan arguments it encountered in the legislature.[25]

The most dramatic battle over local option legislation in Ohio, and the one that eventually discharged a governor and firmly implanted the league as a powerful political organization, began in the legislative session of 1904. The league was gaining support because wet cities were annexing formerly dry suburbs. Moreover, the intense market rivalry among the brewers had led them to open new saloons in residential areas. The league measure, introduced by Representative Charles A. Brannock, initially provided for local option elections by wards, but friendly legislators convinced Wheeler to rewrite the bill. Ward boundaries could be changed at will so as to thwart league ambitions, but a "residence district" defined by petitioners apart from other minor civil divisions could not.[26]

Wayne Wheeler, now promoted to state superintendent of the league, approached the legislative session confidently. Although he knew that the brewers, distillers, and dealers had donated substantial sums to the Republican party in exchange for a promise from Mark Hanna that there would be no temperance legislation in 1904, a presidential election year, the league was now powerful enough to override the loyalty of a number of legislators upon whom Hanna could usually rely. So Hanna approached the league with an offer: in exchange for restraint in pushing for any temperance legislation, he would support a ward local option bill in 1906. "He speaks to us of

25. *Ohio State Journal*, Feb. 7, Mar. 27, and April 3, 1902; *Columbus Dispatch*, April 5, 1902.
26. *American Issue*, Jan. 1, 1904, p. 3; Jan. 29, 1904, pp. 8–9; Sept. 22, 1905, pp. 2–7, 10–13; E. Lee Howard to Warren G. Harding, Jan. 13, 1905, WGH. The original bill provided for local option by petition. This method would allow intense church pressure on individual parishioners and obviate the opposition argument that special elections were a burden on the taxpayer. But Wheeler changed the method to special elections when he was advised that the wets might intimidate and boycott persons who publicly petitioned for dry territory.

the 'socialistic' tendencies of the times," the *American Issue* reported, and the need therefore to leave the Republican party undisturbed and entrenched. The league officers refused the deal. "The churches cannot consent to being placed in the attitude of a mere annex to the Republican or any other party, or to wait attendance upon party plans . . . . The churches consider moral and spiritual issues supreme."[27]

As the Brannock bill went through the legislative process in the House and Senate, it clearly had strong support. The drys beat back every attempt to weaken it, and in mid-March the bill survived a crucial test in the House by a comfortable twenty-vote margin. In the Senate the story was the same, with league-approved amendments attached. Then, Governor Myron T. Herrick announced that he would veto the measure unless it was substantially changed. Herrick was the first Ohio governor to command the veto power, and his message that the bill was "unfair" shocked the drys. Indeed, the league, which in 1900 had praised the appointment of Herrick to the Republican National Committee in place of Cox, had hoped that the governor recognized the pitfalls of alienating "the church vote."[28]

The difference between Herrick and the league related to the definition of what comprised a residential district and how its size should be determined. As the bill had passed in the legislature, the wets had complained that it practically amounted to "prohibition." Herrick insisted on changes that would substantially reduce the areas of cities to which it might apply and allow virtually all saloons of long standing (as opposed to those recently opened in the brewers' marketing wars) to survive. "I take this stand in the interest of the Republican party," he said. Working with the head of the liquor dealers, the governor engineered a conference committee that did his bidding. The league was able to change the final bill only slightly. Despite the bitter disappointment that Wheeler and his followers suffered, the dry leader claimed the bill was "a most decisive victory . . . when we stop to consider the forces opposed to it." The new law "will limit and centralize the saloon area, and make it easier to enforce ordinances and laws regulating saloons."

27. Cleveland *Plain Dealer*, Feb. 9, 1904; *American Issue*, Jan. 22, 1904, pp. 5–9; Jan. 29, 1904, p. 1; Mar. 17, 1905, pp. 1–2; Wheeler to John D. Rockefeller, Dec. 29, 1904, PPMR.

28. *Ohio State Journal*, Mar. 17, 1904; I. W. Metcalf to Herrick, Mar. 22, 1904, IWM; F. L. Dustman to Herrick, Mar. 30, 1904, MH; *Cleveland Leader*, Apr. 13, 1904; *American Issue* 9 (Aug. 1900):14; Apr. 1, 1904, p. 8; Apr. 15, 1904, p. 1; *Cincinnati Enquirer*, Apr. 16, 18, 19, 1904.

Wheeler vowed to continue to press the fight to grant "the people of Ohio . . . the right to protect their homes in any political division without any exemptions."[29]

Herrick's actions presented the league with both a problem and an opportunity. The league had always proclaimed that it would work to defeat its enemies, first in obtaining nomination for office, and second in winning election. But the application of that policy was a much more serious matter in the case of a governor who headed the majority party in the state than it was with an obscure legislator in a rural county. Herrick commanded large resources. As a prominent Cleveland banker he was personally wealthy, with access to other party contributors, and through his patronage the governor commanded much of the party machinery around the state. Republican newspapers were likely to help him in any fight with the Anti-Saloon League. Defeating Herrick's bid for renomination would be next to impossible unless some popular leader came forward. Once Herrick was renominated, there was no assurance that the Democrats would choose a satisfactory dry candidate. Meanwhile there was always the danger that Republican drys would rebel against the league's interference in such important party affairs, costing it access to pulpits and financial support. But if such were the problems, if the league was able somehow to defeat Herrick's bid for a second term it would present temperance people across the nation with a dramatic triumph of popular single-issue, nonpartisan politics and establish the league firmly as a major political force. Even if Herrick were successful, if the league could noticeably reduce his vote total from that of other candidates, it could still claim a victory.

Herrick was aware that he was in serious political trouble. As the first governor to command the veto power, he had enraged farm groups by his reduction of appropriations of agricultural education. He tried to placate temperance Republicans by vetoing a bill, which he had earlier promised privately to support, that allowed race track betting. In private letters to old supporters who were drys his claim of only having searched for a "fair" bill that the courts would approve was unpersuasive. At their November meeting, the league's board of trustees, and soon after the state convention delegates, unanimously declared their opposition to the governor's renomination and reelection. "Whether he is elected or defeated," the editor of the *American Issue* wrote, "the lessons of his bad break will remain

29. *American Issue*, Apr. 5, 1904, pp. 1, 3; Apr. 22, 1904, pp. 1, 5; Apr. 29, 1904, p. 3.

a heritage for other politicians in the future." He promised a "stir-
ring up" not seen since the constitutional amendment campaign of
1883.[30]

The next step for Wheeler and Baker, the latter now working as
national superintendent, was to try to secure a candidate to oppose
Herrick within the party. They quickly settled upon Warren G.
Harding. Harding, who as a state senator had voted favorably on
local option measures, was serving as lieutenant governor, nominated and elected in 1903 as a bow to the temperance forces as well
as to the Foraker faction. A number of party officials were urging
Harding to enter the race, and Foraker gave his private blessing.
Both Baker and Wheeler pressed Harding to come forward, circulating petitions around the state, but in the end he refused. From
Cincinnati George Cox announced his support of the governor, and
Herrick quickly moved to ensure that the county organizations
would send friends to the state Republican convention. With the
governor successfully maneuvering to prevent participation by the
party rank and file in the delegate selection process, and no prominent leader willing to fight openly for the nomination, Baker and
Wheeler had to turn to the Democrats to find a dry candidate.[31]

The Democratic party was also divided on the issues of temperance. But as the minority party, having failed for nearly a generation
to control the statehouse, some of its leaders had developed good
relations with the Anti-Saloon League. Democratic legislators helped
to pass the local option laws pushed by the league, and on occasion
they consulted with league officers and rejected candidates for
nominations deemed unacceptable. So although all of the important
league staff members in the state were Republicans, true to their
nonpartisan strategy they had developed good lines of communication with the Democratic party. This enabled them to persuade the
party to nominate for governor in 1905 John M. Pattison of Cincinnati. Pattison was an insurance executive and a former member

30. Herrick to I. W. Metcalf, May 10, 1904; Metcalf to J. C. Jackson, May 23 and
27, 1904; Tod B. Galloway to Metcalf, June 3, 1904, IWM; *American Issue*, Nov. 25,
1904, p. 2; Dec. 9, 1904, p. 12; Jan. 6, 1903, pp. 8–9, Mar. 10, 1905, p. 4.

31. L. B. Cherrington to Harding, Jan. 3, 1905; Wheeler to Harding, Jan. 4,
1905, Jan. 16, 1905, Feb. 17, 1905; Baker to Harding, Feb. 3, 1905; Foraker to
Harding, Jan. 20, 1905; Charles Dick and John R. Malloy to Harding, Jan. 19, 1905,
WGH; *Columbus Dispatch*, Jan. 16, 1905; *American Issue*, Feb. 24, 1905, p. 5. One of his
aides advised Harding that as a candidate, "You will have to have somebody at
Columbus to keep in touch with the enemy and to advise with Wheeler." Malcolm
Jennings to Harding, Jan. 6, 1905, WGH.

of the legislature and U.S. Congress who had served for a time in the 1890s on the league's board of trustees. The contest between Pattison and Herrick was clear-cut: a dry Democratic challenger versus a wet Republican incumbent.[32]

The campaign was bitter. Despite the efforts of some wet Democrats, most notably in Columbus, to hurt Pattison, by late August one league employee was referring to Herrick as a "gone goose." When Pattison stumped the state, he found welcoming committees that included prominent Republicans. Most of the state's Protestant church magazines were openly calling for Herrick's defeat. The *American Issue* published detailed accounts of how the governor had seriously weakened the Brannock bill. League speakers were instructed to be "in the position of the prosecutor, the saloon system is the prisoner at the bar of justice, and the audience is the jury." Saloons that remained open because of his action were "Herrick Saloons." The league and the WCTU cooperated to canvass voters.[33]

To counteract these efforts, the Herrick organization tried to discredit the Anti-Saloon League. Never before had the league been so bitterly attacked in the media of general circulation. The papers of the liquor dealers and brewers had villified "the Rev. Purely A. Faker," but those had small circulations. Now the Republican literary bureau was sending boiler plate material across the state, and articles and editorials were appearing that cast the league as an organization of a few well-paid agitators who had appointed themselves to arouse emotions about the saloons. The league was a "blind pool" that sucked hard-earned money from rural churches and their ill-paid ministers so that Baker, Wheeler, Russell, and the others could live in grand homes on fashionable Columbus streets. They allowed no real voice to the churches or to their pledge-signing members in determining the course of league affairs and were interested only in prolonging political issues so that they could retain their salaries and stay in the limelight instead of preaching to small congregations and ministering to farmers in remote villages. Meanwhile, so the line went, all they wanted was to hurt the Grand Old Party, which was responsible for all Ohio temperance legislation. Despite the agitators' claims, the Brannock law as passed and ap-

32. "Board of Trustees," undated typescript, ASLA; *American Issue*, July 7, 1905, p. 8; Jan. 12, 1906, p. 2.

33. *American Issue*, Jan. 27, 1905, p. 8; Jan. 12, 1906, pp. 1–6; *Why Be an Independent Voter?*, 1905 campaign leaflet, IWM; E. L. Skeel to Ernest Cherrington, Aug. 28, 1905; Cherrington, "The Local Option Address," 1905 typescript, ECg; Moon to Dick, Nov. 3, 1905, CD.

proved by the governor was an effective, fair instrument. According to the Republican propagandists, the real danger to Ohio was socialism, and the only effective way to fight it was to maintain a powerful, elected Republican party.[34]

These attacks did Herrick little good. John D. Rockefeller, a friend of the governor, cut his league donation from $5,000 to $3,000, and a few pastors may have been induced to refuse league speakers access to their pulpits, but there was no visible suffering by the league. Instead, it was bigger, better financed, and more active than ever before. In 1905 the Ohio league raised and spent $73,000 and paid its 2½ percent levy to the national organization. The Ohio league maintained five district offices, forty-two full-time and twenty part-time clerical employees, thirteen full-time officers, and a large band of Sunday speakers. Baker was so confident of the Ohio league's ability to employ able staff members that he sent Assistant State Superintendent Ernest Cherrington to Seattle to head the Washington league when the gubernatorial campaign was just beginning. The league was leading a reform wave of "home rule" and "the people" against "party bossism," and it rode the crest to victory. In spite of a heroic effort by the distilling and brewing firms to use their staff to turn out wets to vote for Herrick—and despite reports that wet Democrats were doing likewise—in the largest turn-out to date in a gubernatorial election in the state, Pattison was elected by a 45,000-vote margin while every other Republican candidate for state office won.[35]

This victory attracted national attention and did more than anything else to convince Americans that the league could turn its rhetoric concerning nonpartisan politics into practical action. The victory provided league strategists with another opportunity to demonstrate how a single-issue, popular reform organization should operate. Shortly after the votes were counted, the headquarters in Columbus began to receive requests from aspiring patronage appointees for league endorsements to the governor-elect. But the *American Issue* announced that the league had notified Pattison that it had no "political requests for appointments to make of him," and that it would endorse no other requests. "The League, in all its

34. *American Issue*, Oct. 21, 1904, p. 7; Dec. 16, 1904, pp. 8–9; Feb. 17, 1905, pp. 8–9; Mar. 10, 1905, pp. 8–9; June 2, p. 3; *Elyria Republican*, Apr. 6, 1905.

35. John D. Rockefeller to F. T. Gates, Feb. 17, 1905, PPMR; *American Issue*, Nov. 17, 1905, pp. 4–5; Nov. 24, 1905, p. 14; Dec. 22, 1905, p. 12; Jan. 12, 1906, pp. 1–6; Jan. 19, 1906, p. 12; "Status and Record of the Ohio Anti-Saloon League," 1905 typescript, ECg.

efforts," the editors told their supporters, "is not actuated by any desire for the spoils of office for its members or its friends. . . . We propose to remain entirely aloof from all political alliances, and to operate with an eye alone single to the advantage of the temperance cause." When other reformers who sympathized with the drys asked the league to support their causes (such as woman suffrage), it refused to take an official stand. The *American Issue*, however, praised changes that were related to the temperance reform, such as the WCTU's advocacy of a bill to allow woman suffrage in local option contests. As to the problem of "party bossism," the league paper suggested that its defeat might prove temporary unless a direct primary law were passed. In dry eyes the old party system was intimately linked with the saloon system, with the latter funding the former.[36]

What the league wanted most of all was an improved residence district local option law that would close the Herrick Saloons and an additional "Blind Tiger and Speakeasy" law to provide enforcement tools. With help from both Democratic and Republican leaders, the league achieved those measures easily in the 1906 session of the General Assembly, which also increased the saloon tax to $1,000 annually. The league immediately announced that the "next thing. . . is county option," which it achieved in 1908. By the close of that session, the Ohio Anti-Saloon League was triumphant, ready to solidify its forces for some future push for statewide prohibition.[37]

The Significance of the Ohio Local Option Campaigns

The political wars over local option legislation in Ohio were important experiences in the history of the Anti-Saloon League. The charges and countercharges among church spokespersons, partisans, and the state's wet trade and political associations produced both a clarification of prohibition propaganda and changes in the formal structure of the Ohio league that were part of a national pattern for the entire league movement.

In the view of the league's propagandists, the liquor traffic needed to keep its marketing apparatus intact. The league was

36. *American Issue*, Dec. 22, 1905, pp. 6, 10–11; Dec. 29, 1905, pp. 1–2; Feb. 9, 1906, p. 2; Apr. 13, 1906, pp. 4–5.

37. *American Issue*, Dec. 22, 1905, p. 1; Mar. 2, 1906, p. 9; Mar. 23, 1906, pp. 3, 8–10. The league was against the licensing of saloons, and thus any special taxation of them, so it took no official position on the tax increase. *American Issue* (Ohio), Mar. 7, 1908, p. 1.

trying to strike at the liquor traffic as a system, and damaging part of
that system, by reducing the geographical areas in which Ohioans
allowed the saloon to operate advanced the dry cause, and not just
symbolically. The most zealous drys in Ohio, usually claiming leadership in the Prohibition party, complained that winning local option
campaigns, especially in remote rural counties, was insufficient; that
only the election of the Prohibition party to the control of state
politics would provide a substantial victory. The leaders of the
league, of course, disagreed sharply with this contention, and in
their eyes the Ohio political battles confirmed their beliefs. League
spokesmen pointed to the vigorous and expensive resistance
mounted by the various business associations connected with the
liquor traffic as evidence that the prospect of local option was hurtful. At every step in the legislative process the whiskey and brewing
interests had offered amendments designed to preserve their marketing system. This evidence convinced the league leaders that they
were on the right course, that the liquor traffic was a business system
whose restriction, in whatever form, substantially advanced the dry
cause. By restricting the marketing apparatus of the liquor traffic,
they reasoned, the dry movement was striking at the heart of an evil.
Thus, prohibition, as a movement that used every opportunity, however gradual, for enlarging government power over the traffic, was
deserving of support from all citizens who sought to improve society
and free individuals from the temptations of evil.[38]

The verbal vitriol poured on the league by the Republican organization in the 1905 campaign forced some modifications in the formal structure of the Ohio Anti-Saloon League. As has been noted,
the league was formed from the start as a self-perpetuating organization controlled by its own staff, and the league's defense against
the charges that it was a blind pool were shallow and unconvincing.
The leaders simply insisted that all members of the league's board of
trustees were outstanding men to whom the staff was accountable.
The churches, so the counterargument ran, were clearly behind the
league. They appointed ministers to league work, and the Protestant
bodies of the state passed formal resolutions of support. Nor were
the salaries of the league staff high, especially in comparison with
comparable positions in public and business life; the wet complaint
was baseless. Moreover, the *American Issue* began to publish financial
reports to refute the charges that the league commanded enormous
financial resources.

38. *American Issue*, Feb. 17, 1905, p. 13; Wheeler to Starr J. Murphy, Jan. 11, 1907,
PPMR.

But after the heat of the battle in 1905, Wheeler arranged for changes in the league's formal structure. Now the board of trustees would have representatives directly chosen by the state's church denominations. "The policies of the League will be guided more and more by the church," Wheeler told the board, and "this will unite the church more firmly to the temperance cause, and hasten the day of final victory." The change obviated charges of "self-perpetuation." But the action made no visible difference in the league's policies or in the activities of its employees. Like other kinds of private associations that were becoming such a prominent feature of twentieth-century society, the league, now formally democratic at its top level, was susceptible to "the iron law of oligarchy."[39]

With the passage of the county local option bill in 1908, the Ohio Anti-Saloon League had risen to become a dominant influence in the state's politics. Although it never extended as far as the county level, as Russell had originally envisioned it would, the Ohio league maintained five district offices in addition to its Colulmbus head-quarters. Nationally, the movement had grown sufficiently to re-quire separate editions of the *American Issue*, and the Ohio edition circulated widely across the state and supplied copy for editions elsewhere. The Ohio league could comfortably budget its opera-tions annually for over $70,000.

Now, furthermore, Wheeler could boast of the league's strength. The Ohio league had become so powerful by 1906 that all of the major party candidates for statewide office, except one Democrat, expressed support for local option legislation. "The liquor dealers were placed in the last election in the same position that the temper-ance people were thirteen years ago." Wheeler reported. They "had to choose between candidates at the head of the dominant tickets both of whom had expressed themselves openly in favor of the strongest temperance law ever proposed to the General Assembly." The defeat of the lone wet Democrat showed that "no sane man in Ohio any longer doubts that the liquor support is a blight rather than a blessing at the polls."[40]

Wheeler's confidence was unwarranted. There was a political problem on the horizon that he and his advisors failed to foresee. Despite the protestations about nonpartisanship, events led the league to become linked to the fortunes of the Republican party.

39. *American Issue*, Mar. 10, 1905, pp. 8–9; Jan. 19, 1906, pp. 10–12; Mar. 30, 1906, p. 11; Dec. 21, 1906, p. 11.
40. *American Issue*, Dec. 21, 1906, pp. 10–12.

Governor Pattison died in 1906, and his successor, Republican Andrew Harris, openly supported local option legislation, as did the next state Republican party convention. This support may have helped speed the passage of county option in 1908, but it would soon cost the league dearly. In 1909 the Democrats elected a wet governor, Judson Harmon. At the same time the Ohio Brewers' Association began operating under a new strategy of persuading Ohioans to retain the saloon, and another era in prohibition politics in the state had begun.[41]

41. Wheeler to Starr J. Murphy, Jan. 17, 1908, PPMR.

John Dough, saloon keeper.

The liquor traffic.

How our public watch dogs are fed.
Series H poster distributed by the Anti-Saloon League.

Universal suffrage (limited).
Series H poster distributed by the Anti-Saloon League.

Protection and free trade.
Series H poster distributed by the Anti-Saloon League.

Who's to blame?
Series H poster distributed by the Anti-Saloon League.

Store front, Dayton, Ohio.

The literature room at the
headquarters of the
Ohio Anti-Saloon League.

Store front, Toledo, Ohio.

Anti-Saloon League office, Seattle, Washington.

The downward path. Series H poster distributed by the Anti-Saloon League.

The army of drunkards.
Series H poster distributed by
the Anti-Saloon League.

Not in the Peace Treaty—
Still Your Enemy

5

THE EVOLUTION OF THE NATIONAL LEAGUE, 1895–1913

The events in Ohio during the formative years of the Anti-Saloon League were important for the national movement, for they demonstrated the development of an effective nonpartisan organization and lent substance to league publicity calling for the adoption of its strategy and structure elsewhere. Each state, of course, had peculiar political traditions, and there were regional differences in the patterns of partisan politics. As was common in the Middle West, Ohio was a closely contested state, whereas the South, a bastion of dry sentiment, was a one-party system during this period. Such peculiarities meant that the Ohio league was not always duplicated. Nevertheless, it remained the most completely organized and best-funded state league, the embodiment of Howard Russell's idea of adapting business methods to reform politics, and a model for others to emulate.

The American Anti-Saloon League, as has been discussed, was initially formed to combine Russell's ideas, then in embryo, with the perceptions of other dry leaders that a new national temperance organization was desirable. The American league began slowly, was always closely tied to the Ohio headquarters, and never became the unified, omnipotent organization that was sometimes portrayed to politicians and voters. But it did perform important functions. The national league developed to become much like the central office of a diversified corporation. It set the strategy for winning national legislation and exercised considerable control over the pace of dry agitation in the hinterlands. The national office collected resources for the state affiliates and allocated them according to the leaders' observation of political opportunity. It lent cohesiveness to the national prohibition movement by publishing periodicals and propaganda materials.

Before 1913 the national officers saw prohibition as a goal for state and local action. A campaign for national prohibition seemed premature. Meanwhile, they believed that the fastest means to victory was through adaptation of the methods of the Ohio league to conditions elsewhere and the fostering of appropriate organizations. The main task was to promote the movement outside of Ohio. This goal dictated the other functions of the national organization. It raised funds. It developed publications to teach the uninitiated or inexperienced just what nonpartisan politics entailed and to promote temperance ideology. It fought for national legislation, both to encourage the hopes of temperance supporters that eventually their views might prevail and to provide the federal statutes that were needed for state and local prohibition laws to have any effectiveness against the devices of the liquor traffic. These functions, of course, were all interrelated. Winning a law encouraged donors, just as the growing number of state leagues increased the number of congressmen with constituencies agitating for dry legislation.

Although these functions were apparent, the best means of putting them into effect was not. The American Anti-Saloon League, as an organization, evolved through experience and expedience. But while its formal structure changed, the domination by the salaried staff was remarkably immutable. And that staff, the cast of characters that determined the course of the league's history, changed very little.

Democracy and Authority in the League

In devising the constitution of the Anti-Saloon League, the leaders were continually plagued by a major problem. On the one hand, Russell and the other founders thought of the organization as something akin to an army. Victory would come only after a long struggle against large odds, and it would require a steady, disciplined effort among the temperance legions. Russell used business and military rhetoric to express these observations. On the other hand, the league had to operate in a society with a democratic political tradition. It had to appeal to ministers and laymen in churches with a tradition of lay and congregational control. Other fraternal and associational activities of the time often included provisions for the membership shaping their destiny. So there was a competing need for the Anti-Saloon League to be democratic or at least to be so structured that its component parts had a genuine feeling that they were helping to control the league's destiny.

The reconciliation of these competing needs in the formal, constitutional structure took many years. The league underwent major constitutional changes in 1903 and again in 1913 on the national level and, beginning in 1903, on the state level as well. The result was a complex, evolving mix of authority embodied in the salaried officers, especially the general superintendent, and control of league direction by its constituency.

This problem did not appear in the first years, when the only task at hand was promoting the development of state organizations. The first constitution provided that each national temperance society or church denomination "cooperating with the League" would appoint a member to the board of direction. The board, in turn, hired Russell as a part-time general superintendent and chose an eight-person executive committee to offer guidance between annual conventions. Russell spent as much time as he could traveling and organizing state leagues. An amendment passed in 1896 gave the convention delegates more authority.[1] This simple organization was suitable for the fledgling organization, but as Russell succeeded in organizing more state leagues he found it cumbersome. There was no formal mechanism for them to control national affairs. So in 1900 he recommended the creation of a board of trustees composed of persons from the state leagues, and biannual national conventions in order to save expense. He wanted "a system of general government" that was both "elastic and advisory" and capable of providing management discipline over state and local work.[2]

The new constitution was finally adopted in 1903. Under its provisions, the convention elected officers, most of whom were honorary, and a general and legislative superintendent. The national league was to have two boards. The board of direction consisted of one representative from each member organization, and its only real duty was to decide the time and place of the biannual convention. The board of trustees included two representatives from each state league, one of whom was the state superintendent. The trustees had much more power. They approved budgets and the appointment of the state superintendents. The board of trustees had a headquarters committee that advised the

1. *Proceedings, National Anti-Saloon Convention, 1895*, p. 18, and *1896*, p. 38; *American Issue* 5 (Jan. 1900):6.

2. "Annual Report of Superintendent Russell, Dec. 10, 1902," HH; *Proceedings, Fifth National Anti-Saloon Convention, 1900*, pp. 33–34; *Proceedings, Sixth Annual Anti-Saloon Convention, 1901*, pp. 5–7; *Proceedings, Seventh Annual Anti-Saloon Convention, 1902*, pp. 36–37.

general superintendent and helped prepare the budget. The board decided how much money the states would forward to the national office. The general superintendent, by this time Purley A. Baker, chose the state superintendents, so he, in effect, controlled half of the members of the board of trustees.[3]

But the authoritarian nature of these provisions was mitigated by another important development on the state level. In 1903 the salaried staff recommended that the state boards of trustees be reconstituted so that the church denominations would elect their members. State constitutions began to be changed accordingly. So in the important matter of appointing and disciplining state superintendents, there was a mixture of representative democracy from below and authoritarianism from above, with both levels approving basic staffing decisions. There were procedures for the removal of a state superintendent when either the national office or the state board found him unsatisfactory.[4]

The constitution of 1903 was seldom amended before 1913. The organization changed its name in 1905 to the Anti-Saloon League of America and gave the larger church denominations additional representatives on the board of direction. In 1909 an important element of national discipline was added to the bylaws. Now any state league, prior to initiating a major statewide effort for advanced temperance legislation, had to receive the approval of the national office. The national headquarters committee felt this rule was essential lest financial resources become too strained. But the only enforcement power of the national officers, in cases where state leagues refused to follow their direction, was that of publicity. This greater discipline was mitigated in 1911 by an amendment that allowed each state league three representatives on the board of trustees.[5]

This constitution was completely revised in 1913 in preparation for the drive for national prohibition. The changes were, on paper, dramatically to make the league a representative democracy. There was to be only a board of directors, with two to five representatives from each state, depending on population. The board elected of-

3. *American Anti-Saloon League Constitution* (Columbus, n.d.).

4. Ibid.; *Proceedings, Eighth National Anti-Saloon Convention, 1903*, p. 26.

5. *Proceedings, Tenth Annual Convention, 1905*, pp. 6–7, 43, 51–52; *Proceedings, Thirteenth Convention, ASLA, 1909*, p. 56; *Proceedings, Fourteenth Convention, ASLA, 1911*, pp. 7–8; William H. Anderson, *The Church in Action Against the Saloon*, rev. ed. (Westerville, Ohio, 1910), p. 42.

ficers, including the general superintendent. The board chose the trustees of the American Issue Publishing Co., established in Westerville, Ohio, in 1909 to print the enormous volumes of literature that the movement required. The board elected a sixteen-member executive committee apportioned according to geographical districts. This committee met at least quarterly, appointed necessary subcommittees, submitted the budget, fixed salaries, and approved the appointment of state superintendents and their salaries. These changes in structure were accompanied by an entirely new budgetary system that had the national office paying the salaries of all the state superintendents, and state leagues paying a percentage of their income to the national office graduated according to their wealth.[6] This scheme did two important things. It precluded wet charges that the Anti-Saloon League was simply a self-perpetuating group of staff members enjoying high salaries at the expense of struggling church members. And the scheme insured that the well-organized states, like Ohio, would carry the organization in states where the league was weaker, but where votes were essential if a constitutional amendment were ever to be secured.

Leaders and League Management

These structural changes mattered little, however, in determining the direction of national league affairs. Regardless of the constitutional changes, a small group of men made the important decisions about which bills to support in Congress, what election contests to enter, new publication ventures, and the allocation of funds. The national leadership changed over the years, but only slowly, and then because of infirmity or managerial decisions, not because of the views of the dry constituency. It was not that the structural changes were unimportant. As the movement grew in scope, and especially as the volume of monetary transactions increased, the leaders sought advice from wealthy volunteers and made certain that wealthy laymen were on the executive committee to offer their advice.[7] State superintendents were usually appointed after negotiations between the national office and local trustees. But there

6. *Constitution of the Anti-Saloon League of America* (Westerville, 1913).

7. In 1912 Baker asked William Anderson, Maryland superintendent, to resign from the headquarters committee so that he could appoint another millionaire. Anderson to Cherrington, Dec. 24, 1912, ECe. Anderson to John Lewis Clar, Oct. 24, 1906, WA.

were also instances in which the national headquarters dictated staff appointments contrary to local wishes. The views of the salaried officers prevailed when they chose to exercise their power.

The national management of the league changed in 1902 when Howard Russell resigned as general superintendent. He then became New York state superintendent, seeking to build the movement in the most populous state with the nation's most powerful wet political organization, Tammany Hall. Russell remained in that post until 1909, while continuing to serve as an influential member of the national headquarters committee. But his administration of the New York league was a failure financially and politically, and after 1909 the national league used his talents as a speaker to raise money and enlist abstinence pledges. From 1909 until his death in 1946, Russell lived in Westerville, Ohio, where the league had established its printing plant and offices. As assistant general superintendent he had no significant managerial role.[8]

Purley Baker replaced Russell as general superintendent in 1903, and until his death in 1924 was the most powerful individual in the organization. Born in 1858, Baker had little formal education. He was embarked on a successful career as a Methodist minister in Columbus when Russell recruited him for the league staff. He enjoyed revivalist preaching abilities, was effective in goading wet politicians, had an eye for adminstrative details, and commanded intense loyalty from his coworkers. Some league men saw Baker as pugnacious, even bullheaded; in any event, he demanded good performances from his staff and removed from office those who, like Russell, did not measure up to his standards of excellence. The superintendents under him were required to cooperate with league policies. "Reformers must preach a shut-fist Gospel," he told the convention in 1906, "which develops within them a spirit of fight-righteous warfare, and when engaging the enemy they are in danger of engaging each other." He reported that prayer helped overcome disagreements among league leaders. But Baker was also prepared to fire men who challenged his instructions. The men directly under him knew this trait, and although they might disagree with Baker's view on a subject, they acceded to his wishes.[9]

8. Baker to Russell, May 22, 1907, HH.

9. *Standard Encyclopedia of the Alcohol Problem*, 1:258–60; James Cannon, Jr., *Bishop Cannon's Own Story* (Durham, N.C., 1955), p. 170; Baker to S. E. Nicholson, Jan. 10 and Jan. 17, 1912, ASLAN; *Proceedings, Eleventh Annual Convention, ASLA, 1906*, pp. 40, 45.

The two men with the greatest ability to influence Baker's actions were Wayne Wheeler and Ernest Cherrington. When Baker's health failed in the 1920s, they became the most important league officials. Of the two, Wheeler was the less popular among league workers. But in his devotion to prohibition, his zeal for law enforcement, and his ability to influence press coverage of league political activities, Wheeler was unexcelled. Wheeler replaced Baker as superintendent of the Ohio league, serving in Columbus until 1915, when he went to work for the Washington, D.C., office as general counsel and later legislative superintendent.[10] Unlike Wheeler, Cherrington owed his career chances initially to Baker's patronage. A graduate of Ohio Wesleyan University, he had taught school and edited a small Ohio newspaper when Baker recruited him for the league staff in 1902. In 1905 Baker sent Cherrington to superintend the Washington league in Seattle and then recalled him in 1908 to take over the *American Issue* when the health of its editor, J. C. Jackson, began to fail. Cherrington served as the general manager of the American Issue Publishing Company, assuming overall charge of all of the league's publications. In his career at various times he served every department except legal affairs. Cherrington set up and directed the national fund-raising programs beginning in 1912, served as secretary to the executive committee after 1913 and was on the national legislative committee during the drive to secure the Eighteenth Amendment. While he lived in Washington, Wheeler received more attention from the press than did Cherrington, but the latter was at least equally important in the shaping and execution of league policies.[11]

The headquarters committee before 1912 was dominated by salaried superintendents. Of these, three men were prominent in the national movement. Edwin C. Dinwiddie served as legislative superintendent in Washington, D.C., from 1899 to 1907 and again from 1911 to 1919, but in the latter period he was not part of the inside circle of officials.[12] Before 1912 Samuel E. Nicholson was. He had successfully fought for a local option bill in the Indiana legislature prior to the inception of the Anti-Saloon League and then went on to serve the league as its superintendent in that state and in Pennsylvania and as national legislative superintendent from 1909 to 1911.[13] William H. Anderson became the Illinois league's attorney

10. *Standard Encyclopedia of the Alcohol Problem*, 6:2832−35.
11. Ibid., 2:565−66.
12. Ibid., 2:806−09.
13. Ibid., 5:1982−83.

in 1900 and later was superintendent there, in Maryland, and in
New York. As a layman he was a leader in the Methodist Church's
Temperance Society as well as of the Anti-Saloon League. Anderson
enjoyed a facile pen, expressed buoyant optimism for his favorite
causes, and was outspoken in his convictions. Never close to Baker,
nevertheless he was admired for his administrative and public relations abilities and continued as a force in the league until convicted
by a New York jury of fraud in 1924. More than any other person
Anderson was responsible for changing the league structure so that
the church denominations elected representatives to its governing
bodies.[14]

A State-by-State Strategy

The purposes of the Anti-Saloon League of America were clear in
the minds of its leaders. Their gospel of nonpartisan, ongoing
political action conducted by expert men, based on a system of
organizing voters at the precinct level, first tried and then proved
successful in Ohio, had to be spread around the nation so that in
state after state the economic power and the grip of the liquor traffic
on the political system would be broken. Convincing the dry constituency to adopt league methods required a number of steps. The
national league had to persuade able men to assume leadership
positions, raise funds, start publications, and win political victories—
emulate the Ohio experience, in short. The system of internal governance and the selection of national officers pointed toward those
purposes. Nevertheless, mistakes were made and controversies
aroused in both governance and the selection of leaders. The national leaders, Baker, Russell, and the rest were fallible and limited
men. They were engaging in a pioneering effort of citizen reform
action outside of the political party system and had no precedent or
experience to draw upon.

Before 1906, when the potential of the league methods was revealed in Ohio politics, the role of the national office was chiefly to
start state leagues by raising funds and recruiting leaders. After
1906 the national officials also demanded performance from those
state organizations. Initially, the league spread among the states
through opportunistic means. Wherever there was some form of
nonpartisan interdenominational temperance organization, the
league pressed to have it change its name and employ at least one

14. Ibid., 1:164–65.

full-time state superintendent. Thus the Anti-Liquor League in Indiana, led by state legislator S. E. Nicholson, became the Indiana Anti-Saloon League, and Nicholson a lifetime staff member in the national movement.[15]

This method of coopting existing organizations and strengthening them was partly successful. It gave the national movement a way of entering into the religious and political life of a state, an opportunity to build the kind of organization it envisioned. The method also allowed Russell, in the first years, to make large claims about the number of state organizations in existence and the large sums of money being raised and expended. In 1902 he proudly reported to the national convention that the movement, with thirtynine states and territories organized and two hundred full-time employees, was annually spending $250,000. This was a substantial enough effort to alarm the wholesale liquor dealers and prompt them to renew their own political initiatives.[16]

But in important ways the league failed to fulfill its leaders' proclamations of success. In 1902 the South was largely unorganized, and there were states, most notably Connecticut, in which the temperance organization, although affiliating with the league, kept to an independent course, operated by volunteers promoting a broad range of reforms, not just the single issue of temperance. Soon after taking over the national office from Russell, Baker complained of his inability to attract enough able men to league positions. Too many ministers and too few men with business and legal experience were in charge, he felt. The clergymen might have taken their league posts because of failed pastorates. Or they might be dishonest; the Washington superintendent left Seattle after embezzling league funds. Both Russell and Baker used the Ohio league as a source of staff members to be placed elsewhere. But one state could not supply the entire movement with superintendents. In their annual reports a common refrain from the state offices was that little had been accomplished by way of concrete political results, but that the ground was being prepared for future victories. Exasperated, in 1906 Baker informed the national convention that the time had passed for such reports. "The seed has been sown," he warned. "In due time there should be a harvest."[17]

15. *Christianity in Earnest* 7 (July–Aug. 1895):147.

16. Russell, "Annual Report, Dec. 10, 1902," Russell papers; Cherrington, *History of the Anti-Saloon League*, p. 57.

17. *Proceedings, Eleventh Annual Convention, ASLA, 1906*, p. 40; Blocker, *Retreat from Reform*, p. 161; *Proceedings, Eighth National Anti-Saloon Convention, 1903*, pp. 53–54.

Baker's biggest headache was the South. This was a region with a strong tradition of church piety, local option laws, and sizeable power in national politics. But the league, for most practical purposes, was not there leading the prohibition cause. Russell had been optimistic as early as 1896 about prospects for league organization in Virginia, and that state, with the energetic and able leadership of James Cannon, Jr., who after 1913 was one of the most prominent prohibitionists nationally, did develop an effective league. But the course of league affairs was not so happy elsewhere in the region. The problem in Cannon's view was that Baker and other northern leaders simply did not understand southern conditions. They were too impatient with southern social customs, did not understand the operations of the one-party system, and disagreed with the local practice of race relations.[18]

Whatever the case, Baker recognized that he needed help in organizing the section. "We must have a Southern man" in the field, he noted, "because of the race problem." He asked G. W. Young, the Kentucky superintendent, to become assistant general superintendent for the league's southern affairs. With Cannon's advice and Young's leadership, the national league wanted to have the southern church denominations promote the organization. This approach worked in some places and failed in others. In Alabama and Tennessee strong leagues appeared that engineered state dry laws. But Young had to return to Kentucky in 1906 because the national office could no longer pay his salary. Mississippi in 1907 and Georgia in 1908 enacted prohibition statutes without much help from the league.[19] The Texas Anti-Saloon League had great difficulty and operated ineffectively until 1914, when Rev. Arthur J. Barton became superintendent under a closer affiliation with the national office.[20] Prohibition legislation swept through the South in the

18. Cannon, *Own Story*, p. 170; Russell to Lillian Russell, June 28, 1896, HH; C. C. Pearson and J. Edwin Hendricks, *Liquor and Anti-Liquor in Virginia, 1618–1919* (Durham, N.C., 1967), p. 252. The Virginia league, according to Pearson and Hendricks, adopted the Ohio techniques of publishing the positions of candidates and organizing dry voters in groups of ten, each with a "captain" (p. 274). In 1908 Anderson, while serving as Maryland superintendent, asked Cherrington to remove all references to secession from the *American Issue*. Anderson to Cherrington, October 15, 1908, ECg.

19. *American Issue*, March 11, 1904, p. 13; *Proceedings, Ninth National Anti-Saloon Convention, 1904*, pp. 26–27; *Tenth Convention, 1905*, pp. 18–19; *Eleventh Convention, 1906*, p. 40; *Fourteenth Convention, 1911*, p. 125.

20. Lewis L. Gould, *Progressives and Prohibitionists: Texas Democrats in the Wilson Era* (Austin, Texas, 1973), pp. 44, 53–56, 145, 166. There is a substantial scholarly

early twentieth century, but apparently not so much due to league organization as to the zeal of the churches abetted by league propaganda. After 1913, when the Democratic party came to power in Washington, D.C., southern votes were an essential ingredient in the drive for the Eighteenth Amendment.

Chronic shortages of funds overshadowed even the league's difficulties in organizing the South. The South went dry, with or without the leadership of the league, but the problems of raising money never receded. The national office struggled to remain solvent, sometimes doing so only because of the willingness of the officers to forego part of their salaries. The financing scheme before 1913 provided for each state to pay the national treasury 2 ½ percent of its total collections. But when collections lagged in a major political campaign, the officials sometimes failed to submit its assessment. Since these funds were used to pay salaries and printing costs, the movement suffered generally. Nor was the national office always helpful to the states. Sometimes it sent into a locality fund raisers who collected monies that otherwise would have been donated to the state league.[21]

Until 1909, at least, publication of the *American Issue* was a constant source of financial concern. The paper was established by the Ohio league and became the national organ as well after 1895. The *Issue* changed to a weekly schedule in 1900. Because Ohio news dominated its columns, other states began establishing their own papers. Then, in 1907, the national league began to publish a general monthly, *American Issue*, with separate editions, either weekly or monthly, for each cooperating state league. Advertising revenue, which grew with circulation, helped defray expenses. But the purpose of the paper was to promote prohibition, not turn a profit, and

---

literature on the southern prohibition movement. Four states are covered in the following monographs: Paul E. Isaac, *Prohibition and Politics: Turbulent Decades in Tennessee, 1885–1920* (Knoxville, 1965); Pearson and Hendricks, *Liquor and Anti-Liquor in Virginia*; James B. Sellers, *The Prohibition Movement in Alabama, 1702–1943* (Chapel Hill, 1943); and Daniel J. Whitener, *Prohibition in North Carolina, 1715–1945* (Chapel Hill, 1946).

21. *Proceedings, Seventh National Anti-Saloon Convention, 1902*, p. iii. One fund-raising technique was to borrow from wealthy patrons and later to ask them to forgive part of the debt. Russell to Starr J. Murphy, Feb. 24, 1902, HH. When some local churches demanded that they retain a percentage of funds raised by league men, Baker responded that the practice "will paralyze" the movement. He also railed against the desire of some churches to budget their donations to the league. *American Issue* (Wisconsin ed.), 4 (May 1909):15.

so it was always a drain on resources, especially during political campaigns when thousands of free copies were distributed.

In 1909 the league took a major step by incorporating the American Issue Publishing Company and establishing its printing plant as well as the national league headquarters in Westerville, Ohio, accessible to Columbus by street railroad. This decision required the league to obtain special donations from wealthy benefactors and to incur a significant debt. Under Cherrington's management, the firm grew, and its presses turned out enormous volumes of printed matter.[22]

During this period of state and local prohibition strategy, Baker realized that the league needed to enlarge its constituency. "If we simply continue to enter the churches we have been entering each year," he reported in 1909, "we begin to move in a circle, with the circle growing steadily smaller." The two groups he wanted to approach were the "country people" and "wage earners." The way to gain and hold the attention of rural Americans was twofold. The league organized college students to canvass in the summer and place the *American Issue* in homes. It established a press "bureau" for weekly releases to small-town papers. "We can get into the press of the country free, as news, what the other fellows have to pay for," Baker told Cherrington. To reach wage earners, Baker wanted to adopt modern advertising techniques—billboards and posters displayed in streetcars and other public places. "It is siege work," Baker noted, "but it brings lasting results."[23]

National Politics and the Churches, 1903–1913

The strategy of the Anti-Saloon League in this pre-1913 period, of course, was to advance the areas of the nation that appeared as "white"—or dry—on the league's maps. The league hoped to establish itself as the political arm of the churches on the temperance question—"the church in action." The structure that Russell, Baker, and others thought was necessary for the conduct of the political campaign, one that the salaried staff essentially controlled, however, was not necessarily appropriate for convincing either the national denominations or individual congregations that the league was, in

22. Baker to Cherrington, Dec. 12, 1907, ECg; Cherrington, "Report of the Committee on Financial Management, 1916," ECe.

23. *Proceedings, Thirteenth National Convention, ASLA, 1909*, pp. 44–46; *Fourteenth Convention, 1911*, pp. 22–23; Baker to Cherrington, Dec. 24, 1907, ECg.

fact, their agency, or, as it styled itself, a church "federation." It was success, as much as any other factor, that finally convinced the churches to accept the league's direction of the prohibition movement, combined with the policy after 1903 of having state church bodies select the members of state boards of trustees. It was not until after the national league strategy shifted in 1913 from an emphasis on state prohibition to national constitutional amendment that the structure of the Anti-Saloon League of America was changed so that nationally, as well as in the states, the body was formally representative of the denominations.

The constitutional changes of 1913 came after bitter struggles over federal legislation. The league changed its constitution after remnants of the Prohibition party seriously challenged the league's claim of representing the churches in prohibition politics. The changes came after the disruption of league lobbying efforts in Washington. The institutional history of the national league in this pre-1913 period, thus, was bound up with its efforts in national politics to break the grip of the party system in the Congress and establish prohibition as an issue to be dealt with outside of the political party system.

In the first years the league not only had to convince American drys that its approach to political action was appropriate, but it also needed visibility as the organization pushing federal temperance legislation. Initially events forced Russell to set up a legislative office in Washington before the league could properly support it either with funds or an organized national constituency. The WCTU had introduced a measure to abolish the canteen on U.S. military bases, and if the league was going to press its claim as the leader of the temperance forces, it had to involve itself in the lobbying effort. So at the end of 1899 Russell appointed Dinwiddie national legislative superintendent. He worked closely with the District of Columbia league and the WCTU, and in 1901 Congress outlawed the sale of whiskey and beer on the posts.[24]

Dinwiddie proved an able lobbyist. He eschewed his clerical collar and rhetoric for ordinary business dress and the practical language of politics to cultivate friends in Congress. He cooperated with other dry groups, especially the WCTU, in establishing legislative priorities and the policy of pursuing one goal at a time. The priorities included appropriations for recreational facilities for enlisted men

24. Edwin C. Dinwiddie, "Story of the League's Washington Bureau," *The American Patriot* 2 (May 1913):11.

that would stymie efforts to bring back the canteen, funds to enforce liquor regulations on Indian reservations, and a requirement that the Treasury Department provide state and local law enforcement officers with the names of people and firms who purchased liquor tax stamps in dry territory. These victories were won by 1906, together with a provision in the Oklahoma statehood bill for a prohibition referendum there. The other priorities were to obtain local option legislation for the District of Columbia and, most important, legislation under the interstate commerce clause of the U.S. Constitution to prevent the shipment of alcoholic beverages into dry areas where the local law forbad them.[25]

Serious problems arose after 1906, however, that disrupted the federal legislative effort and even threatened the league's claim to national leadership. They arose initially from inept leadership by Purley Baker. From the general superintendent's viewpoint, Dinwiddie was not cooperative. Dinwiddie preferred to work alone, even secretively, and he failed to provide regular financial and written reports of his activities. Dinwiddie did not owe his appointment to Baker, and his friendships with powerful and wealthy friends and politicians both in Washington and in temperance groups around the country allowed him considerable independence.[26] The differences between the two men came to a climax in 1907, and Dinwiddie resigned as national legislative superintendent.

The issue that brought about the resignation involved the prohibition referendum in Oklahoma. After passage of the statehood bill, Dinwiddie went there to take charge of the dry campaign. Baker and his associates on the headquarters committee wanted to control local expenditures and whom the league brought to Oklahoma to speak on its behalf. One member of the committee even suggested that Dinwiddie was guilty of indiscretion when he took his secretary to Oklahoma but not his wife and children. In the middle of the campaign effort, Dinwiddie was summoned to a meeting in Columbus, where, failing to convince the committee that he and others on the scene needed a large measure of autonomy, he resigned his national post. He returned to Oklahoma (with his wife, children,

25. Ibid.; *Proceedings, Eighth National Anti-Saloon Convention, 1903*, p. 83; *Proceedings, Eleventh Convention, 1906*, pp. 58–59; *American Issue*, Feb. 5, 1904, p. 1.

26. Dinwiddie to Russell, July 12, 1907; William Anderson to V. G. A. Tressler, Nov. 20, 1911, ASLAN. Dinwiddie was heavily, and successfully, involved in raising funds in the critical, debt-ridden early years. *Proceedings, Tenth Annual Convention, ASLA, 1905*, pp. 49–50.

and mother in tow!) to serve as state superintendent, winning a dry victory.[27]

Baker and his associates subsequently sought to discredit Dinwiddie by insisting that he was insubordinate. Baker claimed that he had forced the resignation. The national office refused to pay the salary of Dinwiddie's secretary, although it had no evidence of impropriety. Not only were these actions dishonest, but they were potentially harmful to the league's cause. There were great stakes in the Oklahoma referendum, the first in seventeen years; prohibitionists thought that a dry victory would encourage similar results across the South. Most serious, however, were the national implications of the episode.[28]

Dinwiddie returned to Washington to resume lobbying work on behalf of the Good Templars, the Oklahoma Anti-Saloon League, the National Temperance Society, and a new group, the Inter-Church Temperance Federation. The league, meanwhile, had difficulty filling its own position. William Anderson took some time from his duties as Maryland superintendent to be acting legislative superintendent in 1907 and 1908, and in 1909 Baker persuaded S. E. Nicholson to leave his post in Pennsylvania for full-time service in Washington. While the league was operating its Washington office on an ad hoc, part-time basis, Dinwiddie was present, maintaining his contacts with congressmen, encouraging league rivals, and working at cross-purposes with the league's efforts on important matters.[29]

This temperance schism in the lobbies of the nation's capitol and the part-time effort that the league was mounting conformed neither to its claim of providing effective political leadership and practical results nor to the goal of breaking the grip of the party system on national affairs. The party system in Congress was under widespread attack by 1908 from a number of reform sources. The focus of the criticism was the Republican Speaker of the House of Repre-

27. Correspondence relating this episode from May 20 to July 15, 1907, and "Resolutions of the Board of Trustees of the Oklahoma Anti-Saloon League, April 9, 1908," appears in the Nicholson subseries. Baker reported to the convention of 1906 that the league, "deeply interested" in the Oklahoma outcome, had sent Dinwiddie. "More and more must the American League be left free to devote its energies and experienced leadership into crucial contests." *Proceedings, Eleventh Annual Convention, ASLA, 1906*, p. 42.

28. Although both had written Dinwiddie asking him to withdraw his resignation, Russell and Nicholson told Illinois Superintendent James K. Shields that Dinwiddie had been fired. Nov. 12, 1908, Nicholson subseries.

29. "Resolutions of the Board of Trustees of the Oklahoma Anti-Saloon League, April 9, 1908;" Dinwiddie to Nicholson, Aug. 1, 1911, ASLAN.

sentatives, Joseph G. Cannon of Illinois. Cannon and his supporters were opposed to a variety of reforms, including prohibition. Uncle Joe, as he was disapprovingly called, believed that parties should present important issues to the voters in their platforms and enact important legislation only after receiving a mandate. In part this view rested in the traditions of democratic government as they arose in nineteenth-century America, but in part they were rooted in a self-interested resistance to substantive changes in federal legislation. Cannon used his power as Speaker to control the membership and actions of the House committees, where bills of which he disapproved were buried, and to regulate the order of business on the House floor should reformers try to circumvent the committee system.[30]

These practices became a major issue in national politics in 1908, and the Anti-Saloon League was in the forefront of the critics. As far as the league was concerned, the problem with "Cannonism" was that it was effectively preventing consideration and passage of a bill to regulate the interstate shipment of liquors. This bill had been of highest priority to temperance people since the 1880s. Federal law and court decisions allowed persons living in dry territory to import liquor across state lines and even resell it, so long as it stayed in its "original package." The league and its allies wanted a bill to forbid such shipments. It was an emotionally charged issue, for local prohibition statutes mattered little to the distilling industry so long as it could operate across state lines. Cannon, who was personally wet, opposed the legislation, arguing that it was unconstitutional because it allowed the states to regulate interstate commerce. The league responded that the constitutional issue was for the courts, not the Speaker, to decide. League leaders were convinced that if their bill ever reached the House floor it would pass.[31]

But the league could not get the issue squarely before the Congress for a roll call vote. In fact, under Cannon's control of the House, the league and the WCTU had learned that the only way

30. Cannon's own views are expressed in L. W. Busby, *Uncle Joe Cannon* (New York, 1927). George A. Pearce, a representative from Maryland, was convinced he lost his seat on the Judiciary Committee because of his dry views. Pearce to A. E. Shoemaker, Sept. 17, 1909, DCASL.

31. *American Issue* (Ohio ed.), May 30, 1908, p. 11; Sept. 26, 1908, p. 8. A problem was that Representative Charles Littlefield of Maine, the measure's sponsor, was close to Cannon and cooperated with the Speaker in refraining from calling a committee vote. E. J. Webb to John A. Oates, Feb. 5, 1908, ECg.

they could obtain action on temperance legislation was by attaching it to other bills as amendments. That is how they were able to abolish the canteen. In the Oklahoma issue they showed sufficient support to hold up statehood, which the Roosevelt administration sought, until the bill was written to their liking. But their interstate bill was another matter. It was a separate issue that could not logically be attached to some other bill. But Cannon shrewdly insured that it would not come up for a vote. He even changed the membership of the Judiciary Committee to bury it there.[32]

By 1908 the league's only hope of obtaining the interstate bill appeared to lie in breaking the grip of the Speaker over the House and weakening the grip of party government in the Congress. That summer the headquarters committee decided to oppose Cannon's bid for reelection in his downstate district. Realistically, Baker, Anderson, and Cherrington, along with Illinois Superintendent James K. Shields, knew that they had little hope of defeating him; Cannon's previous victory margins were substantial. His district included loyal Republican farmers and small townsmen, and it contained railroad shop workers and coal miners, most of whom had Republican sympathies carefully cultivated by Cannon with his patronage resources. Complicating the league's effort was the bitter opposition of Samuel Gompers of the American Federation of Labor to Cannon. The main legislative goal of the union movement was enactment of a federal law to prevent the use of court injunctions against strikers under the Sherman Anti-Trust statute. Gompers and other labor leaders would campaign against Cannon and thereby alienate rural voters upon whose help the league relied. But even if the drys could not defeat Cannon, the effort seemed necessary. It would encourage George Norris in Nebraska, Cherrington advised, and other insurgent Republicans. If Cannon could not be beaten, other congressmen who did his bidding were more vulnerable, and the league also decided to enter those races, even though its funds were drained in the process. By helping to defeat some of his henchmen and by cutting Cannon's own margin, the House Republicans would have "an object lesson." The fight would present party leaders with "a predicament." They would either have to pass the interstate bill as a party-endorsed measure or suffer the continuing wrath of the prohibitionists. "In short," Anderson noted in outlining this rationale, ". . . there is every reason for fighting him

32. Nicholson to J. S. Dancey, Oct. 24, 1908, ECg.

in his district, regardless of the outcome, and no special reason on the other side."[33]

The campaign effort began in Baltimore in May, where the General Conference of the Methodist Church (North) was meeting. The conference appointed a committee, which included Baker and Anderson, to interview Cannon and express the demands of the "moral forces" for an effective interstate bill. The meeting was unfriendly. Cannon kept trying to obscure the issue by raising arguments about the Constitution and by avoiding direct questions. The delegation reported its failure to the church and urged that all Methodists work to elect representatives who refused to follow the Speaker's lead. As electioneering began in the late summer, the *Northwestern Christian Advocate*, the church's paper published in Chicago, printed condemnations of Cannon by fifteen bishops. The Prohibition party candidate for Cannon's seat withdrew and asked his followers to vote for H. D. Bell, a dry union supporter nominated by the Democrats. The local chapters of the WCTU prepared to lend their assistance. When the league and the La Follette organization in Wisconsin defeated John Jenkins, the chairman of the Judiciary Committee, in the Republican primary, the drys were hopeful that they might actually retire the Speaker as well.[34]

But the optimism of September soon waned, and the national leadership schism that Baker and the headquarters committee provoked in 1907 came back to haunt the league. The problem was that Cannon's actions against league legislation were covert, and it was difficult to explain them to the Republican voters in his district with whom the Speaker had long curried favor. After naming Cannon "the most effective dam to the temperance stream," the Illinois league asked Nicholson, who was serving as both the Pennsylvania superintendent and as national legislative superintendent, to give concrete grounds for the league's opposition. Nicholson disagreed with the decision to enter the race, and he responded with an equivocal statement couched in general language. Privately he complained to Baker that the whole effort endangered his own work in

33. Anderson to Baker, Sept. 10, 1908; Cherrington to Baker, Oct. 14, 1908, ECg; Baker to Nicholson, Oct. 13, 1908, ASLAN. The fight against Cannon led Rockefeller to reduce his league contribution substantially. F. T. Gates to Rockefeller, Oct. 22, 1908; Starr J. Murphy to Rockefeller, Jan. 5, 1909, PPMR.

34. *American Issue* (Ohio ed.), May 16, 1908, pp. 8–9; June 13, 1908, p. 12; July 4, 1908, pp. 11–12; *American Issue* (National ed.) 16 (Sept. 1908):10–12; William R. Gwinn, *Uncle Joe Cannon, Arch Foe of Insurgency* (New York, 1957), pp. 145–58; Blair Bolles, *Tyrant from Illinois* (New York, 1951), pp. 111–12, 150, 161–64.

Pennsylvania, where he was trying to convince Republicans that the league was not antagonistic to the party. So the drys did not have available the kind of specific charges that made good campaign material, only the general complaint against Cannonism. Cannon, concerned about the charges of despotism, arranged to have union leaders endorse him, and most important, for Dinwiddie publicly to deny the league's charges. The lobbyist stated that Cannon had allowed passage of the Oklahoma statehood bill in the form the league had wanted and had not stacked the Judiciary Committee against the drys. The interstate bill could be brought before the House, under the rules, for a vote at any time.[35]

Dinwiddie's statements contradicted ones he had made privately while in the league's employ. While technically they were not falsehoods, they certainly harmed the league's campaign. Cannon won reelection, of course, albeit by a smaller majority than before, and went on to rule the House for the next year and a half before insurgent Republicans took away his power to control the powerful Rules Committee. Dinwiddie's actions discredited the league and encouraged division in the national temperance movement. They also indebted Cannon to him. The debt was paid off in part in 1909 when Congress, with the Speaker's blessing, changed the federal criminal code to forbid COD liquor shipments and shipments to fictitious parties and to require that all packages in interstate commerce be plainly marked with the name of the purchaser intact. Although not a measure it had proposed, the league pronounced the bill a victory for its campaign efforts of 1908, when it forced the congressional Republicans to realize that they must do something on behalf of interstate temperance legislation.[36]

The other part of the debt to Dinwiddie caused more difficulty for the league. The nation's temperance groups had for decades been calling for a federal inquiry into the liquor traffic. But when a bill to

35. *Illinois Issue*, Oct. 2, 1908, p. 1; Nicholson to Cherrington, Oct. 12, 1908; Cherrington to Baker, Oct. 10, Oct. 14 and 16, 1908; Baker to Cherrington, Oct. 13 and 17, 1908; Nicholson to James K. Shields, Sept. 18, Oct. 10 and 30, 1908; Nicholson to J. S. Dancey, Oct. 24, 1908; E. M. Sweet to Cherrington, Oct. 24 and 30, 1908; Cherrington to Sweet, Oct. 31, 1908, ECg; *Chicago Tribune*, Oct. 22, 1908.

36. *American Issue* 16 (Dec. 1908): 7 and 17 (March 1909): 6 (Ohio ed.); Dec. 5, 1908, p. 8; Feb. 27, 1909, pp. 10–12; (Wisc. ed.), IV (May, 1909), p. 10. The fight against Cannon may have actually harmed the league's lobbying efforts in the short run. The name of Charles Littlefield of Maine had been attached to the bill, but he was a Cannon supporter. Littlefield discredited the bill in order to help Cannon as Speaker. In any case, in 1909 Wheeler drafted a new bill for the league. *Proceedings, Thirteenth National Convention, ASLA, 1909*, pp. 26–28.

provide such a commission was introduced at Dinwiddie's request, the league was in the embarrassing position of having to oppose it and of persuading other groups, especially the WCTU, that it was a dangerous measure. The bill would have had the Speaker and the President of the Senate appoint a ten-member commission to inquire into the traffic. Dinwiddie, supposedly, would serve as its chief staff officer. The existence of such a commission would have allowed the distilling and brewing industries to argue that all temperance legislation should be held in abeyance until its findings were complete, and that might well take years while the commissioners and their staff enjoyed federal sinecures. The Republican leaders might well appoint enemies of prohibition and issue a "biased" report. So the league claimed that no such inquiry was necessary, as it once had been, because the prohibition movement had over a generation privately collected more than sufficient information to condemn the liquor traffic.[37]

At the same time the prohibition movement was being divided in the quest for federal legislation, the Anti-Saloon League was facing a serious challenge to its claim to leadership. There had always been prohibition advocates who disliked the league from its inception. Samuel Dickie, national chairman of the Prohibition party, had refused to attend the convention that founded the league in 1895, asserting that it was nothing but a move to protect the established two-party system. The National Temperance Society intensely disliked the new league, which its leaders viewed as a usurper of the society's functions. These elements began to combine in 1906 and 1907 under the leadership of Charles Scanlon, head of the national Presbyterian temperance committee and a party prohibitionist. Their attack on the league struck on its unrepresentative character. The league was an "outside" organization that had improperly imposed itself on the Protestant denominations, its leaders more interested in collecting money from the faithful than in building a grass roots movement for prohibition, these critics said, repeating the usual charges. The movement among the state leagues to have their trustees elected by the churches was insufficient to mollify these critics, who claimed that the league should never have been "im-

---

37. *American Issue* (Ohio ed.), Mar. 6, 1909, p. 11; (Wisc. ed.), IV (March, 1909), pp. 10–11; *Proceedings, Thirteenth National Convention, ASLA, 1909*, pp. 29–31. Wet papers were endorsing the federal inquiry, and in some states they were introducing local versions of the bill that would have suspended all local option elections until findings were issued. William Anderson to E. Y. Webb, June 9, 1909, EYW.

posed" on the churches from the start. Despite the league's claim that the churches could "take it over" at any time they chose, Dickie as late as 1912 complained that the league was "a trust and a monopoly controlled by a few men and utterly undemocratic in its plan of organization."[38] Clearly he and his supporters understood the original intent of the league, even as they disagreed with it.

When Scanlon schemed to have the denominations reject the Anti-Saloon League and form a new organization called the Inter-Church Temperance Federation, he became the unwitting tool of the liquor interests. They had been secretly financing a Rev. U. G. Robinson of St. Louis, who had been fired as Missouri superintendent by Baker, to publish a paper, the *National Issue*, whose principal theme was that the league enriched itself at the expense of the nation's congregations. The wets may also have financed a Detroit investigator, Charles Mabee, at the same time. Mabee surreptitiously tried to gain access to the books and contributor lists of the New York league and, when he failed, he demanded that the national league open its accounts for public inspection. Scanlon used these attacks to fuel his charges that the churches must disaffiliate from the league and form a new organization. In 1907 he arranged for the General Synod of the Presbyterian Church to ask the new Federal Council of Churches to investigate the Anti-Saloon League. The council refused, stating that it had no jurisdiction and did not want to multiply church agencies in any case.[39]

But the federal council's refusal and Baker's offer to open the league's books for inspection by any legitimate church or temperance group did not stop Scanlon. He informed the local Presbyterian synods that the church constitution did not allow them to elect members to the league's board of trustees or to allow league fund raisers access to the local churches. In 1909 the Presbyterian General Synod recommended that local churches refuse access to league fund raisers, and it endorsed the Inter-Church Temperance Federa-

38. Nicholson to Baker, June 2, 1910; Robert N. Turner to Nicholson, Nov. 29, 1911; Dickie to U. G. Robinson, May 13, 1912, ASLAN; Blocker, *Retreat from Reform*, p. 203. William Anderson, "The National Inter-church Temperance Federation," 1911 typescript, ECg. *Proceedings, National Anti-Saloon Convention, 1895*, p. 17. Scanlon had opposed the Pennsylvania league's decision in 1906 not to seek a county option bill. Nicholson to Cherrington, Oct. 18, 1910, ASLAN.

39. Blocker, *Retreat from Reform*, p. 220; *American Issue* (Ohio ed.), Nov. 7, 1908, pp. 11–12; Dec. 5, 1908, pp. 11–13; Dec. 12, 1908, p. 11; Dec. 19, 1908, pp. 11–13; Mar. 6, 1909, p. 11. W. E. Johnson to Cherrington, Mar. 17, 1918, ECe; Charles R. Mabee form letter, Oct. 15, 1908, ECg.

tion. The federation proceeded to arrange with the National Temperance Society and the Good Templars to hire Dinwiddie as superintendent of the bureau of information and legislation.

This situation was hardly conducive to successful lobbying for an interstate bill. Dinwiddie and Nicholson worked at cross-purposes as bitter personal enemies who rarely communicated. Dinwiddie claimed responsibility for the revised penal code that gave state enforcement officers some relief and told congressmen that it should be given a trial before they enacted additional legislation. Nicholson continued to press for the league's bill, working with "regular" Republicans associated with Cannon. This strategy backfired when the insurgent Republicans and the Democratic majority curbed the Speaker's powers in 1910, and the representative who sponsored Nicholson's measure was defeated for renomination that summer, partly because of league opposition. As far as the Senate was concerned, Nicholson learned that he could not arrange for a favorable committee report. The Democrats elected a House majority in 1910, and Nicholson decided to spend the better part of 1911 trying to persuade them that it was to their advantage to enact the league's bill.[40]

Not only was the political complexion of Congress changing rapidly, but so too were the attitudes of prohibition leaders. The Federal Council of Churches endorsed Dinwiddie's work, and pressures mounted from the denominations to end the schism. Congress appointed Nicholson, Dinwiddie, and Cherrington to the American delegation to the International Congress on Alcoholism in 1911, and the three men agreed to suspend their differences and travel together. Members of the headquarters committee discussed holding a conference to unite the Inter-Church Temperance Committee with the league; they saw that Scanlon's group was gaining ground with the churches in its opposition to the league. Cherrington advocated reemploying Dinwiddie as national legislative superintendent. Finally, in conjunction with the league's national convention at the end of the year, the two groups met and settled their differences. The league rehired Dinwiddie; it seemed the simplest way of preventing harm. Nicholson became assistant general superintendent with unspecified duties. To stem criticism, amendments to the

40. Charles A. Littlefield to Mr. Taylor, Oct. 29, 1910; Nicholson to Baker, Aug. 8, 1910, Jan. 19, 1911; Nicholson to Anderson, July 6, 1911, ASLAN; W. M. Grafton to Cherrington, June 26, 1908; Cherrington to Grafton, July 6, 1908; Cherrington to Anderson, July 14, 1909, ECg.

league constitution provided for additional trustees chosen by the churches.[41]

It took more than a year for the reunited temperance forces to achieve a substantial legislative victory. When it came, the victory demonstrated the spectacular strength accrued by the dry coalition in Congress. In January of 1912 a committee of temperance leaders met and agreed on a draft of what eventually became the Webb-Kenyon Act, outlawing interstate liquor shipments into dry areas. Dinwiddie arranged for the bill's introduction in both houses. The danger of wet opposition was twofold. Opponents might somehow hold the bill in committee or delay consideration on the floor by parliamentary maneuver. Once the measure came to vote, the wets would surely offer weakening amendments. Of a veto from President Taft the league had no fear. Taft had invited Baker to consult with him during his term and assured him that he would not oppose interstate regulation of the liquor traffic if Congress desired it.[42]

The bill followed a tortuous path through Congress. Dinwiddie arranged for simultaneous hearings by both Judiciary Committees in March and urged the state leagues to send representatives "to make it the biggest demonstration . . . ever made in behalf of any piece of legislation." But the House Committee reneged, and the Senate postponed a vote until the session that began in December. The delays seemed interminable for the drys. They scheduled a large public gathering in Washington in December designed to impress senators of the wisdom of speedy passage. But once again consideration was delayed. Finally, President-elect Wilson passed the word that he wanted the issue decided, as the league explained, "so that it might not hang over" into his administration and embarrass the incoming Congress.[43]

Finally, in early February 1913 passage came in both houses. Cherrington jubilantly telegraphed the *American Issue*: "Party lines were cut to pieces. Speaker Clark gave a square deal straight through." His euphoria was short-lived: President Taft vetoed the bill on constitutional grounds. Baker charged that the action re-

41. *American Issue* (Ohio ed.), Dec. 23, 1911, p. 10; Nicholson to Cherrington, Aug. 12, 1911, ECg; Anderson to Cherrington, June 27, 1921, ECg; draft form letter, July 17, 1911; Nicholson to Baker, Aug. 14, 1911; Nicholson to Headquarters Committee, Aug. 17, 1911; Nicholson draft letter, Dec. 26, 1911, ASLAN.

42. *American Issue* (Ohio ed.), Jan. 27, 1912, p. 10; Mar. 8, 1913, p. 9.

43. Ibid., Feb. 24, 1912, p. 7; Oct. 12, 1912, p. 11; Dec. 7, 1912, p. 7; Feb. 8, 1913, p. 9.

sulted from a corrupt bargain. In his 1912 reelection bid, faced with the split with Theodore Roosevelt, the president had made a deal with the brewing interests: in exchange for their substantial campaign contributions, he promised to stop any interstate regulation of the liquor trade passed while he was in office. His was a "blundering administration," Baker wrote. Taft was "more to be pitied than blamed."[44]

The president reckoned not with the support of the league in Congress, however. Within two hours of receiving the veto message, the Senate voted to override by a margin of 63 to 21. The next day the House provided "tonic to the temperance forces of the whole country" by its 244 to 95 vote to enact the new law. Now a new wave of prohibition would sweep the nation. The league reported that twelve states were ready to enact prohibition, for no longer could the wets successfully argue that such statutes would simply produce "blind-tigers." Cincinnati distillers were quoted as saying that the law would cost them from $8 to $10 million annually in business.[45]

In 1913 the league's show of strength in the Congress was spectacular. By the time of the victory over President Taft, in spite of organizational difficulties and the constant worry over obtaining funds, the advance of prohibition legislation was widespread. Most of the South and the rural areas of the North and the West were dry either from state laws or successful local option efforts. One-half of the American population lived under some form of prohibition law. The state and local prohibition strategy was successful and now would be abetted by the new interstate shipment law. There was a solid core of dry support in Congress as more and more constituencies expressed their approval of prohibition. The league proceeded almost immediately to prepare for national prohibition by constitutional amendment.

44. Ibid., Feb. 15, 1913, pp. 10–11; Mar. 8, 1913, p. 9.
45. Ibid., p. 4.

6

NATIONAL PROHIBITION STRATEGY

The decision of 1913 to seek what became the Eighteenth Amendment signified that the Anti-Saloon League was in a position to operate on a national scale as a political arm of American envangelical Protestantism. The decision, moreover, was taken at a time of general reform, "progressivism," that proved, in retrospect, special in American history. Public sentiment favorable to prohibition appeared to be growing as part of a more general reform consensus among Protestant Americans. Most important for the league as a reform organization, almost all prohibitionists were accepting its leadership and nonpartisan methods. With the league's own internal problems in its Washington legislative office apparently resolved, with a new administration entering the White House determined to achieve important social and economic reforms, and with so much of the nation's territory already under dry statutes, not only did conditions seem favorable for the national campaign, but a constitutional amendment was apparently the only practical method of exercising control over the large urban areas that resisted all dry reform efforts.

The campaign for national prohibition involved much more than electioneering and lobbying. The campaign reshaped the Anti-Saloon League in important ways. The league needed to enlarge the dry constituency, a task that required a far larger organization and one supplied by adequate funds. The league needed to reach out to persons who did not attend services regularly in the Protestant churches. The league had, in short, to mount a tremendous educational and propaganda campaign to expand public support while maintaining its strength in the areas that had already chosen to outlaw the liquor traffic. The requirements that flowed from the decision to seek the amendment led to the creation of an organization that rested less on local efforts and more on the work of a staff

139

organized and funded by the national office. The national campaign also led to the rapid rise of Ernest Cherrington.

National prohibition was not a new goal, but before 1913 it remained a dream. The league had always asserted that the liquor traffic was national, even international, in its operations, and with other temperance groups it had argued that control required the power of the federal government. Russell and the other men and women who had founded the league had consistently and publicly asserted that national prohibition was their ultimate objective. But now, after twenty years of struggle on the state and local level, and with a major congressional victory in hand, for the first time it seemed possible.

Nevertheless, there was some inconsistency in league rhetoric on the subject. League publicists were opportunistic, and when the organization was a fledgling and struggling to achieve local option legislation, they played down their interest in more sweeping legislation. Local option laws, they told legislators who were reluctant to antagonize wet voters and business organizations, were simply a device to allow "home rule" so that a neighborhood or community could decide for itself whether or not it wanted saloons. But when the focus of the reform shifted away from the local level, those arguments no longer applied. In fact, after 1913 the league found itself facing its own "home rule" arguments from the brewing and liquor interests, who were defending the rights of cities to enjoy saloon services. When the battleground changed to statewide and then national prohibition, the league claimed that those Americans, increasingly a majority, who lived in dry territory should not have to pay the social costs of the remaining saloons. This was the classic doctrine of modern American reformers, that the majority had the right to impose its will on the minority, however recalcitrant, in order to achieve the higher social good. State prohibition became, in league rhetoric, just another form of local option, limited in effectiveness so long as the liquor traffic was allowed anywhere in the nation.

But there was another, more practical political consideration that may have entered into the calculations to seek national prohibition. In individual election campaigns the league customarily had followed a "balance of power" strategy, mobilizing dry voters to favor selected candidates in hopes of providing the margin of victory. The technique was successful in building dry majorities in state legislatures. But beginning in Ohio in 1908, the wets were sometimes able to circumvent it by shifting the issue to public referendums.

The league was among the reform organizations that had promoted the referendum as a device allowing "the people" to rule themselves apart from the machinations of the party system and its links to "special interests" like the brewers and distillers. But now in states where urban and wet populations were rapidly growing, the referendum, always a two-edged sword that both reformers and their opponents could use, threatened to damage the dry cause, and the league's hopes of drying up districts heavily populated by immigrants dimmed. But in a national amendment campaign the balance of power strategy would again be effective as the league worked for the election of sympathetic congressmen and then for ratification by state legislatures.[1]

The Decision for National Prohibition

League leaders began to express thoughts of taking advantage of the traditional balance of power technique in a national prohibition campaign at least a year before enactment of the Webb-Kenyon bill. Then the congressional victory convinced Baker that it was time to propose the new venture seriously. "The Time Has Come," the *American Issue* announced in March 1913, and in April, when the headquarters committee met, Baker suggested "The Next and Final Step," testing reaction to such a momentous effort. He reminded the committee of the policy always "to go just as fast and just as far as public sentiment would justify." All signs were favorable. One-half of Americans living in two-thirds of the nation had the benefit of dry laws. The liquor traffic "no longer has advocates; it must depend for its existence upon partisans." The old argument that liquor taxes were essential revenue sources no longer applied in view of the ratification of the federal income tax amendment. Congress had shown its capability of responding to the people's clearly expressed wish. Nevertheless, he told the league's constituency to expect the campaign to last for twenty years.[2]

1. Lloyd Sponholtz, "The Politics of Temperance in Ohio, 1880–1912," *Ohio History* 85 (Winter 1976): 4–27, suggests that the brewers' successful use of referendums pushed the league toward seeking national prohibition. For a general study of the uses of both the initiative and the referendum, key parts to what historians have traditionally construed as "progressive" reform, see Lloyd Sponholtz, "The Initiative and Referendum: Direct Democracy in Perspective," *American Studies* 14 (Fall 1973): 43–64. One example of the league's continuing success with the referendum was the state of Washington. See Clark, *The Dry Years*, pp. 128–43.

2. W. E. Johnson, "Columbus Convention 1913," typescript, July 19, 1932, HH; Minutes, Headquarters Committee, April 22, 1913, ECe.

It was the American city that most concerned Baker and that led
him and the committee to agree that the "next step" for the league
was the "final" one. We face "peril" from the cities, Baker warned.
The vices of cities were always "the undoing of past empires and
civilizations," and some in America were "well-nigh submerged." To
make matters worse, the general superintendent and his advisors
were aware that the political sophistication of the brewers was
growing. They were engaged in a self-reform movement that was
removing some of the more objectionable features of the saloon.
Their investments in political activities, heavier than ever, were
holding off the league in states with large urban populations unsympathetic to the evangelism of the prohibitionists. The only way to
break the grip of the saloon in states like Ohio, where the wet and
urban population balanced closely with the dry and rural peoples,
was to turn to a federal solution. "If our republic is to be saved,"
Baker warned, "the liquor traffic must be destroyed."[3]

The headquarters committee "enthusiastically adopted" the new
strategy and recommended it to the league's trustees. After the
board's approval, Cherrington and Baker began to orchestrate the
public announcement, to climax at the national convention in Columbus commemorating the league's twentieth anniversary. Cherrington asked local churches to enroll as "outposts" in the campaign,
their pastors reading the league proclamation to their congregations
on Sunday, September 7. Each outpost church would display a new
league poster each week, presenting arguments for national prohibition. Prohibition Sunday was November 9. Each preacher would
have a thirty-two page league booklet providing material for ser-
mons, while Sunday school members signed the abstinence pledge
and young people's societies enjoyed a special prohibition program.
Then, from November 10 to 13 was "The Mammoth Twenty Year
Jubilee Convention" in Columbus. The 5,000 delegates were expected to report on its events in their home churches on the following Sunday.[4]

When the delegates gathered in Columbus, Baker related some of
the considerations that had led to the announcement. Dry workers
would have to discipline themselves as never before for the fight.
"Reforms cannot move in a circle—they must progress or die
speedily." The state and local campaigns had succeeded in building
dry public sentiment, but victory awaited national action lest "polit-

3. Minutes, Headquarters Committee, April 22, 1913, ECe.
4. Johnson, "Columbus Convention 1913."

ical exigencies or the delinquency of party candidates" imperil dry laws. Dinwiddie noted that other organizations had called for national prohibition, even succeeding on one occasion in the 1880s in having such a measure reported to the Senate. The difference now was that the league was placing the issue "squarely before the people in a practical and effective form." It was not "a mere paper declaration."[5]

To press the issue, the prohibitionists formed a Committee of 1,000 to meet on the steps of the Capitol in Washington. There Cherrington presented a draft of the resolution to Congressman Richard P. Hobson of Alabama, who would introduce it in the House. Malcolm R. Patterson, the wet governor of Tennessee who had converted to the dry cause, gave it to Senator Morris Sheppard of Texas. "It was a great event," one observer recalled. "Thousands stood in the chill December air."[6]

Apart from the public symbolism of gathering on the Capitol steps, the league leaders believed that their national campaign would be long and hard, lasting for upward of a generation. "The same political policies that have won township, municipal, county and state prohibition will win national prohibition," Baker advised his followers. Two steps were required: a vote by two-thirds majorities in both houses of Congress to submit an amendment, followed by successful campaigns in thirty-six states for ratification. The first step would prove most difficult for the league. The drys had to interrogate each candidate for House and Senate, publish, and, where necessary, interpret his replies. This in itself was a mammoth task, made all the more difficult by the intrusion of other large national issues. The politicians, Baker noted, will tell us "that there are other very important issues" that should take precedence. "We have been told that for fifty years," he reminded his listeners. "Experience has proven that the nearer men are right on this question the nearer they are right on every great question that affects the welfare of humankind." After the league elected sufficient majorities to have Congress submit the amendment to the states, it could concentrate its resources on them one at a time. In the meantime, the league had to maintain agitation for statewide prohibition to enhance its chances of electing cooperative congressmen.[7]

5. *Proceedings, Fifteenth National Convention. ASLA, 1913*, pp. 51, 56−70.

6. W. E. Johnson, "The Council of 100 and the Committee of 1,000," typescript, July 20, 1932, HH.

7. *Proceedings, Fifteenth National Convention, ASLA, 1913*, pp. 56−70; *American Issue* 21 (March 1913): 3−4.

Cherrington and National Strategy

It was one matter to decide to seek an amendment to the U.S. Constitution and then orchestrate the announcement. A far more important task was the consideration of the appropriate winning strategy for the complexities of national politics. Ernest Cherrington was the central figure in the planning of the campaign and in rearranging and adding to the league's structure for its conduct. Less well known to subsequent generations of Americans than to reformers and churchmen during the Progressive era, Cherrington, by the time the Eighteenth Amendment was submitted for ratification, had involved himself in every aspect of the league's work, save its legal affairs, to the point of personal exhaustion and bitter criticism from his patron, Purley Baker. In fact, after 1916 Cherrington was de facto in charge of the headquarters while Baker lived in semiretirement in Alabama.

Cherrington was most visible as general manager of the *American Issue* and the *Yearbooks* that appeared annually after 1908. Cherrington's position led him into other roles: gathering the information upon which the league based decisions, shaping those strategy considerations, and raising the money and organizing the personnel to carry them out.

A devout Methodist, Cherrington was a layman who brought a levelheaded sense of the practical to Howard Russell's dream of a great, businesslike temperance organization. Like so many other college-educated persons of his generation, Cherrington was a pragmatist who looked at the facts of political power, constituent support, and the financial requirements of political victory. Throughout his career with the league, which did not end until his death in 1950, Cherrington developed a consistent viewpoint toward the movement to which he dedicated his life. He combined a sense of reality with an idealistic vision of society freed from the vices of the liquor traffic. Prohibition would eventuate only after an ever-larger proportion of Americans was persuaded that it was a wise policy for them personally, for their state and nation, and eventually, for all mankind. Moreover, winning dry laws helped education work, just as the reverse was true. As more and more citizens witnessed the social benefits of prohibition firsthand, they would agree to obey the law as well as to seek it. Cherrington's special contribution to the prohibition movement was to express this vision. The Anti-Saloon League failed to follow his advise only after the Eighteenth Amendment was ratified, and that failure in the 1920s contributed to the organization's decline.

Cherrington and other national league leaders defined their political problem as a city problem. Their rhetoric was full of references to an urban-rural division in American society, with the cities resisting the rural desire for prohibition. Subsequent observers, some of them scholars, adopted this rhetoric to analyze the conflict over prohibition as one between country and city. But for Cherrington and his contemporaries, the description was simply a shorthand way of observing religious and ethnic differences within the population that had to be conquered to secure the reform. They recognized their political problem as not one simply of cracking the resistance of cities—the Anti-Saloon League had large support within cities—but of somehow reaching out to the burgeoning immigrant populations who had come to live and work in urban America. Cherrington explained this situation in a series of tables in the 1913 *Yearbook* and analyzed the problem in *A New Plan of Campaign*, printed in 1913 for consideration by league officials.[8] The perception of the tidal waves of immigrants coming to American cities shaped the decision to seek constitutional prohibition, the strategy of the campaign, and the timetable required.

Cherrington's observation of America's teeming immigrant populations led him to conclude that the league's work had barely begun. Prior to 1913, he asserted, even the "splendid victories and successes" of the drys had been "mere skirmishes." Those immigrants—the workers and working-class families—had to be reached in a sophisticated and coordinated effort. He realized that there would remain Americans who were recalcitrant wets, and that the league was unlikely to achieve majority support in immigrant neighborhoods. National prohibition would involve an element of coercion. But at the very least, he continued, the league needed to provide convincing arguments to the wet people of the cities for them to understand prohibition as a reasonable approach to serious social problems, to the betterment of mankind. Otherwise their resistance would allow the liquor traffic to retain a foothold of corruption. It was of little use, he warned in 1911, to enact prohibition laws in places where public sentiment made enforcement unlikely. In his view, the league

8. *A New Plan of Campaign in the Interest of National Prohibition* (n.p., 1913).

must pay attention to law enforcement but its "real mission" was to insure wide public support for the dry policy.[9]

As Cherrington explained in his *New Plan of Campaign*, the requirements of national dry strategy were thus first and foremost educational. The league needed literature prepared in twenty languages and placed in the hands of every city resident. Billboard advertising along thoroughfares and inside streetcars would reach the masses who did not, or could not, read. The league needed to help Americans already convinced of the righteousness of the dry cause to prepare to speak effectively when they encountered doubtful or dissident citizens in the course of their daily lives. It the league could own ten daily mass circulation newspapers in strategically chosen urban centers it would insure a fair hearing for prohibition.

Cherrington was not proposing, however, to convert the league from a political organization to a crusading temperance propaganda mill, but rather to combine the two functions effectively. The drys had to win new converts and then mobilize them on election day. He observed that successful political machines had knowledge of each individual voter, his preferences, affiliations, friendships, and occupations. The league should marshal an organization reaching every sympathetic voter if it was to win outside of the existing partisan framework.

The vision was grandiose—but Cherrington argued that it was realistic. As he examined the required budget, he concluded that the league needed to raise $5 million a year for five years to accomplish the task. Such an amount contrasted sharply with the more modest current expenditures of the state and national leagues of $1 million per year, but the $25 million goal was still achievable. American churches annually raised $30 million for foreign missionary work. Surely, he asserted, the appeal, properly presented and organized, of destroying the organized liquor traffic within America's borders would provide one-sixth of that amount.[10]

The league never adopted Cherrington's *A New Plan of Campaign* as an official strategy statement. But the plan had Baker's backing. The general superintendent had already warned of the need to expand dry sentiment.[11] So the league proceeded on the course Cherrington outlined in 1913, embarking on new fund-raising and publishing ventures under his direction. These policies led to a

9. Ibid.; untitled speech, ECg.
10. *A New Plan of Campaign.*
11. *Proceedings, Thirteenth National Convention, ASLA, 1909,* pp. 44–46.

reorganization, not only in the addition of new departments but in the reshaping of the league as a national institution that did not necessarily rest on state and local bodies.

Structural Changes for a National Strategy

Cherrington, Baker, and the other members of the headquarters committee knew that the national campaign required some important structural changes. Some developments they planned in 1913, but others evolved slowly over the next several years. Some educational programs never fully materialized because the campaign lasted but six, not the expected twenty years.

The leaders realized even before they launched the national strategy that the league faced serious internal problems. Simply expressed, the league was well organized in some states, most notably Ohio, to raise money and mobilize voters. But in other areas it was little more than a paper organization. Nicholson was most concerned, warning that "public sentiment that is unorganized . . . amounts practically to no public sentiment at all." Some southern states had enacted prohibition without developing a grass-roots political movement, and others, like Kansas and Oklahoma, saw the involvement of citizens wane. In fact, in 1914, the Illinois and Ohio leagues led the nation in fund raising, and the majority of states paid less to the national headquarters than they received. The league virtually had to write off some wet strongholds like Wisconsin, whose league president reported in 1915 that his office was in debt and suffering politically in the legislature. "We all rejoice in the great progress the work is making," he told Cherrington, "and we believe Wisconsin will share in this success, though more slowly than most states.[12]

The national office tried to strengthen state organizations, with mixed results. New York and New England were weak spots. Russell had failed to build a successful league in New York. Finally, in 1914 Baker assigned Anderson, one of his two or three most able officers, as state superintendent. Anderson wrote off the Empire State Democratic party as hopelessly under the influence of Tammany Hall. Working with the Republicans, he won a local option law in 1917 and, most important for the national effort, enlarged the organization, erased its debt, and began contributing substantial sums to the national office. But elsewhere the story was less happy for the

12. *American Issue* 20 (October 1912): 10–11; "1914 Receipts"; L. H. Keller to Cherrington, ECe.

league. When Wayne Wheeler visited Vermont just before its 1915 referendum on prohibition, he found that the local league was not prepared for the campaign. Alarmed, the national headquarters rushed a man to the scene, but it was too late, and the measure failed.[13] In fact, all New England leagues disappointed Baker.

If the problem was an uneven distribution of zeal and organization, the solution that emerged was for the national headquarters to dominate the league more and more. After 1913 the league became less a movement rooted in specific locations, addressing itself to political conditions peculiar to individual states, and more a centrally directed national organization. This evolution conformed to the dictates of a national campaign, of course, but it did not result from conscious planning. Instead it was a practical response to immediate problems. The result by the time the United States entered the First World War in 1917 was a national hierarchy funded and administered on national terms.

The most noticeable change was the adoption of a new constitution in 1913. This action, as we have seen, was partly a response to the persistent cricitcism that the league was an oligarchy of a few self-appointed superintendents, but it was also partly a plan to insure that the drys could reach down to the local level in every part of the nation. The new constitution did not empower new leaders— the same men were running the league—but rather transformed the method of financing their work. Whereas in the past state leagues had customarily turned over 2½ percent of their total receipts to the national headquarters, now they were to pay a much larger share, on a sliding scale according to the amount collected. The national league in turn assumed the burden of paying the salaries of the state superintendents, insuring the appointment of an active person in every state. The funding scheme removed control from the states, while forcing the better organized, more populous states to send funds to support operations in the less populous, more poorly organized regions. The latter states would provide a significant share of the congressional support for prohibition.[14]

At the same time the system of distributing funds was changing, the method of collecting money was undergoing a dramatic transfor-

13. Wheeler to National Executive Committee, March 18, 1916, ECe; William H. Anderson to Superintendents, May 22, 1917, HH.
14. There were some state leagues that resisted approving the new constitution. The executive committee used its ability to raise funds "to insist" on cooperation. Minutes, Executive Committee, June 3, 1914, ECe.

mation. The national headquarters assumed an ever-growing share
of the task of raising money, and after the adoption of the new
constitution it was the national office rather than the states that
systematically raised the large sums necessary to promote national
prohibition. In 1912 the american league was still troubled by debts,
especially in its publishing operations. The dry leaders had been
aware of the large sums that the brewers, distillers, and dealers had
invested in politics over the years. To offset their economic power,
Baker wanted to appeal for more substantial contributions from
wealthy patrons. So, as general manager of the American Issue
Publishing Company, Cherrington arranged for a special fund-
raising campaign to occur outside of the annual Anti-Saloon Sunday
solicitations in the churches. The Westerville office arranged special
meetings with potential contributors and provided a prominent
speaker. These appeals allowed the league to cancel its debts and still
enjoy continuing payments on pledges.[15]

This success turned the leaders to thoughts of restructuring
league finances entirely. The executive committee saw the role of
small contributors as central to the work of building electoral support. The result in 1913 was the creation of a new department, a
committee on financial management, headed by Cherrington. In
this role, Cherrington sought to expose the general public to
speeches, to increase the circulation of league publications, "to secure a contributing constituency different and larger than the regular constituency of the State organizations," and, of course, to supply
a steady flow of large sums. The league needed more money, as
Cherrington noted, "on account of the rapidly increasing public
sentiment over the country and the pressing and insistent demands
for more aggressive work."[16]

Under Cherrington's management, the new department quickly
and efficiently began generating large numbers of contributions. By
1916 it employed sixty persons and spent from $27,000 to $30,000
monthly to enlist subscriptions averaging $250,000 monthly. League
employees arranged for meeting halls, bought advertising, and
booked speakers for regional tours. When a person pledged to give
money, he received a subscription to the *American Issue* or some
other publication in return. When the Westerville headquarters

15. Cherrington to Filmore Condit, April 21, 1916, ECe.
16. *Ibid.* Baker appealed to wealthy patrons by advising them that it did little good
for them to finance YMCA halls and other urban missions without also eliminating
the saloon scourge that made those missions necessary. *Proceedings, Fifteenth National
Convention, ASLA, 1913*, pp. 56–70.

actually received the money, it deducted the expenses of the campaign, paid its bill to the American Issue Publishing Company, and turned half of the balance over to the league in the state where the contributor resided.[17]

The flow of large sums that resulted, along with the legislative success of the prohibition movement, worked to reshape the league structure. In dry states, local leaders reported that they were unable to sustain popular interest except insofar as supporters saw the need to maintain the amendment campaign. This led to a movement toward the "nationalization" of the state league. Under this scheme the national headquarters assumed all responsibilities for a state anti-saloon league, whose staff members became national employees. They then devoted at least half of their time to the national fund-raising efforts. By the end of 1918 there were thirteen nationalized states where local interest in the state league had dimmed, but where the national officers wanted to maintain a presence "to keep in line the Congressional representation . . . on all National prohibition legislation."[18]

Propagandizing a Nation

By 1913 there were indications that public sentiment for prohibition was growing. Not only were the congressional victory and the extension of dry territory under state and local laws signs of the popularity of prohibition, but support in the popular media seemed to be on the upswing. In 1910 American writers had become fascinated with the potentialities of achieving a more "efficient" nation of social harmony and industrial progress based upon the insights of scientists and engineers. Articles appeared in mass circulation magazines that coupled prohibition with the larger social good. Cherrington promoted prohibition as part of the popular search for efficiency. Under his direction the prohibition movement became involved as never before in the dissemination of knowledge about alcohol abuse. That dissemination would take several forms, all shaped by the American Issue Publishing Company.[19]

17. Cherrington to Condit, April 21, 1916; Milo G. Kelser to Cherrington, April 12, 1917, ECg.
18. H. B. Carre´ to Baker, Mar. 8, 1917; Minutes, Executive Committee, April 5, 1917; Boyd P. Doty to Condit, June 18, 1918, ECe; Kelser to Cherrington, Dec. 3, 1918, and Feb. 8, 1919, ECg.
19. On the interest in efficiency, see Samuel Haber, *Efficiency and Uplift: Scientific Management in the Progressive Era* (Chicago, 1964). On its relationship to the prohibi-

The firm was the central league agency for the conduct of the campaign. It had begun in 1909 when the citizens of Westerville, Ohio, donated $10,000 to purchase land for a building to house printing presses. No longer having to rely on job printers proved a bonanza for the league. Now owning its own plant, it scheduled the printing of the many state editions of the *American Issue* efficiently and kept the presses constantly producing pamphlets and books. In 1915 Cherrington reported assets of $164,000 and a regular payroll of 156 employees. During the autumn of 1914 the Westerville presses produced ten tons of printed matter each day.[20] The assets and staff permitted the company to perform two essential functions. The firm's capital carried the league between the time pledges were made and donations were actually received. Its staff handled the large volume of mail and bookkeeping that the committee on financial management generated and served as a research arm for the collection of information and the preparation of articles, pamphlets, and posters.

One aspect of the widespread public concern with efficiency related to industrial and personal safety in a society where technological complexity was rapidly increasing. Part of the concern, moreover, related to the efforts of manufacturers to gain greater control over their industrial workers, to rationalize factories not only with machinery, but carefully and "scientifically" to integrate the workers' routine with machinery. The league skillfully adapted the traditional dry ideology to this modern movement.

In 1912 Cherrington established the safety and efficiency bureau. It prepared materials "dealing with the scientific phases of the liquor question in simple and easily understandable terms." Its audience was "laymen of all classes" but especially of "the industrial class." The bureau developed a course of study with monthly lessons and distributed it to classes across the United States and Canada. It worked through employers, most notably the U. S. Steel Corporation and the Reo Motor Car Company, to distribute circulars in pay envelopes. Reo Motor even paid for its 4,500 employees to hear an hour's lecture on prohibition, efficiency, and safety on company time. Cherrington considered the program so successful—in 1915 it

tion movement, see Timberlake, *Prohibition and the Progressive Movement, 1900–1920*, pp. 39–66. On educational plans, see H. B. Carre´ to Baker and Cherrington, July 26, 1916, ECe.

20. "Report of the General Manager, American Issue Publishing Company, July 5, 1915," AIP, roll 13.

circulated 600,000 leaflets among industrial workers—that in 1916 he urged each state league to form its own department of safety, health and child welfare.[21]

Cherrington hoped to reach workers and their families through the union movement as well. The league leaders, along with so many social gospel advocates, were sympathetic toward organized labor, which Baker once termed "fundamentally a holy crusade." There was, moreover, a tradition of temperance sentiment in the American union movement. The unions belonging to the American Federation of Labor, for the most part, promoted temperance among their members and sought in their meetings and publications to counteract the influence of the liquor business. Prominent members of the AFL's executive council favored suppression of the saloon. But by 1908 the union leaders were placing highest priorities on achieving legislation exempting unions from the federal antitrust law and providing for a cabinet-level Department of Labor. Nevertheless, Cherrington hoped to mobilize the movement's temperance sentiment by creating a special labor bureau, publishing a special paper, *The Worker*, and employing Charles Stelzle, the nation's most prominent labor minister, to run them. Stelzle, who had grown up in the tenement district of New York's Lower East Side, was a machinist before studying for the ministry and operating the Presbyterians' department of church and labor. He was devoted to prohibition and to the scientific "survey" of social conditions. Stelzle had a successful career in urban missions designed to reach the poor and the worker.[22]

Stelzle's message was clear, both in the pamphlets and in the monthly paper he prepared for the Westerville presses. Prohibition helped the workingman escape poverty and achieve security. "Every time [a worker] comes out of a saloon he's a lot poorer than when he went in." Prohibition would result in higher wages because employ-

21. "Report of the General Manager, American Issue Publishing Company, June 26, 1916," AIP, roll 13. On employers' concerns with rationalizing work routines with technologically advanced machinery, the studies of labor historians are especially instructive. See Herbert Gutman, "Work, Culture and Society in Industrializing America, 1815–1919," *American Historical Review* 78 (June 1973): 531–88, and, for the workers' responses, David Montgomery, "The New Unionism and the Transformation of Consciousness in America, 1909–1922," *Journal of Social History* 7 (Summer 1974): 509–27.

22. Charles Stelzle, *A Son of the Bowery* (New York, 1926), pp. 167–75; *Proceedings, Thirteenth National Convention, ASLA, 1909*, pp. 44–46; Minutes Executive Committee, July 5, 1915; Cherrington to William F. Cochran, Jan. 28, 1916, ECe; Timberlake, *Prohibition and the Progressive Movement*, pp. 87–94.

ers preferred to hire the sober; the less qualified drinking class held down pay scales. "The efforts of Trade Unionists to maintain a fair standard of wages are made more difficult by the men who drink." Workers suffered from an unfair share of the tax burden; prohibition would lower the costs of police and jails and thereby reduce taxes. The brewers and distillers were simply "greedy capitalists" complaining that dry laws were ruinous. But prohibition would help workers, for money formerly spent in saloons would create jobs elsewhere. Stelzle understood the opposition of the skilled brewery workers but told them that they should readjust to jobs in other industries rather than be part of the moral evils of the saloon system. When the Brewery Workers' Union influenced the AFL to protest the prohibition movement, Stelzle asked, "Shall the saloon dominate the labor movement, when every decent organization and institution is breaking loose from the power of the saloon?" He wanted workers to believe that the prohibitionists were simply concerned with their welfare.[23]

But Stelzle's work was frustrating. He was unable to establish a solid link with the AFL. The problem was threefold. The Brewery Workers' Union fought him. The league had a poor reputation among workers, who generally viewed it as an employers' agent trying to control their lives. Nor was the league in a position to cultivate the favor of union leaders. When Stelzle surveyed the state superintendents asking for names of labor leaders to whom he could explain the labor bureau's plans, almost all state headquarters ignored his request. "It seems that comparatively few of the State Superintendents desire to conduct their work upon a larger social basis," he concluded, "having in mind a constructive program, as well as a destructive propaganda."[24]

Without a solid base of support within the league, Stelzle made little headway with the unions. In 1909, at the AFL convention, he had suggested the formation of a temperance fellowship, modeled on one in Great Britain, among labor leaders. About half of the delegates expressed an interest, but Stelzle dropped the matter when Samuel Gompers warned that interjecting the prohibition

---

23. *The Worker* 1 (Jan.–Feb. 1916): 1–4. Stelzle's arguments appear in a series of undated pamphlets published by the American Issue Publishing Co. See "Why Should the Workingman be Liquor's 'Goat?' "; "Why the Workingman Must Be Interested in the Liquor Traffic"; "Poverty. The Principal Product of the Saloon"; "Shall the Saloon Dominate the Labor Movement?"; and "Will One Million Workingmen Lose their Jobs If the Saloons are Closed?"

24. Stelzle to Cherrington, May 4, 1916, ECg.

issue would seriously split the labor movement. In return, Gompers promised to use his influence to have the federation refrain from passing the brewery workers' resolutions condemning prohibition. Gompers did so until 1919, when prohibition was an imminent reality. Frustrated on all sides, Stelzle left the league to work with the Federal Council of Churches on matters of broad social concern, including prohibition, and the labor bureau was abandoned. Not until the campaign to secure ratification of the amendment did the national league again attempt to establish links with union officials.[25]

The league's educational efforts among urban workers went beyond the abortive efforts to gain the help of the unions. In cooperation with other temperance organizations, the league sought to reach immigrants directly in their native languages, as already noted. The prohibition movement worked to supply pastors in churches serving immigrant neighborhoods with temperance materials, including the "best European scientific arguments for abstinence." The league planned to employ foreign language lecturers to visit immigrant communities. By 1916, working with the Federal Council of Churches, the American Issue Publishing Company was printing pamphlets in fifteen languages. "I hope the time may come," Cherrington told a correspondent, "when the League will be strong enough financially to have a German paper of its own and perhaps a paper published in three or four other languages." His dream, however, never materialized.[26]

In sharp contrast to its experience with the unions, the league enjoyed a fabulous success in attracting the support of American businessmen. The work of the safety and efficiency bureau was attractive to industrialists, and in 1915 the league issued a special invitation to businessmen to meet with the league at its national convention in Atlantic City. Under the leadership of S. S. Kresge, the dime store magnate, the manufacture and business committee of the league developed rapidly. By mid-1918 it consisted of about 14,000 businessmen who had responded to Kresge's appeal for funds.[27]

25. Timberlake, *Prohibition and the Progressive Movement*, p. 90; Cherrington to William F. Cochran, Jan. 28, 1916; Cochran to Cherrington, Feb. 3, 1916; Cherrington to James Cannon, April 18, 1918, ECe.

26. Cherrington to L. E. Kirkpatrick, Feb. 18, 1916, ECe; Minutes, Executive Committee, Council of 100, Dec. 9, 1913, STF, roll 42; *Annual Reports of the Federal Council of Churches of Christ in America* (New York, 1915), p. 128.

27. Undated, Untitled document, ECg; Minutes, Executive Committee, ASLA, Jan. 6, 1916; Anna W. Demart to Cherrington, June 12, 1918, ECe.

The main business of the publishing company, of course, re-mained the production of regular league papers, by 1915 at the annual rate of eighteen million copies. "The movement for national prohibition is really just beginning," Cherrington reported. Even that large volume was "insignificant" when compared "to the work which must be done before national prohibition is possible." He recognized that the *American Issue* had limitations. The *Issue*, he noted when he took charge in 1909, reached one of every twenty-seven families in the United States, or one in every three hundred persons. This circulation was insufficient. The problem, apart from limited financial resources, was that the paper had too little space and alone could not do the full job of reaching new readers. In some states it was published weekly; in others monthly—but in any case it was too infrequent to serve as a newspaper. "It is peculiarly a class paper, published in the interests of propaganda," he noted. Yet it had to cut across the line of party, social class, and religion in its appeals.[28]

The solution that Cherrington chose was diversification. In 1912 he established a new monthly magazine, the *American Patriot*, as a general interest, "educational periodical" that included depart-ments for women and children. In 1913 he recruited William E. "Pussyfoot" Johnson to serve as managing editor of all publications and to begin a new weekly, the *New Republic*, and, eventually, the *National Daily*. Johnson was both an experienced journalist and a famous prohibition fighter. As United States marshall in Indian territory under Presidents Roosevelt and Taft, he had earned his nickname with stealthy night raids on bootleggers and speakeasies. Quick on the draw in capturing bandits, he fearlessly confronted the saloon interests, first as a worker for the Prohibition party and later as editor for the league. The *New Republic*, which the league pub-lished from 1913 through 1916, was "most popular" for use in special fund-raising campaigns. The *National Daily*, on the other hand, distributed national political and temperance news to the editors of general interest magazines and newspapers. Its purpose, noted a contributing editor, was "to challenge the vision of busy men and women at their breakfast tables to higher things than wars and stocks and sports and offices to the *REAL VICTORIES THAT OVERCOME THE WORLD*." The publishing company even purchased a building in Washington, D.C., to house its presses. But by the end of 1916 it was apparent that capital was insufficient, and with the widespread

28. Cherrington, "The Year Book, the National Issue, and the Printing Plant," 1909 speech, ECg; "Report of the General Manager, July 5, 1915," AIP, roll 13.

victories in state prohibition campaigns that autumn, the comfortable majorities apparently elected to the next Congress, the league consolidated all its papers into an expanded edition of the *American Issue*.[29]

New Temperance Alliances

The campaign for national prohibition involved more than changing and expanding the organization, publishing, and fund raising of the Anti-Saloon League. Other temperance groups were still in the field, and closer cooperation among them would assist the victory. The Anti-Saloon League was the dominant political and propaganda organization, but other groups were still important in swaying the nation to adopt an amendment.

In the spring of 1913 Cherrington began working with Daniel A. Poling to form the National Council of One Hundred as a coordinating body. Poling, who ran for governor of Ohio in 1912 on the Prohibition party ticket, had close links to all of the church temperance groups as well as to the league. A minister in the Reformed Church, he served for many years as the temperance superintendent of the United Society of Christian Endeavor, a large interdenominational evangelical organization that encouraged young people to model their lives according to church precepts. Poling served as chairman of the council, Cherrington as secretary, and they quickly succeeded in enlisting the support of well over a hundred other prominent persons. Poling and Cherrington called a convention of all temperance leaders to follow the league's twentieth anniversary celebration in Columbus. The plan was to coordinate all educational efforts and aim them at the cities.[30]

The meeting attracted widespread support, and the group, which soon called itself the National Temperance Council, voted to confer regularly. As it evolved, the council served as a clearinghouse of information and propaganda techinques. At the end of 1915 the council appointed a committee of nineteen, headed by James Cannon of the league, to revise the wording of the proposed amendment.[31] By this time there was close cooperation among all

29. *Standard Encyclopedia of the Alcohol Problem*, 3:1408–13; "Valourous Pussyfoot," unmarked clipping, Otterbein College Library; *National Daily*, June 3, 1915, p. 4; "Report of General Manager, July 5, 1915 and June 26, 1916," AIP, roll 13.

30. Daniel Poling et al., form letter, June 20, 1913, ECg; "An Epoch-Making Call," STF, roll 42; *Standard Encyclopedia of the Alcohol Problem*, 5:2175–76, and 6:2717–18.

31. Minutes, Council of One Hundred, Dec. 10, 1913, and National Temperance Council, Dec. 11, 1915, STF, roll 42.

prominent temperance organizations, except for a minority in the Prohibition party.

Some Prohibition party leaders remained bitterly hostile to the league throughout this period. In California, at a time the league believed was premature, they were powerful enough to force a referendum on statewide prohibition. Nationally they recognized the tremendous growth in prohibition sentiment and hoped to capitalize on it and revive the flagging party fortunes. Some party leaders proposed merger with the Progressive party, whose candidates usually favored prohibition. Then, in 1916, as the movement's propaganda programs began to return tremendous political dividends, party officials began the Five Million Movement. Their goal was to enroll five million voters in a pledge to assert "their independence of all candidates and political parties not committed by platform declaration to state and national prohibition." Since in the larger states the Democrats and Republicans alike refrained from dry declarations, the pledge would require support of the Prohibition party. As one league man expressed his concern, "This goes all the way."[32]

After this effort failed, the party made a last, desperate attempt to capture leadership of the dry movement while the states were considering ratification. In February 1918, Charles Scanlon formed the National Dry Federation and enlisted William Jennings Bryan as president and Senator Arthur Capper of Kansas as treasurer. Both men were apparently unaware of the enduring hostility between Scanlon and the league. The dry federation, which falsely claimed a number of churches as its constituent bodies, urged donors to fund an organization extending to over 2,000 counties. But just as the party's appeal that only its candidates promised adequate enforcement of prohibition statutes failed, the dry federation never amounted to more than a letterhead with prominent names. Very simply, after 1913 no other dry group was in a position to challenge the national leadership of the Anti-Saloon League.[33]

In one case the league actually came to control another temperance organization. In 1913 it assumed financial responsibility for and majority control of the board of directors of the Scientific Temperance Federation. The federation was the heir to Mary Hunt's WCTU work for scientific temperance instruction in the

32. Gilman M. Ostrander, *The Prohibition Movement in California, 1848–1933* (Berkeley, 1957); *Mida's Criterion*, Feb. 1, 1913, p. 62; Virgil Hinshaw to Richmond P. Hobson, July 17 and July 27, 1915; L. B. Musgrove to Hobson, undated 1915, ECe.

33. S. S. Kresge to Arthur Capper, May 21, 1918; Claudius B. Spencer to Cherrington, May 27, 1918; Cherrington to Spencer, May 31, 1918, ECe.

schools. After Hunt's death in 1906, her secretary, Cora Frances Stoddard, following a disagreement with the WCTU's department of scientific temperance instruction, started the federation as an independent organization headquartered in Boston. Always in a difficult financial position, it promoted the study of alcohol and its social effects and published a quarterly *Scientific Temperance Journal*. In 1913 Stoddard arranged with Cherrington for the American Issue Publishing company to publish the *Journal* and to assume formal control of the federation, although she continued to operate independently. Her work achieved national prominence, and she helped persuade scientists, physicians, social workers, and industrialists to support prohibition.[34]

During this period the Intercollegiate Prohibition Association also came increasingly under the league's influence, although the Westerville headquarters did not assume financial responsibility for it until 1924. The association had begun in 1892 as the collegiate wing of the Prohibition party, trying to educate college students through temperance oratorical contests to serve as future party leaders. In 1910 the association dropped its affiliation with the party prohibitionists. Harry S. Warner was the key person in the organization by this time, and as one of the organizers of the Council of One Hundred, he saw to it that the campus work conformed to the educational goals of the amendment campaign.[35]

The largest, most important organization with which the league cooperated, of course, was the WCTU. After Willard's death in 1898, the union, as we have noted, dropped its endorsement of the Prohibition party and began reaching new heights, not only in numbers of membership but also in range of activity. Retaining its democratic structure and its interest in a variety of reforms, the union between 1913 and 1915 alone gained 61,000 members. In 1895 Willard had established a department of legislation in Washington, D.C. Margaret D. Ellis served as superintendent until she

34. Minutes of June 9, 1913, meeting, Scientific Temperance Federation, ECg; *Standard Encyclopedia of the Alcohol Problem*, 5:1279–80, and 6:2535–36. Timberlake, *Prohibition and the Progressive Movement*, pp. 39–66, reviews "The Scientific and Social Arguments" that the league, the Scientific Temperance Federation, and other dry groups were advancing.

35. *Standard Encyclopedia of the Alcohol Problem*, 3:1327–28; Harry S. Warner, *An Evolution in Understanding of the Problem of Alcohol. A History of College Idealism* (Boston, 1966), pp. 30–32; "Records, 1892–1904," and Minutes, Executive Committee, 1904–20, IPA. I completed research in the IPA records prior to their preparation for the microfilm edition and cannot therefore list exact locations.

retired in 1917, when Lenna Lowe Yost replaced her. Ellis proudly informed the National Temperance Council in 1915 that within twenty-four hours she could contact a member in every county in the nation to begin agitation as needed. That was a more complete network even than the league's. Both Dinwiddie and the league's legislative committee respected the WCTU and were careful to include its officers as equal partners in consultations regarding lobbying strategy.[36]

The growth of the WCTU and its important contributions to the amendment campaign were but one sign of the widespread support for prohibition. Equally important for the league was acceptance of its nonpartisan methods. The Federal Council of Churches and its director, Charles S. MacFarland, helped the league develop and distribute propaganda materials. Charles Stelzle joined the council in 1916, lending his talents to the broad social concerns which included prohibition. In 1917 the council's commission on temperance even took over the old National Temperance Society, which had once so bitterly opposed the Anti-Saloon League.[37]

The acceptance of nonpartisan methods, the fantastic fund-raising accomplishments, the reorganization of the Anti-Saloon League, and the support of the WCTU and the prestigious Federal Council of Churches mattered little, however, unless they could be translated into favorable votes in the Congress and in the state legislatures. The political task would be difficult, certainly, probably lasting, the drys believed, for at least a generation. Moreover, the congressional victory of 1913 served not only to encourage the prohibitionists; it also spurred the liquor industries to reorganize the defense of their business and finance a massive counterattack.

36. Minutes, National Temperance Council, Dec. 11, 1915, STF, roll 42; *Standard Encyclopedia of the Alcohol Problem*, 3:906.

37. *Annual Reports of the Federal Council of Churches of Christ in America* (New York, 1913), p. 106; MacFarland to Cherrington, Jan. 23, 1917, Gen. Office file; Stelzle to Cochran, June 12, 1916, ECe.

7

THE WETS
STRIKE BACK

The defense of their industries by the brewers, distillers, and dealers was an incredible exercise in futility and shortsightedness. For the first time in American business history, two sizeable industries faced extinction, without any financial compensation, as a result of the deliberate efforts of a reform movement. They had a common interest in uniting for their defense. Prominent and outspoken leaders in both industries clearly understood the peril, yet they continued to find themselves unable to devise and manage effective political programs to forestall it. In the end, the prohibition movement reinforced the commercial rivalries between the distillers and brewers, and internal dissension splintered the nascent political and propaganda union between them. The organizational, commercial, and political rivalries of the capitalists who owned the breweries, distilleries, marketing organizations, and most saloons eased the way for the triumph of the Anti-Saloon League.

Yet if the rivalries among the components of the liquor industries ended up prevailing over a need for a common defense of common interests, there was a phase in their histories during which the liquor men, led by the brewers, developed successful political techniques. The phase began in Ohio, where the brewers cooperated with the distillers, wholesalers, and retailers to reverse the fortunes of the state's Anti-Saloon League. After 1908 the wet territory actually expanded in the state. The Ohio Democratic party allied with the liquor industries and drove the league into the arms of Republican leaders, some of whom were reluctant to accept the prohibitionists. National brewing industry leaders began to adopt the program of their counterparts and, after the enactment of the Webb-Kenyon law, there was a brief period when it seemed that a "liquor trust" would abate the movement for national prohibition.

In the end, however, the national union of a liquor trust proved illusory. The main problem was the welter of disagreements in the brewing trade. The brewers traditionally had promoted a laissez-faire strategy, convinced that in the absence of government interference their beverage would gain public favor. That gain would occur in part at the expense of whiskey. Nevertheless, rivalries between local and interstate shipping firms led some small brewers to hope for protection from the large firms through state regulation. Some brewers, observing the increasing sales of beer in America's growing cities simply could not agree to spend their fortunes to fight dry zealots in remote rural regions. And sometimes men of German ancestry simply did not believe that anyone could really want to outlaw the distribution of beer. Some national brewers, most notably Gustav Pabst and Adolphus Busch, realized the serious national threat that the Anti-Saloon League posed. It was they who, after 1908, arranged for a more vigorous and better planned defense and who worked for closer cooperation with the distillers and dealers. But they were unable to develop the necessary support within the United States Brewers' Association (USBA) for a consistent political strategy. In 1916 men who simply could not abandon the notion that beer was a benign temperance beverage, who looked to the continuing popularity of beer in urban markets, gained control of the trade association. They were willing to allow the destruction of the distilling industry in order to save their own. Their strategy, which reflected their inability to perceive the true nature of their opposition, abetted the destruction of both the spirits and brewing industries.

Initiatives of the Distilled Liquor Industry

The distilled liquor men were unencumbered by notions that they might somehow persuade the prohibitionists that their product was in any way benign. As was the case in the prohibition wave of the 1880s, they took the initiative in the national effort to reduce the appeal of the Anti-Saloon League and reverse its progress. The protective bureau was the first manifestation of the industry's clear perception of the Anti-Saloon League threat. But it was not the last. As its name implied, the bureau was formed with a defensive strategy. But by 1908 the industry took the offensive under the National Model License League. It sought coalitions with other businessmen in support of a program of state regulation. The distillers and dealers invited the brewers to a joint campaign under its auspices.

The brewers refused. As one of their trade journals expressed it, "the beer business has nothing in common with the whiskey business. Quite the contrary. Their interests are apart and, under present conditions, antagonistic." When some brewers called for a distinction in the law and separate licenses for beer and spirits, the National Wholesale Liquor Dealers' Association (NWLDA) reported that "a line of demarcation . . . has never received any recognition or encouragement from the prohibitionists." The result of the brewers' delusion was that the liquor industry fought a lonely battle on the national level, achieving real cooperation from brewers only on an ad hoc basis in state and local contests.[1]

The losses of 1907, 1908, and 1909 shocked the spirits industry. Six states, including Oklahoma, adopted prohibition, and the legislatures of Ohio and Indiana passed county option bills. "The trade was demoralized," recalled one participant, "and could see nothing but disturbance and ruin ahead." The protective techniques, so successful in the 1880s, were not working. The protective bureau distributed funds in states where there were few dealers or inadequate organization among them. It produced literature to persuade voters of the prohibitionists' fallacies. But the bureau had neither the staff nor the funds to extend to every locality, much less to organize successful political movements. When NWLDA officers analyzed the situation, they concluded that part of the problem lay within the industry. Dealers who did not face an immediate threat did not necessarily see the advisability of contributing money to the national effort. In their eyes the problem also extended to the commercial situation: for some houses, set up to handle a mail order business, prohibition laws— which did not prevent the possession or use of alcoholic beverages—potentially increased their volumes. The industry leaders realized that the dry campaigns were unlikely to disappear. They believed that although truth and justice lay on the wet side of the argument, the officers of the Anti-Saloon League were "unprincipled mercenaries" who would maintain agitation for no other reason than to secure their salaries.[2]

The solution was evident. American industries in the early twentieth century were often turning to government regulation as a way of solving their internal problems and of assuring the general public and customers of the safety and soundness of products. Just as the passage of pure food and drug laws allowed established meat pack-

---

1. *Wine and Spirit Bulletin* 23 (July 1909): 19; *American Brewers' Review* 23 (July 1909): 315.
   2. *Wine and Spirit Bulletin* 24 (Jan. 1910): 33, and (June 1910): 18.

ers and canners to guard their markets, so did government regulation of the retailing of beer and spirits seem to the distillers and
wholesalers the solution to the ills that beset them. So in 1908 they
embarked on a new political strategy of seeking to persuade state
and local governments to license saloons and regulate their numbers
and operations. This was a positive program to eliminate the abuses
that arose from competition among the brewers, protect legitimate
businessmen, and extinguish the fires of prohibitionist rhetoric in
the process.[3]

The National Model License League, formed in 1908, was the
agency through which the spirits trade advanced its new regulatory
strategy. Although it was officered and financed by men prominent
in the liquor industry, and headquartered in Louisville, Kentucky,
the business center of the bourbon trade, the new league was designed to involve a much broader constituency. The model license
league appealed for the active support of clergymen, politicians, and
businessmen from all industries, "a campaign of education and
organization outside of the liquor trade," in the words of President
Thomas M. Gilmore. "I feel safe in saying," he told his supporters,
"that the only solution of the liquor problem lies in a proper regulation of the liquor traffic." The model license league tried to enlist the
brewing industry in a joint program of regulation, but when the
league called a unity conference early in 1909, no brewers' representatives appeared.[4]

The model license league was an innovation that enjoyed some
initial success. Its spokesman argued that prohibition nowhere had
ended alcohol abuse. "We know, and experience shows," Gilmore
asserted, "that prohibition will not solve the liquor problem." Nowhere was prohibition really enforced, and never had it actually
reduced the consumption of alcoholic beverages. All that prohibition legislation had ever accomplished, in his view, was the destruction of legitimate business and the creation of illicit, and therefore
untaxed, systems of production and distribution. The only effective
social control of the liquor trade, argued Levi Cooke, general counsel of the NWLDA, was "thorough regulation" of the distribution

3. Ibid. 23 (May 1909): 50–52. For a general discussion of the business use of
government in this period to escape internecine competition, see Gabriel Kolko, *The
Triumph of Conservatism: A Reinterpretation of American History, 1900–1916* (New York,
1963).

4. *Wine and Spirit Bulletin* 23 (July 1909): 19; (Jan. 1910): 33; Gilmore to Texas
Brewing Co., Aug. 14, 1911, in *The Brewers and Texas Politics*, pp. 1517–18.

system. "Beyond that, remedy can be found only in the constitution of the individuals in whom lurks the danger in and to the community." Law simply could not reach that far.[5]

In order to achieve regulation, the license league, working closely with the protective bureau, entered political campaigns. It presented itself not as a self-interested organization of the distillers and wholesalers but as a public-spirited group with positive answers to real problems who refrained from challenging the basic liberties of Americans. It preferred to work with associations of local people who faced victimization by the Anti-Saloon League. In Oregon in 1910, for instance, the model license league helped local wets form the Greater Oregon Home Rule Association and sent speakers and literature to assist it. The wets there, by enlisting support from a large number of businessmen unconnected with the trade and by working closely with mayors and town councils, persuaded a majority of the voters that local option had only increased social abuses; the solution was a "home rule" measure that allowed towns to adopt license laws to regulate the traffic. In the 1910 Missouri campaign, the wets won by a large margin because it was not an issue "between the Prohibitionists and the liquor element, but a fight between the Prohibitionists and the business element."[6]

By the autumn of 1910 the development of the model license league and its strategy seemed promising. Not only had important victories been won in Oregon, Florida, and especially Missouri, but, as the editor of the *Wine and Spirit Bulletin* expressed it, "the model license seed" was "taking root" in "cities and towns here and there." The spirits men approached the future with confidence and realism. "The belief in the theory of prohibition is undoubtedly on the wane," one dealer noted. "The state-wide prohibition wave that started with Georgia in 1907 did not represent the sober sense and conviction of the public, but was brought about by a frenzy, created through buncombe, that has had no parallel in the political history of the country." Nevertheless, the dry attacks would continue. "[We] will never be free from insidious attacks, from secret machinations, from far-reaching plans to rob us of the fruit of our victories." Their realism led the distillers to seek to improve and extend their organization. They wanted to have strong leagues in at least two dozen states to fend off the prohibition movement.[7]

5. *Wine and Spirit Bulletin* 24 (Jan. 1910): 33; 25 (July 1911): 36.
6. Ibid. 24 (Dec. 1910): 47–49; 25 (Feb. 1911): 44–47; (July 1911): 43.
7. Ibid. 25 (Feb. 1911): 44; (July 1911): 30, 43–43; 26 (June 1912): 23.

State associations of firms engaged in the spirits business were especially important because it was on this level that the brewers were willing to cooperate. The liquor men learned from bitter experience that they could expect little, if any, help from the USBA, but in individual states, when both the brewers and distillers faced an immediate crisis from a state dry campaign, they did cooperate. One of the places where this alliance developed most fully was Texas. The Texas Anti-Saloon League, although it was organized much more loosely than the national officers advised, threatened to impose statewide prohibition, and it succeeded in drying up most of the state's northern counties by using local option laws. The Texas Brewers' Association responded as early as 1902 by seeking help from the distillers and wholesale dealers. The Texas brewers were experiencing competition from the Milwaukee and St. Louis shippers and were appalled by the growing number of saloons in the state. Restrictions on the opening of new retail outlets would both serve their commercial interests and help to overcome the arguments of the prohibitionists. This was common ground upon which they could unite with the spirits men, and they succeeded until state prohibition came in 1917. In Texas, and elsewhere where the two industries cooperated, the financial arrangement was for the brewers to contribute two-thirds and the distillers one-third of the costs. George F. Dieterle, while serving as president of the NWLDA, expressed the hope that such cooperation on the state level would build national friendships.[8]

Wet Politics and the Travail of the Ohio Anti-Saloon League

Nowhere was cooperation between the brewers and the liquor men more successful than in Ohio. When the Ohio brewers reversed their laissez-faire strategy, engaged in a vigorous policy of self-reform, and obtained the wholehearted cooperation of the spirits industry, they reversed hard-won victories of the Anti-Saloon League. The wet successes were all the more important because they occurred in the state where the national league maintained its headquarters and had most completely perfected a system of state and local organization. If the brewers and liquor men could win victories in Ohio, it seemed, they could win them in any populous state with

8. Ibid. 23 (July 1909):19; G. H. Luedde to Otto Wahrmund, April 18, 1902; J. W. Riggins to Liquor Dealers' Association of Texas, July 7, 1902, *Brewers and Texas Politics*, pp. 513, 1150–51; Drescher, "Opposition to Prohibition," pp. 144–46.

an important market. And win they did: by the end of 1912 in a
license clause the new Ohio constitution recognized the right to
manufacture and sell alcoholic beverages, and a wet politician of
national stature held the governorship. These developments were
probably partly responsible for the league's decision to launch the
campaign for a national prohibition amendment and for its strategy
of enlarging its dry constituency. Once again the Ohio experience
had important national implications.

The early political triumphs enjoyed by the Ohio Anti-Saloon
League had shocked the Ohio Brewers' Association. Not only had
the league exhibited its political power with Herrick's defeat in 1905,
but following the adoption of county option by the 1908 legislative
session sixty-three of the state's eighty-eight counties voted to outlaw
the saloon that autumn. The number of victories exceeded even
Wayne Wheeler's expectations. It appeared to the brewers that the
only places where the league was not a controlling political influence
were Cincinnati, Cleveland, Columbus, Dayton, and Toledo. Something had to be done lest the league achieve statewide prohibition,
clearly its next goal.[9]

In 1907 the Ohio Brewer's Association reversed its attitude toward the use of governmental authority regarding the industry. It
began a two-pronged strategy of self-reform and achieving state
regulation of the number and operation of saloons. The Ohio
brewers borrowed their new policy from Texas brewers, who in
1904 had promised voters that they would work to insure that
saloons operated according to legal restrictions. The Texas association went to considerable expense to employ a team of private
detectives who made certain that saloons obeyed restrictions on their
hours of operation and allowed no gambling or prostitution on the
premises. The Ohio brewers established a vigilance bureau to
cleanse the retailing businesses of the abuses that the Anti-Saloon
League delighted in highlighting. Percy Andreae, an officer in a
Cincinnati brewery, was chosen to guide the effort, and within
eighteen months he was employing a force of twenty detectives to
fight saloon abuses of the law.[10]

Andreae approached his new assignment with a pragmatic spirit.
Customarily, industry spokesmen had denounced the Anti-Saloon

9. *Brewers' Journal* 33 (Nov. 1, 1908):13; Wheeler to John D. Rockefeller, Jan. 11,
1910, PPMR. Five of the sixty-three counties were already dry under the previous
local option law.

10. Paget to Hugh Fox, Aug. 27, 1908, *Brewers and Texas Politics*, pp. 1400–01;
Percy Andreae, *The Prohibition Movement* (Chicago, 1915), pp. 81–83.

League leaders and their arguments in the bitterest language. In contrast, Andreae told the liquor men that "the fallacies are not all on one side, nor are the morals." The arguments on both sides were too often a "bewildering mass of contradictions." Nor were the brewers and distillers correct when they thought of the prohibitionists as ". . . lunatics. They are not." More accurately, he said, they are almost always reasonable men and women "who merely recognize the existence of the same evil that we recognize, and seeing no way of curing it, conclude that it is incurable" and requires "complete destruction." The answer was self-regulation within the industries affected. "There is only one way for a man to put his house in order," he told the brewers. "It is to do it himself."[11]

Andreae did not stop simply at making a call for a reversal of the industries' "defensive attitude" or at adopting the self-reform program of the Texas brewers. He began a sophisticated program to reverse wet political fortunes. The vigilance bureau between 1908 and 1913 spent $1 million on politics. Its staff, ignoring hopelessly dry areas, carefully surveyed the state's political conditions district by district. The bureau identified sympathetic organizations, charted ethnic populations, and ascertained the attitudes of priests and ministers. It funded fraternal groups and other organizations not connected with the industry. As for political candidates, it intensively investigated their backgrounds and records and sought to insure, on a nonpartisan basis, that supporters were running in every important race. This operation was so well developed that by 1912 Andreae, through the Personal Liberty League which he headed, could inform 150,000 voters within twenty-four hours of issues and candidate positions on matters affecting the industry.[12]

The self-reform movement used the law to end the integration of retailing and production. The Dean Character Law of 1909 regulated the operation of saloons and required saloon keepers to be local residents with no other connection to the liquor traffic. They had to respond to an annual questionnaire, assuring the state that they were not convicted felons, allowed no gambling or prostitution on the premises, and did not serve minors, drunks or habitual drunkards. A false answer constituted perjury. The vigilance bureau enforced these strictures by turning evidence of violations over to local

11. Andreae, *Prohibition Movement; Wine and Spirit Bulletin* 24 (June 1910):180–81.

12. *Brewing and Liquor Interests and German and Bolshevic Propaganda*, Hearings, U.S. Senate, Subcommittee on the Judiciary, 65th Congress, 2nd Sess. (1919), pp. 349–99; Drescher, "Opposition to Prohibition," pp. 219–46.

prosecutors. By divorcing retailing from the breweries, the law struck at one of the sources of saloon overpopulation; no longer could a brewer use his capital to open new outlets.[13]

The new strategy of the brewers, who were acting in complete harmony with the Ohio Wine and Spirit Association and the Liquor League, very quickly began to pay substantial dividends. In 1908, with Republican Governor Andrew Harris openly receiving support from the Anti-Saloon League, the Democrats nominated a wet, Judson Harmon, who, with support from Andreae, was elected. Nor was the legislature any longer firmly within the grip of Wayne Wheeler. Not only did it pass the regulatory bill pushed by the brewers' association in 1909, but in its 1911 session Andreae could count majorities for a bill that would exempt municipalities from the operation of the county option law of 1908. Eventually this measure was defeated, but only after Governor Harmon informed his supporters in the General Assembly that his own presidential ambitions would force him to veto it if it were passed. Only through the wish of the governor to avoid a divisive veto was the Anti-Saloon League saved from an embarrassing reversal. "We are having strenuous times in Ohio," one league official remarked privately.[14]

Conditions in the state continued to worsen from the viewpoint of the league. The county option law allowed a new referendum every three years, and in 1911 Andreae's organization immediately pushed to place the issue on the ballot in twenty-seven dry counties. By June 1912 eighteen of them had reentered the wet column. The only way the Anti-Saloon League could win a referendum, chortled one liquor man, was by calling new elections in safely dry areas where Andreae had no interest in contesting the results. Clearly the Ohio prohibition movement, the flagship organization of the Anti-Saloon League, was on the defensive. "Cincinnati liquor men," a trade journal reported, "are rejoicing over the way Ohio is getting out of the rut of county options."[15]

The evidence of that political strength encouraged the state's brewers and liquor men to press to have their industry granted a right to exist under a license clause in the constitution. The electorate approved the call of a convention to meet in 1912 to revise the

13. Sponholtz, "The Politics of Temperance in Ohio."

14. *Wine and Spirit Bulletin* 25 (Feb. 1911): 26, 44, and (Mar. 1911): 42; John S. Rutledge to Charles Dick, Feb. 4, 1911, CD.

15. *Wine and Spirit Bulletin* 25 (Dec. 1911): 55; Sponholtz, "The Politics of Temperance in Ohio."

charter. "We are getting ready to meet [the wets] and lick them to death," Wheeler boasted, but when the constitutional convention assembled, license delegates were in the majority. The liquor traffic committee split twelve to nine in favor of the wets. Andreae appeared before it to appeal for a general clause allowing licenses for the trade but leaving the specific restrictions to legislative action. Wheeler, knowing that he could not control the convention, argued in favor of a licensing clause that severely restricted the number and operation of saloons. The result was a compromise satisfactory to the brewers that limited the number of saloons in wet areas to one for every five hundred residents. Wheeler was uncertain as to the recommendations he would make to league supporters when the clause was submitted to the voters for approval in September. Finally, the *American Issue* asked its readers to express their views, and when they did so, in a proportion of forty to one against any constitutional license, the league campaigned against the new provision—and lost. The new Ohio constitution, while not disturbing existing local option statutes, required the licensing of saloons in wet territory. Wheeler tried to assure his followers by saying that "there is nothing in the amendment which will prevent the people from securing state-wide prohibition whenever they desire to do so." In the words of his biographer, "this was making the best of a bad situation."[16]

In the years to come Wayne Wheeler had to continue to offer such explanations. The Anti-Saloon League was very much on the defensive. Andreae's strategy had taken away the league's ability to follow its time-tested balance of power strategy. Not only was Ohio now the only state with a license provision in its constitution, but the wets continued to dominate state politics. The new governor elected in 1912 was James Cox, who scorned the prohibitionists. In 1913 Cox, working with the Democratic majorities in the legislature, created a system of state licensing that provided the party with a new source of patronage and firmly allied it with the wet businessmen. Wheeler did succeed in having enacted legislative restrictions on the saloon that were more severe than those of the constitution. But he could not control the politicians on the issues that were most vital. So he and the league decided to use the new provisions for initiative and referendum to obtain statewide prohibition. In 1914, when the league placed the issue on the ballot, however, the wets countered

16. Sponholtz, "The Politics of Temperance in Ohio"; T. J. Steuart, *Wayne Wheeler, Dry Boss* (New York, 1928), p. 71; *Proceedings, Thirteenth National Convention, ASLA, 1909*, pp. 142–43.

with a "home rule" amendment that would repeal the county option law and forbid prohibition measures in any units larger than townships or municipalities. That autumn the league measure lost by an 83,000-vote margin, while the home rule amendment won by 12,000 votes.[17]

The problem with the initiative and referendum, from the league's point of view, was simple. Wheeler estimated that of the state's 1,250,000 voters only 400,000 were firmly committed to prohibition. But he had little choice except to try to utilize the referendum to achieve statewide prohibition. The 1912 constitution had reduced the relative strength of small town and rural votes in the General Assembly, which was certainly unlikely to enact prohibition in the foreseeable future. Referendum campaigns were propaganda ventures, moreover, that conformed to the national policy of education. Their use had one important advantage to the league: the zeal of the prohibitionists offset the heavy expenditures of the liquor trades. "What we plan to do is to make the saloon, the distillery, and the brewery elements bankrupt themselves trying to keep Ohio wet," Wheeler said when he announced an initiative in 1915. "And we will succeed. We will wear them down, and we will wear them out." The Ohio league followed that strategy with campaigns in 1915 and 1917 before finally winning in 1918. The wets tried to block the strategy with a ballot measure in 1915 that would prevent any issue, once defeated, from arising again for six years, but it lost.[18]

The Ohio league did not rely solely on the zeal of its followers. The league fine-tuned its political and fund-raising organization. Wheeler assumed full-time duties as national general counsel in 1915; his successor, attorney James A. White, organized the Ohio Dry Federation to coordinate the efforts of all supporting groups. Operating from the league's Columbus office, the federation budgeted large sums for the effort: $450,000 for the 1917 campaign and $500,000 for 1918. The funding system had each county raise one dollar for each vote cast in the preceding referendum. These funds went for salaries—each county had a manager—publicity, and the support of affiliates specially formed to reach new voters with the

17. *Proceedings, ASLA, 1909*, pp. 76–77; *Mida's Criterion*, Jan. 16, 1913, p. 40; USBA, *Yearbook and Proceedings of the 54th Annual Convention* (New York, 1914), pp. 52–53.

18. Sponholtz, "The Politics of Temperance in Ohio"; *Wine and Spirit Bulletin* 29 (April 1915):36; 29 (Aug. 1915):59–60; Steuart, *Wayne Wheeler*, pp. 72–79.

dry message. On election day each precinct had an inspector and two challengers working for the cause.[19]

These campaigns showed the sophistication of the Ohio league's program to enlarge its constituency. The drys' funds were too limited to purchase as much advertising as the liquor and brewing trades could afford, but they did allow the placement of posters in streetcars and billboards in prominent locations, each carrying a pithy prohibition message designed by a professional advertising agency. The American Issue Publishing Company supplied ample literature. The sophistication did not stop, moreover, at the use of the latest publicity methods. The dry federation budgeted funds for the formation of special organizations to reach Republicans, Democrats, Catholics, women, farmers, and especially workers and their families. Its working men's department in 1917 formed the Trade Union Dry League of Ohio and arranged to set aside a Labor Week around Labor Day, with appropriate speakers addressing assemblies of workers and their families. In 1918 it worked with management to appoint a "keyman" in factory departments to distribute literature and display posters. In 1917 and 1918, when wartime conditions brought a large number of transients to the state's factories, the dry federation prepared to check their registration while placing absentee ballots in the hands of sympathetic soldiers and sailors.[20]

The danger in all of this effort, of course, was that the state's prohibitionists might tire of the fight. As one long-time league supporter expressed it, "some of us are inclined to get weary in well-doing." But the league leaders were able to maintain support from their basic constituency in the evangelical churches. When prohibition met defeat in 1915, the *New Republic* assured its readers that it was worth the cost in educational benefits. Most important for maintaining zeal were the declining margins by which the wets won. The 83,000 wet majority of 1914 shrank to 55,000 in 1915 and to only 1,137 votes in 1917. "We are all convinced that with a little closer organization, a little more sacrifice and service," White told his followers, "we can win a splendid victory." Finally in 1918, with

19. White form letter, Oct. 9, 1915; Minutes, Ohio Dry Federation, Jan. 26, Feb. 6, March 6, Sept. 11, 1917, Mar. 5, 1918, OASL, rolls 1 & 5; *Manual, Ohio Dry Workers* (Columbus, 1917).

20. White form letters, Aug. 17, 1917, Jan. 15 and July 19, 1918, OASL, roll 1; Report of Wheeler, 1915, ECe.

White's efforts reducing wet majorities in Cincinnati, Ohio voters approved prohibition by a margin of 25,000.[21]

Changes in the Ohio League

This victory on the face of it resulted from a successful application of the single interest politics of direct appeals to hundreds of thousands of voters. Behind this impression, however, were important political developments that reshaped the Anti-Saloon League, making it different from the model first envisioned by Russell in 1893. Russell had spoken of the league as both an omnipartisan and nonpartisan organization, working with all political parties where possible or with none. The events of prohibition politics in Ohio, however, along with the new intervention led by Andreae, linked the league closely with the state Republican party. Wheeler, White, Russell, Baker, and Cherrington were all Republicans personally, and Wheeler in particular forged ties with Ohio Republican politicians that remained significant when he worked on the national level in the 1920s.

The alliance between the Ohio league and the Republican party was in part of Wheeler's making and in part a matter of circumstance. In 1905 Pattison's election as governor meant that the league was influential in the statehouse through the Democrats; but his untimely death brought a Republican dry, Lieutenant Governor Andrew Harris, to office. Harris assisted Wheeler in obtaining the county option bill in 1908, and the league in turn endorsed his election effort. But it was Judson Harmon, the wet Democrat, who was elected. He owed his victory to Hamilton County—termed "that filthy ditch in the back corner of Ohio" by the *American Issue* editor. The Cincinnati Republican machine had worked for William Howard Taft and Harmon in 1908. Nominating wet candidates seemed the path to statewide victory for Democratic leaders, especially with Andreae's resources available. Both James Cox and U.S. Senator Atlee Pomerene opposed prohibition legislation.[22]

21. E. R. Root to King, Sept. 28, 1915; *New Republic*, Nov. 12, 1915, p. 1; White form letter, Nov. 20, 1917, OASL, roll 1; *Standard Encyclopedia of the Alcohol Problem*, 5:2053.

22. J. C. Jackson to Cherrington, Nov. 6, 1908; Cherrington to Wheeler, Nov. 9, 1908, ECg. The *Wine and Spirit Bulletin* (26 [July 1912]:21) commented that the Democrats had won in 1908 and 1910 "through the influence of the liberal forces." *American Issue* (Ohio ed.), Nov. 14, 1908, p. 5; *American Issue*, Mar. 17, 1905, p. 13. In

The problem that faced the Ohio Republicans was clear. The Republican organization in Cincinnati was both wet and, in terms of votes, the state's largest. Elsewhere in the state many Republicans supported the Anti-Saloon League. In 1914 both the party and the league wanted to defeat Cox. But the Republican nominee, Frank Willis, tried to placate both wet and drys by making vague statements that there should be no backward steps in temperance legislation. The response of Wheeler and the league was to endorse the Progressive James R. Garfield for the governorship, finally forcing Willis at the end of the campaign to come out for prohibition. He won. But as governor, Willis failed to receive support from Cincinnati Republicans, and Cox defeated him in 1916. That year the league faced the embarrassing situation of endorsing the candicacy of Myron T. Herrick for the U.S. Senate seat occupied by Pomerene, who opposed submitting the amendment to the states for their ratification. Pomerene, Cox, and Woodrow Wilson carried the state in spite of the league's endorsement of their opponents.[23] Clearly in the machinations of Ohio politics the league was having difficulty advancing its cause.

These Ohio developments were significant for more than the future ties between Wheeler and the national Republican party in the 1920s. They showed that the league could be beaten by a well-organized, ably led, and adequately funded opposition. Just as the league's experience in Ohio helped shape its national strategy, so too did the success of Andreae and the Ohio Brewers' Association affect the policies of the USBA. Eventually, after the passage of the Webb-Kenyon bill shocked both industries, the brewers united with the distillers and employed Andreae to lead the opposition to the national prohibition movement.

Changes in the USBA

Within a year of the Ohio brewers' adoption of regulation and self-reform, the USBA followed suit. The awakening of the associa-

1905 the Democratic party had allowed the league to veto a potential nominee for secretary of state.

23. *Wine and Spirit Bulletin* 29 (Nov. 1915): 30; 30 (Dec. 1916): 49–50; Harry M. Daugherty to Fairbanks, Nov. 12, 1913, NF. Because of his failures, the wets heard rumors that Republicans forced Wheeler to leave his post as Ohio superintendent. *Wine and Spirit Bulletin* 29 (Mar. 1915): 40. In 1917 the Coalition of Ohio Dry Republicans, working on behalf of the prohibition referendum, asserted that large donations by the liquor and brewing trades to the Democrats had "brought our party defeat after defeat." Charles A. Reid form letter, 1917, OASL series, roll 1.

tion to the realities of the power of the prohibition movement followed the statewide victories in the South and in Oklahoma in 1907 and was announced at the group's convention in 1908. President Julius Liebmann, a New York brewer, opened the meeting with an analysis of the current attack on the saloon and the brewing industry. He recognized the Anti-Saloon League as the cause of the trouble and advocated that the association work in concert with local police, judges, landlords, bonding companies, and licensing authorities to control what, in his eyes, was the small proportion of saloons that disturbed the social order.[24]

Liebmann's address reflected both changing sentiment within the industry and the appointment of a new association secretary, Hugh Fox. As the vigilance committee told the delegates, the past year had been "a tale of war." The board of trustees reported that it was changing the association's strategy. Its new antiprohibition literature would recast the industry's arguments in a more usable, forceful, and appealing format. The *Yearbook* would address a general audience, not just the industry. Most important, the organization would promote licensing laws as the best means yet devised for the social control of alcohol sales.[25]

Fox, replacing Gallus Thomann, who had served the industry for twenty-five years, brought a fresh approach to the task of battling the Anti-Saloon League. He was the key person in the industry's associational activities until the advent of national prohibition in 1920. Soon after taking office, Fox studied the successful policies of state brewers' associations. He acknowledged that "keen competition has in the past led to the multiplication of saloons beyond the actual requirements of the market." The 1909 *Yearbook* announced that the industry sought regulatory laws to assist it in self-reform efforts. Fox emphasized that the fight would be a long one, requiring substantial appropriations annually from the brewers. Even if the Anti-Saloon League were to disappear, public sentiment was such that major problems would remain. The appropriate strategy was a continuous educational effort to change public opinion, coupled with regulatory laws.

Fox instituted significant changes within the USBA to put his strategy into effect, all recognizably of a bureaucratic variety. Fox developed a large clipping service to keep track of events and changing sentiment. He established a professionally managed library at

24. USBA, *Proceedings of the 48th Convention*, 1908, pp. 31–67.
25. Ibid.; Drescher, "Opposition to Prohibition," pp. 102–12.

association headquarters. Fox believed that the gathering of data and its proper presentation would enable the industry to obtain a fair public hearing. He retained John Koren, a prominent statistician, to scrutinize USBA publications and Dr. E. H. Williams, an authority on the medical problems of alcohol abuse, to study the effects of prohibition laws. Fox believed, in short, that a careful, calm, and scholarly presentation of the industry's positions and of the nature of its products would eventually replace prohibitionist claims in the free marketplace of public opinion.[26]

The other important aspect of Fox's new approach was the enlargement and reorganization of the USBA staff and committee structure. He was only partly successful in accomplishing this goal. Within two years of his appointment, the board of trustees saw a reorganization plan that would create four separate functional departments guided by an executive committee. The legal department would deal both with the prohibition statutes and business affairs such as trademarks. The labor department would help member firms write contracts for their employees and establish permanent relations with the unions in the American Federation of Labor. The education, or publicity, department would maintain the library, prepare and publish literature, and develop exhibitions for public gatherings. "Recognizing our natural limitations," the board was told, "we must, first of all, reach and teach the teachers," especially journalists. The political department would maintain a trained staff to help wet organizations mobilize for campaigns. Fox was critical of the existing USBA policy of supplying funds to local groups on an ad hoc basis as "expensive and wasteful."[27]

Under Fox's leadership, for the first time the brewers had a plan for the adaptation of the managerial skills of modern business to their associational and antiprohibition efforts. The shipping brewers were among those businessmen who had done so much to change the way American firms conducted their affairs in important sectors of the economy. But in comparison to their modern management practices in production and marketing, the brewers' associational

---

26. Drescher, "Opposition to Prohibition," p. 168; "Report of the Secretary to the Board of Trustees, USBA, Nov. 9, 1908; "Meeting of Executive Officers of State Brewers' Associations, Dec. 29, 1908, *Brewing and Liquor Interests*, pp. 786–93; O. Paget to Fox, Aug. 27, 1908, *Brewers and Texas Politics*, pp. 1400–01; USBA, *Yearbook and Proceedings of the 49th Convention,* 1909, pp. 147–50.

27. USBA, *Yearbook*, 1909; "Skeleton of Reorganization Plan," USBA files, 1910, *Brewing and Liquor Interests*, pp. 810–11.

and political structures were organized primitively. Fox proposed to change that state of affairs.

But even now, in the face of growing dry power, the USBA failed fully to follow Fox's modern managerial scheme. The association failed to appoint a separate publicity department until 1914. The most significant change occurred in political work, coincident with Fox's appointment. In 1908 the organization committee, which had been a part-time group of brewery executives, became the organization bureau. Under John A. McDermott it employed a full-time staff and had access to larger sums of money. The bureau used its resources in states where local brewers' associations were weak. Its staff worked to anticipate prohibition campaigns, laying the groundwork for alliances with sympathetic organizations, which might include unions, immigrant groups, hotel keepers, and other businessmen commercially tied to the brewing industry. They worked with existing groups whenever they could and when necessary formed new organizations. When a campaign came, McDermott formed an ad hoc campaign organization with a temporary but experienced staff. Most important of all of these efforts was the relationship that developed with the German-American Alliance, which claimed to represent the 10 percent of the American population of German ancestry. The alliance received substantial grants from the brewers, who preferred to work indirectly, to petition against prohibition legislation, interrogate candidates, circulate endorsements, and turn out the vote on election day.[28]

Although the appointment of McDermott and Fox breathed new life into the activies of the USBA, the brewers themselves remained divided in their perception of the Anti-Saloon League threat and the need to spend large sums fighting it. Some members argued that nothing was more essential. Adolphus Busch warned a Texas brewer in 1911 that the state's campaign was "a struggle for existence. If we lose, we lose everything. We can not afford to lose." Busch consistently pressed his competitors to rally to the national fight, but others remained lulled by the growing sales volumes of their product and the local successes in states like Ohio. In 1910, USBA President Carl J. Hoster, experienced in the Ohio political wars, asserted that "we have finally succeeded in breaking the backbone of the prohibition wave." For evidence he cited the prohibitionists' inability to obtain legislation from Congress. Hoster repeated the

28. Drescher, "Opposition to Prohibition," pp. 31–74; Testimony of McDermott, *Brewing and Liquor Interests*, pp. 401–24.

assurance in 1911, and his successor, Jacob Ruppert, told the annual meeting that "for the future, I have no plans, no policy, no promises." He would simply "meet conditions as they arise." These men could not comprehend the notion of a public rejection of beer. One of Fox's main tasks as association secretary was to try to arrange compromises between the factions of the USBA, compromises that would maintain a steady pressure on the drys. It was hardly a situation conducive to a consistent effort against the determination of the Anti-Saloon League.[29] In the end, the downfall of the brewers involved a failure to pursue a managerial and bureaucratic procedure countervailing to that of the Anti-Saloon League.

Brewers and Distillers, Union and Fracture

The spectacular success of the prohibitionists in overriding Taft's veto and enacting the Webb-Kenyon bill sparked repercussions within the brewing industry, temporarily ending arguments about the seriousness of the Anti-Saloon League's threat. Then, less than two years later, came the vote on the Hobson resolution, which revealed the league's national power. Even before the drys achieved their simple majority in the House of Representatives on behalf of submission of a prohibition amendment, the political events of 1913 had brought renewed pleas from the spirits men for joint efforts among the industries' trade associations. Eventually, leaders of the distillers and brewers agreed to a joint effort, to have the spirits firms support the National Association of Commerce and Labor (NACL), initially formed by the brewers to engineer a new wet politics. Led by Percy Andreae, the NACL received enormous grants and forced the trades allied to the liquor industries to help in the effort. But in the end the unity was abortive, dissolving under the continuing victories of the prohibition movement, the disagreements among the brewers, and the ancient competitive rivalry between spirits and beer.

Neither the brewers nor the spirits men expected the congressional action of 1913. Spokesmen for both industries believed that their educational efforts were paying dividends, that prohibition

29. Busch to Zane Cetti, Feb. 1, 1911, *Brewers and Texas Politics*, p. 151; USBA, *Yearbook and Proceedings of the 50th Convention* (New York, 1910), pp. 18–19; *Yearbook and Proceedings of the 51st Convention* (New York, 1911), pp. 7, 143; Drescher, "Opposition to Prohibition," p. 113; Fox form letter, Jan. 17, 1911, *Brewing and Liquor Interests*, pp. 1022–23.

sentiment was on the wane. After the southern dry victories, the prohibitionists added no new states to their column. Alabama had overthrown its prohibition statute in 1911. The brewers' regulatory policy was making substantial progress, capped by the Ohio license victory in 1912. Their abilities to persuade politicians in the lobbies of legislative chambers and party caucuses seemed great enough to prevent the interstate legislation that, as Adolphus Busch wrote privately, "is most dangerous and antagonistic to our industry and which makes prohibition possible." Reviewing the developments of 1912, one liquor journal commented, "we enter upon 1913 with a feeling of optimism."[30]

The liquor men had always favored working with leaders of both major political parties in order to protect their interests. Like other shrewd businessmen whose firms faced threats of hostile legislation, they had contributed to party treasuries and employed lobbyists to cultivate sympathetic responses from individual legislators. The use of the referendum by the prohibition movement had forced them to engage in single-interest political action directed at individual voters as well. But neither the brewers, the distillers, nor the dealers had pioneered in the kind of voter mobilization in which the Anti-Saloon League engaged. The brewers' funding of the German-American Alliance, for instance, for purposes of political organization on the precinct level, began at least a decade after Russell founded the league. To be sure, the industries had insured that their customers knew about election issues, and they sometimes corrupted the political process with the outright purchase of votes.

The nonpartisan strategy of the wet industrialists emphasized working within the party system, not disposing of it or working outside of it as the league and other reform groups were attempting to do. Levi Cooke, who as general counsel of the NWLDA was responsible for overseeing that organization's legislative interests in Washington, D.C., expressed the policy most clearly. He told the group's convention of 1911 that both Republican and Democratic leaders knew that their task was to guard the public interest against the solicitations of special interest lobbyists who might enjoy the closest access to the politician's ear. "It is to this legislative spirit," Cooke asserted, "that the public and trade unitedly seeking proper regulation, may confidently leave the solution of the problem."[31]

30. Busch to Zane Cetti, Oct. 19, 1905, *Brewers and Texas Politics*, pp. 92–93; *Mida's Criterion*, Jan. 1, 1913, p. 55.
31. *Wine and Spirit Bulletin* 25 (July 1911): 35–42.

Both the brewers and the spirits men remained confident that this strategy would prevent the enactment of the Webb-Kenyon bill. Levi Cooke informed his association that the distilling industry ranked next to flour milling "within the group of vegetable products" in the national economy. The trade was "of the warp and woof of the national commerce," providing "the largest single source of tax revenue." These considerations alone should cause the Congress to be reluctant to damage it. Moreover, distinguished and powerful senators and representatives had argued authoritatively that the bill was an unconstitutional delegation of power to the states. If these arguments were insufficient to carry the day, the wets believed that President Taft was on their side.[32]

Their success with congressional lobbying in the past and their confidence in the correctness of their position meant that up until the last moment the distillers and brewers could not believe that Congress would pass the law. It "will never see the light of day" one journal told its readers. When the bill did obtain a date on the Senate calendar, it was "by a fluke" due to a temporary lapse in the opponents' watchfulness. The NWLDA officers were startled by the speed of the bill's consideration and by the size of the favorable majorities, especially the overriding of Taft's veto.[33] The shock of the interstate legislation was expressed immediately. "Prohibition is no longer a local issue," warned the *American Brewers' Review*. "The last stage has been reached. *Prohibition is a national danger.*"

In their public statements spokesmen for both industries tried to reassure their members. The league's victories and its announcement of the campaign for national prohibition were simply devices of its leaders to insure a continuing flow of contributions. "Rather than admit the inherent evils of prohibition and the practical impossibility of enforcing it," the USBA trustees stated, "they have insisted that the one sure remedy was to prohibit the inter-State business in alcoholic beverages." In spite of the law, one editorial assured, "the brewing industry as a whole will continue to prosper" because of market demand. Nor was the Webb-Kenyon Act likely to have much impact on the distribution of spirits, unless states suddenly forbad the possession and use of alcoholic beverages. To be sure, wholesale dealers were shut off from supplying speakeasies, but the market for their products was still present. The houses could supply that mar-

32. Ibid. 26 (June 1912): 49–52.
33. Ibid. 26 (July 1912): 49–50; *Mida's Criterion*, Jan. 16, 1913, p. 92; Feb. 1, 1913, p. 100; Feb. 16, 1913, p. 86; *American Brewers' Review* 27 (Mar. 1913): 114–16.

ket directly even under the law. If they did not, and the law was enforced, a brewer argued that the "indignant command of an overwhelming majority of the American people" would have it "revoked."[34]

But their private actions belied these expressions of confidence. Soon after the 1913 dry victory, when the brewers began the NACL, the distillers and dealers pressed upon them the critical need to achieve a united front. While the Webb-Kenyon bill was pending, Hugh Fox called an emergency meeting of USBA leaders to discuss ideas about a new effort. When the USBA formed the NACL later in 1913, the brewers closely controlled it, although it was to operate independently of their trade association and even of their own organization bureau. They wanted the NACL to appeal to a broad range of businessmen, labor unions, and fraternal groups, to transfer Percy Andreae's successful Ohio techniques to the national level.

Initially Andreae began his national work with enormous financial support and encouragement from the brewers. They agreed to pay him an annual salary of $40,000 for five years. The USBA asked its members to contribute three cents for every barrel of beer they sold, in addition to the half-cent assessment for the regular educational and political campaigns of the association. To add to the NACL treasury, they developed a sophisticated boycott system to force the firms supplying equipment and materials to the breweries to contribute. The industry had long argued that these firms should donate funds on the grounds that none of the profits made in brewing should go to the Anti-Saloon League. The NACL developed a system wherein it sold stamps to supplying firms; cooperating breweries refused to accept invoices that did not carry these stamps.[35]

Andreae used these funds to develop the NACL as an organization representing itself as independent of the businesses that supported it, as one that would appeal to businessmen and members of the general public who were fearful of "freak" and "confiscatory" legislation. His program was both educational and political. He began a monthly magazine, *The Hearthstone*, to reach a general audience. He established close ties with Louis N. Hammerling,

---

34. *Brewers' Journal* 37 (Mar. 1913): 219; *Mida's Criterion*, Mar. 1, 1913, pp. 55—56; USBA, *Yearbook and Proceedings of the 53rd Convention*, 1913, pp. 5—6.

35. Fox to Brewers of U.S., Jan. 17 and 27, 1913; "Report of USBA Trustees Meeting, April 10—11, 1914," *Brewing and Liquor Interests*, pp. 937—39; Drescher, "Opposition to Prohibition," pp. 210—17.

president of the Foreign Language Newspaper Association. Andreae prepared biweekly essays for distribution under Hammerling's byline for 683 papers that reached 7,500,000 subscribers. For rural audiences Andreae created a weekly news service that by the end of the year was placing items in hundreds of local papers in thirty-two states. For political action, he created an organization department to make a complete survey of conditions in each state. Early in 1914 he called a meeting of brewers and distillers who pooled their knowledge of congressional districts. Andreae's idea was to explore in detail the complexion of Congress and then to work with his allies to improve wet representation. He expressed confidence that the propaganda campaign coordinated with political activity would soon produce results.[36]

Representatives of the distillers and dealers were delighted that the brewers had finally launched a sophisticated action program. They used the shock of the Webb-Kenyon bill and the majority support for the Hobson resolution to press for united action. In a face-to-face meeting with leaders of the USBA at the end of 1914, the NWLDA officers were sharply critical of the brewers' attitudes. They warned that the prohibitionists were never going to accept the notion of beer as a temperance drink; that the two industries were mutually faced with extinction in spite of whatever hopes some brewers expressed. They forthrightly stated that the saloon system was the principal cause of the problem, and the brewers were responsible for it. They called upon the two industries to combine their resources, and they agreed to share the costs of the NACL on a one-third, two-thirds basis and to allow it to direct the activities of the National Model License League. The spirits men emphasized that the new, united effort had to counter the Anti-Saloon League with regional political headquarters of its own, staffed by permanent employees knowledgeable in political operations. In short, they asserted that the antiprohibition fight required the application of the same resources and skills that a modern business firm used. But when they asked for joint control of the NACL to insure a steady and fully coordinated program, Hugh Fox calmly told the liquor men that they were wasting words; the brewers would never agree.[37]

36. Drescher, "Opposition to Prohibition," pp. 190–217; E. T. Busch to Galveston Brewing Co., June 12, 1914; *Brewers and Texas Politics*, p. 104.

37. Andreae form letter, Jan. 3, 1914; Andreae to Edward A. Schmidt, Jan. 23, 1914; L. H. Gibson and Gale M. Harley to Andreae, Nov. 14, 1914; Andreae to Fox, Nov. 15, 1914, *Brewing and Liquor Interests*, pp. 455–62, 941–43, 953.

Some of the brewers rejected this advice and refused to accede to Andreae's efforts. The apparent national strength of the prohibition movement was not sufficient even to solidify support for the NACL within the brewing industry, much less to allow some brewers to overlook their market rivalry with the distillers in a defense of their common interests. The disagreements among the brewers meant that the NWLDA had little choice, if there was to be a united front, but to allow the rival industry to control it. From the distillers' viewpoint only the brewers could reform the saloon system, and their financial resources were necessary to any successful campaign of either reform or politics. The problem was that internal disagreements in the USBA soon ended both the NACL's initial burst of activity and the confidence that Andrea expressed. By the time officers of the two trade associations were meeting, there was a movement afoot in the USBA to have the industry go along with prohibition and have beer and wine excluded.[38]

Andreae was already having trouble maintaining his support from the USBA. In 1914 the NACL received $525,000, but in the first half of 1915, a year of major state prohibition victories, it obtained only $70,000. At a time when the Anti-Saloon League was spending far larger sums, Andreae complained to his patrons that he had to reduce his operations to one-fifth of what he had originally planned. Even so, some officers in the brewers' association were sharply critical of the expenditures. They stopped publication of *The Hearthstone* shortly after it began, rejecting the argument that advertising revenue would soon make it self-sufficient. They criticized his close ties with the foreign language press. Andreae tried to explain that where foreign language voters were well organized, as in Ohio, they insured the defeat of prohibition. Andreae complained that he had only ten men working in politics, and the German-American Alliance three, and the Ohio prohibition referendum occupied them all. Part of the problem lay in lowered beer sales—the 1914 dry victories cost the industry 1,500,000 barrels annually—part in the distrust of the NACL affiliation with the distillers.[39]

The dispute among the brewers came to a climax shortly before the autumn elections of 1915. With national beer sales falling, the majority on the USBA board refused to grant Andreae additional

38. E. A. Schmidt to Andreae, Mar. 2, 1914; "Report of Conference Between Brewers and Distillers, Dec. 29, 1914"; "Report of Meeting of the Joint Harmony Committee, Mar. 6, 1915"; *Brewing and Liquor Interests*, pp. 1049, 1059–61, 1066.
39. "The Trend in the United States," *Brewing and Liquor Interests*, pp. 1057–58.

funds. Their action split the association. Gustav Pabst warned that "unless you get an organization and stick by it and stick to what you do and support the man you have chosen, you had better disband and let this whole industry go to the devil." The Anheuser-Busch Brewery, which had pledged $100,000 to continue the NACL work, in disgust withdrew its membership from the USBA. In 1916 the choice of Christian Feinspagn as association president signaled the final triumph of the faction that wanted a complete disassociation from the spirits industry. That fall the brewers in Oregon, Washington, and Colorado tried to obtain exemptions from prohibition statutes and failed. Even in the face of the sweeping prohibition victories that year, there were brewers who believed they could still convince Americans that theirs was a "temperance beverage." The spirits men were bitterly disappointed, but there was little they could to to dissuade them. When wartime restrictions in 1917 cut off grain supplies to the distilling industry while allowing brewing on a limited basis, the separationist brewers believed that their position was vindicated.[40]

In the end the money, time, and attention that the wet businessmen spent in fighting the prohibition movement proved inadequate. A significant number of brewers failed to understand clearly the motives, arguments, and determination of the Anti-Saloon League and the WCTU. They assured themselves that Baker and his subordinates were simply professional agitators intent on keeping their hands in church collection baskets. They spent a considerable fortune in trying to convince the public that theirs was a benign industry. A group of brewers even secretly purchased the *Washington Times* and hired Arthur Brisbane, a prominent journalist, to edit it, thinking that it was important for the wet viewpoint to be heard in the nation's capital. But the decision for prohibition was not made in Washington; it was made on election days in the precincts and townships across America. The dealers and distillers were joined by prominent and powerful brewing firms in developing a clear vision of the requirements of a successful defense. But the shortsightedness of other brewers, for whom the thought of national prohibition of brewing was simply too incredible to believe, insured that their

40. J. Ruppert, Jr., to Andreae, Sept. 29, 1914; Andreae to President and Board of Trustees, USBA, Nov. 14, 1914; Fox to Andreae, Feb. 12, 1915; "Minutes of an Executive Session of the USBA, Oct. 15, 1915," *Brewing and Liquor Interests*, pp. 455, 928–32, 948, 1073–77, 1182–99; Drescher, "Opposition to Prohibition," pp. 147–49; *Wine and Spirit Bulletin* 30 (Dec. 1916): 36; *American Brewers' Review* 30 (Dec. 1916): 341–49.

industry's strategy vacillated between cooperation with the spirits industry and the hope of profiting from its destruction. The brewers' expenditures surely delayed the imposition of prohibition in some states. But nationally there was no delay. The leaders of the Anti-Saloon League were themselves surprised at how quickly they gained national legislation aimed at destroying the merchants and manufacturers of alcoholic beverages.

8

PROHIBITION VICTORY
1913–1919

On December 18, 1917, Congress submitted the Eighteenth Amendment to the states for their ratification. A little more than one year later, on January 16, 1919, Nebraska became the thirty-sixth state—the last needed to reach a three-fourths majority—to approve the amendment. It would go into effect in one year. In this short time the United States had outlawed the liquor traffic in what prohibition advocates believed was a permanent victory.

Although this remarkable social policy was the product of a century of agitation, the events of the last two years of the campaign moved in a rush that surprised the Anti-Saloon League, its allies, and its opponents. While the years of antidrink agitation had paved the way, it was the politics of wartime mobilization that provided the impetus for the speedy approval of the amendment by the states. The drys had triumphed in the 1916 elections and were prepared to press for submission in the 65th Congress, scheduled to meet the following December. Then Germany resumed unrestricted submarine warfare, and in April Congress declared war. Suddenly a whole new element, charged with emotion, dominated American politics: mobilization and how best to expedite it. Peacetime political disputes did not fade away in a flurry of patriotism but instead were reshaped by the war as Americans tried to attach their particular ideologies and values to the clearcut national interest of achieving victory. During the emotionally charged months when Americans battled "the Hun," prohibitionists urged their cause upon the Congress in the national interest of food and fuel conservation. The brewers and distillers pleaded that their industries, while providing solace for terrified soldiers and weary factory workers, would supply much-needed war revenue.

In the efforts to attach themselves to wartime requirements, the drys had the advantage over the wets. Prohibition sentiment had been spreading like wildfire, faster than even the Anti-Saloon League could organize it. When the delegates to the league's twentieth-anniversary convention met in Columbus, nine states were dry. When the 64th Congress assembled for its final session in December 1916, nineteen states were in the dry column, four of them joining in 1916 alone. The greatest victory was the decision by a majority of Michigan voters to abolish the traffic in that state, the first crack in the wet bastion of the industrial North and East. Detroit would be the largest American city where the saloon was outlawed.[1] These dry triumphs meant that the league was prepared to press Congress for further restrictions, especially prohibition in the District of Columbia, even before the new members took office.

The speed at which the state victories occurred was significant enough in its own right, but it also had important implications for national politics. Even in states where the Anti-Saloon League and its allied organizations might not be well enough organized or financed to mobilize voters according to the balance of power strategy, dry victories came. Those victories instructed politicians that the voters wanted prohibition, that a record vote against a prohibition measure was suicidal for a future career.

If the state victories were not enough to convince skeptical politicians of the popularity of prohibition, they also witnessed a burst of public declarations in support of the reform. The dynamics of these endorsements were inseparable from the spread of dry territory after 1913. By the end of 1916 the weight of business, medical, scientific, and social science opinion was favorable to prohibition, expressed either in formal resolutions or in the informal assessments that American professional and business elites made in the course of their daily activities.[2] All observers of American opinion, wet or dry, realized that the Anti-Saloon League and its allies had won the propaganda battle. This realization prompted a split in the USBA, which was controlled henceforth by those who believed they could salvage the industry with the old arguments that beer was a benign temperance beverage, not associated with spirits. The realization meant that the leaders of the spirits industry, despairing of help from the brewers, turned away from their public campaign toward trying to influence the president and to check the dry tide with legislative and court maneuvers.

1. Larry Engelmann, *Intemperance: The Lost War Against Liquor* (New York, 1979), pp. 2–30.
2. Timberlake, *Prohibition and the Progressive Movement*, pp. 39–99.

Prohibition National Political Strategy

The speed with which the United States placed prohibition in the Constitution and the ease of the Anti-Saloon League's successes in 1918 and 1919 obscured the problems that the league encountered in seeking to win the necessary two-thirds support in both houses of Congress and the difficulties the drys expected in achieving affirmative votes in three-fourths of the states. In devising their political plans, league leaders observed that the fight would not only be difficult, but might fail. They saw the rapidly growing immigrant populations in the cities and the realignment of political power that would result as a forbidding hurdle. This basic demographic trend shaped the league's educational strategy and profoundly affected its political plans.

Most significant, immigration dictated the timing of the league's political efforts. When Baker had announced the decision to seek the constitutional amendment in 1913, he wrote of it as a twenty-year effort. So did Howard Russell. But when Ernest Cherrington examined the requirements of victory more closely, he concluded that the campaign had to be planned for a five-year period. He sought a favorable submission vote in the 66th Congress, elected in 1918, and, failing that goal, after the next round of biennial elections.[3]

Cherrington's planning emerged from his perception of political conditions, immigration and its results, and the state of public opinion. An off-year election seemed the best target, when the considerations of presidential politics and national party maneuvering would be a less powerful influence on the results. The elections of 1918 seemed a desirable goal because the 66th Congress would be the first with all senators chosen by popular ballot, free of the wet corruption funds that the league believed had historically influenced the decisions of party caucuses in the state legislatures. If the league's educational campaign progressed as he planned, public opinion favorable to prohibition ought to be powerful enough to insure the election of supportive senators.

But the House of Representatives was the key to the situation.

---

3. *Anti-Saloon League Yearbook, 1913*, p. 32; Cherrington to Cannon, March 26, 1915, ECe. Subsequent scholarship would tend to confirm Cherrington's analysis of the difficulties facing evangelical Protestant reformers in the 1920s. See, for example, J. Joseph Huthmacher, *Massachusetts People and Politics, 1919–1933* (Cambridge, Mass., 1959).

Cherrington was confident that the progress of the prohibition movement in the southern and western states would ensure a two-thirds majority in the upper chamber. In the House, on the other hand, there were potentially enough urban districts to make the achievement of a two-thirds majority difficult if not impossible. The league was weakest in the industrial cities, in the very places that were gaining in political power as the demography of the nation changed rapidly. The reapportionment of seats in the House of Representatives following the 1920 census would reflect the population growth of the cities. At worst, the resulting wet strength, possibly augmented by gerrymandering, would make impossible the securing of a submission vote. Constitutional prohibition would then require the more difficult and time-consuming politics of having enough dry states call for a constitutional convention for consideration of the issue, a procedure which the league wished to avoid. At best the reapportionment would require the league to engage in a very long educational campaign among immigrant families that might drain the churches' resources. In fact, Cherrington expected the worst. His experience with the league's lack of response to Charles Stelzle's efforts with the labor bureau only served to reinforce his gloomy expectation.

These considerations were still in the future when the league decided to embark on its national campaign in 1913. They awaited a cold, hard look at the political realities, at the vote count in Congress. Insofar as Congress was concerned, the league political strategy was to obtain record votes on two issues that would serve as a benchmark for the congressional district election campaigns. One issue, by far the more significant, was the resolution submitting the constitutional amendment to the states. The other was prohibition in the District of Columbia, where states' rights rhetoric did not limit congressional power. In 1914 the league began working on both measures.

Prior to 1914 the prohibition advocates had made some progress toward reaching the goal of prohibition in the nation's capital. They had put pressure on the licensing authorities in the District government to enforce restrictions on the operation of saloons. The drys had eliminated sales from government buildings and had sharply restricted the number of saloons. But thanks in part to skillful parliamentary maneuvers by the wets, a dry District of Columbia still eluded the league and the WCTU.[4]

4. *The Anti-Saloon League Yearbook, 1917*, pp. 11–31.

More significant, however, was the submission of an amendment. The league worked for that objective in 1914, hoping to have a vote in the House of Representatives in time to place appropriate pressure on individual politicians during the year's election campaigns. The effort was a failure. President Wilson was himself unsympathetic to any prohibitory legislation that extended beyond local option, and he and his advisors did not want prohibition to intrude on the attention of Congress when matters they considered more vital were at stake. So the Sheppard-Hobson resolution, as it was called, so dramatically presented to the congressmen on the Capitol steps, languished in the House Judiciary Committee. The resolution was finally reported, without recommendation, after the 1914 elections.[5]

Nevertheless, the league considered the events that took place in the House on December 23 a victory. In fact, the drys had little to lose and everything to gain. Even if the vote failed to achieve a simple majority, the league could still trumpet the unprecedented consideration of constitutional prohibition. As it was, the simple majority achieved allowed the league to broadcast its "victory" to every corner of the nation, using it to maintain sentiment favorable to the conduct of the national campaign and to whip up enthusiasm for donating funds. This was especially important in those bastions of prohibition sentiment that had already enacted dry laws. The church folks there were told that the Hobson resolution vote indicated the desirability of continuing donations to the league in order to conquer the liquor traffic elsewhere.[6]

The principal consideration in pushing for the vote in the first place was that it would provide a record of prohibition's friends and enemies in the House. The league wanted to use this roll call as a guide for future work in the congressional districts. Cherrington and the other members of the legislative committee knew that there was at best a slim chance that the resolution might receive the needed majority.[7]

The problem with this strategy was that the NACL received the same data as the league and planned its defensive politics in the congressional districts accordingly. Shortly after the vote on the Hobson resolution, Cherrington somehow learned the wet strategy.

5. *Union Signal*, May 14, 1914, p. 2; May 21, 1914, p. 2. Cannon failed to convince William Jennings Bryan and Wilson that the league would not allow prohibition "to impede in any way any of the administration measures." *Bishop Cannon's Own Story*, pp. 176–77.

6. *Union Signal*, January 1, 1915, p. 2; H. B. Carre´ to Baker, March 8, 1917, ECe.

7. Minutes, ASLA Executive Committee, January 28, 1915, ECe.

It was the direct opposite of his own: to hold enough congressional districts to prevent a two-thirds majority in the House. The wets decided to concentrate their attention on nine states with a combined total of 196 representatives. They were New York, New Jersey, Pennsylvania, and Massachusetts in the East; Ohio, Indiana, Illinois, and Missouri in the Middle West; and California in the West. These nine had provided 113 votes against the Hobson resolution, just 55 in favor. If the wets could hold those votes they were a long way toward ensuring the 146 votes they needed to prevent the amendment from ever being submitted to the states. By their own conservative estimate, the wets thought that they were assured of retaining 29 votes in other states without making any special effort. Only four more members from the target states were needed to keep the drys at bay.

When Cherrington learned of this strategy and looked at the figures that emerged from the vote on the Hobson resolution it seemed to him that the league's task was well-nigh impossible. He observed that there were "129 representatives in Congress from large cities where any kind of prohibition, national, state or city, would have a poor show" if the issue were clearly drawn. There were "140 congressional districts . . . which the liquor traffic can control . . . . This alone means that the anti-saloon forces must control in the next Congress or in any Congress, every district which is considered prohibition territory and practically every doubtful district." This reality required some sort of "heroic effort" lest all the "splendid progress" of the dry movement "go for naught . . . in spite of the rapidly rising public sentiment all over the country in favor of prohibition."[8]

The NACL had chosen its nine target states carefully. The New York Anti-Saloon League, despite making some progress, had never succeeded in achieving the control desired. In Pennsylvania the Republican organization led by Senator Bois Penrose was bitterly antagonistic toward the prohibitionists. In New Jersey the league considered the enactment of a local option law a major victory. In Massachusetts, as in the rest of New England, the league was never organized adequately according to the standards of the Westerville headquarters. In the Middle West, the skillful use of the initiative and referendum had tied up the league's resources and caused it to lose ground. The Indiana Democratic party had ridden to victory by criticizing, and then repealing, that state's county option law.

8. Cherrington to Cannon, March 26, 1915.

Indiana's thirteen-member congressional delegation had voted solidly against the Hobson resolution. Wet strongholds in Chicago and Peoria insured the NACL of votes from Illinois. Missouri voters had soundly defeated prohibition in a statewide referendum; the brewers and liquor men there were skilled at organizing business resistance to prohibition and combining it with the solidly wet urban labor vote. California had not seen the kind of solid organization that Russell and Baker wanted to achieve, and the San Francisco Bay area seemed sure of continually sending wet representatives to Congress.

As he analyzed the situation, Cherrington concluded that it was time to change the league's basic political strategy. He observed that the league had always billed itself as an organization apart from the political parties. The league had variously used the terms *nonpartisan* and *omnipartisan* in its organizational rhetoric. Now it was time to turn to the latter slogan and seek platform declarations from all parties, especially the Democratic and Republican, for national constitutional prohibition. This seemed the only way to overcome the obstacles in the path of a two-thirds majority in the House of Representatives. Platform declarations for prohibition would place the party caucuses on the side of the Anti-Saloon League.

Cherrington realized that such a course of action was both dangerous and controversial and gave careful thought to it. If the league succeeded in obtaining an endorsement from one major party but not the other, there was nothing to prevent it from working for dry candidates on the old basis while, after the election, using the endorsement in one party caucus to increase its majority. If the league tried and failed in both major parties, it had lost some respect from its supporters, perhaps, but it should also have gained esteem from making the fight and clarifying the issue. If the league succeeded in obtaining platform endorsements from both parties, there might be little reason to continue the existence of the league on its current basis. But that, as he told Cannon, mattered little. "The League's fight, after all, primarily is not to perpetuate institutions but to solve the liquor problem, and whatever will do this in the last analysis is the policy to pursue, whether that policy be partisan or nonpartisan."

This recommendation was but one alternative—the one he personally preferred—that Cherrington drew from the analysis of the political situation. His second choice was to concentrate on fights for statewide prohibition, while still "holding the flag" for national prohibition. This choice had the advantage of bypassing the House of Representatives and the ominous effects of the post-1920 reap-

portionment altogether. After the league achieved prohibition in
thirty-six states, it could work on petitions for a constitutional convention to consider the issue. This alternative would require the
educational campaign to show urban workers the benefits in terms
of industrial efficiency and safety and fit in with Cherrington's
plans of working toward a national consensus of acceptance, if not
advocacy, of national constitutional prohibition. But it was a time-
consuming and risky strategy. The convention procedure for amend-
ing the constitution had never before been used.

The third alternative that political realities offered was to use the
dry majorities in Congress to destroy the liquor traffic through
legislation. The best route lay in Congress's power to tax, already
used against other evils. There were two problems with such a
strategy, however. The appeal of an amendment was its permanence,
something that no statute enjoyed. Even more serious were the
quarrels that a tax policy was sure to produce within the prohibition
movement. "Some of the radical temperance people will strongly
oppose such an effort on the score that it is a compromise and that it
savors of the liquor traffic's plan of regulation and license."[9]

In the end the league rejected Cherrington's proposal to seek
platform declarations from the major parties. Instead, Baker warned
President Wilson that if the wets obtained his endorsement, and the
Republicans nominated a man satisfactory to the drys, "there will be
new faces in the White House windows after the next presidential
election." Baker conferred with Bryan, now no longer a member of
Wilson's cabinet, and Bryan in turn urged party leaders to remain
silent on prohibition lest it "surrender the great economic advantage"
they had gained over the Republicans. The league posted men at the
conventions to insure that the wets did not influence the platform
committee.[10]

Wilson and the Republican nominee, Charles Evans Hughes,
remained silent on prohibition during the campaign. They justified
their silence by citing the absence of a prohibition plank in their
party's platform. The league, meanwhile, threw its resources into
the congressional races. "We went into every congressional district
where there was a chance to elect a dry," Wheeler recalled ten years
later, "and waged as strong a fight as candidates have ever seen."

9. Ibid.
10. Bryan to Hobson, August 12, 1915, in L. B. Musgrove correspondence, ECe;
Baker to Cherrington, March 1, 1916, ECp; *National Daily*, June 3, 1915, p. 1; May 30,
1916, p. 1; June 12, 1916, p. 4.

The campaigning went on simultaneously with petitions and personal meetings with incumbents. Victorious in November, in its postmortem of the races the league's *New Republic* concluded, "Crepe is now hanging on the door of every rum shop in the land."[11]

The league's victories in 1916 occurred mostly in the Republican party, resurgent after the split of 1912. The league publicized the 1917 victory appropriately as a nonpartisan one. Republican representatives favored submission by a vote of 138 to 62, Democrats by 140 to 64. But the nonpartisan nature of the vote obscured an important partisan trend that allowed the league to achieve the victory in the 65th Congress that had eluded it three years before. The 63rd Congress, elected in 1912, was heavily dominated by Democrats thanks in large part to the Progressive party revolt led by Theodore Roosevelt. Republican wounds healed sufficiently for the 1916 races to elect a plurality in the House of Representatives, although the Democratic caucus was able, after considerable maneuvering, to organize its committees. The resurgence of the Republican party brought 65 more persons to the House willing to vote for submission than had been there in 1914; in comparison the Democratic dry gains numbered only 20.[12]

The other difference between the vote in 1917 and that of 1914 lay in the nine states that Cherrington had learned were the NACL targets. He reported to Cannon in 1915 that the wets counted on 29 votes from other states as safely on their side. The wet calculations were accurate. They gained 28 of those 29 planned votes. The wet disaster came in their nine target states. In 1914 those states had produced a wet majority of 113 to 55. In 1917 they produced a dry majority of 98 to 81. The most dramatic shift came in Indiana, solidly Democratic and solidly wet in 1914, but solidly dry in 1917 with a bipartisan vote.

In spite of the dramatic proclamation of demon rum's funeral crepe in 1916, the submission resolution was not a sure thing in the 65th Congress. Parliamentary maneuver could still defeat it, as could intervention by the party caucuses. Immediately following the 1916 election, Baker issued public statements warning both the Democrats and Republicans against allowing either wet strategy. Never again would the league allow the parties to avoid prohibition

11. *National Daily*, November 9, 1916, p. 1; *New Republic*, November 17, 1916, p. 4; *New York Times*, March 30, 1926.

12. The roll call votes are conveniently displayed in Odegard, *Pressure Politics*, pp. 267–69.

in their platforms. "Henceforth, the political party that is not willing to put a plank in its platform, and the candidate, from the President down, who is not willing to stand squarely on that plank, are not worthy [of] support by patriotic American citizens." The wisest course for the national parties on the horns of a constituency deeply divided by prohibition was to remove the issue by voting for submission.[13]

War, the Wilson Administration, and Prohibition

The league's opposition appraised the situation similarly. The wets were aware that their hold on one-third of the members of the House was uncertain at best. Their strategy thus was the opposite of the league's: to influence the Wilson administration to intervene on their behalf. What confused the political situation in the Congress and in the Wilson administration was the American declaration of war in April 1917. Events thereafter occurred in an atmosphere of national crisis. The 64th Congress, meeting in its lame-duck session, banned the liquor traffic entirely in the District of Columbia. It also provided some surprises. When the 65th Congress convened in a wartime session, prohibition became enmeshed in the complexities of mobilization.

When the 64th Congress convened in December 1916 for its final session, the league hoped to ride the wave of statewide prohibition decisions to legislative victories. The legislative committee listed the submission of the constitutional amendment to the states, the destruction of the liquor traffic in the District of Columbia, a federal ban on the distribution of liquor advertisements in any form in the U.S. mail, and prohibition in the territory of Hawaii as its goals for the session. The drys had withheld pressure for these measures in the earlier sessions, heeding the advice of Democratic leaders that preparedness measures had to take precedence. But now, with their new strength, and the clear signals for prohibition that the voters had just relayed, the dry lobbyists were no longer willing to wait.[14]

The league leaders, acting in conjunction with other temperance organizations through the National Temperance Council, went to work quickly. They arranged with Edwin Yates Webb, chairman of

---

13. *New Republic*, November 17, 1916, p. 1.
14. *National Daily*, November 17, 1916, pp. 1–2; Margaret Dye Ellis, "Report of Washington Superintendent," *43rd Annual Report of the NWCTU, 1916*, pp. 331–32; Cannon, "Report of the Legislative Committee, January 11, 1917," ECe.

the House Judiciary Committee and a member of the board of trustees of the North Carolina Anti-Saloon League, to have the constitutional amendments reported with a favorable recommendation. They worked with supporters in the Senate to have a bill sent to the House banning the saloon in the nation's capital. By securing passage in the Senate first, the dry tacticians hoped to avoid the wet House District of Columbia Committee, which had blocked earlier legislation by refusing to meet. Webb and his supporters in the House planned to attach the bill to an appropriation measure.[15]

But this tactic failed, and the bill almost went down to defeat. The issue that the wets raised was the referendum. The residents of the District, they argued, should enjoy the same right of self-determination on the liquor traffic as their fellow Americans in so many states that decided the controversy with a referendum. Their amendment for a referendum failed in the Senate on a tie vote that the vice-president did not break. When the bill went to the House, the District Committee held hearings designed to delay a floor vote. The league succeeded in having the district committee discharged of its duties only by intervening in the Rules Committee. Then, after the bill passed the House, the wets sought President Wilson's veto. They claimed they were "looking at that higher principle—the right of the people to participate in their government." At the very least the president should appoint a commission "to devise some equitable plan of compensation" for the businessmen who stood to lose their investments to the prohibitionists. Cannon was on guard, however, and had already received the president's assurance that he would sign the bill. Wilson told his secretary, Joseph Tumulty, himself a former attorney for the liquor interests, "how impossible this is for me, particularly at [the] present." Prohibition went into effect in the District on November 1, 1917. The new law closed 356 licensed liquor establishments.[16] On other measures, however, the league was much less successful. The bill to outlaw the liquor traffic in Hawaii never reached the floor of either chamber for a vote. Webb's committee reported the amendment favorably, but that was as far as it ever went in the session. Most important, the effort to ban liquor and beer advertising matter from the U.S. mails backfired on the league.

15. Webb to R. L. Davis, December 6, 1916; Webb to R. B. Glenn, December 20, 1916, EYW.

16. *Union Signal*, January 18, 1917, p. 2; March 8, 1917, p. 2; John F. Wescott to Wilson, February 26, 1917; William F. Ande and Charles J. Columbus to Wilson, March 1, 1917, WW; *Bishop Cannon's Own Story*, pp. 184–85.

The prohibitionists fell into a wet trap that not only embarrassed them, but damaged the eventual success of their cause. The Senate had passed a bill on January 11, 1917, to exclude advertisements of or solicitations for alcoholic beverages from the U.S. mails. This measure was designed to strengthen the prohibition movement by reducing the profits of the wholesale liquor dealers. Most states that had enacted prohibition statutes had struck at the organized liquor traffic and the saloon. They had scrupulously avoided forbidding the personal possession or use of liquor. The Webb-Kenyon Act had given impetus to such state measures because it allowed them to police the interstate traffic within their borders. The result was a healthy one for wholesale liquor dealers who were prepared to engage in a mail order business. They could advertise their products in a dry state and ship their goods to the individual customer for his or her personal use. All prohibition did in most states was outlaw the saloon, strike at the local business system that encouraged Americans to drink. Wholesalers prospered and used their profits to fight the prohibition movement. Both wets and drys were well aware of these conditions. Hence the drys sought to reduce the profitability of the mail order business by striking at its ability to advertise and distribute its products.

Suddenly in Congress, however, they were taken by surprise by Senator James Reed of Missouri. Reed was a bitter foe who yearned to humiliate the drys in any way possible. When the measure excluding the wholesalers' access to the mails came before the Senate as a rider to the post office appropriation, he offered a "bone-dry" amendment that forbad the ordering, purchase, or sale of intoxicating beverages, except for sacramental or medicinal purposes, in any state that had outlawed the liquor traffic.

This amendment was an acute embarrassment to the league. By striking at the individual's right to purchase alcoholic beverages, the bone-dry amendment conformed to the propaganda of the brewing and spirits industries, and it also went much further than Anti-Saloon League rhetoric. The wet businessmen had long complained that prohibition laws did not really prohibit, that even in supposedly dry areas consumption remained rampant. From their perspective this reality called for an abandonment of prohibition measures and the adoption of government regulation and licensing of the traffic. The point of the Anti-Saloon League, however, from its very naming through all of the rhetoric that it had used for twenty-five years to persuade Americans, was to prohibit the organized, legal liquor traffic that was corrupting American life. Although the league leaders clearly advocated abstinence, they were not prepared to use the law to try to impose it. They had consistently followed a strategy of legislative restraint, of not seeking measures until public opinion was prepared to accept them. Suddenly Reed proposed to make it a federal offense for anyone residing in a dry area to order, purchase, or transport alcoholic beverages no matter what the local or state laws said on the subject.[17]

When Reed offered his bone-dry amendment, both Wheeler and Cannon were sitting in the Senate gallery. Dinwiddie was out of town, not expecting an important vote on that date. The two leaders were alarmed and undecided as to the wisest course of action. The Senate had approved the amendment, but the House could still block it. Wheeler drafted a letter to dry representatives urging them to defeat the measure. He expressed fears that as an affront to the doctrine of states' rights, so often emotionally used by southern politicians who were also among the strongest supporters of prohibition, Reed's amendment endangered the entire movement for a constitutional amendment.

Wheeler's letter was never forwarded. Instead, the next day he, Cannon, and A. J. Barton, a prominent Texas Baptist and a member of the legislative committee, sent a letter to every member of the House in which they avoided making a league commitment and suggested that the members follow their own consciences. Then William E. Cox, chairman of the House Post Office Committee, requested a personal audience with the league leaders, during which he directly asked them, "If you were a member of Congress, would you vote for or against this bill?" Both Cannon and Barton, as southern Democrats ostensibly in favor of states' rights, indicated that prohibition took precedence in their minds, and they responded "for the bill." Word of their answer quickly spread through the capital, and the House concurred in the bone-dry amendment by a vote of 319 to 72.

Although at the time he knew the Reed amendment was a "wet joker," Wheeler later claimed its passage as a league victory. In briefs to the attorney general, he argued that carrying even one small bottle of liquor from a wet into a dry area was a federal offense. The attorney general upheld this contention.[18] Meanwhile, Cannon

17. Engelmann, *Intemperance*, pp. 25–30, explains the impact of the bone dry measure on Michigan.

18. Wheeler, Report of the Legal Department, April 4, 1917, ECe; Steuart, *Wayne Wheeler*, pp. 90–93.

called at the White House to urge the president's approval. He
informed Wilson that the political realities in Congress were such
that if the nation were to maintain its postal system, the president
would have to approve the bill.[19]

By the close of the 64th Congress the White House had become an
important center of national prohibition politics. The spirits and
brewing industries read the election returns of 1916 along with
other interested Americans, and the leaders observed the large dry
majorities that the league enjoyed in the battle over prohibition in
the District of Columbia. They turned their attention on the White
House, hoping to influence Woodrow Wilson to use his power in
Congress to impede the prohibition stampede, his veto power to
stop it at crucial points, and his ability to command public attention
to save their industries. These wet efforts were under way before the
American declaration of war, and they continued throughout the
war as prohibition intruded on the problems of mobilization.

The wet leaders' hope of influencing the president was not an
unrealistic one. Wilson had always attempted to avoid the prohibition issue lest it damage his slim hold on public favor. As the leader
of the Democratic party, he was aware that its claim to majority status
was tenuous at best. The party was a coalition of southern and
western Americans who largely adhered to the dry cause, and of
eastern, big city organizations, most notably New York's Tammany
Hall, that were the bitter foes of the Anti-Saloon League and the
WCTU. For a time, first as governor of New Jersey and then during
his first presidential term, Wilson was able to avoid having the issue
impinge on his political career and to keep the lines of communication open to both sides. But during his second term, and especially
after he led the nation into the war, wet pressures on Wilson
mounted, and he showed his opposition to prohibition.

The Anti-Saloon League had applauded Wilson's early political
career in New Jersey. He presented himself as a progressive, reform
governor, and his support of local option legislation endeared him
to the drys. After he was elected president, when called upon to take
a stand on statewide prohibiton, Wilson equivocated. He tried to
straddle the issue by saying that such laws were appropriate in some
states but not others, depending on their homogeneity. In 1911 he
had written that prohibition, a highly divisive issue in the Texas
Democracy, was appropriate for the state, a position he retracted in
1915 as national party leader. His behavior as a president interested

19. Cannon et al., to Wilson, March 3, 1917, WW.

in achieving congressional majorities for the reform of business and the beginnings of federal support for the trade union movement was consistent with the view he had taken toward prohibition legislation while governor of New Jersey. Such questions, he had written, were "social and moral," not properly a part of a party program.[20]

This kind of equivocation would no longer work in 1917. Prohibition bills were now being presented to the president for his approval or rejection. Representatives of the distilling industry were appealing to the president to help them avoid the destruction of their property without just compensation. Trade union locals were flooding the White House with appeals for presidential rejection of prohibition, while the WCTU mounted countervailing campaigns. Compounding Wilson's political difficulties with the issue, the American entry into the war suddenly made the "social and moral" aspects of prohibition seem highly relevant for federal legislative action.

The mobilization for World War I reshaped American politics. Despite the rhetoric of politicians to the effect that a suspension of politics should occur in the interests of national unity, special interest groups of all kinds tried to turn mobilization policies to their particular advantage. The wet and dry forces were no exception, and the "social and moral" prohibition issue became embroiled in wartime affairs.

The drys initiated efforts to turn the war into a compelling requirement for reform. Congress had established the Council of National Defense in 1916 as a group of six cabinet members, with a civilian advisory panel, to coordinate preparedness efforts. Its tasks, of course, assumed a new urgency in April 1917. Irving Fisher, a prominent professor of economics at Yale University, volunteered his services to the council. He expected an assignment related to his professional specialty but was surprised instead by a request that he call a conference on alcohol to meet in conjunction with a conference on venereal diseases, addressing the effects of both on the efficiency of the military.

Fisher had not been actively involved in the prohibition movement, although he was convinced of the evils of alcoholic beverages, in part through personal experience with his own health. The Con-

20. *Proceedings, Fourteenth National Convention, ASLA, 1911*, p. 132; Wilson to Thomas B. Shannon, May 5, 1911; to Hardin Mallard, June 28, 1911, *Papers of Woodrow Wilson*, ed. Arthur Link, (Princeton, N.J., 1976–77), vol. 22, p. 599, and vol. 23, pp. 175–76; Wilson to W. B. Haldeman, May 14, 1915, WW.

ference on Alcohol recommended the establishment of dry zones around military bases and the imposition of prohibition for the duration of the war as a means of saving grain for foodstuffs, coal for factories, and of improving the efficiency of industrial workers. The council approved the first recommendation, but the brewers blocked the second. It was so divisive an issue on the council that its chairman, Daniel Willard, agreed to keep it off the agenda in the interest of preserving harmony.

This was far from the end of the matter, however. The council formed a permanent Subcommittee on Alcohol and named Fisher as the chairman. The subcommittee prepared an analysis showing that the barley used in brewing could potentially provide "eleven million loaves of bread a day." To press the issue, Fisher formed a Committee on War Prohibition, which he headed, and entered the ranks of the nation's temperance leaders. The new committee's authority came from the long list of prominent Americans that supported its goal.[21]

Fisher's leadership and the agitation of the temperance organizations insured the continuing liveliness of wartime prohibition as a political issue. By the summer of 1917 it required presidential intervention. Mobilization strategists informed the American people that food was critical to victory. Wilson called Herbert Hoover, who had enjoyed success and popularity as the administrator of the relief effort for war torn Belgium, to Washington to head a prospective Food Administration. In Congress, Representative A. F. Lever introduced the administration's bill for food and fuel conservation. It would create the Food Administration, empowered to coordinate the production, conservation, and distribution of foodstuffs.

The prohibition organization began agitating to ban the use of grains in distilling and brewing as a food conservation measure. Fisher took a delegation of temperance leaders to a meeting with Wilson, who referred their plea to Hoover. Hoover told them that he was personally sympathetic toward wartime prohibition; that his study indicated that barley, an essential ingredient in brewing, was more useful in stretching wheat supplies in food manufacture than was corn, the staple of the distilling industry.[22] With this kind of backing, the dry amendment to the Lever bill quickly passed in the

21. Irving Fisher, *Prohibition at its Worst*, rev. ed. (New York, 1927), pp. 5–12.

22. *The Cabinet Diaries of Josephus Daniels, 1913–1921*, ed. E. David Cronon (Lincoln, Nebraska, 1963), p. 148; *Union Signal*, May 3, 1917, p. 6; Fisher to Wilson, May 24, 1917, WW.

House. But when the bill went over to the Senate, the early hopes of the prohibitionists encountered a determined wet filibuster.

In the politics of wartime prohibition, the distillers and brewers were working at cross-purpose. Gone was the vision of the distillers for joint efforts in defense of the industries. Those brewers who had long believed that beer could be separated from whiskey, thus saving their industry, were seeking an exemption from the food bill. They had Arthur Brisbane, who listed himself as "owner and editor" of the *Washington Times*, promote the brewers' cause in public editorials and private correspondence and meetings on Capitol Hill and in the White House. Labor unions appealed to politicians to save beer. In this stragtegy the brewers were more than happy to suggest that the distilling industry be sacrificed.[23]

The distillers' strategy was to pose as responsible financiers of the war. They wanted the tax on spirits doubled from the peacetime rate of $1.10 per gallon. The quantity of grain used in the manufacture of spirits, they noted, was infinitesimal when compared with the total production of American farmers. Besides, cattle feed was an important by-product of distilling. But their pleas were ineffective against the combined onslaught of the brewers and the prohibitionists. Thomas Gilmore of the Model License League did not help matters when he wrote to congressmen that issuing spirits to soldiers "will insure that steadiness of nerve that wins battles." He concluded that "the man who rushes a rapid fire gun should be given the relief from terror that alcohol imparts."[24]

Aided by such inept actions from their opponents, the drys were convinced that they could eventually defeat the wet filibuster and insure that no foodstuffs would go into beverage alcohol production for the duration of the war. Even the president let it be known that, although he frowned on extraneous amendments, he considered the dry provision germane to food conservation. But the league leaders had their suspicions of Wilson's wet sympathies confirmed at the end of June. The president was angry that he had to appeal to a special interest to obtain passage of legislation that seemed clearly in the national interest. In private meetings with James Cannon and Senator Thomas Martin the president asked the league to withdraw its pressure and allow the bill to pass as originally written. But Cannon, sensitive to the strong emotions of the prohibition move-

23. John L. Eddy to Webb, May 14, 1917, EYW.
24. *Union Signal*, May 3, 1917, p. 2; President, Distillers Securities Corporation to Webb, May 2, 1917; Gilmore to John G. Cooper, May 22, 1917, EYW.

ment in the war crisis, refused to back down without a public request from the president. On June 29, Wilson wrote the league, appealing to "patriotic motives" and urging that "time is of the essence." The depressed prohibition leaders responded the next day that "we will not for our constituency offer any obstruction to the prompt passage of the Food Control Bill." Wilson replied that their action showed "a very admirable proof of their patriotic motives." The filibuster stopped, the Senate acted favorably, and the resulting conference committee reported a measure that banned the use of grains in distilling and allowed the president discretion in determining the volume of grain to be allocated to the brewing industry.[25]

This compromise speeded the drive for national prohibition. The prohibitionists vowed to obtain a separate measure to impose prohibition during the war. They were concerned lest the brewers use their victory in the food bill to challenge prohibition measures in the dry states. Dry Democrats informed Wilson that the wets were using his action to indicate that the president personally favored the continued use of beer and wine, that the episode made the dry task in Ohio's referendum campaign all the more difficult. "I am very much afraid," William Jennings Bryan wrote to E. Y. Webb, "that the separation of beer from whiskey will give to beer a prestige that will reopen the liquor question in all the prohibition states." He urged Webb to have the Judiciary Committee submit the constitutional amendment "at once."[26]

Webb was unable to do so, however. As the league leaders counted their supporters in the Senate, they realized that they had little if any margin to spare for the needed two-thirds majority. They decided to push the issue in the upper chamber first. There was no trouble with the Judiciary Committee. Its chairman, Wesley L. Jones, in asking Knute Nelson to attend the meeting, noted that "no doubt each member had his mind made up. . . . Why not report it promptly?" In August, the Senate voted by a margin of sixty-five to twenty with eight votes to spare for the prohibitionists, to submit the amendment to the states. This victory did not come without compromise, however. Senator Warren G. Harding, who personally was wet and whose support the league could not count upon, suggested to Wayne Wheeler a change in wording to require ratification within

---

25. Odegard, *Pressure Politics*, pp. 167–71; Cronan, ed., *Diaries of Daniels*, pp. 169–70.

26. Bryan to Webb, July 27, 1917, EYW; William P. Halenkamp to Wilson, Aug. 3, 1917; Tumulty to Wilson, Sept. 5, 1917, WW.

five years of submission. Suspecting wet trickery, Wheeler was non-committal until he studied the schedules of all the state legislatures. When he learned that six years would provide the league with several chances in key states to obtain affirmative ratification votes, he agreed to that designation. Harding then added the provision to the submission resolution and, along with seven other Senators on whom the league had not counted for support, voted favorably. Some were won over, apparently, by the appeal that submission was not a declaration on the merits of prohibition but an action that allowed the states to follow popular wishes.[27]

The Senate's action came too late for Webb to push the measure during the special session of Congress. He knew that he had the necessary votes in the Judiciary Committee and believed that such was the case in the entire House. But absenteeism during the late summer and autumn might cost the drys a victory. So he postponed consideration of the measure until the regular session convened in December.[28]

In the meantime prohibition politics in the federal government did not abate. They only shifted from the legislative to the executive branch. Appeals began to pour into the White House demanding that the president use his powers under the Lever bill to stop grain from being used in brewing as well as distilling. The WCTU complained that the distillers were purchasing huge quantities of grain in anticipation of federal intervention. They were also withdrawing whiskey from bonded warehouses at unprecedented rates in order to escape the doubled federal tax. An officer of United Cereal Mills informed the president that distillers were "driving up" the cost of foodstuffs fourfold. "It would seem to us," he concluded, "that the people running the government are more interested in taking care of the drunkards than taking care of the starving."[29]

Wilson paid no heed to these appeals. Instead he listened to Tumulty and the appeals that the availability of beer was essential for the well-being of industrial workers. When Hoover decided that it was best for the Food Administration to have an advisory committee for the issue, and asked the president for advice on whom to appoint, Wilson replied, "On the whole, I think for the present we

27. Jones to Nelson, June 2, 1917, KN; *Union Signal*, August 9, 1917, pp. 2, 8; *New York Times*, March 31, 1926.

28. Webb to Bryan, July 26, 1917, EYW; *Union Signal*, August 16, 1917, p. 2.

29. Arthur Dunn to Wilson, July 17, 1917, WW; *Union Signal*, August 23, 1917, p. 2.

had better leave the brewing trade alone until the situation develops more clearly." The brewers continued to operate through the autumn. Then Hoover wrote the president suggesting a reduction of the alcoholic content of beer to under 3 percent, and a halving of the use of grain from peacetime levels. The president agreed on the alcohol reduction but suggested that the restriction on grain allocations was too severe. It would increase the price of beer and "be very unfair to the classes who are using it and who can use it with very little detriment when the percentage of alcohol is made so small." Finally, Hoover reduced grain allocations for brewing to 75 percent of their peacetime levels. Conscious that this would not placate prohibition supporters, he had Food Administration officials inquire in local communities to learn if a ban on brewing would bring public favor. Hoover wanted the public to cooperate voluntarily with conservation programs, and he was concerned that the continuation of brewing would not elicit it. The outcry over the continuing use of grain for brewing continued to plague Hoover and the Wilson administration until the separate wartime prohibition bill went into effect.[30]

The only interruption in the dispute over the administration's wartime beer policy was the submission of the prohibition amendment. The wets made two last desperate attempts to hold it up in the House. Samuel Gompers appealed directly to the president on behalf of the members of the AFL. Gompers was part of a general wartime policy of exchanging worker's cooperation for improvements in wages, hours, and working conditions. In tune with Wilson's appeal for social harmony during the war, he urged the president to intervene in the House fight to stop the submission vote. The prohibitionists were "eaten up with egotism and fanaticism," he wrote. "Their project is not calculated to unite our people." But Wilson refused to intervene. When a "non-partisan committee" of representatives asked to see the president, he told his secretary, "I should very much like to keep out of the prohibition mix-up."[31]

The brewers used another approach to try to delay the vote. They had been raising the issue of the expropriation of their property

30. Hoover to Wilson, August 28, 30, and 31, 1917; Wilson to Hoover, November 20, 1917, *The Hoover-Wilson Wartime Correspondence*, ed. Francis W. O'Brien (Ames, Iowa, 1974); P. G. Selby to Warren G. Harding, March 5, 1918; to Cherrington, March 6, 1918; Cherrington to Selby, March 9, 1918, ECe.

31. Gompers to Wilson, December 14, 1917; Wilson to Tumulty, undated (December 1917), WW.

without compensation. One brewer asked the Anti-Saloon League to allow them to operate for five more years, with the federal government in the meantime collecting additional tax revenue from beer that it would use to compensate the industry for its losses. But when the advocates of this approach discovered that the USBA leaders refused any compromise, adamant that they could still somehow save their industry, the plan fell through. Its only result was an extension of the period allowed for ratification to seven years, in return for the amendment not taking effect until one year from the date of its ratification. The House passed the submission resolution in a bipartisan vote of 282 to 128, and the Senate quickly agreed to its changes. On January 8, 1918, Mississippi began the ratification process.[32]

The Politics of War and Ratification

Whatever hopes that senators and representatives may have had for their action removing prohibition from the Capitol soon evaporated. Although the Anti-Saloon League and the WCTU turned their attention to the ratification controversy in the state legislatures, they did not fail to continue pressing the federal government to stop the production of alcoholic beverages during the war. They pressed their attack on two fronts: the food policy of the Wilson administration and the enactment of wartime prohibition legislation in its own right.

The persistent attacks on the use of scarce coal and grain by the brewing industry finally forced the Wilson administration to respond. Hoover suggested that the president inform the nation that a cessation of brewing would simply grant the entire market to the whiskey dealers, who had a large supply in storage. Not only would such a policy be "demoralizing," but it would give the whiskey men a monopoly in the market. This response to the dry complaints fit neatly with the arguments of the brewers that theirs was a "temperance beverage," and it satisfied the labor unions, whose complaints the USBA and the brewery workers were orchestrating. When Representative Charles H. Randall, the sole Prohibition party member in Congress, sought to amend the agricultural appropriation bill to require the president to ban the manufacture of beer

32. *Ratification Hand-Book*, 2nd ed. (Westerville, Ohio, 1919), p. 8; *New York Times*, March 31, 1926.

and spirits, Wilson asked Morris Sheppard "to let the situation stand as it is" at least until Hoover advised otherwise.[33]

Finally, after the November armistice, Wilson affirmed his support of the brewers. Technically the nation remained at war, so the president could continue wartime conservation efforts. But the Food Administration informed the White House that there was no longer a need for conservation, and Wilson, in Versailles for the peace conference, asked his cabinet for advice. Would a continuation of restrictions serve as a temperance measure? The majority advised him to keep the restrictions. Representatives of the USBA, on the other hand, pressed the White House for permission to continue operation. Claiming that the wartime beer containing 2.75 percent alcohol was not an intoxicating beverage, Hugh Fox told the president that without a resumption of brewing many consumers would turn to whiskey. Restrictions threatened to increase unemployment. Wilson finally agreed to allow the breweries to continue operating.[34]

This controversy of 1919 was more symbolic than substantive because Congress had already voted to outlaw brewing after May 1 in what was known as the Wartime Prohibition Act. It forbad the sale of all intoxicating beverages after June 30, 1919. Congress passed this measure ten days after the Armistice, but its legislative history extended back to the controversy over the Lever Act of 1917.

When Wilson obtained the league's agreement on the food conservation bill, the prohibitionists vowed to press for a separate wartime law. Wilson opposed this measure, as he did all such measures, and used his influence with Democratic leaders in Congress to try to prevent its consideration on the grounds that it "might operate seriously to disturb and delay the necessary business of the session." But the president was not able to control the congressional situation, and the drys arranged to attach their bill to the agricultural appropriation measure. It was almost killed by parliamentary maneuvering in the Senate, but in the end the league's pressure was sufficient to have it sent to Wilson, who had to sign it if he wanted funds for the

33. Hoover to Wilson, May 27, 1918, *The Hoover-Wilson Wartime Correspondence*, pp. 200–01; Wilson to Sheppard, May 28, 1918, WW.

34. Edmund W. Pugh to Tumulty, January 15, 1919; Wilson cablegram, January 17, 1919; "Memorandum for Mr. Tumulty," January 23, 1919; Hugh Fox to Wilson, February 25, 1919, WW; Cronon, ed., *Diaries of Daniels*, pp. 369–70; J. J. Stream to Detroit Federation of Labor, December 18, 1918, USFA.

Department of Agriculture. Thus the United States actually went dry on June 30, 1919.[35]

As events turned out, the Wartime Prohibition Act speeded up the abolition of the legal liquor traffic by little more than six months. On January 16, 1919, Nebraska became the thirty-sixth state to ratify the Eighteenth Amendment. In 1917 the Anti-Saloon League was concerned lest the seven years allowed for ratification should prove insufficient. The dry organizations geared up for a massive publicity campaign to promote the amendment, while Wheeler and Cannon arranged for a Senate investigation of the brewing industry and its German connections in hopes of discrediting the league's opposition while wrapping the mantle of patriotism around ratification. Twenty-one states had enacted their own prohibition laws, and the league expected little difficulty securing positive votes from their legislatures. But it needed thirty-six states and was not at all sure of that number.[36]

The speed at which ratification occurred surprised the league leaders. "We thought it would take three or four years to get the amendment ratified," Dinwiddie told a reporter in 1918. "Instead, one wet state after another is coming in and the thing's become as simple as 'A.B.C.' " Filmore Condit, chairman of the league's executive committee, told one colleague in the autumn that the process would be complete by April 1919, when state legislative sessions were ending. "The liquor interests of America seem without hope," he wrote.[37]

The alcoholic beverage industries engaged in the politics of desperation during 1918. The distillers tried to appeal to other businessmen by raising the spectre of government expropriation. "It has become a sort of fad for businessmen to look with more or less complacency on the goring of the liquor man's ox," Gilmore wrote to President Wilson, "but the time had arrived when every businessman must look for the gore of his own ox. The . . . amendment bids fair to start a landslide that will grow into an avalanche carrying private ownership of property over the brink of socialism and thence

35. Andrew Sinclair, *Era of Excess: A Social History of the Prohibition Movement* (New York, 1962), pp. 157–58; Wilson to Sheppard, March 22, 1918, WW.

36. Steuart, *Wayne Wheeler*, pp. 116–38; Cherrington to Filmore Condit, January 3, 1918, ECe. For example, Charles Stelzle, *Why Prohibition!* (New York, 1918), was a book-length effort of the Federal Council of Churches to persuade Americans to ratify the amendment.

37. Condit to H. B. Carre', October 4, 1918; undated clipping, *New Orleans Item*, 1918, ECe.

into the gulf of anarchy." He hoped the president would lead a popular campaign to resist ratification.[38]

The desperate appeal to the capitalist sentiments of the president and other businessmen failed. The Anti-Saloon League was well prepared for the confiscation argument. "There will be no confiscation of property because no property will be taken from anyone," the league assured its business supporters. Instead, the law will require the brewers, distillers, and dealers to use their property in other ways. Nor did Wilson follow the wet appeals for presidential intercession in the dispute. William Jennings Bryan, conveying the league's message to the president, reminded him that the amendment sentiment was strong in those states that were the bedrock of Democratic strength. It was prudent for him to stay out of the fight. If the amendment was ratified and proved beneficial, the administration would share in the credit. If the states failed to ratify, there would be no reason to criticize Wilson. Wilson listened to this advice and took no visible part in the controversy.[39]

The other part of the wet desperation strategy was to cloud the ratification process with legal confusion. The wets claimed that such an important matter, so closely touching the lives of individual Americans, should not become part of the Constitution without direct popular action. The ratification question should be submitted to the voters directly. While the opponents attempted to stage referendums in fourteen states, the test occurred in Ohio. The state had recently approved an amendment to its constitution that the action of the legislature on a federal amendment could be submitted directly to the people. When the General Assembly approved the Eighteenth Amendment in a lopsided vote on January 7, 1919, the wets proceeded to collect sufficient signatures to require a referendum. A dry attorney from Cincinnati, George S. Hawke, sought an injunction to prevent Ohio Secretary of State Harvey C. Smith from placing the measure on the autumn ballot. While the question was in the courts, Ohio voters, by the slim margin of 479 votes out of a total of 1 million cast, rejected national prohibition. But this proved only a psychological victory for the wets. On June 1, 1920, the U.S. Supreme Court, in *Hawke v. Smith*, ruled unanimously that the provision in the federal constitution for ratification by state legislatures prevailed over local laws. After this ruling, there was little reason to proceed with popular referendums on the amendment,

---

38. Gilmore to Wilson, May 22, 1918; Gilmore to Tumulty, May 28, 1918, WW.
39. Steuart, *Wayne Wheeler*, pp. 113–14; *Ratification Hand-Book*, p. 23.

already ratified by all legislatures save those of Rhode Island and Connecticut.[40]

So by early 1919 the needed states had ratified the Eighteenth Amendment. One year later the evangelist Billy Sunday preached an oft-quoted funeral oration of John Barleycorn. In Chicago, in an event staged for the press, Hinky Dink's Saloon saw some of its last customers, O. G. Christgau, E. J. Davis, and F. S. McBride of the league, who purchased empty beer tubs as souvenirs.[41] The liquor traffic in the United States was no longer legal. With the ban placed in the Constitution, the prohibitionists were convinced it was permanent. American political controversy concerning prohibition, however, did not disappear. Instead, it entered a new phase, one that proved much more difficult for the Anti-Saloon League to organize and lead. With prohibition in place in the Constitution, what was the proper course for "the church in action against the saloon"? That question, never satisfactorily answered, plagued Cherrington, Wheeler, Cannon, Baker, and all the other officers of the league. Their failure to agree on a strategy of prohibition after 1919 led to the decline of the Anti-Saloon League as a political force able to shape events.

What was happening in the rush of events during the war years was imporant for the future of the Anti-Saloon League and its cause, prohibition. Confusion was arising over the question of personal drinking versus outlawing the liquor traffic as a business. All of the league leaders believed in the desirability of total abstinence from alcoholic beverages for themselves and for other persons. But they had never presented a political strategy designed to force abstinence on individual drinkers. The league had always followed a policy of never pressing legal measures in advance of public acceptance. Abstinence was a behavior that league rhetoricians believed would be enhanced by abolition of the liquor traffic. Now, however, with the passage of Reed's "bone-dry" amendment, those persons in the league, led by Wayne Wheeler, had cause to argue for law enforce-

---

40. "Report of the Legal Department," May 8, 1919, ECe; David Kyvig, *Repealing National Prohibition* (Chicago, 1979), pp. 14–16. In New York, when the wets tried to force a referendum, Samuel E. Nicholson was able to have it blocked by the Republican leaders. As he told Senator Nelson Aldrich, a referendum might set a poor precedent for other issues that might threaten "the substantial business interests" that were "in large degree the backbone of the Republican party." Such controversial matters were best left to "a deliberative body." Anderson to Governor Charles S. Whitman, August 23, 1918, WA.

41. *Chicago Post*, February 3, 1920, clipping in OGC.

ment measures that were intended to force drinkers to stop purchasing and possessing alcoholic beverages. Within the ranks of the Anti-Saloon League's top leaders, therefore, confusion was emerging over the very purposes of prohibiton. In that confusion and in the law enforcement battles of the next decade lay the seeds of the public discrediting of constitutional prohibition itself and of the organizations that supported it. The failure of the Anti-Saloon League leaders to agree on a strategy for the postwar years meant that when another national crisis, the Great Depression, occurred, the league was in no position to stop the repeal of the Eighteenth Amendment.

9

THE LEAGUE DIVIDED, 1920–1927

In 1919 the Anti-Saloon League stood at a peak of success that almost overwhelmed it. During its dramatic rise to national power, culminating in the ratification of the Eighteenth Amendment, Baker, Cherrington, and the other national officers and executive board members had given precious little consideration to the future either of the organization or of the prohibition movement in general. They realized that an enforcement statute was needed, but beyond pressing for that, they had not thought about strategy in a dry America. Uncertainty concerning the role of the pressure group that no longer seeks reform nearly destroyed the Anti-Saloon League altogether during the forthcoming decade. That uncertainty and competing perspectives on the needs of the Protestant church movement led to internal disputes. Not the least of the results was a new relationship between the league and its constituents.

At one level the source of uncertainty about the role of the league was simple enough. Before 1919 the league was a coalition of persons seeking a clear reform goal, the legal prohibition of the liquor traffic. However much different factions of dry Americans may have disagreed about the kind of organization they thought was best for destroying the liquor traffic, the Anti-Saloon League was always able to maintain a clear purpose. Some aspects of the purpose, prohibition, may have aroused some controversy among dry Americans—certainly there were still third-party advocates who bitterly and faithfully maintained a vision of the devout elected to office, and there were others who wanted the possession and consumption of alcoholic beverages outlawed. Nevertheless, the league arrived at a common denominator and persuaded most evangelical Protestant leaders and their congregations that there was a clear and achievable objective. Constitutional prohibition of the liquor business, and the

211

lesser steps preceding it, united millions of dry Americans. But once the goal was realized, the point of union disappeared.

The union of dry reformers, furthermore, had obscured competing perspectives during the campaign for the Eighteenth Amendment. So long as the goal remained unobtained, any leader who could persuasively argue that a program he favored would advance the cause had a reasonable expectation of winning support from other league officers. Thus Cherrington achieved prominence within the organization not only because of his managerial skills, but also because of his programs for education and propaganda. The views of uplift that Cherrington and others espoused might have had less appeal to other officers if those views had stood apart from the political goal. But stand apart they did not, at least before 1919. Once the goal of prohibition was realized, however, the officers of the league began to divide into factions because there no longer was an overarching legislative goal to unite them.

The Anti-Saloon League, in brief, had grown as a coalition of like-minded persons whose common political goal before 1919 hid underlying differences of perspective and of basic values. One powerful element within both the league's leadership and its constituency, as we shall see, advocated a coercive role for the prohibition organization after 1919, one in which the league would seek to enforce the law and make recalcitrant persons conform to evangelical Protestant norms. But another element, led by Cherrington, approached the problems of a legally dry America with assimilative values. This element attempted to maintain the spirit of optimism that had pervaded the campaign for the Eighteenth Amendment. The second group of league leaders and constituents believed that the organization had accomplished the main political task and now should turn its attention to educational work both at home and abroad. Their approach would involve a grand temperance campaign to gain understanding and acceptance of the law and gradually but steadily gain conformity to dry norms.[1]

---

1. Gusfield, *Symbolic Crusade*, esp. pp. 69–70, explains the differences between "assimilative" and "coercive" reform. Gusfield argued that the Anti-Saloon League represented coercive reform. But he had no access to the league records, which reveal a much more complex mixture of assimilative and coercive goals within the modern prohibition movement.

Unlike the woman suffrage movement, which formed the League of Women Voters as an organization appropriate for new tasks once the Nineteenth Amendment was in place, the Anti-Saloon League leaders did not agree upon beginning new structures for sorting out and pursuing new goals in a dry America.

The problem that the Anti-Saloon League faced as an organization, however, was that its structure, designed for the focus on achieving prohibition, provided precious few means for clarifying or resolving disputes over policies in a dry nation. In fact, establishing mechanisms for arguing about the future of the prohibition movement would have contradicted a fundamental league principle. The pressure group, after all, was most effective when it was single-purpose, when it united the largest possible number of persons around a common goal no matter what their disagreements were on other matters. The league, thus, was basically unsuited for action after 1920. The result was a seven-year period of factional disputes in which one group of leaders attempted to wrest control of the league from the other group. The factional disputes occurred in a framework not designed for the resolution of competing goals, coercive or assimilative strategies.

No one closely involved with the league recognized this situation in 1919. The leaders never questioned maintaining the organization. From their viewpoint the fight was unfinished. At the least, they believed, the league must still maintain dry majorities in the legislatures and the Congress and hold politicians accountable for administering and enforcing the amendment. They realized that the liquor traffic and the social customs associated with the imbibing of alcoholic beverages were far from dead. Continuing vigilance, in their view, was necessary. The league officials saw the liquor business as a determined foe whose death would not occur instantly with the passage of the new law.

But the followers of the league did not necessarily agree. From the perspective of countless supporters, the league strategy had succeeded; the victory was won. As emotional involvement in the fight for reform receded, so too did support for the Anti-Saloon League. Collections dropped off precipitously after 1919, and league officials forevermore struggled to develop and meet realistic budgets. Because the officers failed to enunciate a clear, unifying role or even strategy for the organization as the keeper of a reform, rather than its advocate, the league crumbled rapidly.

Leadership and Strategy

If the nature of the league's structure, designed for uniting somewhat disparate Americans behind a legislative goal, was ill-suited for resolving differing views about future activity, part of the organization's problem in clarifying a postamendment strategy stemmed from an accidental failure of leadership. Purley Baker, who had served as general superintendent since 1903, was aging, failing in health, and unable to devote full vigor to the cause. Since 1916 he had resided in Alabama, managing the Black Belt Farms Corporation in which he and the league associates had invested. Baker was frequently absent from the league offices in Westerville. At one time he had set an example of selfless sacrifice for the cause and had provided feisty political leadership. But with his semiretirement, which occurred without forethought as to clear lines of authority or succession, there was a vacuum at the topmost level.[2]

It was not just the semiretirement that created the vacuum but Baker's own suspicions of Cherrington as well. The two men had developed a very close personal relationship over the years, and when Baker decided to move to Alabama, Cherrington, as well as Russell and Wheeler, had assured him that they were capable of handling daily operations. But within three years Baker was expressing antagonism toward Cherrington, telling him that he had assumed too large a leadership role. In 1919 Baker falsely accused Cherrington of trying to oust him from office so he could become general superintendent.[3]

This falling out had far-reaching repercussions for the future. Other personal disputes and suspicions began to divide the league's departments and their officers. The main conflict arose between Cherrington and Wheeler, who were never close personally. Both men were ambitious, but in the last years of the national campaign the former Ohio superintendent had played a subservient role in his post in Washington. After 1920 Wheeler's views and ambitions, sharply conflicting with Cherrington's, led to deepening schisms. Wheeler became the spokesman for those who would use prohibition to coerce behavior. Cherrington complained about the emphasis and proposed that the league embark on an assimilative temperance campaign.

Russell's presence did not help assuage disputes. Although he had no role in daily management, the league founder was still active as a publicist and fund raiser. Both he and Cherrington resided in

2. Baker's decline became a subject of discussion. See Cannon to Board of Directors, Mar. 28, 1924, ECe. Referring to a conference with President Harding in 1923, Arthur J. Davis remarked, "I think the fact of the matter is that Doctor Baker is no longer a suitable person to handle matters of this kind." Davis to Cherrington, May 21, 1923, ECg.

3. Baker to Cherrington, June 9, 1919; Cherrington to Baker, June 25, 1919, and July 16, 1920, ECe.

Westerville, and Cherrington had helped Russell with personal financial problems. Their conferences provided a forum for Cherrington to express personal misgivings and hopes.[4] What the younger man failed to realize until 1924, however, was that Russell disagreed with his views. Russell's views were more like Wheeler's, and as Wheeler gained influence after 1920, he and Russell quietly opposed Cherrington's leadership.

Cherrington by temperament was more interested in education, proselytization, and propaganda than he was in legal matters. His background in journalism, his rapid rise to head the league's publishing house, and his perceptions of strategic needs conformed to those interests. The enactment of prohibition served to reinforce Cherrington's view of the urgency of reaching immigrant peoples with the dry message. In his eyes the Eighteenth Amendment seemed an important instrument for educational purposes. Cherrington reasoned that the law had damaged the liquor traffic and had broken the vice by which those businesses had gripped American society. The saloon was gone. Cherrington realized that important goals had been achieved; no longer could large, wealthy corporations advertise their evil wares; no longer could they seek to enlarge their markets by establishing saloons; no longer could the liquor business openly ply youth, women, and untutored immigrant laborers with drink and the dissolute life that too often accompanied visits to the saloon.

But Cherrington believed that, important as the new law was, it would not by itself kill the liquor traffic. The habits of drink and its institutions were simply too imbedded in social customs for the traffic to disappear easily. In his view the law was, thus, an important instrument of the criminal justice system to bring manufacturers and dealers to court and to end their activities. But in his mind the law was of an importance that transcended the criminal justice system. Cherrington believed that the Eighteenth Amendment was an instrument for education, education that could root out the ancient habits of drink. He reasoned that, with the liquor traffic broken, driven underground and there pursued by police officers, the churches had an unprecedented opportunity to accomplish their fundamental work of moral suasion, reaching out to all Americans with a symbolic standard of proper social behavior. The main task of the prohibitionists, therefore, was to use the law as a symbol in a broad campaign to follow through on the promise of individual

4. Cherrington to S. S. Kresge, Apr. 27, 1923, ECe.

uplift. In this way, Cherrington remained true to the optimistic reform spirit that had caught the emotions of so many evangelical Protestant Americans during the Progressive Era and the World War. In this way, furthermore, Cherrington drew logical conclusions from the large volumes of rhetoric produced by the prohibition movement over the preceding decades, rhetoric so forcefully summarized by Richmond P. Hobson when he first pleaded with Congress to initiate the constitutional reform.[5]

Wayne Wheeler and, as subsequent events later showed, Howard Russell fundamentally disagreed with Cherrington. They never disregarded educational work, but they believed that the purpose of education was to teach obedience to the law. Achievement of the amendment was the pinnacle of league success, and the purpose of the organization was now to insure the law's enforcement. All else was subservient. In their view the league was from its inception a political organization, mobilizing the churches to change and then enforce the law. Although he had given little thought to the problems the league might face once it achieved the goal of national prohibition, Russell had always thought of the "temperance trust" in political and legal terms. In Wayne Wheeler he had found an able follower who agreed with those principles and who himself took time from league work to earn a law degree and admission to the bar. Wheeler, in short, was a politician and a lawyer with a keen sense of the right and wrong behavior that the law was not just to describe, but to enforce. Thus the proper strategy after 1920 was to maintain political power and secure ever stricter enforcement.

During his last years as general superintendent, Baker did not attempt to resolve the fundamental differences between the two approaches. Instead he allowed both Wheeler and Cherrington to pursue their separate strategies. Baker personally favored Wheeler's emphasis on law enforcement, however. Appalled by what he saw as a decline in the vision and the quality of league leadership on the state and local church levels, he warned the executive committee in 1921 of its enormous task. There seemed a growth in lawlessness as the traffic in drink failed to disappear, especially in the cities. This condition required that "violators of the law . . . be arrested, fined, sent to prison and justly punished." But such was not the work of the church. Its great task was to fan the fires of pa-

5. This notion of the law as an instrument creating educational opportunities was a constant refrain in Cherrington's rhetoric for a decade. See his "The Unfinished Task," *The Adult Bible Class Monthly* (July 1925), pp. 193–96, clipping in ECg.

triotism, "to create a condition and establish in the minds and hearts of men the spirit of right thinking and right action, which will compel the enforcement of law through the regularly constituted authorities." Baker, thus, clearly agreed with Wheeler's views. The general superintendent subordinated religion and education to the law. In his mind, therefore, the league was always a political organization.

But if Baker thought of the league as a purely political organization, in practical terms the general superintendent left room for those who agreed with Cherrington's ideas of uplift. Before the passage of the Eighteenth Amendment, Baker was willing to allow Cherrington to pursue a larger educational strategy. Baker expressed his belief, moreover, that the task of the church was not to preach to the faithful. "Filling the pulpits of the land on Sunday morning and evening will not bring about the desired results," he noted. "We must go to the people who do not come, *and they are in the majority*." Leave the pulpit, in other words, go to the people wherever they are, and address them in their own language to demonstrate the scientific truths that undergirded prohibition. Baker understood that such work was essential for winning elections before 1919, and it still remained significant in compelling government officials to enforce the dry law. In short, Baker concluded, "the second great period of a great nation-wide propaganda is upon us, and we dare not refuse to meet the conditions."[6]

Cherrington and the Vision of World Prohibition

Although Baker's purpose was law enforcement, the methods he urged were similar to those that Cherrington espoused. This similarity meant that the general superintendent permitted Cherrington some room to operate on behalf of his vision of education and uplift. In spite of the personal falling out with Baker, Cherrington continued to serve as general manager of the American Issue Publishing Company, secretary for the executive committee, and head of the league's financial affairs throughout the 1920s. He traveled widely, spoke often, wrote important league documents, and addressed large audiences through religious publications. Cherrington's prominence in the league, although largely unnoticed in the mass circulation newspapers and magazines of the day, assured that his views commanded attention among the clergymen and state

6. Report of Baker to the Executive Committee, July 14, 1921, ECe.

superintendents whose activities and dedication were so important. As early as 1911 Cherrington told listeners that statute books might be changed, "but unless back of those laws exists a living public sentiment powerful enough to enforce them, such laws are not worth the paper upon which they may be written."[7]

This view was hardly controversial, for it conformed to the sentiments of Baker, Wheeler, and Russell. They knew that public support—sympathetic jurors, legislators willing to appropriate funds, and party leaders ready to appoint zealous administrators— was needed for effective law enforcement. But Cherrington did not stop at that point. He tied his commitment to education with the international character of the temperance movement and called for the league to adopt a worldwide strategy. He advised dry Americans to reach out and assist in the destruction of the international liquor traffic.

American temperance reformers were part of a movement that was international in scope. For decades they had communicated with like-minded reformers across the Atlantic, especially in Great Britain. The international aspect was institutionalized in 1885 with the convening of the International Congress Against Alcoholism, meetings that continued biennially until the World War interrupted them. Cherrington had attended the congresses of 1911 and 1913 and during the amendment campaign had devoted some attention to the international character of both the liquor traffic and the movement to suppress it. He believed that international work was one means of reaching wet immigrant voters in the United States, essential both to winning prohibition and gaining acceptance of it.[8]

The American involvement in World War I elicited considerable idealism. When the Wilson administration spoke of the war as a kind of crusade, of American intervention as based on principles of international law and brotherhood, churchmen, including Ernest Cherrington, agreed and tried to help shape the postwar world. Even before the armistice in 1918, Cherrington had arranged for a meeting to found the World League Against Alcoholism. His idea was for the committee on financial management to shepherd this

7. Cherrington, untitled speech, 1911, ECg.
8. There is no full-scale history of the international aspects of the temperance movement, but for an able beginning that focuses on the 1920s, see Susan M. Brook, "The World League Against Alcoholism: An Attempt to Export an American Experience" (M.A. thesis, University of Western Ontario, 1972). Ross Evans Paulson, *Women's Suffrage and Prohibition: A Comparative Study of Equality and Social Control* (Glenview, Ill., 1973), discusses the prohibition movement in Scandinavia.

new organization carefully. "If the National League can go forward
with its world-wide program," Cherrington wrote his friend S. S.
Kresge early in 1919, "without making serious mistakes in the early
stages of the enlarged movement, we believe that great service can
be rendered by this organization in the next few years to the cause of
civic righteousness and Christianity throughout the world."[9]

The World League Against Alcoholism, as Cherrington envisioned it, would allow the Anti-Saloon League to reach out and
assist reformers in other nations. As opportunities arose and funds
were available, the world league would place field agents to "bear
testimony," explaining the benefits of prohibition, telling how the
Anti-Saloon League political methods worked, and helping to organize reformers to adopt its techniques. It would call upon American
businessmen and labor leaders to secure the cooperation of their
counterparts abroad, prepare and circulate literature in English and
other languages, coordinate the temperance work of missionaries,
and insure that U.S. consulates were properly informed of the
benefits of prohibition. The world league would raise funds in the
United States to nurture foreign groups.[10]

During the year following the founding of the world league,
Cherrington sketched his grand design for the Anti-Saloon League
and its postamendment strategy. His forty-five page *Plan of Financial Reorganization of the Anti-Saloon League of America for State, National and International Work* was a renewed call to arms for the
nation's evangelical churches. "The greatest danger which today
threatens the Prohibition movement in America and throughout the
world," Cherrington began, "is that in this hour of victory the
faithful friends of Prohibition may conclude that the fight against
the liquor traffic in America is at an end." No law, however highly
placed or strictly enforced, he went on, can "of itself solve the liquor
problem, or any other great moral or social problem." What was
required was the changing of minds, the persuasion of the millions
of Americans who had opposed prohibition that the law and its
enforcement was a wise and beneficial social policy.

This accomplishment, he believed, required expansion of the
Anti-Saloon League. Cherrington recognized that the natural tendency of league contributors was to think of the work as done. But

9. Cherrington to Kresge, Jan. 21, 1919, ECe. On the world league, see *Standard
Encyclopedia of the Alcohol Problem*, 6:2910–16.

10. *Proceedings, Nineteenth National Convention, ASLA, 1919*, p. 34; *Plan of Financial
Reorganization of the Anti-Saloon League of America for State, National and International
Work* (Westerville, 1919), pp. 16–17.

he argued forcefully that it was not. The enforcement of the law through education and the establishment of the world league were enormous tasks that required larger budgets and more thorough organization, especially at the state level. "Large classes of the American population," the foreign born and Negroes, had largely been "neglected" in the league's legislative work. Now they could be ignored only at the peril of the churches. "The enforcement and maintenance of Prohibition in the United States depend to a very large degree upon the ability of the League to harmonize the ideas of these people with the justice of the prohibition amendment," he asserted. Moreover, this educational work would benefit the world prohibition movement, as American immigrant peoples influenced the attitudes of their relatives and friends "in the lands whence they came." The league had been spending about $1½ million annually before ratification. Now Cherrington argued the necessity of expanding operations on a budget reaching $5 million by 1925.[11] Time was to prove that Cherrington's whole assessment was all too accurate. But his opinion was not soon to prevail.

Wayne Wheeler and Law Enforcement

Cherrington's call for a worldwide campaign of education, for a church mission against the evil kingdom of the liquor traffic, to result in observance, as opposed to mere enforcement, of the Eighteenth Amendment, was too grand a scheme for many league leaders. Indeed, Cherrington's opponents among the league officers mistakenly perceived his views as impractically idealistic. Essentially Cherrington was asking the Anti-Saloon League to transform itself into a great temperance organization that transcended political action in favor of uplifting and assimilating all Americans and extending the reach of evangelical Protestant values abroad. Cherrington's opponents did not recognize that the league was already in part such an uplift organization. So in arguing his case Cherrington was flying in the face of the traditional and conscious league strategy established by Russell in the early years. One of Russell's earliest recruits to a lifetime of league work, Wayne Wheeler, came to personify this more traditional and more narrowly political approach.

Wayne Wheeler had always been one of the most important men employed by the Anti-Saloon League, but his career took on added

11. *Plan of Financial Reorganization*, pp. 16−17.

luster in the 1920s. After Wheeler left the Ohio league for the post of general counsel, he did not play an especially visible role in the drive for national prohibition. While the Democrats were in power in Washington, James Cannon headed the legislative committee. Although Wheeler served on the committee, it was Cherrington, also a member, who articulated the overall strategy. The situation changed in 1919. With the Republicans returning to power, it seemed logical for Wheeler, living in Washington and identified with the party, to head the committee while continuing to serve as the league's national attorney.

Wheeler used his positions in the league hierarchy to advocate his own views and at the same time to gain notoriety as America's "dry boss." He relished a reputation of great personal political influence and carefully nurtured it with well-placed newspaper articles and timely interviews with reporters. Wheeler's rise after 1919 to greater public visibility and to enlarged power within the league was directly parallel to Cherrington's diminishing influence with Purley Baker. Wheeler's rise was also caused, however, by his skillful promotion of a law enforcement approach to prohibition.

Wheeler agreed with Howard Russell's earliest prescriptions for league strategy: the league was strictly a political organization, not some transcendent temperance education movement against the kingdom of evil. Agitation (or education) served strictly political ends, in Wheeler's view. Agitation aroused voters to action on election day and threatened reluctant prosecutors and policemen with retirement. The goal of the league, as a political organization, was not just to write an ideal into the nation's basic law, but to express righteousness vigilantly through detailed enforcement statutes and their careful administration. "To avoid complications," Wheeler told the league convention of 1921, "the purpose of the organization should be to enforce prohibition. Singleness of purpose is just as essential in this as in securing the Prohibition law."[12] Wayne Wheeler's view could not have contrasted more sharply with Cherrington's vision of a sober world.

When first employed in 1894, Wheeler had brought tireless zeal to the work. He studied law while assigned as Cleveland superintendent, and after his admission to the bar he never stopped stressing the importance of law enforcement work as an integral part of the league's operations. Tutored by Russell and Washington Gladden that the league, to be effective, must avoid the vigilante practices

12. *Proceedings, Twentieth National Convention, ASLA, 1921*, pp. 113–19.

of some earlier, local prohibition groups, he proposed the establishment of a legal department that would assist law enforcement authorities in the conduct of their tasks, always, of course, with an
implied threat that the league would use its political muscle against
them if they faltered. As early as 1898 Wheeler was pointing out to
supporters the effectiveness of this strategy in bringing the liquor
business to heel.[13]

Wheeler brought this thinking to his national post in 1915. "The
most important work," he observed, "is to help outline a workable
law enforcement program for the different states." After surveying
state laws, he concluded "that prohibitory legislation has not been
followed up by a practical law enforcement program." League supporters, Wheeler cautioned, must not be led to believe that the
league was an enforcement agency—"that will wreck any organization."[14]

The guiding principles in Wheeler's "practical law enforcement
program" were to designate the responsibility of officials, to provide
them with adequate funds, and to remove them if "derelict." He
recognized that law enforcement was traditionally a local responsibility, but when local officers were wet in their sympathies, and
the league was powerless to remove them, the state had to invoke its
police power. This principle conformed to the dictum that the
league not become a law enforcement organization itself—some sort
of updated vigilante committee—but instead use its political power
most effectively.[15]

The Volstead Act

Wheeler adhered faithfully to these principles when the time came
to push for a national enforcement statute. In this endeavor, the
league was caught unprepared. Expecting a long ratification fight,
Wheeler had paid little attention to the detailed requirements of a
federal enforcement measure. Nevertheless, early in 1919 he compiled a list of the features in state enforcement laws that were most
appealing and submitted them to the House and Senate Judiciary
Committees as a legislative proposal.

Wheeler's measure was introduced as a bill in the Senate, but on

13. Wheeler to E. W. Metcalf, Nov. 19, 1898, IWM; *Minutes of the Twenty-Sixth
Annual Meeting of the Non-Partisan Temperance Women of Ohio* (n.p., 1899), p. 58.
14. Report of Wheeler, 1915, ECe.
15. Ibid.

the House side, Andrew J. Volstead, the new chairman of the Judiciary Committee, substantially rewrote it. Volstead included the language Wheeler had taken from state enforcement statutes. "The problem," Volstead later recalled, "was not to embody in a bill old statutes, that was easy, but to devise a scheme that would fit into Federal law and Federal conditions, and that would make that scheme air tight." Volstead spent several months—"as hard work as I ever did"—writing succinct language that would avoid court tests and survive those that inevitably would come. The result, known popularly as the Volstead Act, followed Wheeler's guiding principles regarding important provisions. Volstead included a system of permits for withdrawing industrial alcohol from storage and of record-keeping requirements. One of Wheeler's close associates noted later that Volstead "drafted the entire bill." The congressman himself, however, recognized that the law bearing his name was imperfect. In 1921 Volstead told John Nance Garner, a House colleague, that while "we will gradually work out the machinery that will, with the cooperation of the states, make the country fairly dry, we can not hope that this law can be enforced so as not to be violated. All laws will be violated."[16]

Even before violations became evident, however, some parts of the Volstead bill were controversial. The bill placed enforcement of prohibition in the hands of the commissioner of internal revenue in the Treasury Department, not with the attorney general. Early in 1919 Wheeler wrote about the desirability of having enforcement assigned to Treasury. The department was "obviously the choice" because, as a taxing authority, it had experience with the liquor business. "The machinery is already built." Internal revenue officials understood how the alcoholic beverage traffic operated, and they had a history of cooperating with the states. So the Volstead Act created a commissioner of prohibition who reported to the commissioner of internal revenue. He was to report violations to the Department of Justice for prosecution. This arrangement did not provoke

16. There is a detailed legislative history of the Volstead Act in *Standard Encyclopedia of the Alcohol Problem*, 6:2777–83. Charles Merz, *The Dry Decade* (Garden City, N.Y., 1931), p. 48, explains incorrectly that Wheeler's draft "was introduced in the House of Representatives by Mr. Volstead of Minnesota." Merz based his account on reports in the *New York Times*, and subsequent writers have wrongly accepted its veracity. See Volstead to Garner, Feb. 16, 1921; Volstead to William F. Shea, Feb. 10, 1934, AJV; E. S. Shumacher to Foulke, Oct. 9, 1923, WDF.

opposition in 1919, although it later became the subject of a long controversy.[17]

Three other provisions, however, sparked disputes in 1919. The bill placed responsibility with elected and appointed officials, not with civil servants. The Volstead Act thus followed the traditional Anti-Saloon League policy of holding elected officials responsible for law enforcement. Authority should reside primarily at the local and state levels, but, as Wheeler reported, "if there is any part of this nation so lacking in patriotism that it will defy the law," then federal authorities must have the power to intervene. By having them appointed outside of the civil service, the league, with its awesome political muscle, could insure their dutiful compliance.[18]

The two biggest battles in the legislative history of the Volstead Act regarded the definition of *intoxicating* and the possession of alcoholic beverages. Wheeler and the league insisted on a definition of *intoxicating* that prevented the legal distribution of beer. The brewers fought the provision bitterly and battled for a decade to allow beverages containing less than 2.75 percent alcohol by volume. But Congress agreed with the league and set the standard at ½ percent. But Wheeler lost on the issue of possession. He wanted to go beyond the amendment and outlaw the possession of beverage alcohol as well as its manufacture and sale. "There will be a determined fight," Wheeler told the league. "If we do not get the measure that we need, we will have the standard set and will obtain it in a later session of Congress." He was correct about the fight but wrong about the outcome. A majority of congressmen saw the ban on possession as stepping beyond their mandate. The league, after all, had always used rhetoric against the liquor business, not the individual drinker. Wheeler did not have a good case politically for his personal preference, and the issue of possession never again arose seriously.[19]

17. *Philadelphia North American*, Jan. 14, 1919, quoted in Steuart, *Wayne Wheeler*, p. 132. The placement of enforcement in Treasury seemed to have another benefit. Alcohol was produced for industrial and medicinal purposes. The Volstead Act thus allowed for its continued manufacture, under federal supervision, with permits issued for sales to industries and pharmacies. Commissioner of Internal Revenue Daniel C. Roper, personally sympathetic to prohibition, opposed assigning enforcement to the Treasury Department. A precedent was the assignment of narcotics control to Treasury. One reason for placing the two drugs under the same administrative unit was the widespread fear that alcohol prohibition would lead to greater use of narcotics. Musto, *The American Disease*, pp. 134–43.

18. Report of Legal Department, June 3, 1919, ECe.

19. Ibid., Feb. 27, 1919.

In spite of the setback on possession, the Volstead Act closely followed Wheeler's desires. The law conformed to the principle of empowering federal officials to enforce prohibition when state and local officials were unwilling or unable to do so. The law narrowly defined what were "intoxicating" beverages and seemed to provide a well-regulated system for supplying alcohol for legal uses. It exempted sacramental wines, not offending the religious customs of important segments of the American population. For the most part, the Volstead Act included the best-tested features of state enforcement statutes.

The enactment of the Volstead Act was more than a substantive victory for Wheeler. It also vindicated his desire to maintain the league's traditional political focus. The enforcement statute created a situation wherein Wheeler and other league leaders could reasonably argue that the Eighteenth Amendment made little difference to the basic thrust of the organization and that there was a continuing need to maintain the drys' political power. This was the case in two ways, both political, not educational, in nature.

The Volstead Act required that a well-organized dry lobby concerned about possible amendments keep constantly alert, and the act also required the appointment of officials to administer it. Amendments were always a threat. President Wilson had vetoed the law before the Eighteenth Amendment went into effect; he did so on the ground that it enforced wartime prohibition, and this at a time when hostilities and mobilization had ceased. Congress quickly overrode the veto, but the episode was clear enough evidence that the league's enemies remained powerful and had friends in high office. They would continue to try to change the law, especially to allow the sale of beer. Therefore, Wheeler concluded, the league was needed to thwart them.[20]

In Wheeler's view the law also required a vigilant league to make elected officials accountable for the administration of prohibition. Wheeler called upon local leagues to keep track of the activities of law enforcement successes and failures and to report them to his office. He believed that they should also maintain surveillance over wet propaganda efforts and be ready to counteract them rapidly. This sort of vigilance, backed by a network of communication and a

20. Prior to vetoing the bill, Wilson received urgent pleas from Samuel Gompers, Samuel Untermeyer, who represented distilling interests, and advocates of civil service. Untermeyer to Wilson, Aug. 19, 1919; George Keyes to Wilson, Oct. 14, 1919, Gompers to Wilson, Oct. 20, 1919, WW.

mobilization of voters on election day, would insure that the grip of the liquor traffic was finally broken.[21]

Wheeler and the Politics of Enforcement

Enactment of the Volstead Act was only the beginning of the controversies over prohibition enforcement, which, until his death in 1927, centered on Wayne Wheeler. Wheeler not only promoted his "dry boss" image but arranged for his research assistant, T. J. Steuart, to ghostwrite an autobiography. Not completed until after Wheeler's death, Steuart published the book in 1928 as a biography titled *Wayne Wheeler, Dry Boss*. The author closed the book, in words that Wheeler had instructed him to use, with a statement that the success of prohibition depended on the "health and strength" of Wayne B. Wheeler. "He desired to be pictured as a dictator," Steuart observed privately.[22]

Steuart was convinced that Wheeler suffered from megalomania, a trait that took the practical form of his desire that the government, backed by the league, would use force to secure compliance. Wheeler played down the moral sources of the reform and was therefore of course out of sympathy with Cherrington's advocacy of an educational strategy. Power was what mattered to Wheeler, and the use of that power to regulate the behavior of recalcitrant citizens. Frustrated in his personal desire to achieve governmental power over the individual citizen's right to possess alcoholic beverages, Wheeler remained steadfast in his conviction that the drys must use power to break up the liquor traffic. He never expressed doubt that he himself was the person best able to exercise that power. Tireless in his own work, Wheeler sought arrangements whereby he could control the public image, the strategy, and the power of the Anti-Saloon League.

One league action unwittingly enhanced Wheeler's dry-boss image. In 1919 the executive committee had authorized him, as attorney, to be the league spokesman in recommending individuals for appointment to federal enforcement posts. This action meant that Wheeler was the principal watchdog of prohibition. The league expected politicians to clear their appointments with Wheeler. Wheeler in turn expected to help them by collecting information on

21. *Proceedings, Twentieth National Convention, ASLA, 1921*, pp. 113–19.
22. Steuart, *Wayne Wheeler*, p. 304; Steuart to Cherrington, May 24, 1928, filed with Minutes, Administrative Committee, May 28, 1928, ECe.

the successes and failures of prohibition enforcement. He planned a newsletter that would keep prosecutors informed of the latest legal developments. The Volstead Act had deliberately refrained from imposing civil service regulations in an effort to insure that officials and the politicians who appointed them would respond to the wishes of a powerful league. The whole strategy was, of course, explicit from the beginning.[23]

The executive committee's designation of Wheeler as the watch-dog of prohibition was ironic. In the Progressive Era the league had campaigned, alongside other reformers, for the destruction of "boss" power. The Ohio league, as we have seen, had followed its triumph in the 1905 gubernatorial election by refusing to accept any spoils of office. The league officers could have chosen that alternative in 1919, but they did not. The league could have stood aside from the routine concerns of law enforcement in favor of informing the politicians of their responsibility and warning them that failure would lead to trouble on election day. But instead the temptations, apparently, of exercising national power were too great to deny. Wheeler, true to his belief in coercive reform, maneuvered to become the nation's arbiter regarding the liquor traffic and alcoholic beverages.

But Wheeler's dream of becoming the nation's dry boss did not work out quite as planned. President Wilson's commissioner of internal revenue, Daniel C. Roper, and the first prohibition commissioner, John F. Kramer, were sympathetic and took advantage of the wave of popular enthusiasm that accompanied ratification. But this situation changed dramatically after the election of Warren G. Harding, and controversy over the staffing of the enforcement agency quickly emerged.

Andrew Mellon, Harding's choice as secretary of the treasury, was the first subject of controversy. The prospect of having Mellon in charge of the prohibition bureau appalled some drys, for he was known as a wet whose vast investments included the Overholt Distillery. Wheeler, who believed the appointment was inevitable, did not voice opposition. William H. Anderson accused the attorney of "pussyfooting" on the matter; public opposition was a wiser course, he argued, for it would keep Mellon honest. But Wheeler, fearing a weakened influence in the administration, remained silent.[24]

23. Minutes, Executive Committee, Sept. 18, 1919, ECe.
24. Anderson to Baker, Feb. 17, 1921, ECe; Robert K. Murray, *The Harding Era* (Minneapolis, 1969), pp. 99–101.

Although Wheeler and other league men involved themselves with a broad range of posts, from ambassadors to prosecutors, they were mainly interested in the appointment of the prohibition commissioner. Wheeler urged Roy Haynes on the Harding administration. Haynes was an Ohio Republican of no stature, and Wheeler's action provoked hundreds of protests. The league's executive committee disassociated itself from Wheeler's recommendation, which proved disastrous. Wheeler apparently thought that having a weak person who owed his appointments to the dry boss would serve him well. But the opposite proved true. Haynes, whose hold on his office smelled of intrigue, enjoyed no personal influence in the White House, and neither he nor Wheeler was able to control the naming of subordinates. Patronage considerations and petty politics were the rule under Haynes's administration, which soon evoked scandal. But having a weak person in charge enhanced Wheeler's ability to promote his own dry boss image, which in turn angered other league leaders.[25]

The controversy soon focused on the absence of civil service rules in the prohibition service. Civil service advocates had accused the Volstead Act of being a "spoils raid," and subsequent developments seemed to verify the charge. The National Civil Service League documented the hiring of corrupt and incompetent officials and led a mounting chorus of criticisms. Wheeler and Volstead held to the ground that the classification of enforcement employees would protect wets. But finally, as complaints of incompetence continued from both inside and outside of the Anti-Saloon League, Wheeler was forced to retreat. Still, he tried to trick the civil service reformers. In 1921 Wheeler proposed that Congress classify lower-level employees and leave state directors outside of the civil service. The reformers were not deceived and finally forced Wheeler to accept the principle of civil service for the entire prohibition bureau. But obtaining the change proved no easy task, as the spoils system served politicians well, and it was not accomplished until 1927.[26]

Meanwhile, Wheeler continued to support Haynes, even though his incompetence had become a national joke. The problem, he

25. Murray, *The Harding Era*, pp. 403–07; T. J. Steuart to Cherrington, May 24, 1928, ECg; *Bishop Cannon's Own Story*, pp. 304–05.

26. The main events are documented in Merz, *Dry Decade*. See also Keyes to Wilson, Oct. 14, 1919; Volstead to John H. Bartlett, Feb. 22, 1922; Imogen B. Oakley to Volstead, Feb. 13, 1922, AJV; Harry W. Marsh to Wheeler, Oct. 3, 1923; William D. Foulke to Marsh, Oct. 5 and 30, 1923, WDF.

asserted, was that Haynes's directives were countermanded by his superiors. "It is . . . true," Wheeler reported to the executive committee in 1924, "that there are many failures of prohibition," but "supervising officers, district attorneys, and derelict judges" were at fault, not the prohibition bureau. Haynes had led "an aggressive fight." Wheeler's defense forestalled a campaign from inside the league to have the commisioner fired. To the end of his life, Wheeler stood by Haynes.[27]

Wheeler's motives were apparent, and they conformed with his desire to maintain a strong enforcement stance in Congress. Haynes's removal and the introduction of civil service rules would eliminate opportunities to negotiate patronage appointments with congressmen in exchange for their votes or for party nominations of drys. Wheeler was concerned about both matters, for proper law enforcement required dry majorities to appropriate funds and prevent the wets from weakening the codes. Wheeler was proud of his political record. Although he was unable to prevent the defeat of Volstead in 1922, he reported after every congressional election that dry support in both houses of Congress had increased. This happened not because the league was well organized in most states but because he was able to work with the congressional party leaders as well as individual members and to manipulate the attention of newspapers.[28]

Public opinion was important for Wheeler's law enforcement approach, not only to obtain congressional votes, but, at the local level, to secure the conviction of offenders. So Wheeler and his league supporters worked to rally public support for obedience to the law. "We must broaden the scope of our appeal and reach those who believe in constitutional government and the orderly processes of law to sustain it," he told the executive committee in 1922. "The people of this country are going to choose between orderly government and lawless methods . . . within the next few years." The league had to organize public support for obedience lest "law and order" societies arise and "muss up the whole law enforcement work."[29]

There were league men who shared Wheeler's fears and who developed campaigns to capture and encourage public concerns over foreign radicalism in hopes of fostering support for law enforcement. In Ohio, Superintendent James White gathered evi-

27. F. S. McBride to David McBride, Feb. 23, 1925, FSM, roll 6.
28. Report of the Legal and Legislative Department, Nov. 14, 1922, and Nov. 25, 1924, ECe.
29. Report of the Legal Department, Mar. 3, 1921, and Nov. 14, 1922, ECe.

dence of bootlegging as early as 1919. "In the large cities the prohibition amendment is being violated with impunity," he observed.
Early in 1920, tying the league's cause to the current red scare,
White declared that "the liquor trade makes for Bolshevism. In the
saloon is found the spirit of anarchy." He began a campaign whose
slogan was "Obedience to law is liberty." The Wisconsin league, in a
"campaign for Americanism" titled *Constitution or Revolution*, called
for spreading "the 'Gospel of Americanism'—common sacrifice for
common service" among the state's immigrant peoples.[30]

The national league attempted a comparable program. In 1922
Russell announced formation of the American Bond. He envisioned
it as the "Loyalty Department of the Lincoln-Lee Legion," an organization of local clubs "to promote patriotism and loyalty to law."
Russell wanted the bond to become a regular department of the state
leagues, with a staff officer specializing in "agitation and education."
The national office, which he headed, would provide materials and
training and arrange for prominent citizens to send letters of endorsement to 100,000 "civic leaders." Especially important was providing speakers for public schools and naturalization classes. But
this vision of rallying patriotic Americans behind law observance
fizzled, and within six months the American Bond died for lack of
funds.[31]

The failure of the American Bond—and of a similar effort in New
York State called Allied Citizens—presented the league with the
very problem it had feared. The Ku Klux Klan, rising so rapidly in
the early 1920s, began mobilizing vigilante actions against the illegal
liquor traffic. "The Ku Klux Klan . . . is doing many things which we
would have liked to have done," Indiana Superintendent E. S.
Shumaker wrote in 1924, "but we are not working with them in
either an official or unofficial way." But other state leaders were less
cautious. When the Federal Council of Churches informed Wheeler
that the South Carolina superintendent was helping the KKK in that
state, Wheeler urged the general superintendent to investigate. The
association of the league and the Klan had aroused criticism;
"it would be very detrimental to have this going on," Wheeler
advised.[32]

30. White form letters, Dec. 23, 1919, Jan. 7, 1920, OASL, role 1; *Constitution or Revolution*, ECe.

31. Minutes, Executive Committee, Feb. 1, May 17, and June 29, 1923, ECe.

32. Wheeler to McBride, July 12, 1924; E. S. Shumaker to McBride, July 25, 1924, FSM, rolls 8, 10.

Not only did Klan activites violate league policy of refraining from vigilante tactics, but any association with the KKK hurt Wheeler's efforts to arrange support from respectable groups for his law enforcement policies. In 1924 he was busy coordinating a lobbying campaign in Washington. Wheeler helped form the Woman's National Committee of One Hundred for Law Enforcement, which included leaders of women's clubs, church officials, and educators. During the spring the committee sponsored a convention of 1,362 delegates addressed by Harding's widow and the wives of President Coolidge and Secretary of Commerce Hoover. "It is a good omen for victory," Wheeler reported. The meeting had forced the attorney general to express his support for prohibition and had "impressed upon both the Congress and the Executive and Justice Departments that the American people will insist on enforcement of the law." Later that year the General Federation of Women's Clubs resolved that "reverence for law and obedience to law are fundamental to stable government and a well-ordered society."[33]

Important as such expressions were for Wheeler, even more essential was his ability to control the leadership of the Anti-Saloon League. Purley Baker allowed Wheeler a free hand, and those who wanted an emphasis on law enforcement were in control as long as he remained general superintendent. For instance, even though the theme of the convention of 1921 was "A Sober World," Cherrington was not allowed to speak, and the addresses were all keyed to a law enforcement strategy. But Baker was not healthy. Wheeler needed to control his successor lest Cherrington become his superior.

Choosing a New General Superintendent

The board of directors of the Anti-Saloon League of America was scheduled to hold its biennial meeting on January 12, 1924. Purley Baker's health was rapidly failing, and the men who were operating the league realized that the time had arrived to name a new general superintendent. Although several candidates were sure to emerge, Ernest Cherrington enjoyed wide support among the state superintendents who knew of the energy and skill he had devoted to the national organization since 1908. His election to the post would produce a ringing endorsement of the education strategy and of the World League.[34]

33. Report of Legal Department, May 17, 1923, ECe; Wheeler to McBride, April 16, 1924, FSM, roll 10.
34. Steuart, *Wayne Wheeler*, pp. 214–16.

That situation presented a serious problem to the men who did not want to see Cherrington elected to the office. Of all who had received considerable national publicity for their prohibition work, only James Cannon favored Cherrington. The others, for a variety of motives, wanted someone else. Wheeler, of course, wanted to block Cherrington's election. Some state superintendents, most notably F. S. Shumaker of Indiana, simply opposed Cherrington's strategy, to the point of not allowing the World League to raise funds in their state. Others feared that Cherrington doubted their competence and, once in power, would remove them. E. J. Moore, who was serving as Baker's assistant general superintendent, hoped to obtain the position for himself. Francis Scott McBride had a successful record as Illinois superintendent and was a logical alternative, at least to his friends, who included White of Ohio, Chalfant of Pennsylvania, and Shields of New Jersey.[35]

But none of these men controlled enough votes on the board to block Cherrington or elect an alternative. So, following the lead of Wheeler and with the active complicity of Russell and Baker, they conspired to manipulate the choice. Their first step was to postpone the decision. When the board met, it received a message that Baker had rallied from his illness and seemed likely to recover. Loyal to the man who had for so long led the league, the board elected him to another two-year term.[36]

After the board meeting, Moore began traveling from state to state to round up support for a candidate to oppose Cherrington. Late in February Baker again publicly denied rumors of his impending resignation, and Wheeler issued a statement that when the time came for Baker's retirement, the successor should be a clergyman with experience as a state superintendent. The conspirators chose McBride as the alternative. Although he had a fairly wide circle of friends among the league staff, he had little involvement in its national affairs and had never, therefore, been in a position to make enemies. From Wheeler's viewpoint he seemed a desirably weak choice who, in office, could easily be manipulated if not ignored.[37]

Not knowing that there was a conspiracy at work against him,

35. Thomas Nicholson to William F. Anderson, Mar. 22, 1924; Boyd P. Doty, "A Few Facts Concerning the Election of a General Superintendent," typescript, May 24, 1924, ECg; *Bishop Cannon's Own Story*, pp. 325–26.

36. Steuart, *Wayne Wheeler*, pp. 214–216; Doty to W. J. Herwig, Mar. 24, 1924; Emmet McBride to Cherrington, June 21, 1926, ECg.

37. *Columbus Dispatch*, Feb. 28, 1924; Doty, "A Few Facts."

Cherrington did little to seek the post. He and his supporters had every reason to feel confident, knowing that the majority of state superintendents and board members favored his leadership. Then, on March 7, Cherrington met in Columbus with Baker, Russell, and Michigan Superintendent Holsaple on routine business matters. The next morning Cherrington read in the newspaper that Baker had resigned and that a special meeting of the board of directors was to be held in Indianapolis on April 9 to choose a successor.[38]

In the ensuing month, Cherrington chose to do little to seek the post. His assistant, Boyd P. Doty, however, wrote letters to potential supporters informing them of the facts that led to the conclusion that there was, indeed, a conspiracy at work to keep Cherrington from achieving the office. Cherrington himself finally chose to act on April 5. He wrote a long letter to the president of the league, Thomas Nicholson, a Methodist bishop. Nicholson, a friend who was concerned by the drift of affairs and by Wheeler's activities, was a person whom Cherrington could count upon to act fairly. "The League's past is safe," Cherrington said. "The present and future, however, challenge nothing short of the best possible program for League activites." He chose to refrain from active discussion during the board meeting, and so he asked Nicholson to keep in mind the need for a vigorous strategy looking toward "both the present suppression and the ultimate extinction of the beverage liquor traffic."[39]

In spite of his reluctance to speak, Cherrington made clear that he stood for a vigorous new set of policies for the league that effectively would reverse Wheeler's law enforcement and political emphases. The letter served as a campaign platform for his own election as general superintendent. He divided his thoughts into three categories labeled "rules and methods," "policies," and "immediate program." Cherrington wanted the national and state leagues to meet annually and more carefully coordinate their activities and train their workers. A majority on each board should represent churches. As a church organization, the league should maintain a proper distance from partisan politics. Indirectly critical of Wheeler, Cherrington would have banned efforts to name government officials, and he would have prevented league staff members from resigning to run for public office. (One of Wheeler's allies, James White, ran

38. Cherrington to Nicholson, Mar. 8, 1924, ECe.
39. Doty to George B. Safford, April 4, 1924, ECg; Cherrington to Nicholson, April 5, 1924, ECe.

unsuccessfully for the Ohio Republican gubernatorial nomination.)
No political candidate, he thought, should receive direct financial
support from the league. Whereas Wheeler had raised campaign
funds independently, Cherrington would require all contributions
accounted in the league treasury.

Cherrington not only threatened Wheeler's independence but
would redirect law enforcement efforts as well. Cherrington wanted
a legislative program to improve the federal and state enforcement
codes and especially to increase funding for enforcement. The
league should ask Congress to appropriate not the current $10
million but $50 million annually for enforcement. That goal, how-
ever, was only part of a larger picture. "The League needs, particularly at this time, to emphasize educational policies." He called
for a broad range of activities, including the construction of a radio
transmitter in Westerville capable of reaching all Americans with its
signal.[40]

But in the end it was not the persuasiveness of Cherrington's
arguments or even the majority of the board members who would
carry the day. It was the majority of those present who would decide,
through their choice of superintendent, the future course of the
league. The conspirators had carefully planned the meeting to give
their side every advantage. Since it was not a regular biennial
meeting, distant states supporting Cherrington might not have
funds to send delegates. Scheduled for Indianapolis the day before
an executive committee meeting in Washington, D.C., it prevented
the naming of Cherrington as acting general superintendent. Officials from states near Indiana were sympathetic to Wheeler's views,
whereas Cherrington's supporters were more distant.[41]

When the board members assembled, Wheeler followed carefully
prepared plans. Even though he knew he had no chance of winning,
he had his own name placed in nomination, along with McBride's.
The effect was to insure that no one received a majority on the first
ballot. Rumors were begun that Cherrington did not really want the
post, and that his present work was more important to the prohibition cause. "Other political methods, familiar to men who had
played with caucuses, primaries and conventions for years, were
used," Wheeler's biographer observed. "Enough votes were drawn

40. Cherrington to Nicholson, April 5, 1924, ECe.
41. Doty to A. H. Briggs, Mar. 22, 1924; Doty to George B. Safford, April 4, 1924;
Milo G. Kelser to Cherrington, Mar. 25, 1924; G. W. Crabbe to Cherrington, April 12,
1924, ECg.

from Cherrington to ensure his defeat, while enough of the original Wheeler votes went to McBride to give him the election."[42]

McBride and the Crisis of League Strategy, 1924–27

The conspirators who successfully engineered the election of Francis Scott McBride encountered no surprises from his leadership. They wanted a continuation of the politics of law enforcement and the decentralization of authority. McBride provided both. He had begun league work in Illinois in 1911 while serving the Presbyterian church as a minister. From 1912 until 1924 McBride was Illinois superintendent, a position in which he earned a reputation as a skilled lobbyist and an advocate of strict law enforcement. He had gained little knowledge of the national league's daily operations. As general superintendent, he was inclined to turn to Wheeler, with whose philosophy he agreed, for advice and to avoid confrontations with established state superintendents. The result was continuing drift, with no attempt to resolve league strategy.[43]

Immediately upon assuming his new office, McBride had to face the problem of Ernest Cherrington and the educational vision he espoused. Eventually, the executive committee worked out an arrangement whereby Cherrington, as head of the American Issue Publishing Company, reported directly to it, but as head of the collections department reported to McBride. This may have solved the problem of the lines of authority between an untested leader and an experienced subordinate, but the problem of dealing with Cherrington's philosophy still loomed.[44]

McBride and Wheeler attempted to resolve the internal dispute over league strategy and to undercut Cherrington's influence. They developed the argument that Baker had used, namely that while the league was emphasizing law enforcement, it needed educational programs to secure obedience. On the fifth anniversary of the advent of constitutional prohibition, McBride issued a statement arguing that the stress on law enforcement was a result of a logical historical progression. "We have gone through the stages of the

42. Steuart, *Wayne Wheeler*, pp. 214–216; William Anderson to Cherrington, Mar. 12, 1924, ECe; Doty to Cannon, April 16, 1924, ECg.

43. *Standard Encyclopedia of the Alcohol Problem*, 4:1621. McBride revealed his desire to "stamp out law violators" in a letter to Arthur J. Davis, May 14, 1925, FSM, roll 2. On his weakness in handling an established state superintendent, see Wheeler to McBride, Sept. 26, 1924; McBride to Wheeler, Oct. 4, 1924, FSM, roll 10.

44. A. J. Barton to Cherrington, July 1, 1925, ECe.

historical program of the League of education, legislation, and enforcement," he noted. "We are now majoring on enforcement, but yet need a world of education, [and] some necessary legislation." This doctrine, particularly in view of the circumstances of McBride's election, failed to win over Cherrington or his supporters, who remained convinced that the league required a new strategy.[45]

By the end of 1924 prohibition leaders were expressing alarm about the prospects of the reform. Although there was no doubt of the permanence of the amendment, it seemed that the wets were gaining public support. Federal law enforcement administration remained inept, and a growing number of state legislatures were refusing appropriations for local efforts. New York was the most extreme case. There, under Alfred Smith's leadership, the state was attempting to nullify the Volstead Act. The Association Against the Prohibition Amendment (AAPA) had patterned itself after the Anti-Saloon League. The opposition organization was claiming to have more than 400,000 members across the nation and was accepting financial contributions from persons involved in the liquor business. The AAPA seemed a dangerous opponent. More and more metropolitan newspapers were voicing displeasure over excesses of enforcement officials. Public resistance to prohibition in large cities was apparently growing. Politicians and some church leaders were expressing concern about Wheeler's political methods and were threatening to withdraw support from the league. In short, a crisis prevailed; there was grave danger of further nullification of the Volstead Act.[46]

At the beginning of 1925 the executive committee decided that a clearer plan of action for the league was imperative. It appointed a special committee of McBride, Wheeler, Cherrington, H. B. Carré of Vanderbilt University and the Tennessee league, and Arthur J. Davis, New York State superintendent, to recommend a strategy. Both Davis and Carré were Cherrington supporters, so McBride proceeded to ignore the committee and, with Wheeler, write a document that became the *Programme of the Anti-Saloon League of America*.[47]

45. *American Issue* (N.C. ed.), Jan. 17, 1925, p. 1.
46. A well-crafted study of the opposition to prohibition is Kyvig, *Repealing National Prohibition*. Cannon observed that the Methodist Church, South, was inclined to reduce its support for the league. Cannon to Nicholson, Mar. 17, 1924, ECe. Senators Willis and Sheppard and Representative Barkley were concerned about the league's direction. Sam W. Small to Cherrington, Mar. 28, 1924, ECg.
47. Published in Westerville, 1925. Cherrington to Nicholson, Mar. 3, 1925, ECe.

McBride and Wheeler failed to pacify Cherrington by this action. When revised and printed, the *Programme* was a small, six-page pamphlet that summarized Cherrington's goals and Wheeler's policies, concluding with rhetoric about "The Challenge" to the church. It was neither a detailed agenda nor a policy statement that would restrain Wheeler. "I hesitate to criticize the program presented in view of the fact that I had not been consulted in regard to any part of it," Cherrington wrote to Bishop Thomas Nicholson, the league president. "From the expressions in the Committee [it] did not strongly grip the men," and they doubted there was "much likelihood" of it "receiving much consideration either in the religious or secular press."[48]

Nicholson and Cherrington agreed that the league should have a "council of war on policy and program." The meeting should include the executive committee and all state superintendents. Nicholson urged the idea upon McBride and Wheeler. "In my opinion," he advised, "the Anti-Saloon League and the prohibition cause in the United States have never faced such a crisis as we face at the present time." The league president sought quick action. McBride's response, however, was to avoid such a meeting, which he could not control, and arrange to term the league meeting in 1925 a "Crisis Convention." That suited his purpose; league conventions were never decision-making affairs. Nicholson and Cherrington wanted a smaller, working session to define a specific strategy and the details of its pursuit.[49]

In the meantime, Cherrington was trying another gambit to reinvigorate the prohibition movement and achieve a commitment to his philosophy. As head of the world league, he could provide a forum. He arranged, through the National Temperance Council, for a week-long joint convention in November under the auspices of the world league. The plan was for all the major temperance organizations, including the Anti-Saloon League, to hold their separate meetings in the morning, joining together in a large hall for afternoon and evening sessions. McBride agreed to this plan initially. Then he and Wheeler began acting as if they knew nothing of it. Indiana Superintendent Shumaker implored McBride "to prevent the scrapping of our Anti-Saloon League by a man whose selfishness and selfish ambition are only equalled by his efforts to control everything savoring the name of prohibition." E. J. Moore, now

48. Cherrington to Nicholson, Mar. 3, 1925, ECe.
49. Ibid.; Nicholson to Cherrington, Mar. 6, 1925; to McBride, Mar. 6, 1925, ECe.

Ohio superintendent, argued that local law enforcement conditions were "awful"; prohibition sentiment was declining, and so a joint meeting with the world league was a "colossal mistake." Cherrington's opponents claimed that the joint convention would deemphasize the importance of the Anti-Saloon League while sapping its funds to pay the expenses of foreign visitors. Whatever the joint meeting would accomplish, of course, it would publicize a need for Cherrington's educational strategy.[50]

McBride's reversal of the commitment to meet jointly with the world league strained relations with other temperance groups. Soon Cherrington abandoned the idea. Noting that he had played a large role in the history of the Anti-Saloon League, he told Nicholson, "I am anxious regarding its future." He recognized that his counsel was going unheeded, that there was no commitment to rethink league strategy to meet the problems of wet resistance.[51]

Nothing happened in 1925 or 1926 to ease Cherrington's despair. If anything, Wheeler became more independent of the executive and legislative committees. This independence reached crisis proportions in 1927 when Congress instituted civil service rules and reorganized the prohibition bureau, creating an independent commissioner of prohibition, who reported directly to the secretary of the treasury. Haynes sought the new post, with Wheeler's support. His advocacy of Haynes, after so many years of criticism of Haynes's abilities, both from inside and outside the league, upset many temperance supporters. Wheeler was announcing programs and policies that neither the league's board nor its executive committee had approved.[52]

By the summer of 1927 the discontent with McBride and Wheeler was building. There was alarm that the league was in danger of losing the support of other temperance organizations and of the churches. Cannon thought that "the danger line" was crossed "in promoting the impression upon many good temperance people that the Washington office concerns itself too much with the political fortunes of individuals and is part of the Republican machine." Cherrington agreed but hesitated to speak publicly on the issue lest the audience interpret his views incorrectly. He felt that differences

50. Cherrington to Nicholson, Mar. 31, 1925; ECe; E. J. Moore to McBride, Apr. 4, 1925; Shumaker to McBride, April 6, 1925, FSM, rolls 6, 8.

51. Cherrington to Nicholson, April 10, 1925, ECe.

52. Thomas Nicholson to Cherrington, June 3, 1926; Cherrington to Cannon, July 1, 1927, ECe.

in personality had been injected into the election of McBride in 1924, clouding the more important issue of basic league strategy without seeming to seek a larger position for himself.[53]

Then, unexpectedly, at the end of the summer Wheeler died. His death provoked a crisis. Hostility toward Wheeler's style of leadership and toward the entire politics of law enforcement meant that the choice of his successor threatened McBride's tenure and the law enforcement policies he favored. Both Cherrington and McBride and the factions within the league that they represented moved to replace Wheeler so as to resolve the dispute over basic league strategy. The crisis would come in early December at the league's biennial convention.

In the autumn a group of seventy-five religious and business leaders met in an informal conference not held under league auspices. The agenda was a discussion of the entire relationship of the churches and prohibition politics. The outcome of the meeting was a decision to follow Cannon's advice and question McBride's leadership and the history of the league's political practices since 1919. The participants called upon the league to appoint adequate leaders and adopt an educational strategy.[54]

McBride did not stand idly by while these developments were unfolding. One of Cherrington's complaints was the irregularly held, poorly attended meetings of the legislative and executive committees. So McBride moved to reorganize those bodies. The new executive committee was to exclude salaried officers from serving for longer than two years. The effect was to remove state superintendents who were Cherrington supporters. The legislative committee was to become a four-man administrative committee that would meet every two months. McBride also announced his intention of assuming Wheeler's post, working out of Washington as both general and legislative superintendent.[55]

When the crisis culminated at the December meeting of the executive committee, it tried to compromise between the competing factions while insuring that the league shifted the emphasis of its activities to education. The committee excused Cherrington, Mc-

53. Cannon to Cherrington, June 23, 1927; Cherrington to Cannon, Oct. 18, 1927, ECe. Fred B. Smith to Cannon, Sept. 9, 1927, JC.
54. Cherrington to Cannon, Sept. 14, 1927, ECe. *The California Liberator* 40 (Dec. 1927): 2–8.
55. Cherrington to Cannon, Oct. 18, 1927; A. H. Briggs to Richard J. Hopkins, Dec. 29, 1927, ECe.

Bride, and Russell while it discussed the issues. The committee decided to appoint Cherrington as education, publicity, and legislative superintendent, with an office in Washington, with McBride remaining in charge of general administration. But when the three absentees returned they persuaded the committee to change its decision. The result was, in effect, the adoption of a dual superintendency. McBride would still be general superintendent, but Cherrington was now in charge of a new department of education, publicity, and research in Westerville. He would report directly to the executive committee while also serving with McBride on the new administrative committee. The understanding was that this change meant a new focus on education, not politics. Later, McBride was also appointed legislative superintendent and moved to Washington.[56]

When the board of directors met, however, it almost repudiated this compromise arrangement. A strong move to oust McBride altogether failed, but only by a margin of three votes out of ninety-three that were cast. This close and bitter fight brought the differences between Cherrington and McBride into public view.[57]

By 1927 the disagreement over league strategy had hardened. One journalist observed that McBride represented "the iron-fist school," Cherrington, "the gentle handclasp." Both men issued a series of press releases explaining their positions. McBride called upon church members to organize a larger voter participation in order to strengthen law enforcement. The problem, according to McBride, lay with the administration, not Congress. Prohibition was saving the nation $6.5 billion in costs, so increasing enforcement appropriations to $100 million annually was a small price. His iron-fist would especially strike at aliens and the "naturalized offender," both of whom should "be sent back home to walk up and down the sidewalks of his home city, a living message to the wide world that the United States means business on prohibition."[58]

Cherrington, in contrast, emphasized the adage, "Ye shall know the truth and the truth shall make you free." The task of the league was to inform Americans, including the foreign born, of the truth

56. Minutes, Executive Committee, Dec. 4 and 5, 1927; Proceedings of the Board of Directors, Dec. 5–7, 1927, ECe.

57. Proceedings of the Board of Directors, Dec. 5–7, 1927, ECe; *Baltimore Sun*, Dec. 11, 1927.

58. *Baltimore Sun*, Dec. 11, 1927; Cherrington Scrapbooks, 1927, Ohio Historical Society.

about alcohol, its traffic, and its abuses. This was league strategy before the amendment and should be resumed. Removing the sanction of the law from the liquor traffic had been only one major step in the fight against such a great social evil. The Eighteenth Amendment was "the greatest experiment in social welfare in the modern world." Its objective was not to make men good but to protect society. "Legislation and enforcement . . . cannot alone solve the beverage alcohol problem. That can be done only as enlightened public opinion is translated into law and conduct; and quickened public conscience is expressed in administration or in acquiescence in such law. Therefore, the ultimate realization of the temperance reform depends primarily not on legislation but education. The most important factor in the movement against alcoholism is not the next election but the next generation."[59]

When the convention of 1927 closed, the crisis seemed resolved. Its echoes could still be heard in McBride's press releases that claimed victory, but the league had agreed to Cherrington's philosophy in its future activities while not, of course, abandoning immediate political or legislative problems. Nearly seven years after the Eighteenth Amendment became law, the league seemed finally to have a clear strategy. No one questioned the permanency of the constitutional reform. Now all that lay ahead was the reinvigoration of the temperance movement and its leading organization to accomplish the subtle task of achieving compliance toward a sober nation and world.[60]

Throughout the years leading to the adoption of Cherrington's views about strategy, the inner turmoil had gravely damaged the Anti-Saloon League. When the leaders could not agree on the appropriate uses of their newfound power, they saw that power evaporate. The failure to redefine appropriate goals for a dry America or even to abandon the league altogether for some other institution meant that the officers had little basis for appealing to their constituency. The result was the decline of the Anti-Saloon League as an organization.

59. Cherrington Scrapbooks, 1927, Ohio Historical Society: *Proceedings, 23rd National Convention, ASLA, 1927,* p. 90.
60. Cherrington to Thomas Nicholson, Dec. 29, 1927, ECe.

10

DECLINE OF AN ORGANIZATION AND THE DEATH OF PROHIBITION

The conflict within the Anti-Saloon League over strategy after 1919 was intimately tied to another set of events. During the years following the successful ratification drive, the league crumbled as an organization. A failure to raise money, discontent from the Protestant churches that were its base of support, and a sizeable number of state organizations that existed more on paper than in fact marked the league's decline. The crumbling of the organization was not apparent to the general public, for the league's political power nationally still seemed awesome. But inside league offices and meeting rooms, away from the attention of the press, the organization was only a shadow of its former self. After 1920 there was no tightly organized, well-funded group to defend prohibition.[1]

This decline was much discussed by league leaders. Both sides in the fight over strategy claimed that their approach would reinvigorate the league and restore its former strength. But so long as the fight over strategy was continuing, that reinvigoration was not forthcoming. Not until after the resolution of league strategy at the end of 1927 did organizational recovery seem to occur. To Cherrington and the other officers in Westerville, in 1928 and 1929 the goal of a sober nation appeared to be in sight, although still a great distance away. The league had successfully opposed the wet Democratic presidential candidate, Al Smith. The federal prohibition service

---

1. The information contained in the surviving league archives fundamentally revises a scholarly view of the organization. Odegard, whose study of the league was heretofore standard and whose book is still valuable reading, had to base his observations on printed matter or information that league officers chose to give him, and that information was self-serving. The result, even in the late 1920s, was a picture of an organization still powerful. *Pressure Politics*, pp. vii–ix. This picture was accurate, but, as we shall see, the league's power was very different from what it was before 1920.

was reorganized and placed in the hands of competent leadership. President Hoover was committed to obtaining better enforcement, and the largest dry majority ever in the Congress was in place to support him. The league's department of education was funded and in operation, supported by a counterpart campaign from the federal government. No one could have anticipated the nightmare visited upon the league and the prohibition movement as a whole following the Wall Street crash of 1929.

In the 1880s, when Russell, Commons, and others had spoken of the need to form a "temperance trust," their ideas, as we have seen, came to have widespread appeal. The Anti-Saloon League was the result, and as the league evolved over the years the officers carefully developed its structure so as to promote the long-term goal, national prohibition. Unconsciously the league officers were advancing a principle in modern institutional life, a principle that the executives of successful corporations were learning in the conduct of business affairs. That principle, most simply expressed, was that structure must follow strategy. In other words, once an organization had developed clear goals responsible executives could develop procedures for reaching them. The league's evolution had conformed to that precept as the officers had devised a system of departmentalization, decentralized authority, national and local fund raising and publicity, and representation of constituents on the board of directors. In 1919, when the league had achieved prohibition, the structure that had evolved since 1893 to win the goal was intact. Now that there was no clear goal, or strategy, upon which there was a broad consensus among league officers, church organizations, Protestant voters, and contributors, no basis existed for modifying or adapting the Anti-Saloon League to the new national political conditions. The result for the league, as an organization, was disastrous. The league officers simply tried to keep their organization intact, changing it only when circumstances dictated some emergency or expedient measure. The disaster that eventually befell the league after 1929 was a product in part of expediency in working with Republican leaders and of abandoning the league's own tradition of nonpartisanship. The problems first became apparent, however, in the area of most crucial importance to any voluntary organization, contributions of money.[2]

2. The classic study in business history is Alfred D. Chandler, Jr., *Strategy and Structure: Chapters in the History of the American Industrial Enterprise* (Cambridge, Mass., 1962). For a personal account of how General Motors defined its goals and then struggled to create an appropriate structure, see Alfred P. Sloan, Jr., *My Years With General Motors* (Garden City, N.Y., 1963), pp. vii–249.

Financing Prohibition Work

None of the internal troubles was apparent to Ernest Cherrington in 1919. It was a year of hectic activity, filled with the euphoria of victory and consequent instigation of idealistic vision. As the man in charge of the league's finances, he turned his thoughts to the practical details of raising the money necessary for the final destruction of the liquor traffic. Those details involved the collection of large sums of money and the reorganization and systematization of the methods the league used for raising funds.

Cherrington could not foretell the troubles that lay ahead in achieving agreement to his strategy for the prohibition movement. Nor could he foresee that the plans he was formulating for raising money and budgeting would soon lie in ruins. The league was enjoying the greatest years of prosperity in its history. Hundreds of thousands of church members were pledging donations, and prominent speakers, especially William Jennings Bryan and Richmond P. Hobson, were obtaining large donations in special campaigns. The state leagues were collecting about $1½ million annually, and the national office nearly $1 million more.[3]

What Cherrington and other church leaders could not observe was that these large sums were most unusual. In the second decade of the twentieth century the Protestant churches were enjoying large benevolences, not just for prohibition work but for foreign missions and other activities. The curve of giving from the faithful was on a noticeably upward swing, a manifestation of the concern that so many middle- and upper-class Americans felt about the condition of their own urban poor and of vast reaches of Asia, Africa, and Latin America. There was no reason to think that the concern would abate. It coincided with the patriotic fervor of the war and was abetted by the idealistic rhetoric of making the world safe for democracy.[4]

Building the Anti-Saloon League and the World League Against Alcoholism for the program of education and missionary work that Cherrington envisioned for the eradication of the liquor traffic was an expensive proposition. When he studied the financial situation of the league in 1919, Cherrington determined that it was possible to

3. *Plan of Financial Reorganization*, pp. 13–17, 37–45.
4. Charles A. Fahs, *Trends in Protestant Giving* (New York, 1929), pp. 65–67; Winthrop Hudson, *The Great Tradition of the American Churches* (New York, 1953), pp. 63–136.

project an annual budget, within five years, of $15 million. He based the projection on current experience with fund raising, the total pledged by church members, and the sums actually given to both the state and national leagues. He knew the work was far from finished; he had little reason to doubt that the league would be able to persuade its constituency of the need to continue its contributions. Moreover, there was still a large and largely untapped constituency for the league: the members of small, mostly rural churches. Theretofore the league had not systematically campaigned in churches where the expenses of fund raising exceeded the donations received. The league was using a system of one-year pledge cards. Cherrington proposed the universal adoption of a five-year pledge system, thus making it worthwhile for the league to visit smaller congregations. By this means he believed the regular, pledged donations would increase at least by one-third. The league had about 300,000 regular donors. Surely once the need for a worldwide missionary and educational effort was explained, he believed that the number would increase.[5]

Cherrington spelled out these plans in 1919, and the league adopted them. The national leaders believed that the plan would work, provided four of the largest state leagues concurred: Ohio, Illinois, Pennsylvania, and New York. Budgeting went forward accordingly, and plans were laid to launch the new, more systematic fund-raising program in the southeastern United States as soon as the presidential election of 1920 was over.[6]

The southeastern drive was catastrophic. What Cherrington and other church leaders could not foresee was the sudden unwillingness of American Protestants to continue making donations for benevolent causes. Total donations for mission work and other church projects began dropping off in 1921 as congregations turned inward, pledging funds not for missionaries or for the league but for new physical plants and other local projects. Church benevolent agencies were suddenly competing with one another for scarcer (and inflated) dollars. The Anti-Saloon League was the loser. Although in the 1920s donations for foreign missionary work dropped off only slightly from their previous levels in the 1920s, the prohibition movement was never again to enjoy the success in fund raising that had marked the drive for national prohibition in the preceding decade.

5. *Plan of Financial Reorganization*, pp. 37–45.
6. "Special Report on Plan of Financial Reorganization," Nov. 14, 1922, ECe.

The reason for the relative poverty of the league was clear enough. Part of the trouble lay in the Internal Revenue Service ruling that donations to the league were not deductible. But the biggest problem was that most donors were inclined to think of the prohibition work as finished. Now it was the task of government to appropriate funds for enforcement. Although Cherrington had formulated a strategy that belied that thinking, one that might have persuaded donors of the need for continuing their pledges, he was unable to have it adopted by the league, much less promoted among its constituency.

By the first weeks of 1921 this situation was becoming clear. In planning its southeastern drive the league had borrowed funds from banks and made commitments to speakers, obligations totaling about $360,000. When the returns failed to come in, Cherrington was summoned to a hastily called meeting in Atlanta, where leaders met in an atmosphere of crisis. He was able to draw upon the resources of the American Issue Publishing Company (including the sale of paper in its inventory) to bail out the league. Special efforts to work with state superintendents in tapping wealthy benefactors saved the organization from bankruptcy. But the budget of the league could not be saved. Never again would it be even so large as it was in 1919, much less reach the grand figure of Cherrington's dream for a sober world.[7]

From then on, money shortages would frustrate the Anti-Saloon League and pervade every aspect of its activity. The shortages meant that the world league could consist of little more than an office in London with a single representative. The shortages meant that educational materials were not published, that tracts for schools and churches went unwritten. The circulation of the *American Issue* declined and it was published less frequently. Salaries sometimes went unpaid. Even though the league was emphasizing the politics of law enforcement, Purley Baker was unable to appoint regional attorneys to work in the field with state and local officials. Wayne Wheeler could not publish a legal bulletin to keep district attorneys abreast of the latest developments in prosecutions. When election time came, Wheeler was thwarted by a lack of money and unable to provide support to candidates in races he believed were important for his Washington efforts. In 1922, the national league could meet only

7. "Report of the General Manager, Dec. 31, 1920," AIP, roll 13; Cherrington to S. S. Kresge, Jan. 31, 1921, ECe; Wheeler to King, Mar. 7, 1921, HCK.

half of its budget. In 1927, matters were little better; in ten months the debt of the executive department grew from $33,000 to $66,000.[8]

The financial problems showed up in another important way. The structure of state leagues, never as well established as the national officers desired, began quickly to disintegrate. "There is not any blinking at the fact that the Anti-Saloon League is afflicted with dry rot," William Anderson observed from New York in 1921. With the league emphasizing the politics of law enforcement, donors felt as unwilling to support local organizations as they did the national. By 1921 the national league was carrying twenty-six states on its books as "missionary" leagues. Some, the leaders realized, would never become self-supporting but had to be maintained because their congressmen's votes were important. The number of missionary states was gradually reduced, but the national officers constantly spoke of the need to rebuild state organizations.[9]

The internal dispute over strategy partly caused the money shortage, and it led to a kind of vicious cycle. When pastors learned of Wheeler's political maneuvers to elect McBride, some church doors were closed to league fund raisers. Because some state superintendents were having difficulty even in maintaining their own offices, they were especially bitter about any expenditures for the world league and about any efforts of Cherrington to raise funds in "their" territory for educational and mission work. Their hostility, especially in Indiana and Ohio, only deepened the internal strategy dispute and made it more difficult to resolve, when a resolution might have aided the fund-raising effort generally.[10]

Before Baker's resignation compounded these difficulties, some state superintendents turned to outside help. They employed private fund raisers, promising them a percentage of receipts in exchange for their services. This was contrary to Baker's standing policy; he feared that the practice would turn away wealthier donors. "Organizations that do this do not appeal to businessmen

8. McBride to Wheeler, Sept. 18, 1924; F. L. Dustman to Wheeler, Sept. 12, 1925, FSM, roll 10, McBride series; McBride, "Report to Executive Committee, Sept. 30, 1925; Cherrington to Fillmore Condit, June 27, 1922; Cherrington's notes with Minutes of Executive Committee, Dec. 3, 1927, ECe.

9. Anderson to Baker, May 18, 1921; "Report of the Secretary, Committee on Financial Management, July 14, 1921;" "Minutes, Committee on Financial Management, Jan. 26, 1922," ECe.

10. Anderson to Wheeler, Apr. 24, 1924, ECg; "Report of Ernest Cherrington, Secretary of the Committee on Financial Management, on Behalf of the Subscription Department of the ASLA," June 4, 1925. ECe.

who have money to give to worthy causes," he advised the state superintendents in 1922. Baker, however, contradicted his own statement. When Russell started the American Bond, Baker promised to allow him "to receive personally 5% of the amount over $150,000 that is raised."[11]

Baker's failure to enforce his fund-raising policy hurt the league dearly. William Anderson, New York Superintendent, resorted to the use of commissions in fund raising. Charges that he was pocketing donations for his own personal use led to his imprisonment— Anderson claimed he was framed by a wet jury. Publicity from the case hurt league funding elsewhere. In 1926, the wealthiest benefactors, John D. Rockefeller, senior and junior, stopped their sizeable donations altogether. Since 1919 they had resisted the league's appeals for special gifts.[12]

The League and the Church

The decline of the state leagues and the chronic crisis of the budget were symptoms of failing support from the churches. Needing to pay off mortgages on buildings and other bills, pastors were reluctant to continue the traditional field day services upon which the league had historically relied for the circulation of its pledge cards. The situation was growing worse year by year and threatened the very existence of the Anti-Saloon League. As one Methodist editor observed, the league was becoming divorced from the churches, and if the trend continued, it would "not only fail, but fall." His insight described part of the reason for the eventual collapse of the Anti-Saloon League.[13]

The internal dispute over basic league strategy was very much a factor in this situation. At the national level, the continuing public emphasis on the politics of law enforcement led the Federal Council of Churches actively to consider abandoning the Anti-Saloon League in favor of a council-sponsored group that would conduct a dry educational campaign. In the early years the council passed resolutions advocating strict enforcement of the Volstead Act. But by 1923, with New York having repealed its state enforcement statute and Tammany politicians openly calling for nullification, the coun-

11. Baker form letter, Oct. 5, 1922, ECg; Baker to Russell, April 25, 1923, HH.
12. Anderson to Baker, Mar. 22, 1919, Anderson papers; McBride to Arthur J. Davis, Dec. 1, 1924, FSM, roll 2; Raymond Fosdick to John D. Rockefeller, Jr., Mar. 19, 1925; Fosdick to Russell, Nov. 18, 1926, PPMR.
13. C. B. Spencer to Cherrington, April 17 and 30, 1925; McBride, "Report to the Executive Committee," Sept. 30, 1925, ECe.

cil began to reconsider its position. Aware that in the eastern industrial cities prohibition seemed ineffective, F. Ernest Johnson, head of the research department of its commission on the church and social service, proposed an investigation. The YWCA and leaders in the Baptist, Congregational, and Reformed churches encouraged him. To Johnson it was especially important to investigate conditions in the cities where law enforcement was most ineffective.[14]

Johnson's investigation damaged the Anti-Saloon League, especially the faction led by Wheeler and McBride. Johnson explained his conclusions in *The Outlook* in the early autumn of 1925. He was not against prohibition. In fact, Johnson concluded that Congress should not "liberalize" the Volstead Act "until it has had a fair trial." The problem was, "Such a trial it has not yet been given." The prohibition bureau, however well-meaning its chief officers, was riddled with corruption and swamped with petty offenses. The Coolidge administration remained uninterested in corrective action. The government in general "lacked also a broad-gauge philosophy of social progress that might have won the support of the country." The wave of support that prohibition had received between 1917 and 1920 had receded, and the trends of social indicators of alcohol abuse were unfavorable. Nullification, even in a "small area" like New York City, was "like a cancerous infection."[15]

The problem stemmed from the churches and the Anti-Saloon League that they had created. Johnson believed that the churches should separate themselves from politics now that prohibition law was in place. They should leave the administration of the law to the government. "The churches have been sadly delinquent," he wrote. "They have committed prohibition to the care of a political organization which they created for the purpose and have neglected what is, first and last, the greatest task of all—education in temperate living and in the responsibilities of citizenship." The churches should abandon threats of compulsion to the lawbreaker, he continued and adopt a program of longer-lasting results, "reasoned observance." The people, he concluded, "must be won to prohibition on its merits as a social policy, or not at all."[16]

14. Nicholson to Cherrington, Jan. 20, 1923; F. Ernest Johnson to Cannon, May 14, 1923, ECe.

15. Johnson, "The Balance Sheet of Prohibition," *The Outlook*, Sept. 9, 1925, pp. 49–51.

16. Ibid.; Sinclair, *Era of Excess*, pp. 290–91, interprets these events as a withdrawal of the federal council's support for prohibition, but the league records now available indicate rather that the federal council leaders were upset about the league's emphasis on law enforcement.

The response of the officers of the Anti-Saloon League was defensive. When Johnson told them of his conclusions, McBride tried to persuade him to withdraw the report. When the plea failed, the wet press flaunted the report as support for arguments to change the Volstead Act, the general superintendent became philosophical. He was "satisfied" that the report would "help the entire cause." The league could use it to present the churches with the need for a more definite program of reviving the organization and embarking on an aggressive campaign to convince voters of the need for stricter law enforcement. It provided, in short, ammunition for the league in its forthcoming "crisis convention."[17]

Cherrington reacted differently. Although the report essentially conformed to his own views, it was threatening in two important ways. In the short run, the report damaged the ability of the world league to assist foreign temperance groups because it pointed to the failures of prohibition in the United States. He thought Johnson had cost New Zealand drys a possible victory in 1925. In the long run, the report threatened the very existence of the Anti-Saloon League, for it implied that the supporting churches should abandon the league in favor of educational activities sponsored by the federal council. Johnson's work was, Cherrington privately confided, "the most telling, effective and destructive blow prohibition in the United States has received since its adoption."[18]

Wanting to counteract any move to abandon the league, Cherrington moved quickly to soften the impact of Johnson's conclusions. The world league had gathered data showing that social conditions under prohibition, however ineptly enforced or incompletely observed, were an improvement over former license laws. Cherrington wanted the argument made public but was fearful that under his aupices it would appear self-serving. So he secretly raised a special fund to have Professor Irving Fisher, the prominent Yale University economist and dry, write a book. The world league prepared the research material, which Fisher checked. Fisher invested $5,000 of his own funds to have the Macmillan Company publish his finished manuscript, which he entitled *Prohibition at its Worst*. Fisher candidly admitted to the many problems of enforcement. But he argued that in any case, even the worst case as it really

17. McBride to Wheeler, Sept. 16, 1925; to Arthur J. Davis, Sept. 24, 1925, FSM, rolls 2, 10.

18. Cherrington to William F. Cochran, Oct. 27, 1925; to Cannon, Feb. 16, 1926, ECe.

existed, the nation was benefiting from prohibition. Cherrington
hoped to circulate the book by the hundreds of thousands. In fact, it
went through two editions. Famous as an independent, expert wit-
ness, Fisher was called to testify before congressional committees
investigating prohibition.[19]

The book may have mitigated the impact of Johnson's report, but
it did not prevent the Federal Council of Churches from actively
considering a recommendation for the abandonment of the league.
The council called a Conference on Prohibition and Law Observance in the spring of 1927 to discuss a new educational effort.
Cherrington and Ella Boole of the WCTU attended the meeting,
where they were allowed to talk frankly. Council president Charles
S. McFarland wanted to call a larger, public meeting to act on a
recommendation for a new organization. But Cherrington argued
that the world league, with WCTU support, was already sponsoring
a large meeting in August. Finally, the federal council officers present voted to refer the entire issue back to their policy committee.
Later that year, when the Anti-Saloon League adopted Cherrington's
strategy and created its department of education, talk of replacing
the league waned.[20]

The League and National Politics, 1920–1927

When Johnson and the Federal Council of Churches revealed the
scandalous administration of enforcement, they failed to follow
through on the political implications of their findings. Enforcement
was a disgrace because the league was powerless to change it, to hold
elected officials accountable. The powerlessness of the league,
moreover, was leading to another unanticipated result. In spite of all
the league's rhetoric about nonpartisanship, the organization was, in
fact, becoming linked more and more with Republican fortunes as
the decade unfolded. Although Wheeler may have maintained his
self-styled "dry boss" image, he knew better—that in fact the league
was slipping in its ability to make a direct difference in the outcome
of elections. This slippage soon became apparent in Congress, and it
later became apparent as the nation's two major parties polarized on
the subject of prohibition. Like the strained relations with the
churches, the league's political slippage was a result of the failure to

19. Cherrington to Cannon, Feb. 16, 1926, ECe; Cherrington to Cochran, Oct. 27,
1926, ECe.
20. Cherrington to McBride, April 8, 1927, ECe.

enunciate a clear, consensual strategy. The political slippage was, moreover, very much a result of the consequent decline of the organization.

The results of the congressional polls of 1920 were satisfactory to the league. The drys were confident of maintaining their hold in the Senate, but not in the House. Andrew Volstead in Minnesota provided the key race. The wets knew that if they could defeat Volstead, the next persons in line to chair the Judiciary Committee were sympathizers. The Non-Partisan League rebellion in the northern wheat belt and the discontent of railroad workers over government's failure to nationalize the railway industry permanently seemed to provide an opportunity to unseat the incumbent. So Wheeler sent his top aide to Granite Falls to help Volstead and told the Congressman that if he needed "a few hundred dollars extra to put on the steam in the closing days of the campaign, to do it, and send the bills to us here." Volstead won, and the House and the key committee he chaired stayed in dry hands.[21]

But 1922 provided a different story. Not only was Volstead defeated in the Minnesota primary election, but the dry majority in the House of Representatives dropped by four votes, as the league began to feel the impact of the reapportionment of seats following the census of 1920. Although the drys actually gained four seats in the Senate, both sides knew that the key battleground was in the House. Wheeler warned the executive committee that the press could interpret slippage in the House as the advent of adverse popular reaction to prohibition. Volstead himself had held up amendments to the National Prohibition Act so as not "to stir up any more animosity over the prohibition question than necessary. We cannot afford to have our friends take any extra hazard." Wheeler complained that he did not have enough money for an adequate campaign effort. "It is poor economy and bad political judgment to allow this situation to go by default," he told the executive committee.[22]

Because of the shortage of funds and the decline of local leagues, Wheeler had to depend on other sources to encourage dry voters.

21. Dick T. Morgan to W. C. A. Wallar, June 5, 1920; Frederick C. Stevens to Volstead, June 22, 1920; Wheeler to Volstead, Oct. 8 and 22, 1920; Dinwiddie to Volstead, Nov. 5, 1920, AJV.

22. George B. Safford to Volstead, Jan. 12, 1922; Volstead to Harvey Wood, April 19, 1922, AJV; Report of Legal Department, May 11, 1922; Minutes, Executive Committee, Nov. 14, 1922, ECe.

He worked with the campaign committees of the congressional parties to insure support for dry candidates and with the newspapers to deliver the league's message. After 1922, for the rest of the decade the league was able to maintain, and even increase, the nominally dry majorities in both houses of Congress. Supported by a National Legislative Conference of twenty prohibition and church organizations, the drys obtained increased appropriations for federal enforcement officers and prevented changes in the Volstead law to allow the manufacture and sale of beer and wine. But the prohibition movement was not powerful enough to secure legislation readily. Nor could it command power in presidential elections to insure sympathetic administration of the law.[23]

Before the 1920s, the league had threatened to intervene in presidential races but had never found such action necessary. That situation changed in 1920 with the spectre of the Democratic party nominating on old foe, James Cox of Ohio, while the Republicans chose Warren G. Harding. Harding had once helped the league in the Ohio legislature, but, when facing a larger electorate, had turned into an unreliable vote. In trying unsuccessfully to force both candidates into promising to enforce prohibition effectively, the league received only slightly more cooperation from Harding than from Cox. Knowing that it could control neither candidate, the league simply published the records of both men and concentrated on the congressional races, where candidates in three hundred districts were voicing opposition to the Volstead Act.[24]

Disappointed with Harding's record on enforcement and realizing that Coolidge was unlikely to push the matter, the league leaders in 1924 resisted pressures from the Prohibition party to seek platform endorsements of prohibition. If it tried and failed, the press would brand the league as having lost its mandate. So the strategy was to seek platform endorsements of law enforcement, which, Wheeler argued, would help the league with "the better class of politicians" and give policemen "more courage and determination."[25]

In 1924 the prospect of Al Smith winning the Democratic nomination posed the most serious danger. His leading opponent, William G. McAdoo, was safely dry, but Smith was the nation's best-known wet politician. McAdoo was aware that wet leaders were "exerting all

23. Report of Legal and Legislative Department, Nov. 15, 1924, ECe.
24. Minutes, Executive Committee, July 22, 1920; Report of the Legal Department, Dec. 16, 1920, ECe.
25. Report of Legal Department, July 17, 1924, ECe.

their energies in fighting me in the primaries" by supporting favorite sons and seeking uninstructed convention delegates. "In each
case reported," he told Russell, "we find that the dry forces have
been caught off guard, awakening in some cases only after the
election was over."[26]

The league sought the selection of a dry candidate—McAdoo or
someone else. Wheeler focused his attention on the Democratic
convention, which proved to be the most divisive and longest in
history as the delegates tried on ballot after ballot to break a deadlock between McAdoo and Smith. "The situation is complex, intense
and hard to handle," he told McBride while the delegates were
meeting. "We are doing our best to keep all our friends good
natured." After the convention refused to adopt a wet platform,
Wheeler worked with friendly delegates to insure that when the
deadlock broke they would not turn to a wet candidate.[27]

The compromise selection, John W. Davis, was satisfactorily dry.
Wheeler boasted that the results of both the Democratic and Republican conventions showed that the politicians were finally convinced
of the need to do the league's bidding. "Our winning fight on the
platform policy has given us a stronger hold on the leaders in both
parties than we ever had before." Both conventions had endorsed
placing the prohibition bureau under civil service, actions that
would help win the issue in the Senate. "Everything looks bright for
continued victories," Wheeler told one prospective state superintendent in urging him to accept the post.[28]

The Challenge of Al Smith

Wheeler's words were sheer bravado. The elections produced only a
veneer of power that the league could not translate into desired
legislation. In part, the league's failure reflected its own internal
schism over strategy. In part, the failure resulted from wet skill in
parliamentary maneuver and public relations. Wealthy Americans,
who were the nation's opinion leaders, apparently, were accepting
casual, social drinking. When the league decided it needed to call its
convention of 1925 a "crisis" meeting, the prominent dry politician

26. McAdoo to Russell, April 5, 1924, HH.
27. Arthur J. Davis to State Superintendents, June 4, 1924; Wheeler to McBride,
July 6, 1924, FSM, rolls 2, 10.
28. Wheeler form letter, July 7, 1924; Wheeler to Jonathan S. Lewis, July 10, 1924,
FSM, roll 10.

William G. McAdoo felt obliged to warn the drys to seek better mobilization.[29]

Shortly after the election of Coolidge the league's political weakness became apparent. Not only were the drys failing to realize legislative victories in Congress on the civil service issue, but the Smith forces were gaining ground within the Democratic party. In 1926 Senator James Reed of Missouri, an irascible league critic, chaired committee hearings to investigate the league's financial involvement in politics. The league sent its records to the Senate, only to find information released in a way intended to embarrass the drys. Reed's hearings provided a forum for complaints about abuses of law enforcement authority. Most startling was the declaration by Assistant Treasury Secretary Lincoln C. Andrews, the man to whom Haynes and the prohibition bureau reported, that he supported the legal sale of beer and wine. Andrews argued that modification of the Volstead Act would facilitate action against the distilling industry.[30]

The congressional elections in 1926 provided little relief. The dry majorities were maintained, but McBride admonished Wheeler to issue fewer "glowing" victory reports lest they retard fund raising. To McBride the election results clarified the necessity of resuscitating the league; otherwise, "the wets will win out." He was very much aware that the AAPA was well funded, seemed to have a growing following in large cities, and was aiming its sights on the presidential contest of 1928.[31]

The league officers knew that they had to oppose Al Smith with every means at their disposal, despite their preference for refraining from endorsing presidential candidates lest their actions appear partisan. But the dry leaders could not refuse to speak out against Smith if he were nominated, and they were doubtful of their ability to prevent his selection by the Democrats. The situation was complicated by Smith's Catholicism. To the league leaders, Smith's strategy seemed to involve retaining the traditionally Democratic South while making inroads in northeastern and middle western states with a wet appeal. The KKK was opposing him in the South, and the

29. McAdoo to Russell, Oct. 1, 1925, HH. For an analysis of changing drinking customs in the 1920s, see Joseph R. Gusfield, "Prohibition: The Impact of Political Utopianism," in *Change and Continuity in Twentieth-Century America: The 1920s*, ed. John Braeman, Robert H. Bremner, and David Brody (Columbus, Ohio, 1928), pp. 271–78.

30. Kyvig, *Repealing National Prohibition*, pp. 61–62.

31. McBride to Wheeler, Nov. 8, 1926, FSM, roll 15; McBride, "Report to the Executive Committee," Nov. 16, 1926, ECe.

league wished to avoid any association with that group's politics of prejudice. American Catholics, after all, were the largest group Cherrington and the other advocates of education were hoping to win over to the support of prohibition.[32]

In the past the league had refrained from seeking platform endorsements of prohibition, although they often materialized; in the face of Smith's strength, however, that seemed a viable approach. In 1927 the executive committee actively debated the tactic. If the league could secure a prohibition plank in the Democratic platform, the drys might secure the commitment of the nominee to it. In the end, however, the leaders followed Cannon's advice and rejected the plan. He warned that it was likely to fail and thus destroy the league's credibility as a political organization. Failure would logically lead to calls for support of a third party, something the league was never prepared to accept. Finally, in 1927 the board of directors issued a statement that reminded politicians of the "emphatic" endorsement of prohibition by the public and called upon both parties to affirm law enforcement and refuse the candidacies of any man whose attitude on nullification was "doubtful" or "antagonistic" to prohibition.[33]

In the end the worst possible state of affairs emerged. Dry Democrats in the South were not successfully opposing the selection of Smith delegates. Cherrington believed that the international liquor interests were pouring money into the campaign, "hungry to get at the pie counter." Cannon wanted the league to encourage McAdoo to enter the race to stop Smith, but McBride restrained the league from becoming involved in the candidate selection process. "That is a task," he told the press, "that belongs to political conventions and not prohibition organizations." The Smith campaign went on unchecked.[34]

The best hope for the league appeared to be the Republican

32. A. J. Barton to Roy A. Haynes, Dec. 8, 1925, with Minutes, Executive Committee, Dec. 4, 1925, ECe.

33. "Resolutions Adopted by the Board of Directors of the Anti-Saloon League of America," August 1927, Minutes, Executive Committee, May 19, 1927, ECe.

34. Cherrington to S. E. Nicholson, Jan. 3, 1928, ECg; McBride press release, March 1928, ECe; Cannon to L. B. Musgrove, Feb. 18, 1928, JC. I found no reliable information on the sums the liquor businesses were donating to the political campaigns in the 1920s; that the liquor interests were willing to donate funds, however, there is no doubt. The AAPA leaders felt obliged to prevent more than 5 percent of their group's budget from coming from persons associated with the liquor traffic. Kyvig, *Repealing National Prohibition*, pp. 46–47.

nomination of Herbert Hoover. Hoover's reputation as an effective administrator, humanitarian, and progressive leader gave him more appeal in the South than other possible candidates, and so he seemed to have the best chance of foiling Smith's election strategy. Hoover had spoken favorably of the economic benefits of the prohibition law. When Samuel Nicholson arranged for Cherrington and McBride to meet with Hoover, they explained the campaign to legalize wine and beer. Hoover assured them, "I am a dry candidate." Both his subsequent nomination and the Republican platform pleased the prohibitionists.[35]

Meanwhile, the prohibition organizations tried to encourage Smith's opponents. At the end of February 1928 they held a conference during which they called upon both parties to adopt platforms favoring enforcement of prohibition and "to nominate candidates who are positively and openly committed to this policy . . . by their utterances, acts and records." The conference formed an ad hoc organization to raise money to develop detailed files on convention proceedings.[36]

The prohibition movement failed to achieve its goal at the Democratic convention that met in Houston. Although the delegates passed a "satisfactory enforcement declaration," they nominated Al Smith. When the governor telegraphed his acceptance, he advocated "fundamental changes in the present provisions for National Prohibition." He said that as president he would "point the way . . . to a sane, sensible solution of a condition which I am convinced is entirely unsatisfactory to the great mass of our people."[37]

Smith "raised the wet issue," McBride later reported. "It was very helpful to our fight to be saved the trouble and embarassment of raising the issue." Smith's choice of John J. Raskob, leader of the AAPA and a Republican, as his campaign manager, was offensive to "loyal Democrats and slapped in the face the dry Democrats of the North and South." These actions gave the prohibition leaders cause to mobilize their opposition. It would be "the greatest prohibition fight ever," Cherrington advised.[38]

35. *Christian Science Monitor*, Mar. 11, 1925; S. E. Nicholson to Cherrington, Jan. 12, 1928; "Conference with Hoover," April 12, 1928, ECg.

36. "Prohibition Enforcement Planks and Dry Democrats," JC; Carlton M. Sherwood to Roper, May 28, 1928, DR.

37. "Report of McBride to the Executive Committee, Nov. 15, 1928," ECe, includes a text of the Smith statement.

38. Ibid.; Cherrington to Thomas Nicholson, July 3, 1928, ECe.

The situation was very alarming to the drys. Smith's strategy of holding the South while making inroads in normally Republican northern states might work. The league officers quickly mapped out a plan to stop the wets from occupying the White House. The way to defeat Smith seemed clear: to inform northern voters of his position on prohibition while organizing dry southern Democrats to vote for Hoover. Cherrington embarked on the first task, using the resources of his new department of education. Cannon and A. J. Barton of the Southern Baptists worked in the South.[39]

The dry effort in the South was especially rancorous. Cannon and Barton organized a group in each southern state to urge Democrats to vote for Hoover while supporting the state and local candidates on their party ticket. They faced bitter opposition from some established party leaders. Smith supporters accused them of anti-Catholicism and of improperly embroiling the church in politics. In Alabama, local Democrats issued a pamphlet titled, "Republican Party and Herbert Hoover are Pledged to Make You Insure the Life of Every Negro Rapist in Alabama for $10,000." Facing this kind of scurrilous campaign, the dry Democrats hoped to carry from three to six states for Hoover.[40]

The election returns were cause for jubilation by the Anti-Saloon League. The drys enjoyed tremendous successes. Not only did Hoover crack the "solid South" by carrying Texas, Florida, North Carolina, and Virginia, he won thirty-six other states in the greatest landslide in United States history. "Al Smith and his liquor crowd," commented one dry Democrat, "have had their referendum on the Eighteenth Amendment. If they are not satisfied, we are ready to go again." The wets lost ground in almost every arena. On inauguration, there would be 80 dry senators and 329 dry representatives, the largest prohibition margin ever. Forty-three states would have dry governors, and in Cleveland and Chicago newly elected officials had promised to enforce the law. McBride believed that the Hoover

39. Cannon form letter, July 9, 1928; McBride to Cannon, July 11, 1928; Cannon to L. L. Yost, July 26, 1928, JC; Cherrington to Kresge, July 26, 1928, ECg. Cherrington's use of education funds to fight Smith's election was expedient, but the action was also a deviation from the stated purpose of a broad educational and uplift program.

40. Carter Glass to Cannon, Sept. 12, 1928; Barton to Cannon, Sept. 24, 1928, JC; E. J. Richardson to Eva C. Wheeler, Sept. 29, 1928; F. M. Jackson to Cherrington, Oct. 26, 1928, ECg; Francis O. Clarkson to Clarkson, Oct. 1928, HC.

victory would encourage law enforcement officials everywhere to pursue violators more aggressively.[41]

The problem with McBride's conviction was the subtle change that had overtaken the league during the national political campaigns after 1920. Just as Wheeler had inadvertently tied the fortunes of the Ohio league to the Republican party after 1906 and thereby produced decided setbacks when the state's Democrats regained power, so too his machinations as dry boss on the national scene had a negative impact on the league's effectiveness in the long run. Always looking opportunistically for victory—and after 1920 facing the seriously diminished capability of the league to mobilize voters for a successful district-by-district balance of power politics—Wheeler had used his office and his own personal identification as a Republican to work with the Republican leaders who controlled Congress in the 1920s. Meanwhile, in the North opportunistic big city Democrats, encouraged by wet organizations, were arranging a new coalition of support among wet immigrant voters. In Massachusetts, for example, before 1928 the parties had become polarized along ethnocultural lines, with the drys able to influence only the Republican party, now consisting almost entirely of native born, old-stock persons. The Smith campaign tended to solidify such arrangements in the nation's largest cities.[42]

None of these considerations were apparent, or a cause for concern, so long as the Republicans commanded the federal government. But when the Republican majority evaporated, as it did after 1929, the prohibition movement was in deep trouble. The political failure of the Anti-Saloon League, thus, came to rest on two factors. The league leaders lost sight of their organization's original political strategy, nonpartisanship. And they lost sight because, having failed to resolve the conflict between coercive and assimilative reform, the league had declined as an organization capable of leading sympathetic churches or mobilizing voters.

41. "Report of McBride, Nov. 15, 1928;" Hugh A. Locke to Cannon, Nov. 15, 1928, JC.

42. The original explanation of the polarization of voters along immigrant-old-stock lines in Samuel Lubell, *The Future of American Politics* (Garden City, N.Y., 1952). See also Huthmacher, *Massachusetts People and Politics*, pp. 131–34, and John M. Allswang, *A House for All Peoples: Ethnic Politics in Chicago, 1890–1936* (Lexington, Ky., 1971), pp. 111–38.

Renewed Hopes, 1927—1929

The sweeping dry victories in the 1928 elections produced a heady optimism within the ranks of the Anti-Saloon League. After nearly nine years of national prohibition, opposition to prohibition, well funded and well organized, had emerged and made progress in a propaganda campaign to persuade Americans that the dry law had cost the nation dearly in tax revenues, personal liberty, and respect for legal institutions. The AAPA had threatened to achieve national political power with the nomination of Al Smith. Now it was turned back, Smith and other wet Democrats repudiated at the polling booth. For the first time, a president who seemed committed to making prohibition effective would serve.

For Ernest Cherrington in particular, 1928 was a remarkable year, one in which the fortunes of the Anti-Saloon League turned in a favorable direction. The league had resolved its internal strategy dispute in his favor, established its department of education, turned back the wet bid for the White House, and in the process helped elect a president whose own attitudes seemed supportive of a campaign to achieve law observance.

The political victory, important as it was to the survival of prohibition, was less significant to Cherrington than the establishment of the league's department of education. Shortly after Hoover's election, Cherrington prepared a plan for the league that combined a sense of realism with long-range optimism. Cherrington by this time was advising American drys that, although "public sentiment" was "emphatically favorable to the Eighteenth Amendment as a standard of conduct, nevertheless there [was] as yet no such degree of sanction on the part of the public for the full enforcement of, and obedience to, that constitutional provision." He claimed that the emphasis of the league, through its department of education, was to build a public opinion from which would flow the necessary government actions for the final eradication of the liquor traffic. Reformers had to remember, Cherrington said, "that time is an essential factor in making effective prohibitions against great social evils." Such was the experience historically in the fight against the slave trade, he observed; such would be the experience of the temperance movement even under the amendment.[43]

43. Cherrington, "The Best and Most Practical Plan to Make the Eighteenth Amendment Effective," Dec. 1928 typescript, ECg; *Education Against Alcoholism* (Westerville, 1929).

Cherrington felt that the league was in a favorable position to achieve stronger and wider public support. He and his staff had been planning the department of education since the early weeks of 1927 and had seen it funded and accepted as the prevailing league strategy at the end of that year. Cherrington and Russell had met with S. S. Kresge and had successfully appealed to him that a spectacularly large donation would both help publicize his business and "kindle" an "inspiration" among temperance leaders and "upon the public throughout the length and breadth of the United States" for renewed efforts on behalf of observance. Cherrington outlined a sweeping campaign to renew scientific knowledge of the social and medical effects of alcohol consumption to influence public opinion leaders, church members, and students at every educational level. The campaign would cost, over a five-year period, $15,472,500.[44]

Kresge responded favorably. When the league resolved its internal dispute over strategy and created the department of education, he pledged a donation of $500,000, spread over a three-year period. Cherrington worked quickly to establish his educational program. The league, hoping to raise as much as $10 million from others inspired by Kresge's pledge, created a separate nonprofit corporation to receive donations for education on a tax-free basis. "We have passed our most crucial period," league president Thomas Nicholson wrote to Cherrington. "We are not out of the woods altogether," he said, but the situation seemed promising indeed. With Kresge's money and other, smaller pledges, Cherrington could realistically plan a first-year budget of $175,000 for his new department.[45]

A progressive philosophy guided Cherrington in the expenditure of those funds. Like so many other educated Americans of his generation, Cherrington believed that the prohibition movement had to rest its case on "truth," scientifically derived. Drawing on his experience of directing publicity work during the campaign for the Eighteenth Amendment, Cherrington asserted that the league should compile and disseminate "impartial data compiled by government bureaus, trade associations and others, who are not partisan prohibitionists . . . to offset the extensive and insidious propaganda" of the wets. He wanted to encourage research and to reemphasize "the real nature and effect of alcohol; the evils of indulgence in beverage

44. S. S. Kresge to Paul W. Voorhies, Feb. 23, 1927; Cherrington to Kresge, April 6, 1927, ECg.

45. Thomas Nicholson to Cherrington, Jan. 1928; Boyd P. Doty to McBride, Jan. 31, 1928; Minutes, Administrative Committee, Feb. 17, 1928, ECe.

intoxicants." The league had to reeducate Americans about the character of the liquor traffic and its exploitations "at the expense of society." In Cherrington's program the staff would catalog thousands of germane publications, assemble the results of medical research, hire foreign language assistants to interpret research in other nations, gather its own social statistics, and coordinate and standardize the research efforts of other temperance societies.

The collection of this information was only the beginning. Dissemination would consume the largest part of the department's budget. Especially important was showing how the changing technological nature of modern society made abstinence all the more imperative. Cherrington observed that the widespread application of electric power to industrial production and the growth of assembly line methods in manufacturing increased the hazards of the workplace, "where a single drinker may throw a whole factory out of step." According to his line of thought, now that automobiles were widespread, drinking had to stop. Furthermore, Cherrington observed that in the modern economy, "the pyramid structure of installment buying" rested "upon the integrity and earning capacity of the abstinent worker," who also, through savings, was maintaining "enormous reservoirs of liquid capital."

Cherrington and his staff shrewdly worked to place their message carefully before the public at the lowest possible cost. They were concerned about "informing our constituency" through church newspapers and magazines but also wanted to reach opinion leaders—professors, ministers, editors, and politicians—with a 4,500 name mailing list. Cherrington preferred to have newspapers print information supplied by the league, rather than having the league publish its own material. He arranged for reviews of books that touched upon prohibition and its social effects and supplied authors and journalists with information that they could use independently of the league. Although the output of the league's own presses was sizeable, Cherrington believed that it was best to have dispassionate information about prohibition's benefits placed before the public under other auspices. Not just printed material but radio programs and motion pictures were prepared as well.[46]

A significant problem existed in the Protestant churches themselves. When a group of church leaders met under the auspices of the Federal Council of Churches, they realized that the amount of

46. *Education Against Alcoholism.*

temperance instruction included in standard Sunday school curricula was woefully inadequate. Little attention was devoted to the subject, and the small amount of material they contained reached only a small proportion of the population, especially in the industrial cities of the North and East, where opposition to prohibition was strongest. So Cherrington used his new department to arrange a national conference of the publishers of church school material in 1928. They agreed to form a permanent committee to cooperate with the temperance organizations with a view toward improving the quality and quantity of temperance materials that reached Sunday school instructors. The committee worked with thirty-nine denominations. Cherrington was pleased with the results. In 1928, he reported, "stronger" material was appearing in "Sunday school publications than in any similar period of time during the past ten years."[47]

One significant way the league could enhance its educational program was to have government at various levels assume some of the burden. The historic programs of temperance instruction in the public schools had lapsed, and the league sought to revive them. Cora Francis Stoddard learned that the WCTU had shifted its emphasis away from working with the public schools in favor of sponsoring essay contests among young people. In 1923, realizing that little effort was being made inside the classroom, Stoddard had the Scientific Temperance Federation embark on a long-range strategy of committing teachers and school administrators to a program of temperance instruction. She prepared new curricular materials appropriate for current teaching methods and worked to have them approved by the National Education Association. By 1931 Stoddard was confident that substantial progress was being made toward producing a new generation of Americans persuaded as to the evils of alcohol consumption.[48]

Cherrington, Stoddard, and the other league educators also placed great hopes upon having the federal government sponsor a propaganda campaign to offset wet arguments. The bureau of prohibition under Haynes had spent only small sums to explain and justify its work. Haynes himself had written *Prohibition Inside Out* to defend his policies while sensationalizing the activities of bootleggers. Wheeler had thought the bureau might spend $50,000 a

47. Ibid.; "Preliminary Report, Investigation of Teaching of Temperance in Curricula for Religious Education," undated typescript, ECg.

48. Stoddard to Boyd P. Doty, April 1, 1931, ECg.

year on educational work, but when Congress appropriated the funds, Assistant Secretary of the Treasury Lincoln Andrews had refused to spend them. The reorganization of the prohibition unit, the curtailment of Andrews's control, and the appointment of Dr. James Doran as its head, however, renewed expectations, following the Hoover landslide, that the federal government might actually enter the field. Secretary Mellon observed early in 1929 that some additional appropriations for enforcement might be spent on educational activities. Finally, in March of 1929, Congress allocated $50,000 for education about the need to observe the prohibition law.[49]

Doran believed it appropriate to leave the moral side of the question to the churches and the temperance organizations and to focus on the economic benefits. He worked with a private lithographic firm to develop a series of posters for display in post offices and other public buildings. The temperance organizations could assist in their distribution. He also had his staff suggest slogans like "Prohibition, Your Duty to Posterity," which the Treasury Department printed on its envelopes. Doran changed the title of an office to Education and Reports and had its head, Alice B. Sutter, attend meetings of the National Education Association to inform delegates of the government's work.[50]

This federal effort together with the activities of the league produced a spurt of optimistic activity that proved short-lived. The government's effort was limited by its small appropriation, but the league was doing little to increase it. The problem lay in the lingering dispute between McBride and Cherrington. McBride was hostile to the new strategy, and his office and the education department did not coordinate their efforts—in fact, their Washington offices were even in separate buildings. Cherrington's assistants in Washington felt constrained in lobbying independently for a larger appropriation, and it was never forthcoming, even though a full-scale poster campaign alone would have cost at least $250,000 annually.[51]

But the worst blow to the education department was its private

49. Roy A. Haynes, *Prohibition Inside Out* (Garden City, N.Y., 1923); A. J. Barton to J. M. Doran, Jan. 21, 1929, ECe; Doran to Philip J. Meany Company, May 14, 1929, IRS, file V-B−10.

50. W. C. McKee to James M. Doran, Mar. 11, 1929; Doran to Isabel S. Hunder, June 27, 1929, IRS, file V-B−10.

51. T. J. Steuart to Cherrington, Jan. 5, 1929; Cherrington to S. S. Kresge, Mar. 14, 1929, ECg.

financing. Donations to supplement Kresge's pledge were not forthcoming in the size anticipated, and Kresge himself began to withdraw his commitment. In the autumn of 1929 he decided to extend
his payments over six years rather than over the three years he had
originally promised. The advancing barrage of wet propaganda
distressed Kresge, who observed open violations of the law at a
Florida resort. He believed his dry reputation was hurting his business in big city markets. Kresge's decision was "a heavy shock" to
Cherrington. Cherrington encouraged his friend to take a longer
view of the effort but was unsuccessful. Finally, in 1930 Kresge
stopped payments altogether. "Any funds that I have given up to
this time I consider wasted," he wrote Cherrington, "because there
has not been the cooperation needed from the better class of monied
people." After this decision the league's department of education
virtually collapsed.[52]

National Prohibition Politics, 1929–1931

The optimism that the drys felt following the Hoover landslide
lasted no longer with regard to federal politics than it did concerning
the strategy of education. The problem was not President Hoover's
public commitment to prohibition, which actually grew stronger in
the first two years of his term. The problem was that political events
were out of his control. After the onset of the Great Depression,
Hoover's popularity faded rapidly, and his ability to influence political affairs receded accordingly. Part of the failure of his popularity
was of course a shrewd negative campaign directed by figures con-
spicuous in the AAPA.

But the agony of the prohibition cause under Hoover's administration lay deeper than the president's inability to retain the
popular mandate of 1928. The agony involved the failure of the
Anti-Saloon League and the other dry organizations to mobilize
Americans on behalf of the president's policies. In short, the politics
of prohibition escaped their influence by the end of 1931, and the
drys were helpless to take the initiative.[53]

52. Kresge to Cherrington, Oct. 2 and Dec. 14, 1929, Sept. 11, 1930; Cherrington
to Kresge, Dec. 26, 1929, Jan. 22, 1930, ECg.

53. All scholars who have recently studied the politics of prohibition in the 1920s
agree that the impact of the Great Depression was enormous. Economic events,
entirely out of the drys' control, were greatly increasing the popularity of the Democratic party, within which the wets had made deep and telling inroads. Gusfield,
"Prohibition: The Impact of Political Utopianism," pp. 257–308.

Part of the Anti-Saloon League's internal problems after the 1928 election were a product of its activities during the campaign. The Democratic South was a bastion of support for the Eighteenth Amendment, but, unwittingly, the league's opposition to Smith damaged its ability to mobilize that support for future political action. Although Cannon and Barton spoke bravely of the need to work within the Democratic party to wrest it from Tammany control, they were unable to do so. Instead, loyal Democratic leaders in the South were outraged by the successful campaign for Hoover in their region. They worked within local churches to reduce support for the league, arguing that its involvement in the presidential campaign had violated the mission of the church. So in effect Cannon's efforts in 1928 backfired, and the effects were compounded when his personal life was touched by scandal (rumors that he was having an extramarital affair with his secretary, whom he married shortly after his wife's death). After the onset of the Depression, southern Democratic leaders, scenting national victory in 1932, sought to hold the prohibition issue at bay in the interests of party unity. Meanwhile, the organizational and financial strength of the Anti-Saloon League in the South virtually disappeared.[54]

The troubles of the league with the southern Democratic party and churches were not apparent at the beginning of 1929. What was evident was the reality that legislative and administrative victories were not easily forthcoming in spite of the Hoover landslide. Shortly after the election, the league, with Cherrington leading the way, had helped form the National Conference of Organizations Supporting the Eighteenth Amendment (NCOSE). The NCOSE replaced the old National Legislative Conference that had been allowed to lapse soon after passage of the Volstead Act. The drys tried to force Treasury Secretary Andrew Mellon to declare a need for larger enforcement appropriations, including funds for public education, and to have Congress provide the incoming president with up to $24 million in additional funds. They thought that, with a president committed to prohibition for the first time in history, it was best to accede to his leadership while providing the necessary resources.[55]

The strategy was only partly successful, and its initial implementation revealed the internal weakness of the Anti-Saloon League. In an

54. Cannon to Anti-Smith Democrats, Feb. 5, 1929, JC; E. J. Richardson to Ellis A. Fuller, June 6, 1930, Barton folder, ECe.

55. McBride, "Report to the Executive Committee," Mar. 5, 1929; E. J. Richardson to Delcevare King, Sept. 24, 1929, ECg.

exchange of published letters, Cannon elicited a statement from Mellon acknowledging the need for additional funds for enforcement and education work. But Mellon and the Republican congressional leadership opposed the $24 million appropriation. The result was that, although the Senate approved the sum, the House, acting on instructions from the majority leaders, did not. At the end of January 1929 the league suffered its first major defeat on a roll call vote since World War I.[56]

This defeat was deeply discouraging. During the time the appropriation was pending McBride vacillated, concurring in his press releases with Mellon's argument that such a large appropriation required a precise budget before Congress approved it. The absence of unified lobbying appalled league president Thomas Nicholson. He tried to discuss with McBride the need for better coordination among the national officers, but he also told Cherrington of his personal disgust and of his determination to resign because of the lack of unity among league leaders. He thought the league needed a president who had more time to devote to its affairs and that he was too busy in his church to devote the necessary attention to improve the situation. Nicholson feared for the future of the entire prohibition cause. He thought the four years of the Hoover administration were "pivotal," that "divided sentiment" would "wreck" the league if not corrected.[57]

Even with the defeat on the appropriation, there was still small consolation. The dispute had forced Mellon to admit the need for more funds and for an educational program. It may have caused the president-elect to think more precisely about reorganizing and invigorating the enforcement apparatus. Hoover let it be known to Cherrington that all of his appointees to the cabinet agreed with the need to enforce prohibition. Most pleasing was his naming of William Mitchell, a committed dry, as attorney general.[58]

One measure that most league officials sought was the transfer of enforcement from the Treasury to the Department of Justice. The move would take the machinery from the hands of Andrew Mellon, always unsympathetic to prohibition, and place it in a cabinet department with a dry leader who could improve the coordination

56. Cannon to Mellon, Jan. 18, 1929; Mellon to Cannon, Jan. 21, 1929; E. J. Richardson to Cannon, Feb. 26, 1929, JC.

57. McBride press releases, Jan. 13, 15, 19, 23, 28, 29, 31, 1929; Thomas Nicholson to Cherrington, Jan. 11 and Mar. 7, 1929, ECe.

58. Cherrington to S. S. Kresge, Mar. 14, 1929, ECg.

of enforcement. McBride, however, opposed the change, arguing instead that the prohibition bureau should become an independent agency reporting directly to the president. This internal disagreement hurt the league and its image as a powerful political force. The disagreement also delayed the reorganization of enforcement and its placement under Attorney General Mitchell until 1930.[59]

None of this uncertainty about league policy seemed ominous. The principle of prohibition was not seriously challenged because of a failure of leadership within the Anti-Saloon League. Prohibition still seemed a permanent reform. No amendment to the Constitution had ever been repealed, and repeal was not a serious threat in 1929. Mitchell spoke for the administration when he explained that improvements in law enforcement had to be steady, over a period of "months and even years, so that the improvement may be fundamental and lasting." President Hoover had the same message for private visitors. Hoover believed that prohibition "would succeed or fail according to the success of its enforcement." He told the league that what most concerned him was the inability or unwillingness of many state and local officials to do their part. The federal government, he explained, could never possibly assume the full burden.[60]

One of Hoover's first actions as president was to obtain authorization to appoint a National Commission on Law Observance, headed by George Wickersham. The president told the commission to make recommendations for obtaining better observance of all law, not just of the Volstead Act, but violations of prohibition were of predominant concern. League officers seemed unconcerned by Wickersham's appointment even though he had, from their viewpoint, served President Taft badly on the occasion of the veto of the Webb-Kenyon bill. Apparently they believed that the benefits of prohibition "at its worst" were so evident that no recommendations would be forthcoming either for repeal or modification of the Volstead Law.[61]

A new congressional investigation appeared much more dangerous. In 1930 wets on the House Judiciary Committee arranged hearings on proposals for changing the Eighteenth Amendment. No new arguments were advanced, except that the hearings gave the

59. Steuart to Cherrington, Dec. 4, 1928, ECg.
60. S. E. Nicholson to Cherrington, April 10, 1930, ECg; "Hoover and Mitchell on the Volstead Act," undated 1929 clipping, WM.
61. McBride, "Statement for the National Commission for Law Observance and Enforcement," undated 1930, ECe.

league's opponents a great deal of publicity. Cherrington and other league officers refused to appear lest their presence dignify the discussion of so basic a matter, but McBride disregarded their advice. His testimony helped open a national discussion of the possibility of repealing prohibition altogether.[62]

Even more damaging was the report of the Wickersham commission, issued in 1931. When he announced the findings, President Hoover asserted that the commission did "not favor the repeal of the Eighteenth Amendment as a method of cure for the inherent abuses of the liquor traffic. I am in accord with this view." The commission's summary of its findings called for larger appropriations for enforcement. But Hoover's characterizations had distorted the report. The commission found that drinking had increased since 1920 and that prohibition had corrupted the legal and political system while encouraging disrespect for all law. These were the arguments of the AAPA. "The facts," observed Pierre du Pont, whose contributions to the association were sizeable, " . . . could not have been put in better words for our purposes."[63]

The Anti-Saloon League hoped that the public would disregard the main body of the Wickersham commission's report and accept Hoover's characterization of it. Even before the report was issued, the drys knew that the AAPA publicity department would "take advantage of every word favorable to them" and "get the eye of the public immediately." When the damage was done, it seemed time to forget old differences between factions and organizations and to support the president in his call for greater enforcement efforts at the state and local levels.[64] The difficulty with this strategy was simple, however. No dry organizations—not the Anti-Saloon League, the WCTU, or any other group—was strong enough to mount local campaigns across the nation. Nor, as the politics of prohibition crumbled around them in 1931 and 1932, were the drys able to mount a coordinated, funded, sizeable national campaign to stem the growing chorus of arguments, not now just for modification of the Volstead Act, but for outright repeal of the Eighteenth Amendment.

---

62. Cherrington to Thomas Nicholson, Mar. 25, 1930, ECe; Cherrington to Kresge, May 31, 1930, ECg.

63. Kyvig, *Repealing National Prohibition*, pp. 111–15.

64. Ella Boole to Cherrington, Jan. 2, 1931, ECg; Cannon to Cherrington, Feb. 23, 1931, ECe.

The Collapse of the Anti-Saloon League

The collapse of the Anti-Saloon League soon followed the Wicker-sham commission report. Increasingly and painfully it was becoming obvious that the drys were losing the battle for public opinion. Metropolitan daily newspapers were voicing opposition to prohibition, echoing the arguments of the AAPA and using data from the government's own report. Referendum results and public opinion samples, unscientific though they were, were all showing a shift of sentiment. The league had long argued that prohibition produced practical, economic benefits. But now when the nation and the world were suffering from economic catastrophe, those arguments were fruitless, turned on their head by the wets, who claimed that a legalized liquor traffic would provide sorely needed jobs and tax revenues. After a three-month absence from the country in 1931, Thomas Nicholson was appalled to find a noticeable change for the worse in public sentiment.[65]

To make matters worse, the league had relied on the leadership and vigor of Herbert Hoover finally to set the nation on the proper dry course. But by the end of 1930 Hoover and the Republican party were no longer capable of leading the nation. Discredited by the Depression, Hoover had suffered a stunning reversal in public favor, and the Republicans had lost control of Congress. In a strict sense this loss was not serious for the league as an avowedly nonpartisan organization. But in reality it was a serious blow. Just as the league had successfully worked with Republican candidates in 1916, the wets had powerful supporters within the Democratic party. The prohibitionists could not hope either to command influence in a Democratic controlled Congress or to restrain the party from nominating another wet presidential candidate.

Still, the situation might have been salvageable. Repeal of the Eighteenth Amendment still required approval of three-fourths of the states. In fact, as late as 1930 even the leaders of the AAPA doubted that they would be able to win enough votes from rural, mostly Protestant states to achieve their goal. They were ignorant of the incredible powerlessness of the Anti-Saloon League and other temperance groups and the inability of their executives to unite on a

65. Thomas Nicholson to Cherrington, Jan. 7, 1931, ECg; Cannon to Cherrington, Feb. 23, 1931, ECe.

common strategy for defending the Eighteenth Amendment. They also misjudged public opinion, which galloped past them.[66]

As the crisis leading the repeal mounted, the prohibition organizations began to dispute the best way to meet the threat. The drys never really agreed on a defense, not that they had the financial resources to conduct one in any case. The NCOSE formed a board of strategy at the end of 1930, ostensibly to coordinate the efforts of the league, the WCTU, and other temperance organizations to fend off the mounting AAPA campaign. The board employed Edwin C. Dinwiddie to serve as its executive secretary. Dinwiddie proved particularly ineffective in this role. When the board approved a "Dry Dimes Will Beat Wet Dollars" campaign to solicit hundreds of thousands of petty donations for publicity work, Dinwiddie used the money for filing cases and for paying his salary. By 1932 his sole activity seemed to have been the solicitation of information on delegates attending the summer's political conventions.[67]

Within the board of strategy, Daniel Poling, whose support in the 1890s had helped establish the league, appealed for the formation of a new, grass roots organization called the Allied Forces for Prohibition. Poling argued that, in view of the decline of the older organizations, including the league, the unification of the Allied Command on the western front in 1918 was the model to follow. The Allied Forces should mobilize voters by election district with pledges to support dry candidates. Each local group, he said, should be self-supporting and democratically organized. Other members of the board, however, disagreed. Cherrington and Ella Boole of the WCTU believed that any defensive strategy had to rest on local congregations. McBride suspected that Poling was attempting to destroy the league and take over its resources for his personal benefit.[68]

Poling proceded to form the Allied Forces in spite of the disapproval of the board. At the end of 1931 he reported the organization of local units in eighty-seven cities in twenty-nine states, with an average membership of 1,000 voters. But by January 1932 Poling

66. Kyvig, *Repealing National Prohibition*, pp. 136–37.
67. Dinwiddie press release, Feb. 9, 1932; Boole to Cherrington, Feb. 11, 1932; William Rufus Scott to Cherrington, Feb. 18, 1932; D. Leigh Colvin to Cherrington, Feb. 18, 1932; Dinwiddie to Cherrington, Feb. 20, 1932, ECg.
68. Boole to Cherrington, July 22, 1931; Poling to Cherrington, July 3, Dec. 4, 1931; Cherrington to Poling, July 7, 1931, ECg; McBride to Cherrington, Dec. 16, 1930, ECe.

was sending out desperate appeals for money, and the Allied Forces never amounted to a significant political force. Poling's actions aroused hostility and charges that his efforts, weak as they were, were undermining the established temperance organizations.[69]

The leaders critical of Poling, however, never settled on an effective alternative strategy. By 1932 the repeal movement was reaching stampede proportions. It was apparent that the Democrats were likely to assume control of the federal government after the elections. Their leading contenders for the presidential nomination were considered wet. The loss of three dry seats in the House of Representatives in twenty-five states—a distinct likelihood—would mean a loss of control over enforcement appropriations and amendments to the Volstead Act. The best that the temperance organizations could hope for was to salvage the Eighteenth Amendment from repeal. But they could not agree even on that program. As a delaying tactic, Cherrington suggested the possibility of seeking an amendment requiring popular referendums for any future changes in the Constitution. But that doubtful idea never was seriously considered. The best hope of the prohibitionists was in the Republican party, but by 1932, even Herbert Hoover was changing his position in favor of basic modifications of the prohibition statutes.[70]

In the end, it made little difference that the board of strategy never really developed a strategy. The board had precious few resources to conduct any sort of campaign. The Wall Street crash had impoverished the collections of the Anti-Saloon League. In 1930 the league had held a convention in Detroit that fifteen state superintendents could not afford to attend. Those delegates who came were mostly elderly; there were no new recruits from the young. In 1930, the American Issue Publishing Company, the league's principal asset, had an income of only $155,000. The Ohio league, once the ablest at raising money, owed the firm $6,800.[71]

If the league was impoverished in 1930, the situation only worsened thereafter. At the beginning of 1932, the Bank of Westerville failed. The bank's demise was a disaster, for it had provided a source

69. Poling to Cherrington, Feb. 13, 1932, ECg; Cannon to Cherrington, Feb. 24, 1932, ECe.

70. McBride, "Report to Board of Directors," Jan. 15, 1932, ECe; Boole to Cherrington, April 6, 1932; Dinwiddie form letter, April 27, 1932; Cherrington to Kresge, July 9, 1932; Edward P. Dunford to Cherrington, Oct. 19, 1932, ECg.

71. Cherrington to Thomas Nicholson, Jan. 28, 1930; to McBride, Feb. 17, 1930, ECe.

of short-term loans to solve problems of cash flow. Now those loans would be called, and in the meantime the league's funds on deposit were inaccessible. The officers of the league became consumed with fund raising. They tried asking wealthy persons to make good on their pledges in hopes that they could use the funds raised to collect smaller pledges. They appealed to wealthy donors to make sizeable contributions. But none of this activity was effective. They asked John D. Rockefeller, Jr., for instance, for a special contribution of $2½ million to conduct an educational campaign. Instead, Rockefeller funded a study of liquor control systems in Europe that might be adapted to American conditions. In 1933 the league received $121,940 and had liabilities of $81,727, mostly in unpaid salaries. The Publishing Company received only $53,000.[72]

The financial disaster that befell the league brought with it petty disputes and left the officers isolated and ignorant of political conditions. The best hope of resisting the repeal movement lay in the rural states. But McBride, ostensibly in charge of the league's political activities, was too busy trying to raise money to have a clear picture of political conditions in those states. Cherrington and Ella Boole argued over the best way of distributing antirepeal literature. Finally, to resolve the dispute, she suggested that the board of strategy dispense funds to state groups for their use. She suggested sums for entire states in the $100 range, so pathetic were the resources of the dry movement.[73]

By 1933 matters were desperate. The Democrats and Franklin D. Roosevelt swept into office, and Congress, even before the inauguration, modified the Volstead Act and allowed the manufacture and sale of beer. The repeal amendment was initiated, using the provision for popular ratification referendum for the first time. "Doesn't the world seem up-side-down these days?" remarked Lena Lowe Yost, member of the WCTU and director of the Women's Division of the Republican National Committee. The drys held a Prohibition Emergency Conference in March and agreed on a unified budget. But that spring events were moving so rapidly that the dry leaders could not keep abreast of them. Finally, by summer they realized

72. Cherrington to McBride, Aug. 5, 1931; McBride press release, Feb. 11, 1933; Administrative Committee Minutes, Jan. 3, 1934, ECe; J. L. Miller to John D. Rockefeller, Sr., Feb. 18, 1931, PPMR; Russell to I. W. Metcalf, Jan. 5, 1932, IWM.

73. Cherrington to Boole, Sept. 28, 1932; Boole to Cherrington, Oct. 3, 1932; ECg; Cherrington to McBride, April 13, 1933; McBride to Cherrington, April 14, 1933, ECe.

that their cause was lost. "The outlook for the Eighteenth Amendment is not good," Cherrington advised Thomas Nicholson. "The principal reason . . . is that even the church forces and the friends of prohibition have lost interest for the time being, evidently because they have concluded that repeal is bound to carry."[74]

They were correct. Utah became the thirty-sixth state to ratify the Twenty-First Amendment, the last needed to complete the three-fourths majority. Prohibition ended on December 5, 1933.

74. Lenna Lowe Yost to Cherrington, Jan. 9, 1933; Dinwiddie form letter, Mar. 29, 1933; Cherrington to Thomas Nicholson, June 12, 1933, ECe.

11

CONCLUSION

Prohibition was a failure. Americans in the late twentieth century repeat the conventional wisdom in many ways. Schoolbooks, university lectures, electronic broadcasts, newspapers and magazines reiterate the popular interpretation that Americans in the 1920s bulged their pockets with hip flasks, brewed gin in their bathtubs, and squeezed wine grapes in their basements. A huge illicit industry, organized by criminals, arose to slake thirsts. Finally, in a society riddled by corruption and missing valuable sources of legitimate employment and tax revenue, Americans overturned the Anti-Saloon League and its blue-nose, pinch-faced zealots who would have them forego the pleasures of drink. The drys, so this line goes, attacked personal liberty and were obsessed with reaching down from their pulpits to control the lives of individuals according to a strictly defined, narrow code of moral behavior.

The conventional wisdom is wrong, although it has insights. Leaders like Wayne Wheeler and Francis Scott McBride, like a number of progressives and other reformers, were willing to disregard traditional human liberties and abandon tolerance in their quest for the eradication of the liquor traffic and the higher social good. The Volstead Act and its enforcement were a legal and administrative nightmare. Some persons agreed with Wheeler's desire to outlaw the possession of alcoholic beverages. Some officers of the law abused their power, and organized crime moved in to direct the now illicit liquor traffic. Prohibition advocates manipulated political affairs to serve their ends while they defined those ends from a particular evangelical Protestant viewpoint. In spite of all the drys' efforts, among some urban Americans, tied more and more to bureaucratic agencies and less and less to extended families and local church communions, drinking apparently became an acceptable custom even while the Eighteenth Amendment was in effect. It would not be too many years after 1933 when even Methodists might imbibe.[1]

Those insights, however, omit other important facets of the American experience under prohibition, considerations—now made possible by access to the Anti-Saloon League's archives—that make judgment more difficult. This book has shown that Wayne Wheeler and Howard Russell were not the Anti-Saloon League— were not even necessarily advocates of a majority view within the evangelical dry movement. Certainly Ernest Cherrington and his staff, a majority of the league's state superintendents, and the leaders of the Federal Council of Churches disagreed with the legalistic, coercive approach to prohibition. Cherrington and the other advocates of a renewed emphasis on uplift and assimilation to evangelical Protestant norms believed that if the churches focused on persuasion, not compulsion, in two generations—by 1950—Americans would voluntarily abstain from alcoholic beverages. As events turned out, they were never given a chance. From this perspective, thus, prohibition was not so much a failure as a missed opportunity to engage in a modern temperance campaign made possible by the absence of a legal, openly conducted liquor business.[2]

The conventional wisdom overlooks one simple yet highly significant fact: prohibition worked. The goal of the reformers was to strike at the liquor traffic, to prevent it from advertising its wares and encouraging consumption. The reformers believed that once the traffic was driven underground, drinking rates would drop. They were correct. From data derived from federal tax revenue, comparing the years before state prohibition laws became effective

1. James G. Hougland, Jr., James R. Wood, and Samuel A. Mueller, "Organizational 'Goal Submergence': The Methodist Church and the Failure of the Temperance Movement," *Sociology and Social Research* 58 (July 1974): 408–16. In 1936 the Gallup Poll began asking Americans if they would vote for a national prohibition law. About one-third of the respondents continued to express approval of prohibition until 1957, when the figure dropped to 26 percent. Dry sentiment was strongest in the South, in rural areas, among women and older persons. In 1942, 45 percent of the respondents indicated their belief that young people would be better off under national prohibition. *The Gallup Poll*, 3 vols. (New York, 1972), pp. 43, 203, 251–52, 322–23, 356, and 1477.

2. Conditional history is usually a fruitless exercise, but one wonders if the Depression had not occurred, if political winds had not shifted so suddenly, what the outcome might have been. No doubt the outcome would have differed from actual events, but even so, the Cherrington approach to persuasion was simplistic in the face of centuries-old drinking customs and newly emerging attitudes.

with the years immediately after repeal, the consumption of beverage alcohol went down, conservatively, by one-third to one-half under the dry statutes.[3]

As presidential candidate Herbert Hoover observed in accepting the Republican nomination in 1928, prohibition was "a great social and economic experiment, noble in motive and far-reaching in purpose." But Hoover's choice of words was unfortunate. Prohibition was a reform, a version of an uplift sentiment that was widespread during the Progressive era and that extended beyond World War I. As a reform, prohibition successfully reduced the consumption of alcohol and the attendant diseases, medical and social. When Americans rejected the prohibition reform in 1933, they acted from motives sharply different from the ideals of those reformers who would destroy the liquor traffic in order to foster the improvement of society. Not the least of those motives were the desires of some powerful businessmen to defeat the prohibition reform lest it point the way toward the acceptance of political values and social regulations hostile to their interests. It was wealthy patrons, after all, who invigorated and reorganized the AAPA for the victorious repeal campaign. Later, the same group, organized as the Liberty League, would fight the New Deal's welfare state innovations.[4]

But, if prohibition worked, we now can tell that the Anti-Saloon League did not. The league clearly was a failure after 1920. So adept at rallying dry sentiment and capitalizing on the wave of social uplift optimism that swept through evangelical Protestant groups during the Progressive era, the league officers became mired in their welter of factional disputes, financial difficulties, and disagreements over strategy. Originally designed to amass and direct the largest possible support for the goal of destroying the legal liquor business, the league structure was ill-suited for resolving the disputes that arose after the victory was achieved. The league's policymakers and administrators were not accustomed to allowing the dry constituency to engage in meaningful discussions about ultimate goals. The goal was clear, the league officials declared. The purpose of the league, as defined by Russell and as it was to evolve as an organization, was to make arrangements wherein there was no room for dissenters and thereby no room for distractions from achieving prohibition. There was thus no room in the league for third-party zealots who refused

3. Aaron and Musto, "Temperance and Prohibition in America," pp. 164–65.
4. Kyvig, *Repealing National Prohibition*, pp. 191–96; Burnham, "New Perspectives on the Prohibition 'Experiment' of the 1920s."

to accept the league's expedient policies. Even as the structure of the Anti-Saloon League was changed in order to give the appearance that it rested on the will of its constituency, the same men remained in power, with the same program.

The same men continued in power in league offices after the ratification of the Eighteenth Amendment in 1919, but now they faced an entirely different situation, one in which there was no clear program. The old league, before prohibition, had united Ernest Cherrington and Wayne Wheeler; it had combined reformers thereby who agreed on the necessity for prohibition but who disagreed about actions to take against those Americans who wanted the liquor traffic to survive. The new league did not have room for both of these men or for both coercive and assimilative viewpoints. The league after 1920, as we have seen, had no structure appropriate for reacting to the new situation being faced because the organization had no consensus about strategy among its leaders.

The new situation that the league faced after 1919 involved more than the continuation of the now illegal liquor traffic. The new situation of the 1920s involved a fundamental decline in the optimistic spirit that had characterized so much reform activity in the years prior to World War I. A disillusionment occurred in American society after the war, as historians have long observed, and the league was one of the victims. Once thousands of Americans had parted willingly with donations of funds, but that support dwindled. With no basis upon which to rekindle the optimism of the prewar reform sentiment, the Anti-Saloon League suffered dearly. The league's lack of money in the 1920s was a manifestation of its failure as an organization.

Another manifestation of the disillusionment that beset American society in the 1920s was the continuation of patronage for the illicit liquor business. While not in itself a sign of disillusionment, this patronage was a symptom of a fundamental change in attitudes away from a more traditional value of combining private behaviors and the public good. Although the data reveal a sharp decline in the consumption of alcohol, they obscure the changing social values of the acceptance of casual, recreational drinking. Americans drank less in the 1920s, for one reason, because the price of liquor was high when only illegal suppliers were on hand. Relative to spirits, beer, the workingman's drink, was difficult to manufacture and distribute under the Volstead Act. Surely some Americans drank less, or not at all, because of the law, but others patronized the bootlegger and the speakeasy. Especially in the cities, recreational drinking flourished even while the nation was under prohibition.[5] Church leaders were appalled by what they observed. Some agreed with Wheeler, others with Cherrington, in their responses, but all were reacting to a new set of cultural values against which appropriate defenses were murky.

If the Anti-Saloon League was a failure as an organization after 1920, its difficulties were only compounded by the fact that the prohibitionists were on the losing side of a cultural dynamic in American life. The league and the evangelical churches it represented voiced genteel values, implicit notions that the individual's private and public lives should harmonize. In this view the individual should discipline personal will to conform to the public good. Reform, the elimination of the liquor traffic with its public enticements of debauchery, would assist Americans in controlling their private impulses and in building a civilization rooted in Christian precepts. Overcoming the Kingdom of Evil would allow the Kingdom of God to bear fruit in a well-regulated society of Sunday schools, ice cream socials, and uplift whose citizens democratically accepted a free, yet orderly, existence.

The problem for the prohibition movement, which its leaders did not recognize except for superficial behaviors, was that their system of cultural values was rapidly fragmenting by the 1920s. At this late stage in the development of industrial society, work and leisure were separating, as were private and public behaviors. Symptoms of the change were everywhere, in the speakeasies of the cities, the liberation of women, and the growth of an economy that emphasized the worker as consumer as much or more than the worker as efficient producer.[6]

The strategies of the league, either education or law enforcement, were unrealistic in the face of this fragmentation. Neither strategy, as proposed by Cherrington, Wheeler, or anyone else, addressed the underlying changes sweeping across America in the 1920s. Neither strategy faced the problem of affecting Americans' motivations. The enforcement of the law, when and where it occurred, was a reaction to the symptoms of change. When law enforcement was administered poorly, as was the case under Roy Haynes, there were excesses that fed the propaganda mills of the wets. By the end of the decade

5. Aaron and Musto, "Temperance and Prohibition in America," pp. 158–61; Gusfield, "Prohibition: The Impact of Political Utopianism."

6. Lewis A. Erenberg, *Steppin ' Out: New York Nightlife and the Transformation of American Culture, 1890–1930* (Westport, Conn., 1981), pp. 233–41.

there was hardly a major metropolitan daily newspaper left that editorially supported the Volstead Act or its enforcement. The new American urban culture of the late 1920s had rejected the proposition that the liquor traffic required legal extinction. And the values of that culture were spreading through the new popular media of the day, motion pictures, radio, and recordings, even as the greater use of the automobile facilitated personal contact with cultural institutions.

If the law enforcement strategy failed to address such changes, neither did Cherrington's education strategy. The educational activity that he proposed flew in the face of these changing customs. The activity reasserted the genteel values of the old evangelical Protestant America without recognizing the disillusionment with those values that was occurring. Cherrington was caught up in obsolete technique, not in trying to analyze why the market for liquor continued to thrive. In the end, desperate to stem the tide of wet sentiment, Cherrington abandoned his hope of using the Eighteenth Amendment as a symbol by which to educate and uplift the untutored masses, turning instead to an effort to reach "opinion leaders, government officials and the like." In this campaign Cherrington tried to shift the level of discourse upward, away from the merits or demerits of prohibition and toward a discussion of the nature of democratic government itself. His new message to the American elite was that any repeal movement threatened the very fabric of democratic government. American leaders should realize, he asserted, that repeal would indicate that representative government could not "cope with crime" or "secure obedience and enforcement of its own laws." Elites should believe that submission to the AAPA and the other wet forces "would encourage the reaction of organized opposition to every law that does not please certain groups."[7]

Cherrington's thoughts were ironic. They hold no hint that he or the other league leaders ever considered the Anti-Saloon League as a representative of a particular group in the American population. All of the league leaders were sure of their righteousness, certain of what constituted the public interest, even if bewildered, defensive, and pathetic at the end. The irony was that the league did represent a particular group of Americans, albeit a broadly based group that through the league expressed and mobilized a cultural strand that several generations of evangelical Americans had woven. That Prot-

7. Cherrington to Steuart, June 3, 1930, ECg.

estant cultural strand included the notion of missionizing and up-lifting other persons for inclusion. But by the time the assimilative ideas of a missionary uplift to acceptance of prohibition won out within the league as the desirable strategy, it was too late; the dry view had become particularistic. Perhaps the dry ideology was al-ways a minority view; certainly it had diminished in cultural impor-tance by 1927.

Thus the league had failed in winning the higher social good. League leaders were prescient in lighting the path of a new kind of politics, but they failed to appreciate how those politics became inappropriate once the reform was won. In contrast, the leaders of the National American Women's Suffrage Association, who had successfully conducted a counterpart constitutional reform in the same period, abandoned their old structure in favor of the League of Women Voters. The situations the two organizations faced, of course, were different. Once woman suffrage became part of the constitution there was no apparent need for maintaining vigilance; whereas, the liquor traffic continued, illicitly at home and licitly abroad. The founders of the World League Against Alcoholism saw the need for a new dry organization to shape the continuing fight against ignorance and against the liquor traffic. But the world league would never amount to much in part because it had powerful opponents within its parent organization.

From outside the organization, critics of the league who defended the more traditional practice of partisan politics argued that the party approach to governance was superior in a democracy. Accord-ing to this criticism, political parties were agencies that reconciled conflicts in a heterogeneous society. After party leaders arranged compromises, so the argument went, the parties presented their record and their platforms to the voters for approval or rejection. The problem with the league as a mass-based, single-issue pressure group, in this view, was its uncompromising stance. In the final analysis, according to partisans, the failure to arrange compromises would lead to a kind of dictatorship in which the powerful dis-regarded the values and customs of minorities. On one hand, the history of the league showed the incisiveness of this criticism, at least insofar as the league represented a coercive tradition in cultural reform and practiced thereby the politics of law enforcement. On the other hand, the league arose initially because of the failure of the parties to arrange compromises satisfactory to dry Americans, who were, on matters of corruption, uncompromising. What the history of the conflict between the traditional partisan ordering of political action and the innovative league ordering revealed was that, in the complex, culturally heterogeneous America of the twentieth century, there were cultural values, particularly prohibition, that were not susceptible to compromise.

The league was marvelously successful before 1919 in pointing the way for enlarging and mobilizing popular support for a cultural value. As his son-in-law, University of California political scientist Thomas Reed, himself once a league employee, told Howard Russell on the occasion of his fiftieth wedding anniversary: "While others argued and exhorted to convince the multitude, you devised a policy of practical achievement for those already converted. Parties have largely failed to give the American people what they want. You have pointed the way by which their desires may be enacted into public policy without the aid of parties."[8]

Reed's observation became wisdom in his own scholarly discipline eight years later when Peter Odegard published *Pressure Politics: The Story of the Anti Saloon League*. What his study failed to show, and what was obscured until recently, was that the league could not follow through on its political success. The league sought to unify Americans and implant particular values. But once the league had won its major political victory it did not develop the structure that might have spread those values. The league did not transform itself to allow even the compromise of views within the dry movement. Instead the league demonstrated that, with the adaptation of modern managerial skills from the business world, determined reformers could unite around a single issue and have a chance to change the nation's basic law. Thus the league was a pioneer in devising the modern structure of single-issue politics. By the late twentieth century countless observers of American politics were wondering how the nation could survive the single-issue, interest group political structure the league had promoted.

As for the league itself, it lived on after repeal. Donations trickled in to the Westerville headquarters, where the printing presses still operated. In the 1930s Howard Russell talked of reviving the league for a new prohibition drive. After the attack on Pearl Harbor, the drys tried unsuccessfully to replicate their experience in the earlier war and stimulate a wave of prohibition sentiment in the interests of efficiency. Eventually some of the league leaders, now all old men, accepted the idea that alcohol abuse was a medical, not a social problem. Others continued an educational campaign intended to

8. Reed to Russell, Aug. 30, 1920, HH.

persuade drivers to refrain from drinking and legislators to restrict sales of alcoholic beverages. Cherrington organized the Temperance Education Foundation to house the old league's scientific, educational, and propaganda activities. Eventually, in 1964, the league itself became the American Council on Alcohol Problems, with state affiliates similarly named. This group continues to seek legislative restrictions on the sale of liquor.[9] The pity of it all is that after 1933 the problem of alcohol abuse grew and ran rampant in American society. It took nearly forty years for the rate of consumption, as measured on a per capita basis of the drinking age population, to reach preprohibition levels.[10] Coincident with those consumption levels, a few American elites became once again concerned with devising policies to ameliorate their effects. No prohibition movement would arise seeking control through eradication of the business system that supplies the beverages. But finally, careful students of the social and human problems associated with intoxicating beverages were willing to recognize that the extreme of prohibition, the system of government-business relations that outlawed the distilling and brewing industries, had been effective by a number of measures. Perhaps in the future new systems of control, rooted in scientific and dispassionate analysis as opposed to religious fervor, will emerge to deal with the social ramifications of drinking, not just treat the individual with symptoms. In 1981 the prestigious National Research Council proposed "preventive measures" of social policy as a kind of middle ground between the old wet and dry positions.[11] One lesson of the Anti-Saloon League's history is that a modern control system must rest on a consensus on the nature of the social problem in order to overcome the fragmentation and narcissism of modern American culture and its politics.

9. *American Issue* 77 (September 1970); Jay L. Rubin, "Shifting Perspectives on the Alcoholism Treatment Movement 1940–1955," *Journal of Studies on Alcohol* 40 (March 1979): 376–86.

10. William L. Downard, *Dictionary of the History of the American Brewing and Distilling Industries* (Westport, Conn., 1980), pp. 227–28.

11. Moore and Gerstein, eds., *Alcohol and Public Policy: Beyond the Shadow of Prohibition*, pp. 3–116. The middle ground is now called neo-prohibition. For a discussion, see Allan Luks, "Uncorking neo-Prohibition," *Commonweal*, August 12, 1983, pp. 426–28.

A NOTE ON SOURCES

When I decided to write this book, I based my decision on the acquisition by the Ohio Historical Society of the remaining archives of the Anti-Saloon League and on my realization that no other scholar had previously attempted a full-scale study of the twentieth-century prohibition movement and its leading organization, the league, from the perspective of unpublished sources. While the footnotes describe the full range of the sources I used, they do not fully explain just how valuable particular records were or, even more important, what records proved disappointing or unavailable. The materials the Ohio Historical Society collected were immense in volume, taking up hundreds of linear feet of shelf space when all of the printed documents were accounted. The staff of the society, together with other persons responsible for the Michigan Historical Collections and the Woman's Christian Temperance Union library, ably arranged, collated, and microfilmed manuscript materials from the three repositories, together with selected printed matter, into the substantial film edition of the papers. Researchers interested in exploring this subject further will find the *Guide to the Microfilm Edition of Temperance and Prohibition Papers* invaluable. The *Guide* has over three hundred pages, and I shall not attempt here to repeat its detailed descriptions of the filmed records.

The heart of both the league archives, acquired in 1974, and this book lies in the papers of Ernest H. Cherrington. The Anti-Saloon League, at least in its last years, occupied a brick house in Westerville, Ohio, and kept, apparently, many of its records in the basement, where they were destroyed over time by flooding and vermin. But Cherrington's papers were kept in his office and so remained intact. But even that situation would not be significant except for the fact that Cherrington and his staff were efficient in keeping copies of materials he either wrote or received, including minutes of meetings and the like. Even so, the Cherrington papers are most complete for the years after 1917. Before that date there are many gaps. Because of the many positions he occupied in the league and its affiliated bodies after 1909, however, and his wide correspondence, the remaining records make Cherrington's papers one of the major archival sources for the study of American history in this period.

Even though Cherrington's papers comprise a large and important source for the study of an important attempt at social reform in the American past, they do not reveal many glimpses at his personality or inner thoughts. The papers show Cherrington as a Progressive, as a man caught up in the intellectual climate of his time and thereby dedicated to encouraging the collection of information (always, of course, colored by his Methodist bias). As his many responsibilities testify, Cherrington was an incredibly busy man who apparently took little time away from a hectic routine for reading and reflection. He did much of his work in face-to-face conferences with people, and so his correspondence only occasionally provides details of events or his elaborated thoughts. Especially important in this regard are the letters he exchanged in the 1920s with Thomas Nicholson and, at various times, with James Cannon, both of whom shared many of the same perspectives as Cherrington. Finally, the papers show Cherrington as an investor, interested not only in personal gain in real estate ventures, but in helping his colleagues as well. Cherrington was also interested in investing in the future of prohibition through his educational strategy, but as we have seen, his thoughts on this approach developed little over the years save for trying to adopt new technologies.

I wished for better sources regarding the activities of other league leaders. The Cherrington materials should be counterbalanced with the papers of Wayne Wheeler, but there is no collection of Wheeler materials. Cherrington and Wheeler were never closely associated, and the surviving correspondence between the two is slim. One occasionally discovers Wheeler letters in other collections, but they never reveal his inner thoughts or important private observations. Apparently Wheeler preferred not to express thoughts in writing or, if he did, not to keep the record for future scholarly study.

If the failure to uncover a collection of Wheeler papers was a disappointment, so too was the lack of private papers from either Purley Baker or F. Scott McBride. Three years of McBride's correspondence from the 1920s came to the Ohio Historical Society, but those years included nothing about his election as general superintendent and little about his private thoughts in the ensuing disagreements with Cherrington. Even more disappointing was the lack of material about Baker. I found letters by Baker, of course, in the Cherrington materials, but they are obviously incomplete. I often had to turn to printed speeches to find out what Baker was thinking. Fortunately, because Cherrington was secretary of the board of trustees and later of the executive committee, his files contain copies of some correspondence and statements by both McBride and Baker as part of the official record.

The collection of Howard Russell's papers is more helpful. The material acquired in 1974 only supplemented the collection of his papers already housed in the Michigan Historical Collections. Russell's papers do not contain a great deal of business correspondence, but his wife saved her husband's letters to her written during his many trips, and they provide glimpses into the private emotions and thoughts of the league founder. I found the I. W. Metcalf collection in the Oberlin College Archives essential for supplementing the Russell collection regarding the league's early years. The Dinwiddie collection in the Library of Congress was also useful in this regard, although it does not contain much about the twentieth century.

In the course of my research I found collections apart from the microfilm project to provide important insights. Surprisingly, the papers of Woodrow Wilson had never been exploited on the subject of prohibition although, as president when the reform was instituted, he kept a separate file on the subject. Nor had the papers of E. Y. Webb been used fully concerning prohibition, even though he was an important figure in the North Carolina Anti-Saloon League and a key person in congressional politics. Similarly, the papers of Andrew Volstead to my knowledge had never been cited by another scholar.

If the riches of the Temperance and Prohibition Papers, as supplemented by other collections, provided fresh insights into the prohibition reform, they should be supplemented by comparable materials from the opposition. Unfortunately no scholar can at present peruse private correspondence regarding the activities of the brewers, distillers, dealers, and their trade associations. I was denied access to the archives of any brewing firm, and none of the trade associations involved left papers in any public repository. One inevitably suspects that they fear that they may have something to hide from outside scrutiny. What made possible my examination of the activities of the liquor business was the public record as revealed in magazines and, especially, by government investigations. On the other hand, I made no attempt to explore the archives of the AAPA because of the excellent work already completed by David Kyvig.

Finally, I should recall the significance of several works already cited in the footnotes. Readers who wish to explore further the more recent interpretation of the temperance and prohibition movement should begin with the seminal book, Norman Clark's *Deliver Us from Evil: An Interpretation of American Prohibition* (New York, 1976). A fine, more recent, and briefer overview is the paper commissioned by the National Research Council, Paul Aaron and David Musto, "Temperance and Prohibition in America: A Historical Overview," in *Alcohol and Public Policy: Beyond the Shadow of Prohibition* (Washington, 1981), pp. 127–81. A more detailed study of the Prohibition party and the Anti-Saloon League, which argues that the league was an instrument that effectively destroyed the possibility of tying more fundamental social reform to prohibition, is Jack S. Blocker, Jr., *Retreat from Reform: The Prohibition Movement in the United States, 1890–1913* (Westport, Conn., 1976). David E. Kyvig, *Repealing National Prohibition* (Chicago, 1979) is essential reading for the 1920s and 1930s. Finally, a colorful account of the popular opposition to prohibition, focused on Detroit, written with the insights of the recent interpretation of the reform is Larry Engelmann, *Intemperance: The Lost War Against Liquor* (New York, 1979).

INDEX